"*The Two Cities* is the among the best general histories of the Church written since Vatican II. Jones ends with an ambitious interpretation of the political and cultural challenges facing Christians in the post-modern West. A must read."

R. R. Reno
Editor, *First Things*

"In the contemporary world, believers tend to share the basic assumption of nonbelievers that the history of the world is an essentially secular story; they differ from nonbelievers only by insisting that Christianity has an important part to play in its unfolding. But in this book Andrew Willard Jones radically reorients our imagination on this point: Christianity is not just one character among others in a larger narrative but *is the story itself*; the history of the world is ultimately the history of the Church because 'the Incarnation is the center of history.' Uniquely situated as a historian with theological depth and a theologian with historical substance, Jones offers an accessible account that will be especially welcome to students seeking to understand more profoundly what it means to be Catholic today. This book is worth reading many times over."

D. C. Schindler
Professor of Metaphysics and Anthropology,
John Paul II Institute for Studies on Marriage and Family

"In the face of so many histories which frame the Church as a religious institution on a secular stage, Andrew Willard Jones challenges us in *The Two Cities* to see the Church—and history itself—for what the believing Christian knows them to be: the locus of our communion with God and one another as we ascend by the grace of Christ out of sin and into heavenly glory. In this way, Jones carries the monumental achievement of Augustine's *City of God* into the twenty-first century, extending the contest between the earthly and heavenly cities, which frames Augustine's reading of biblical and world history, into the middle ages, early modern, modern, and post-modern periods. The result is a compelling, accessible, and powerful account of the perennial drama of which the Church is the protagonist: struggling—as each of her members must always—with the temptation to enthrone the love of power, pleasure, and honor upon the altar of her heart, and yet providentially advancing through movements of 'renewal in continuity' toward the consummation of the ages at the marriage supper of the lamb."

Jacob Wood
Associate Professor of Theology,
Director of the Graduate Theology Online Program,
Franciscan University of Steubenville

THE TWO CITIES

ANDREW WILLARD JONES

THE TWO CITIES

A HISTORY OF CHRISTIAN POLITICS

EMMAUS ROAD
PUBLISHING
Steubenville, Ohio
www.emmausroad.org

1468 Parkview Circle
Steubenville, Ohio 43952

©2021 Andrew Willard Jones
All rights reserved. Published 2021.
Printed in the United States of America.

Library of Congress Control Number 2021935004
ISBN: 978-1-64585-122-6 hardcover / 978-1-64585-123-3 paperback / 978-1-64585-124-0 ebook

Unless otherwise noted, Scripture quotations are taken from The Revised Standard Version Second Catholic Edition (Ignatius Edition) Copyright © 2006 by the Division of Christian Education of the National Council of the Churches of Christ in the United States of America. Used by permission. All rights reserved.

Cover design and layout by Emily Demary
Cover image: *Baal's Altar Destroyed, The Sign of the Fleece, Gideon's Valiant Three Hundred & Building Plans, David Is Satisfied, Syria Subdued* Old Testament Miniatures with Latin, Persian, and Judeo-Persian inscriptions, Paris, France
ca. 1244–1254

For Mary, Agatha, Peter, Christopher, Michael, Edmund, Anastasia, Felicity, and the little boy on the way.

"Thus in this world, in these evil days, not only from the time of the bodily presence of Christ and His apostles, but even from that of Abel, whom first his wicked brother slew because he was righteous, and thenceforth even to the end of this world, the Church has gone forward on pilgrimage amid the persecutions of the world and the consolations of God."

—St. Augustine, *City of God*, 18.51

Table of Contents

Preface	XIII
I. The Foundations of the Church	1
1. Creation	1
2. The Age of Nature	10
3. The Age of Law	15
4. The Age of Grace	28
II. The Ancient Church	53
1. Growth and Persecution	53
2. The Christian Empire	68
Christianization of the Empire	68
Monasticism	83
The Fall of the Western Roman Empire	85
III. The Medieval Church	89
1. The Early Middle Ages	89
2. The High Middle Ages	98
The Reform Movement	98
The Investiture Contest	103
Religious Movements and Lay Spirituality	105
The Crusades and the Temporal Sword	108
The Civilization of the High Middle Ages	117
3. The Late Middle Ages	125
The Fragmentation of Christendom	125
Plague and Famine	129
Conciliarism and the Councils	130
Nominalism	132
IV. The Early Modern Church	139
1. The Reformation	139
The Trigger	139
The Theology of Martin Luther	141
The Spread of Lutheranism	148
The Reformation in France and England	152
The Counter-Reformation	158

  2. Confessionalization   160
   Wars of Religion   160
   Divine Right of Kings and Absolutism   164

V. THE MODERN CHURCH   175
  1. The Twilight of Christian Civilization   175
   The Enlightenment   175
   The French Revolution   183
  2. The Nineteenth Century   198
   The Industrial Revolution   198
   Modern Ideologies   204
    LIBERALISM   205
    SOCIALISM   212
    NATIONALISM   219
   The Alliance of Throne and Altar   224
   National Unifications and Mass Politics   230
   Vatican I   242
   The Formation of Social Doctrine   248
  3. The End of the Modern World   266
   Radical Ideologies and the First World War   266
   The Interwar Years and World War Two, 1920–1945   277

VI. THE POSTMODERN CHURCH   289
  1. The Postwar Situation   289
  2. The Second Vatican Council   294
   The Theological Background   294
   The Liturgy   300
   The Church   302
   Religious Liberty   306
   The World   313
  3. After Vatican II   318
   Turmoil and Confusion   318
   The New Evangelization   329
  4. The Coming Reform   337

BIBLIOGRAPHY   349

Preface

The Incarnation is the center of all history. Everything that happened before the Incarnation was leading up to it, and everything that has happened since can only be understood through it. The Incarnation is what history is about. But if the Incarnation occurred only once, in the first decades of the first century, how is it that all of history is about it? How is this event always with us, shaping our lives? The answer is the Church. The Church, put simply, is the Body of Christ both continuing in history and extending beyond history into eternity. As an explanation, this answer perhaps just makes things worse. How is it that a big group of many millions of people is the body of another, single person? That seems strange, and indeed it is. But the strangest aspects of our world are quite often the most important aspects. The strange bits are the bits that reveal things about us and the world that we wouldn't otherwise see. We should pay extra attention to the strange things. And the Church is very strange. The Church persists through time, and yet it changes. The Church both was here before it really came into being and won't become fully itself until it transitions into something greater. The Church moves through history as a full participant in history, and yet the Church reaches beyond history. There are paradoxes every way we turn.

Modern Christians tend to mistakenly think of the world as divided into two tidy, distinct realms. First, there is the religious realm. This realm has to do with the soul, with miracles, and with God talking to mankind. When we talk about religious things, we tend to be talking about supernatural things and, ultimately, about heaven, which we think of as a perfect place that lies totally outside history and to which people go after they die. Second, we have the secular realm. The word "secular" actually means something like "in time," and that remains pretty close to what we mean by it. For most modern Christians, the secular realm is the realm of things and events, the realm of our life here on earth, of politics and economics, of everything that happens out in public. In our modern way of thinking, we tend to imagine the secular realm as obeying its own rules and following its own course, just trucking along, one year after the next, one human lifetime after the next. In our way of thinking, the religious realm intervenes in this secular world here and there. We are living our life, and then a miracle happens. We are living our life and then a priest stirs us with the words of Christ, and our private life is drastically altered. Religious stuff tries to convince us to believe in God and to be good so that we can go to heaven when we die, but we live in a world that is secular, that doesn't need religion in order to be itself. In this view of things, the world is like a field on which a massive game is being played. The players are nations, corporations, ideologies, even powerful men. History is a sort of play-by-play of the game, which is played on a neutral space, the field of the secular. The Church is typically described, even by Christians, as just one more player on this field, just one more influence or one more factor in the course of history. We can imagine her being pulled off the field, and we have no problem supposing the game to continue on without her because, ultimately, we think of the Church as "religious" while the world itself is secular. This is a typical modern way of seeing things. It is almost completely wrong.

Christianity is not about our private lives, and it is not merely about where we go after we die. Christianity is about everything in the cosmos, and the cosmos moves in time. This means that Christianity is inherently temporal, inherently "secular." Christianity is in time in a similar way that you or I are in time. Who are you? To answer this question, you would ultimately have to tell the story of your life. What happened? What choices did you make? Where have you been? Whom have you known? What do you hope to accomplish in the future? Answering these questions gets at who you are as a real person who lives in time, who is temporal. And yet, you reach past time, don't you? In all the stories about you and your biography, there is a certain "you" that is constant, that is always there, that was there when you were a baby and there when you were twenty and will be there when you are on your deathbed and will continue to be for eternity. You have a soul. You are in history completely, and yet you reach past history. The Church is like this. The Church, then, includes within her everything that is in time, all the moving pieces of the cosmos, all the "secular" things, and yet it points all of this beyond time to what is eternal, to God. Like how our soul and our body are intimately connected in making us who we are, so the natural bits and the supernatural bits of the cosmos are intimately connected in the Church, making her what she is. This should remind us of the Eucharist, when the divine and secular become perfectly united. Indeed, this should remind us of Christ, of the union of God and man.

Here we approach the mystery of the Church as the Body of Christ. But, to really understand this, we must dispense with another modern prejudice: individualism. We tend to imagine the social world as a bunch of individuals going about their lives according to their own wills and according to their own rules. Individuals sometimes decide to come together for various reasons. Maybe they want to trade goods; maybe they want to form a government to protect themselves from violent men; maybe they fall in love and want to have a romantic life together. In this way of thinking, human beings are only accidentally social rather than being social in their very natures. In this way of thinking, you are yourself first and then, later, this self-sufficient self joins with other self-sufficient selves. This, too, is almost completely wrong.

People are born into families and into societies, into social worlds. We learn about the world, about who we are, about who God is, about why we are here, about just about everything through people whom we do not choose and in a time and place that we did not choose. Who we are, in our core, includes these people because our world is built through and with these people. We human beings are social in our natures. Human nature is social in the same sort of way as it is rational. We are in relationships, *as us*, fundamentally. We only really exist as full persons in relation to other persons. This is a hard idea. But it is important. Let's take the example of a mother and her son. A mother is only a mother because she has a son. A son is only a son because he has a mother. They cannot be who they are without the other. Included in the idea of "mother" is the idea of "son" (or daughter), and vice versa. This is a simple example of the complex way human beings are in their very natures. You are only you in relation to those whom you love and who love you. That is simply who you are, and the world you inhabit is the world built in and through these relationships. You are no one else, and the world is nothing else. This is what we mean when we say that human beings are social in their nature. It's not a platitude or a meaningless truism. We cannot discuss persons without discussing society and we cannot discuss either without discussing time.

The Church is a society of persons who are united in this sort of way and who are united to Christ in both his humanity and his divinity. The Church is the relationship between persons and Christ. We sometimes call the Church the bride of Christ. This helps us see what I mean. Like a mother and her son, a groom and his bride can only be what they are in relation to each other. They are different persons and yet totally related to each other. But, as the Bible says, a groom and his bride become *so* intimately united that they become actually one flesh, one body. They are different persons who can never be separated from each other; their lives will forever include each other. Here, again, we approach the mystery of the Church as the Body of Christ.

The Church is redeemed humanity moving toward eternity through time. Or, we might say that the Church is "the redeeming" of humanity in time. In the Incarnation, human nature was perfectly united to the divine nature and, as we have seen, human nature is social. This unity, then, is necessarily ecclesial. Through the Church, Christ remains present and unites us in our natures to his own. The Church is the continuation of Christ's mission. Really, we ought to say that the establishment of the Church was Christ's mission and continues to be Christ's mission. The Church is fundamentally temporal, fundamentally social, fundamentally human, and yet it reaches beyond all of this to the eternal, to the divine. The Church saves us as us, as men and women in the world, bound together in time. It does not wait for us to die to save us. Christ begins his saving work now, in time. God created the world to be in union with him as the world, as our social world. This union was broken in sin, and the Church is the re-union. The Church is the place where the particular, the "here-and-now," is mysteriously united to the universal, to the "in-all-times-and-places." The always-changing particular is, in the Church, an ever-shifting, and yet always true, analogous participation in the universal. The Church doesn't merely have a history; the Church is history. The Church is not a player on the field of history, a contender in the game of human order; the Church is the field, and human history is Church history. "The Church" is the name of the game being played.

This is what this book is about. This topic is, of course, more or less infinite. Any history must pick and choose what is discussed and what is passed over. This book is no different. This book focuses on the Latin Church. When Christianity split into divergent streams, this book sticks with the branch that looked to Rome, and so the papacy, as its head. In the late modern period, the book shifts west to America as the cultural, political, and economic leadership of Western civilization shifted. What is more, I am an American writing for English speakers. As we get closer to our time, the book becomes more about us. Traditionally, history is written mostly about politics, and this book carries on the tradition. Politics, most broadly understood, is the study of social life, of how humans live together. But, in honesty, there is a prejudice here toward the great people and great events of social life: kings, popes, wars, nations, and so forth. This book tries to situate these great people and great events within the more mundane context of normal people in their normal lives, but it is in no way balanced. Similarly, this book tries to discuss changes in thought and culture, in theology and philosophy, art and social mores, but it does so in a totally inadequate manner, bringing in details when they serve the story and passing over them when they do not. This is not a history of Christian thought or doctrine. It is also not a history of the papacy or of the clerical hierarchy. Because of our modern prejudices discussed above, we have a tendency to mistake the priests for the Church, and unfortunately most of our Church histories are really histories of the priesthood. The Church, though, is the society of the baptized. It intrinsically includes the laity. This means that this book does not suppose that "the Church" interacts with laity, such as kings and emperors, as if they were two different actors in a story; rather, the book supposes that the laity are fully within the Church and that sometimes, within this one Church, there are conflicts or different ways of seeing things.

Finally, this book tells the story with a certain plot. All histories are given a plot by their authors. This is how they can make sense to the reader. We think in plots and need a narrative arc to make sense of anything temporal. Most of us carry around a plot line of history that we were given as children and which is reinforced constantly through our culture. This is the plot of progress, progress from tyranny to freedom, from superstition to science, from poverty to wealth, from darkness to enlightenment. This is modernity's origin myth. Within it, history is primarily understood as the overcoming of Christianity. Christians are sometimes tempted to counter this plot by merely asserting that it was actually Christianity that was responsible for all the good things of modernity. Other Christians are sometimes tempted to counter this history by simply reversing who are the good guys and who the bad guys, by asserting that the "tyrants" were actually right, by siding with the Inquisitors and witch-burners. Both of these approaches are flawed because they cede too much to modernity.

As a corrective, in this book I attempt to give Christians a historical narrative that is Christian through and through and which is capable of understanding modernity from within the truth of Christianity and not the other way around, even if remnants of the two approaches discussed above do find a way of creeping in from time to time.

The plot of this book is the rise and fall of Christendom, with a certain (perhaps undue) emphasis on the fall. As for the characters in this story, St. Augustine explained long ago that there are really only two: the City of Man and the City of God. Some communities aim down, seeking happiness in things that they control, in earthly things. Taken together, these peoples are the City of Man. Some communities aim up, seeking happiness in the love of God through grace, through an unmerited gift that they cannot control and can only graciously receive. These communities constitute the City of God. History, the story of the Church, is the struggle between these peoples. This struggle, though, is complex. The two cities are not sealed off from each other, and they are not always easily identified. In fact, they are intermingled and mixed up, and every individual is a citizen of both in certain respects. Nevertheless, they are real. They are the real actors in history. The external Church, the visible Church, should, by rights, simply be the City of God. Its continuous conversion is aimed at this objective. But, in history, during its earthly pilgrimage, it will never perfectly achieve this goal. Rather, the City of Man is always present, always tugging the Church back into the world, always tempting her with whatever allures a particular time and place have to offer. The history of the community of the baptized, of the visible Church, is the history of her yielding to these temptations to various degrees and then her reform, her purification through a return to grace, as she seeks with a renewed vigor to become more perfectly the City of God. The struggle is continuous, but it is not uniform. In some times and some places, the Church is more herself than in other times and other places. The history of the visible Church, therefore, takes on the biblical narrative structure of cycles of fall and redemption, a narrative structure that also shapes the individual's spiritual life. The rise and fall of Christendom is not, then, the final history of the Church. Indeed, it would be the height of foolishness to suppose the history of the Church to be coming to a close. The Church has only recently escaped the boundaries of Europe. Rather, it is far more likely, I think, that in the end, the rise and fall of Christendom will be only an early chapter in a much, much longer story.

Preface

    I would like to thank Marc Barnes for countless hours of discussion, especially concerning the biblical narrative. Marc's ideas have had a profound impact on my own, and my interpretation of Scripture is heavily indebted to his insights. I also thank Jacob Imam, Jacob Wood, Logan Gage, Louis St. Hilaire, Alex Plato, and Alex Denley for discussing with me many aspects of this book and helping me make it better. I have taught a great deal of the material that makes up this book in various classes. I thank all my students, especially the honors students at Franciscan University of Steubenville. I thank *New Polity* magazine for supporting this work both intellectually and financially. I thank Chris Erickson, Madeleine Cook, and the rest of the staff at Emmaus Road Publishing for their wonderful editorial work and near-infinite patience. As usual, I am indebted to my mother, Jerilou Jones, for correcting my grammar and style and for endless discussion. Finally, I thank my wife, Sara, without whom things like this simply wouldn't happen.

I

The Foundations of the Church

1. Creation

When did the Church begin? The answer is that, in a sense, it was always here. In the beginning, God created the cosmos and placed human beings in it in order for them to live in community with each other and in communion with himself. This is a pretty good description of the Church. The book of Genesis tells us about this primordial Church in its account of the seven days of creation and the fall of mankind. There is something profoundly engaging about these first few chapters of Genesis. They capture our imagination and provide an answer to our most fundamental question, the question of "Why?"—the question that even a child knows to ask. In recent years, however, there has been a great deal of controversy surrounding whether or not Genesis's account of "the beginning" really happened. This controversy is profoundly modern and is rooted in the collision between a fundamentalist reading of the Bible and a fundamentalist reading of the knowledge gained through modern science. One side says that God created the world in exactly seven days. The other side says that the world is billions of years old. To both sides, this is an extremely important fight because at root they share an understanding of what constitutes truth, a modern "scientific" understanding. Within this shared understanding, there simply is not room for both the teaching of Bible and the findings of modern science. Both sides agree on this; hence the irreconcilable fight.

Luckily, we need not enter this fray. The Church has a long tradition of accepting different theories of what might have factually happened as being compatible with the Bible's account of creation. The truth of Genesis is not dependent on such things. One can read Genesis literally and believe that the events occurred exactly as described and in the same sequence and within the same duration of time and, in doing so, can capture the truth of things. Or, one can read the book as having layers of metaphor, as being dependent on literary devices, on symbolism, and on the appropriation of myth and, in doing so, can likewise capture the truth of things. This is so because as people of faith, we can assert that Genesis tells us the truth about how the world and mankind came to be, and we can at the same time understand that truth can be communicated in many ways. What we must refuse to believe is that Genesis, or the Bible itself for that matter, in any way misleads us about what happened. God created the world in a meaningful manner, and that meaning is accurately captured in Genesis's account. What this all adds up to is that we can approach Scripture and read it as simply true, and we need not bother ourselves too much with the dating of layers of sedimentary rock or the lineage of trilobites, which I hope the reader agrees is a great relief.

In Genesis, we are told how God created the world and all the animals and plants and that he then created mankind. He created mankind as male and female and he told them to "Be fruitful and multiply, and fill the earth and subdue it; and have dominion over the fish of the sea and over the birds of the air and over every living thing that moves upon the earth" (Gen 1:28). Mankind was created as a family of love, as a communion of persons in relation to each other, male and female. We might think of this as a "horizontal" communion. Adam and Eve were husband and wife, and God instructed them to have children, to build a society of human beings.

But Adam and Eve were also created in vertical communion. They were placed in the garden in order to "till it and keep it" (Gen 2:15). God commanded them to subdue the earth and have dominion over creation. Adam and Eve were placed over the rest of creation, above the plants and animals. This "vertical" relationship was as much an aspect of who they were as was their "horizontal" relationship. In both directions, Adam and Eve were given a mission. They were instructed to build a society of persons, and they were instructed to subdue the earth and have dominion over it, to be kings over it. They were not placed in a static little paradise to live out lives of careless inactivity, like fish in an aquarium. Rather, they were created to spread. They were placed in the garden so that they could extend the garden into the entire world, ordering the animals and plants and things through their dominion. From the beginning, there was going to be history, change over time.

Adam and Eve's vertical relationality went in both directions. They were created with a relationship to what was lower than they, the plants and animals, but they were also created in a relationship with what was higher than they, the angels and ultimately God himself. Indeed, they walked with God in the garden. This relationship was so profound that Adam and Eve were created full of grace. God filled them with grace so that through their dominion, through their kingship over creation, all of creation could come to participate in humanity's holiness, in its communion with God. In this way, human beings sanctified the world through their priesthood. And they performed both these offices in service of the truth, the truth about God, about themselves, and about the cosmos itself. Through their rational natures, they mediated God's reason, the divine Logos itself, to the rest of creation. In this, they were prophets. Creation itself was ordered as a vast hierarchy. At the bottom were non-living things, minerals, chemicals, mere stuff; higher were the living things, plants that grew, and then the animals that moved and acted. The highest living thing was man. Man, though, was not just a complicated animal; he was a spiritual animal, with a rational soul. He was, therefore, the bridge between the material temporal world and the even higher spiritual world, the world of the angels and finally, the world of God. Man moved among the lesser creatures and acted upon them as he elevated them past their natures through participation in his spiritual nature as he sought the supernatural end that his nature made possible. Through man, himself elevated through grace, the hierarchy that stretched from a single grain of sand to the majesty of the angelic choirs found unity.

A good way of understanding this is to imagine a temple. A temple is a place where God dwells with human beings. A temple is where the divine and the temporal meet, where they find communion. But a temple is built by human beings. Human beings take the things of the world, such as stones, and assemble them into a temple. This is human kingship, our dominion, our ordering of things and so their participation in our rationality. Then, human beings worship God in the temple through liturgy. Liturgy is public worship that includes intrinsically all aspects of our temporality: words, motions, things, smells, sounds. We perform a liturgy, like a play. Liturgy is worship of God, performed by human beings and which includes all of creation. In liturgy, we are priests of the world. In liturgy, the things that are below us participate in our worship of God, an act that they cannot do on their own. We might think of the garden as the original temple, and Adam and Eve's royal, priestly, and prophetic mission was to extend this temple to include all of creation, to order creation as a temple, and to lead creation in constant liturgy. From the very beginning, then, God intended a type of Church, a Church that would have included everything. This Church would be built in time by human beings through their reason and creativity, elevated through grace. Human beings had a mission that would have taken time and would have involved unpredictable decisions, as people decided how to construct the most spectacular temple and how to render God-fitting worship within it. So, even if Adam and Eve had not sinned, the Church would have had a history. It also would have had a government. I don't mean that it would have had politicians and policemen. I mean that the human mission would have required coordination and decision making. Considering a temple as a piece of architecture helps us understand this.

Architecture is a universal human endeavor. Why? The answer is that buildings provide us with small worlds that we can control. We can't much control mere nature, the wild animals or the weather, for example. But when we construct a building, we are building a small cosmos over which we have dominion. When we venture out of our buildings, we enter a world over which we have much less control, less dominion. Buildings, then, are microcosms that in some way model and, in a very limited manner, satisfy our primordial mission to subdue and have dominion over the earth.

A very interesting thing about architecture, however, is that it is not simplistically practical. Rather, buildings have both form and function. The function is straightforward: What is the building for? The form is more complicated: What does the building look like? How does it make us feel? What emotions does it evoke? What does the building make us want to do? These are the concerns only of a building's form. Architects are, of course, as much concerned with form as they are with function. In fact, the form, the art of a building, cannot be properly separated from its function, its practical reason. Take, for example, a home. All we need as animals is to stay warm and dry. So, a box, maybe one of those big steel shipping containers, should do the job. But what do we build instead? Houses that are themselves sculptures, that have proportion and flow, that have decoration and detail, that are beautiful and make us happy. But clearly such form considerations are not really distinct from function considerations because, ultimately, the function of a home is to provide a place for human flourishing, a place for us to be happy. We need to be warm and dry to be happy, no doubt. But we also need beauty and joy. In good architecture, then, form and function are inseparable.

This means that human creativity is fundamental to architecture in two ways. First, we need a building to do a job. We need it to be a piece of technology, and this uses our creative rationality in a problem-solving, mechanical sense. Second, we need a building to be beautiful, to be a work of art, which uses our creative rationality in an artistic and aesthetic sense. And these two types of rational creativity clearly cannot be separated. What is more, this creativity is a true, unpredictable, and free creativity. In response to the same need, we could build any number of things, as we witness clearly in the vast architectural diversity across cultures. Our rationality is free in its creativity: We can choose freely between means in the pursuit of our ends. However, this freedom is always subject to the limitations that architecture imposes. A building must stand up. It must keep the rain and the wild animals out. Most basically, however, a building must obey the laws of physics. We cannot build whatever we can imagine—a house that floats in the air, for example. We can do an infinite number of things with a stone, but we cannot do just anything with a stone because it has a nature that we didn't create. In the same way, we must respond to human nature. An ugly building, a structure that makes people feel anxious, threatened, or repulsed, is a failure, no matter how "creative." We must work with what we are given; we must accurately understand the materials of creation and assemble them in creations that work toward the realization of the ends of mankind. We cannot, like God, create out of nothing. We must work within truth and are not the masters of truth. We must mediate into the world a truth that is not our possession. We create little worlds, this is true, but they are always participations in the larger world that was created by God.

The architecture metaphor provides us, then, with an antidote to relativism while retaining the utmost respect for human freedom and diversity. There is literally an infinite number of things that we could build, and the Chinese might build something very different from Americans, but no culture can defy the fundamental reason of the cosmos and be successful. If one attempts to defy reason (which the tradition refers to as the natural law), the building will, in the end, fail. A beam of a certain type of wood and of certain dimensions can only hold so much weight. If a roof doesn't keep the rain out, it is a failure. Architecture is truly relative. Architects have real freedom but without succumbing to a fundamental relativism or indifferentism. The natural law is real, but it is not authoritarian. It is our participation in the divine reason, a participation in God's real creative freedom, and what flows out of that participation is the ability to create within the world and not against it. The natural law is the setting, then, for true liberty.

These considerations help us gain a deeper understanding of mankind's primordial commission to build the cosmos as a temple for God. Mankind was commissioned to be an architect, and all the creative variety that comes along with architecture was attached to the original commission. Man's full creative rationality had to be used, and what he would have built would be as much a work of art as a work of technology: form and function would have remained always united. This means that there is an infinite variety of "worlds," of temples that mankind could have built. The completion of creation, we might say, could have happened in as many different ways as human rational creativity could freely conceive. Here we see the need, even had humanity not fallen into sin, for a government of some sort. As people multiplied, they would have had to be somehow coordinated in order to build together a single world-temple. Different people would have had different notions of what they should do, different creative visions, but only one design could have been implemented, even if that design were extremely complex.

The choice between painting a door blue and painting it red, for example, was a choice that would have had to be made, and it is a choice that would have relied upon some form of authority to be made. However, this authority would not have been arbitrary. It is not merely that a choice has to be made and one is as good as another. If this were the case, we could have just flipped a coin. Rather, human beings were created with different talents, different abilities, and the proper ordering of people according to these abilities would have been integral to the original justice of the primordial society. Some people are better at design. Some people are better at engineering. Other people are better at building. What is more, these talents are not merely innate. They are, rather, developed to a greater or lesser extent through the formation of habits. A man with a phenomenal natural ability to paint, for example, still has to be taught and to practice, and this takes both time and certain personality traits. So, even before the Fall, different people would have had different habitual abilities, different levels of knowledge and virtue, as St. Thomas Aquinas explains.[1] Therefore, had humanity not fallen, the people of society would have been ordered appropriately for the accomplishment of its collective mission with decisions being made and actions performed up and down their social order. There would have been bosses and workers, artists and craftsmen, farmers, teachers, even poets, philosophers, and theologians. Each vocation within such an order would have been creative within itself even as it participated in the creativity of higher vocations and guided that of lower vocations.

So, without any sense of domination or "lording it over" between one man and another, humanity, had it not fallen, would have required organization and hierarchy. But if we can imagine graced and holy people organized without sin, without vanity, without envy, without the lust for power, we can easily see that this organization would bear little resemblance to our governments, and we can see that its laws would be pedagogical and communicative rather than coercive. Such a society's human laws, as St. Thomas Aquinas calls them, would have been the mediation of the natural law through human creativity into a societal plan of action. They would have been the blueprints, we might say, for the temple-cosmos that humanity was building. Human law, Aquinas tells us, is architectonic, and had we not sinned, the primordial Church— which included, of course, absolutely all human activity—would have been built according to our human law's perfectly just plan, according to our true participation in the life of God.[2]

We ought not to imagine this primordial society as a single hegemonic entity, micromanaged from the top through commands. Again, architecture gives us a way to see through this temptation. Buildings are grouped together into cities. The buildings that make up a city have their own designs, their own functions and forms. We can look closely at a single building and see the genius of its architect and its builders. But we can't really understand the building without situating it within its city. The city itself has a function and a form, and simi-

---

[1] Thomas Aquinas, *Summa Theologiae* I, q. 97, a. 3. Hereafter abbreviated to *ST*.
[2] *ST* I-II, q. 91, a. 3; qq. 95–97.

lar to how a doorknob is a piece of a building's design, an individual building is a piece of a city's design. This does not mean that a real city is just a building writ large any more than a house is just a doorknob writ large. It is a different type of thing with a categorically different type of design. A city has a limited number of explicit, positive rules about roads and drainage and things like that. In this regard, it has plans and planners that are similar to architects. But these plans pertain to a higher level of order than the plans of a single building and work in different materials. Indeed, for the most part the city is not "designed" in the same sort of way as a building. Most of it is really "unplanned." It is laid out over time through the execution of many smaller plans. The explicit rules of a city have to do with connecting these plans. They don't constitute the city; they manage it.

However, such explicit rules are not the primary way in which the little plans are connected or managed; positive law is the exception. Rather, as anyone who has visited a city with a long history knows, the individual buildings, the individual little plans, somehow "fit" together within themselves and not through extrinsic regulation. They are governed by a culture that bears within it a motivation and an aesthetic. The architect of a building is free within this aesthetic and not against it. His genius functions through his mastery of this aesthetic, through his participation within it. The architect works in form, but he is not the master of form; he creates an instance of beauty, but not beauty itself. Many of the real "rules" within which he works are, therefore, not explicit laws at all but are, rather, the threads that make up the tapestry of his culture. The city is the setting for this culture, this way of life. In this way, the city is at a higher "order" than the building, not just in scale but in content. Because of this, it has far fewer explicit "plans," even while maintaining far more fundamental and more important "rules." The rulers of a city have far less fine control over a much greater scope of action than does an architect. They have far less direct power over a far greater plan, a plan that includes the vast realm of the cultural, the unplanned. They intervene in order to redirect more than they create and design.

The same dynamic works in the other direction. The architect drafts rather detailed plans for a building, but these plans do not extend to the "rules" that govern the skill of the individual artisan or tradesman. Nothing, for example, is more detailed, more particular and precise, than the rules, the expertise, the plan, that governs the silversmith who crafts a doorknob as a piece of sculpture. The architect dictates that a certain style of doorknob be used, perhaps, but the artisan understands that doorknob from the inside. He understands the rules so profoundly that they have become an integral part of his mind and body. This is categorically different from the control of the architect. The artisan works at a far lower level of order, and so his explicit "control" is drastically greater and categorically different than that of the architect. His vocation's freedom functions, then, within the architect's plan and not against it. Indeed, the architect, whom the silversmith serves, cannot build the doorknob, or really even understand it, but only direct it and judge it from without.

What we are seeing is just how complex architecture really is. It is the process of integrating the most particular, through a hierarchy of participatory, creative rationality, into the most universal and simultaneously instantiating the most universal within the most particular. It would seem that the silversmith, working at the smallest level of detail, is the least powerful, and yet the culture, the aesthetic, that is managed by the city's rulers is constituted by all the details, all the little things, and it is at the level of such little things that innovation most often first occurs. The smallest has more "play" than the largest. Because the smallest is the most finely controlled and the largest is the most generally governed, this hierarchical ordering is not, therefore, the destruction of freedom but the context for its maximization. Autocracy is impossible within such an order because each level operates in a distinct "realm," and the higher levels are ultimately less "powerful" even as they encompass the lower realms within their vision. True creative freedom operates at every level without competition between them. This is the basis of the city's justice. Consider how language constitutes one of the highest orders of unity, and yet it is almost completely beyond the control of men. It is not totally beyond man's control, but this control is highly rudimentary and interventionist rather than constructive. Lower levels of unity work in language, and they do so with increasing amounts of power and control as things get smaller, such as in the specialized language of highly technical fields of knowledge. Such an "inverted" hierarchy is the result of freedom and not what "creates" it.

This whole complex reality forms a single "social architecture," pursuing a shared end through a hierarchical matrix of shared means. Had men not fallen, therefore, they would have built the world as an ever more complex piece of social architecture, with great diversity at lower levels mounting up to a more profound unity. Freedom would flourish at the smallest level because of that level's unity within a larger, more abstract project that would terminate finally in the most general manifestations of the natural law, the love of God and love of neighbor: faith and charity. This would have been a truly magnificent "temple," not just a building but a whole fascinating world, governed through a beautiful and dynamic "human law" that would have shifted in scope and form as it moved from the smallest to the largest, with no one person master of it all and with every person free to exercise his rational creativity in the project of rendering total worship to God, a project that participated beyond itself through grace in the ultimate "plan," the eternal law of God.

Human beings did sin, however. Through the Fall, we used our kingship, our priesthood, and our prophethood not for the worship of God but for the worship of ourselves, as if we were gods. Through the Fall, we set about building the world as a temple to ourselves. This is the basis of idolatry, the worship of creation instead of the creator. When we sinned, we lost the grace that had enabled us to live out both our horizontal relationships and our vertical relationships. We turned on each other. Adam blamed Eve; Eve blamed the serpent. Our multiplying, our building of a human society through procreation, would now be painful, and it wasn't long until Cain killed his brother Abel. Murder is the ultimate breaking of horizontal relations, and murder now strove to dominate history. We also lost our vertical communion with creation. Our dominion, our tilling and keeping, would now be experienced as toil, as labor. Our relationship with God was also shattered. We hid in the bushes, scared of God walking through the garden and looking for us.

2. The Age of Nature

Through sin, mankind's world was shattered. In original justice, man had ruled all that was below his nature, everything physical and temporal. He was at the same time elevated beyond his nature and into the supernatural life of God. When man sinned, he lost grace and simultaneously wounded his nature. Without the help of what was above, what was below slid into disorder. Reason was wounded by ignorance. The will was wounded by malice. Fortitude, the ability to push ahead, became weakness. And temperance, the ability to order goods properly, became concupiscence (disordered desire). No longer ordered by what was above, man's sensuality, the goods perceived by his senses alone, came increasingly to dominate over his rationality. What was lower usurped the position of what was higher. Oriented down to the animals, man became more animal-like.

In this situation, man became divided against himself. His higher powers, such as his reason and creativity, came to war with his passions and desires. Often, his own reason (natural law) came to be felt as a tyrant. Similarly, God was no longer a transcendent Father to whom man submitted in trust and love. Instead, man tended to experience him as a very powerful creature, as a tyrant from whom one is inclined to run and hide in the bushes. Broken off from what is above, the world became closed in on itself, and its powers became frightening. Think of a child who is not afraid of a dog because his father is holding his hand and reassuring him. If the child is alone, however, he is justifiably terrified because the dog is, in fact, dangerous. After the Fall, man perceived himself as alone and as helpless against the forces of nature. Society itself became dangerous. No longer connected through our common love of our Father, we became opaque to each other; we became suspicious and envious, and so Cain kills Abel, as if he were an animal. Our fear was justified. The loss of our vertical order destroyed our horizontal order. Faith was replaced with doubt, charity with suspicion, and hope with fear.

God, of course, did not abandon mankind to this sad fate. Like the loving Father that he is, he moved to save us from ourselves. This was a movement of condescension, of God coming down to our level to move us out of our self-obsessed little world to share again in his world. God's action to save mankind is what we call salvation history. This history is the story of mankind's prolonged struggle between the upward pull of God toward redemption and the downward pull toward an ever more bestial life. St. Augustine told this story as that of two cities: the City of Man and the City of God. What distinguishes these cities is their orientation, up or down. Some people are oriented up toward the angels and God; they are the citizens of the City of God. Others are oriented down toward animals and things and, ultimately, the fallen angels. These are the citizens of the City of Man, the Earthly City.

Both cities are after the same thing. Augustine describes this as peace, which he defines as the tranquility of order. As we have seen, the Fall disorders man's relationship with God, with his neighbor, and with himself. After sin, it becomes the desperate struggle of every man to somehow regain this order, this peace, to resituate the particular within the universal. Peace, Augustine explains, is the opposite of anxiety, of stress, of unfulfilled desire.[3] Such anxiety is what Augustine is talking about when he famously asserts that all men have a restless heart. For Augustine, man's attempts to regain peace, to put his heart at ease, is the deep plot of all human history. This is the struggle to regain in our particular lives the three loves: love of God, love of neighbor, and love of self. The only way to do so, of course, is for our restless hearts to rest again in God. This is the path taken by the City of God. Its citizens strive in this world after the repose given only by God. The City of Man, on the other hand, seeks peace in contrivances of its own making. Its citizens seek peace through total domination, through the hopeless ambition of finishing what Adam and Eve started and finally becoming gods themselves.

In ancient thought, the city was understood as a complete community. Cities have their own human laws, they have their own customs and mores, and perhaps most importantly, they have their own cults, their own gods and liturgies. Ancient cities were temple-states. They were oriented toward the worship of their gods. We can connect, therefore, Augustine's discussion of the cities with our previous discussion of man's primordial mission to construct a temple world. As we have seen, cities are little architectural worlds of man's construction, microcosms, little temple-cosmoses. Augustine shows us that while the world is made of countless little cities, in fact, there are only two ultimate cities. And the history of these two cities spans from Cain and Abel all the way to the final judgment. The downward-looking city will descend through selfishness to perfect misery in complete war with God, neighbor, and self, while the upward-looking city will ascend through grace to perfect peace in perfect love of God, love of neighbor, and love of self. The plot of this history, however, is not a simple progression. It is filled, rather, with ups and downs, with advances and reversals, with corruptions and reforms. Salvation history is marked by God's interventions in this story, with his guiding of the City of God and his constant reaching out to the City of Man.

After the Fall, the City of Man came to dominate over the City of God. Man as a whole descended deeper into depravity. This descent is tragic and yet understandable. Human beings, as we have seen, come to understand the architecture they are building, their society's

---

[3] Augustine, *The City of God*, 19.11–17.

"project," through the education that they are given, through hierarchy, through their society's human laws, where "law" is understood to include customs and manners, mores, and finally even language. Children are raised into all of these cultural habits of their people, and their lives are oriented accordingly. Rather than building a social world that leads people toward the common good and so into deeper virtue and peace, people filled with vice make unjust laws, building an unjust social architecture that leads people away from the common good and so into deeper vice and disorder. After the Fall, mankind was accordingly trapped in a bind. The human laws that mankind needed in order to climb out of vice became harder and harder to make, precisely to the extent that he needed them more. The worse mankind got, the more it needed good government and so good law, and to the exact same extent, the less it was inclined to make it. Mankind became, rather, more and more inclined toward bad governance and toward making corrupt law, toward building a disordered social architecture, leading in turn to ever-deeper vice. It was a downward spiral, a decent into ignorance and malice.

As man fell deeper into ignorance, his reason was clouded by his passions. His animality came to increasingly dominate his rationality. He lived less and less by reason, less and less by the natural law, and more and more by a perversion of that law. His human law, then, rather than creatively expressing the true natural law, came increasingly to express his ever-growing irrational desires. Human law increasingly worked not toward the common good but toward the fulfillment of the selfish desires of whomever happened to control it. The social hierarchy is inverted, with that which is lower serving the power of that which is higher. Law became tyranny. And so, rather than leading people into virtue, it led them into vice. At the same time, because all human cities are ultimately temples, the descent into unjust law was also always the decent into idolatry, which is the worship of man's creations rather than his Creator. This is the origins of what will come to be called paganism. During this period, which the tradition calls the Age of Nature, this City of Man steadily enveloped the City of God until the holy city consisted of only Noah and his family, who "walked with God" (Gen 6:9).

Through the flood, God attempted to wipe the City of Man from the Earth. As soon as the waters subsided, however, Noah got drunk. His son Ham sinned. And the City of Man was reestablished under the line of Ham, while the City of God continued under the line of

Shem. The drama picked up where it had left off. An important aspect of this story is the manner in which all of humanity and, indeed, all of creation, remains bound up together in a single narrative. There is no aspect, no department of creation or of the human race that is not included in the story. This will remain fundamentally the same throughout all of salvation history and in our understanding of the Catholic Church as truly universal. The Bible provides us with no neutral ground, no population of men that falls outside the story of fall and redemption. This, of course, makes perfect sense, but it is easily forgotten as the story focuses more and more on a particular people and then a particular Church. But, throughout the rest of this book, we need to retain the universal perspective provided by Genesis.

Indeed, Genesis relates how all the nations of the world spread out from the sons of Noah. At first, mankind retained a cultural unity, as the Bible states, "Now the whole earth had one language and few words" (Gen 11:1). As the City of Man came to once again dominate, this unity made it exceedingly powerful. In the story of the Tower of Babel, the citizens of the City of Man, united through their shared language, attempt to build a temple-city for themselves and a great tower that will place them in the heavens, in the rightful place of God. Again, we have the architecture imagery, again we have the prideful idolatry of self-divinization, and again we see that men are social in their very nature, working together through their language and customs, through their human laws, to build a temple-world. Here, mankind is once again accelerating the downward spiral that led to the flood.

But God intervenes. He disrupts their cultural unity, the source of their power and the mechanism for the propagation of their vice. He confuses their tongues and "scattered them abroad from there over the face of all the earth" (Gen 11:8). This scattering is profoundly significant. Mankind was not meant to be divided. We were certainly meant to be diverse, but we were not meant to find each other baffling and confusing. What Babel shows us, though, is that the unity that would have made us strong in justice can make us equally capable of great evil. God, therefore, as a mercy, divides us into the nations. He does this, however, not to abandon certain factions of mankind. He is not cutting his losses, casting loose the bulk of humanity to a seemingly secular, national existence. Rather, he is setting the stage for the redemption of all mankind through the election of a particular people, Israel, that will then act as a light to the nations. Breaking humanity up into nations was a part of a bigger strategy to reunite it.

God elects Abraham to be the father of Israel. This is a fascinating plot twist. God takes Abraham out of the line of Shem and instructs him to move away from his kindred, away from his nation. God seems to be starting over with a single family, at the lowest level of the social hierarchy. He is going to give this family new laws and a new way of life, making it a vast and prosperous people. But not merely for its own sake. Rather, God tells Abraham that through him all the families of the earth will be blessed. This is a dynamic that we will see repeatedly in salvation history. God takes what seems to be a step backward in order to collect wayward humanity and pull them forward. God focuses in on one little family so that they might become the means of all of humanity's redemption. God established a covenant with Abraham according to which his descendants would be the Lord's people, and the Lord would be their God. They would not have idols, and their national god would be God himself.

3. The Age of Law

Genesis relates how Abraham's grandson, Jacob, and his twelve sons moved to Egypt during a terrible famine. In security and prosperity, the Israelites multiplied quickly. This troubled Pharaoh, who viewed their strength as a threat, and so he reduced them to slavery. They toiled in bondage for over four hundred years. Understanding this slavery is important. The Church Fathers almost universally taught that it was as spiritual as it was physical. Their bondage was both to sin and to other men. This makes perfect anthropological sense. Four hundred years is a very long time. Four hundred years ago, for example, the first permanent English settlements in America were established. During Israel's centuries in Egypt, the kingdom developed into a massively powerful slave state ruled by a god-king, by a living idol. The society was literally a temple-state constructed for the worship of a man as a god. And after four hundred years, Israel was largely assimilated into this idolatrous culture. They were slaves not only physically but spiritually.

Like Egypt, the nations everywhere were forming themselves as temple-states with god-kings. This is precisely the type of society that we would expect fallen man, increasingly enslaved to his vices, to build. His nature was fallen, but not destroyed. He remained driven to serve as king and priest over a temple that he constructed. Only now, rather than being just and holy and rather than working humbly in freedom within the truth of nature to build a world for the worship of the true God, he toiled as a slave to build a false temple for a cynical priesthood to worship their human king as the source of order in the cosmos. This was an inversion of the primordial hierarchy. Here, the highest levels claimed for themselves the most particular power: They claimed to be the very source of order rather than the servants of order. In effect, they claimed that their will was the eternal law and that, therefore, their power was complete. Each level in this hierarchy, driven by pride, sought to maximize its power and so to dominate the levels below them, even as they were dominated by those above. Slavery to vice was also literally slavery to other men. Idols were not only false gods; they were the mechanism through which vicious men dominated other vicious men.

Consider how the cosmic hierarchy had been inverted: Now the lowest level—things, wood, paint, and stone—was feared as if it was the highest level, the level of God himself. Such a society was ordered by and toward what was lower. It was descending rather than ascending, boxing itself in with the finite rather than opening itself up to the infinite. This is the logic of the City of Man, the Earthly City. The fear and anxiety that men increasingly experienced as they fell further from God was focused on their idols, and the kings and their priests positioned themselves as mediators, as those capable of placating the gods' wrath and winning their rewards. A pagan king's power, of course, was never anything other than the combined power of the people subject to him, and yet the idols allowed the monarch to hide this from them. It was in the ruling elite's interest to increase both the people's fear of the idols' wrath and the people's greed for the rewards the idols dispensed. Through these vices, the kings could organize their societies and so project immense power. This reinforced the people's conviction that the king was himself a god upon whom they relied completely.

Nowhere is the power of the kings and their idols more demonstrable than in the widespread practice of human sacrifice. Throughout the Bible, the most abominable practice of the nations is the sacrifice of their own children to the gods. The parent-child bond is the most fundamental human-to-human bond possible. The practice of child sacrifice is nothing else than the ripping apart of that bond to make room for the power of the god-king. As long as the bond between parent and child retains its integrity, it flows out of their personhoods without reference to external human power. It is a source of true power and justice, a rendering of the common good, which flows from below. It is a remnant of the City of God and the proper hierarchy of being, a lingering just architecture in which power is for the weak. This is an ever-present mitigation of the power of men because it is a space not governed by fear. The idols, then, demanded child sacrifice and sought to produce the fear that made it a reality. This fear is what enables total domination, and the sacrifice of one's own child is the sacrifice of the last vestiges of freedom. Killing babies both enables slavery and is the proof that it exists. The killing of children is the ultimate claim to human divinity. This is why child sacrifice was everywhere in the ancient world, and why it was such an abomination to the Lord.

The story of the Exodus makes it very clear that Israel had become largely assimilated into Egyptian society. They suffered, as all fallen men suffer, as slaves to both vice and to false gods. It was precisely this suffering that led them to cry out to the Lord for help. The patristic reading, that their slavery was as much spiritual as physical, is not, therefore, some "pious" or "allegorized" abuse of the text. Rather, the Fathers understood exactly what was going on. Within the logic of the biblical narrative, slavery to vice, slavery to false religion, and slavery to tyrants are simply different aspects of the same thing. Of course, Israel was not totally lost. Their identity, even if greatly diminished, remained rooted in the covenant between Abraham and God. There remained deep within their peoplehood a fading glimmer of the radiance of the City of God. When the time was right, God intervened through Moses to save his people, his "first-born son" (Exod 4:22), both spiritually and physically. As the Church Fathers insisted, the Passover was a passing over from slavery to freedom and from vice to virtue. Nevertheless, the deep cultural hold that idolatry had on Israel is clear throughout the narrative.

Moses led Israel into the wilderness, out of the civilizations of the temple-states and the god-kings. They were exposed and frightened, without a king and without gods. God, therefore, gives them a law to live by, asserting himself as their king and their God. Through Moses, God first gives Israel the Ten Commandments. St. Thomas Aquinas explains that the Ten Commandments were an expression of the natural law. Indeed, all the natural moral law, Aquinas asserts, was contained within the Decalogue.⁴ This was necessary because Israel's reason was so diminished and so perverted through centuries of slavery, that, like the nations, it no longer knew with clarity even such fundamental truths. St. Thomas asserts that the reason that God waited for centuries before giving the law was precisely so Israel would come to despair of their own intellects, so they would come to give up the "self-reliant" project of the nations and accept the truth of their own intellectual infirmity in humiliation.⁵ Israel was no longer able to reliably tell good from evil, and so God steps in to instruct them. The Ten Commandments, however, were not enough because such general precepts of the natural law must be instantiated in culturally appropriate particular laws in order for a people to obey them. How do we honor our mothers and fathers? How do we worship the one true God? What does it mean to steal? In what does adultery consist? When is it justified to kill another man, and when is it murder? In order to live the natural law, a people must answer countless such questions.

This, we recall, was supposed to be done through what St. Thomas calls human law. But Israel in its servile state was in no condition to make such laws for itself. For the very same reason that it needed the natural law to be given to it explicitly in the Ten Commandments, it was incapable of specifying that law justly. This makes sense. Let's take the injunction, "Thou shalt not murder." Every human society knows this law. They *all* have it. The natural law at this level has not been blotted out by sin. However, the nations disagree profoundly regarding what counts as murder. The Nazis had laws against murder, and yet they had Auschwitz. In the United States, we have laws against murder, and yet we kill millions of unborn children. The natural law must be specified in human law. It is only at this level that it can finally be kept or broken.

Israel had spent four hundred years in Egypt and was more or less idolatrous in its worldview. It needed a human law that was particular to this condition, that could speak to this people in their cultural grammar, using concepts that they understood, so that they could live the natural law. But it was precisely this condition that made it impossible for them to make this law for themselves. The instantiation of the natural law within an idolatrous culture could not emerge

---

⁴ *ST* I-II, q. 100.
⁵ *ST* I-II, q. 98.

from within that culture; it had to be given from above. And so, God again condescends and, acting as their king, makes for them a law code that justly specified the Ten Commandments and through which they could approach the tranquility of order. Through Moses, God instructed Israel in great detail concerning how they should live the commandments. In the Garden of Eden, God gave Adam and Eve few positive commands. The positive Divine Law was minimal. For the most part, they made their own law according to the dictates of their graced reason and their creative application of this reason. They served as king over creation, ordering it according to their just will, designing for themselves their architectural project. Now, the Divine Law was extended to include this kingship. This extension is called the Mosaic or the Old Law. Through it, Israel would be ordered through obedience, even in those areas where its reason and its capacity for justice should have allowed it freedom. But this was the path out of slavery. This law was a mercy, and to live it was to live rationally. It was the first step toward finding happiness through the fulfillment of human nature in justice.

St. Thomas explains how the most fundamental precepts of the natural law are that we ought to love God and to love our neighbor as ourselves.[6] These loves, of course, animate humanity in both its vertical and its horizontal relationality. Concerning the love of neighbor, the Mosaic law included what are called the "judicial precepts." This was what we might think of as the criminal and civil law. It covered everything from murder to loaning money, from marriage law to farming rules. Concerning the love of God, the Mosaic law included the "ceremonial precepts." This was the ritual and liturgical law through which Israel was to worship God. First and foremost, in the ceremonial law, God commanded them to build a tabernacle, a place for worship:

> Moreover you shall make the tabernacle with ten curtains of fine twined linen and blue and purple and scarlet stuff; with cherubim skillfully worked shall you make them. The length of each curtain shall be twenty-eight cubits, and the breadth of each curtain four cubits; all the curtains shall have one measure. Five curtains shall be coupled to one another; and the other five curtains shall be coupled to one another. And you shall make loops of blue on the edge

---

[6] *ST* I-II, q. 100, a. 3, ad 1.

> of the outmost curtain in the first set; and likewise you shall make loops on the edge of the outmost curtain in the second set. Fifty loops you shall make on the one curtain, and fifty loops you shall make on the edge of the curtain that is in the second set; the loops shall be opposite one another. And you shall make fifty clasps of gold, and couple the curtains one to the other with the clasps, that the tabernacle may be one whole. (Exod 26:1–6)

This sort of detailed instruction goes on for two chapters. In order to understand this, I want to go back to our discussion of the primordial mission of man to turn all of creation into a temple for the Lord. We'll recall that in fulfillment of this mission, man was called on to use his full reason and creativity so that the temple that he built would be an outpouring of his personality in freedom, a gift of his love and devotion to both God above and the things and animals of creation below. The world that he created would have been a work of art that flowed out of his worship of God and fulfilled his own nature while elevating through participation the natures of all things, plants, and animals. Man was free, similar to how a master painter is profoundly free with canvas and oil or how a master pianist is supremely free as he sits down at the keyboard. Man's temple-world would have been an expression of that freedom. Through the Fall, however, man maimed himself. He mixed everything up and wounded his rationality, his nature. This is why he built idols and temples for them to live in. Literal temples, special buildings designated for worship, were built first in order to worship false gods. They were built first for the idols through which men enslaved other men, even while progressively enslaving themselves.

What God is doing here, then, is coming to fallen man. Mankind was looking down, and God inserted himself within their line of sight, as if he were a mere god. He is entering into their world, into the space of the still-lingering fundamental inclinations of the natural law, and redirecting them toward him in a manner that will be meaningful for them. He doesn't forbid the building of temples; he instructs them how to build a type of temple that will be just and good, that will be an appropriate place for them to worship the true God. He is showing them how to build a temple for him because they have lost the ability to build it through their own creative freedom. And this temple is a condescension, a humbling of God. God, the creator of the universe, will live in a little temple-tent, like one of the Egyptian idols of wood and stone that the Israelites had grown accustomed to. This is not like the temple that Adam and Eve were to build. That was, of course, the world itself, and we use the word "temple" only analogically when we are talking about the primordial commission. It is here, in the world of fallen men, that we get the actual buildings called temples, and when God deigns to come dwell in one, he is entering into our fallen world to find us. This is how all of the Old Law works.

One of the things that we have to see here, though, is that the judicial precepts and the ceremonial precepts are two aspects of a single law. God is providing Israel with a starting point, like he had with Adam and Eve through the garden. This starting point, however, was appropriate for a fallen people and so included far, far more commands with more threats of punishment. But, nevertheless, it was a starting point from which Israel could presumably resume the primordial mission of turning all the cosmos into a temple. Mankind will start here, with true laws and an acceptable place to worship, and from there they will expand out, ordering the world. This is a vision of Israel as king, priest, and prophet, as a priestly kingdom that could lead the nations back to God and could mediate between God and the rest of mankind.

The tabernacle is a great example of this. The nations everywhere were building temples to their idols. They understood temples. Their fallen world contained temples. God did not, therefore, destroy the very concept of the temple; rather, he appropriated it. He showed the nations, through Israel, that a different kind of temple existed, a temple to a true God, not a mere work of human hands. God gives Israel a law, judicial and ceremonial, that allows them to act as mediator between the nations and himself, as a bridge between idolatry and true worship. This works because the law that God gives is a true specification of the natural law, and it is at the same time a specification that is perfectly appropriate for a fallen, more or less idolatrous people. This is a specification that such a people could never have made for themselves precisely because they were so fallen. It could only come from above, and yet it entered fully into their human life. It was the Word of God being spoken in the language of man. This is why it is incarnational, why the Church has always maintained that the law is the Word of God, an expression of the second person of the Trinity, Christ, God's definitive utterance. The law of the Old Testament is Divine Law as human law, the eternal reason reaching down and becoming a human reason, both human and divine. It is an anticipation of the Incarnation.

Israel was being formed as king, priest, and prophet for the nations. Israel was to be the City of God that would slowly envelop the

City of Man, converting mankind back to itself. But it almost immediately failed: after the Israelites accepted the law that Moses brought down from Sinai, ratifying a covenant with God, they fell back into crude idolatry. While Moses was receiving instructions from God, the people formed a golden calf and began to worship it. This was a second fall. Adam had rejected the Divine Law. Israel now did the same. Israel was supposed to be the priest for the idolatrous nations, the City of God to their City of Man. What the golden calf revealed was that Israel itself was mostly the City of Man. It wasn't ready for the mission. More remedial action was needed.

Rather than serving as a priestly nation, Israel now received a priesthood for itself. The Levitical priesthood was formed as a response to the golden calf, and from here on, Israel would be divided into clergy and laity. The priests now mediated the ceremonial law to the nation. Positive law itself became much, much more extensive. Through Leviticus and Deuteronomy, the judicial and the ceremonial precepts of the Old Law were greatly expanded and came to govern almost every minute aspect of Israel's life. More than just a help, more than just a starting place from which Israel could order itself, this law became nearly all-encompassing. It remained, nevertheless, a perfect specification of the natural law for this particular people. It remained a Divine Law that was a perfect human law, even if it was a human law that attempted to order society in a positive manner from top to bottom, even if it was a human law that carried within it the scars of the pagan nations.

This law was penitential and pedagogical. As St. Thomas explains in great detail, God gave the law so that Israel might move from vice to virtue, that Israel might be led, first through fear of punishment and then through love of righteousness, into a closer relationship with God. The tradition considers Israel here as a boy that must be instructed and disciplined as he grows into a virtuous man. The law, then, is onerous but is entirely true, entirely rational, and so in keeping with the natural law. This means that to become righteous in the law, to become habituated to perform it with love, was to become a virtuous man. The problem, however, was that this law remained external, written on tablets of stone rather than the flesh of the heart. What this means is that while knowledge of the law and the outward performance of the law was possible, righteousness in the sense of a converted heart was elusive. This required grace; this required God to turn man's heart so that he not only performed the actions of the law, but he did so in the right manner, with the right intention, with charity. This grace, Aquinas tells us, was not given through the Old Law.[7]

Because of this, the law could not really be fulfilled. Israel continually fell short. The book of Judges is particularly instructive here. Israel had a priesthood, but it did not have a king. As Judges relates: "In those days there was no king in Israel; every man did what was right in his own eyes" (Judg 17:6). Of course, they didn't have a king because God himself was their king, their lawgiver. The judges were judges, not legislators, judging the law that God had given, not creating their own law. But in the same sort of way that Israel had demonstrated with the golden calf that they needed priests to mediate their relationship with God, so through the period of the Judges Israel demonstrated that they could not live in filial obedience to the divine king. It was a terrible time. Over and over again, Israel fell into disobedience and idolatry, even to the point of human sacrifice; this led to oppression and slavery, which led to Israel crying out for redemption, which led to the emergence of a divinely sent redeemer. This was, of course, the basic plot of the Passover and Exodus being recapitulated, seemingly without end. These cycles dragged on for over four hundred years. Israel demonstrated that it was incapable of free obedience; it needed to be subject to power.

Finally, as 1 Samuel relates:

> All the elders of Israel gathered together and came to Samuel at Ramah, and said to him, "Behold, you are old and your sons do not walk in your ways; now appoint for us a king to govern us like all the nations." But the thing displeased Samuel when they said, "Give us a king to govern us." And Samuel prayed to the LORD. And the LORD said to Samuel, "Listen to the voice of the people in all that they say to you; for they have not rejected you, but they have rejected me from being king over them. According to all the deeds which they have done to me, from the day I brought them up out of Egypt even to this day, forsaking me and serving other gods, so they are also doing to you. Now then, listen to their voice; only, you shall solemnly warn them, and show them the ways of the king who shall reign over them." (1 Sam 8:4–9)

In the same sort of way that idolatry with the golden calf led to the establishment of a priesthood, here a form of idolatry led to the establishment of the monarchy. As we have already seen, in the

---

[7] ST I-II, qq. 98–105.

ancient world, kings were gods. They were living idols that wielded the mechanisms of temple-based slave-states in order to bring military and economic power to bear on their enemies. Israel's begging for a king, "that we also may be like all the nations, and that our king may govern us and go out before us and fight our battles" (1 Sam 8:20), was begging for the "peace" and protection of slavery to an idol. It is not that kingship is bad. Such a conclusion would be to misunderstand this event entirely. Kingship was a great good in and of itself. Adam was a king. But this proper goodness is why kingship as it devolved in the nations was such a great evil. Pagan kingship was, in a sense, the culmination of the Fall, wherein a man was placed in the position of God himself, as if a man's will ordered the cosmos.

It seems strange, then, that God gives them a king. We have to understand this event within the same framework through which we understand God's establishment of the priesthood. It was a remedial action that gave a little room for Israel's fallenness but saved them from the full impact of their folly. With the golden calf, Israel demonstrated that it was still idolatrous at heart, and idolatrous religions have priests to minister to their gods. God, therefore, gave them priests to mediate between them and him. He opens a little space for their fault, and yet because these priests would, in fact, be sacrificing only to the true God according to a just application of the natural law, Israel would be saved from the disastrous consequences of true idolatry. Similarly, here, God gives them a king to rule them. They might, in their sin, treat him as a god-king of power, like the nations, but the king need not himself actually be one. As Deuteronomy explained, the king whom God set over his people

> must not multiply horses for himself, or cause the people to return to Egypt in order to multiply horses, since the Lord has said to you, 'You shall never return that way again.' And he shall not multiply wives for himself, lest his heart turn away; nor shall he greatly multiply for himself silver and gold. And when he sits on the throne of his kingdom, he shall write for himself in a book a copy of this law, from that which is in the charge of the Levitical priests; and it shall be with him, and he shall read in it all the days of his life, that he may learn to fear the Lord his God . . . that his heart may not be lifted up above his brethren. (Deut 17:16–20)

God would give Israel a king, but the king would not be the lord of Israel and would not be the source of their law, of their truth, of the order of the world. He would be a king, most certainly, but nevertheless not a king "like all the nations" (Deut 17:14). The establishment of the monarchy opened a little gap for the fault of the people, saving them from the full consequences of king worship. God was building a new architecture out of the goodness that remained within the cultural materials that Israel had available. The king, like the priests, was established to mediate between God and the people: Both the priests and the king were anointed (*christos* in Greek). Mediating between the true God and the people, the king wasn't truly a king like those of the nations only because he was more perfectly a king, because he was closer to the fulfillment of kingship itself, of which the kingship of the nations was a perversion.

Nevertheless, God warned Israel that they would experience their king as a tyrant. This need not be, however, because the king was actually a tyrant. A disobedient child rants against his just and loving father as if his father is abusive, even though he is not. In the same way, a just king is compelled to rule an unjust people with severity, and they, on account of their injustice, are often blind to his righteousness. There is an irony in this story. Israel finally descends so far from the law that the Israelites want a god-king like the nations. But, for precisely this reason, they need a king to rule them, not the god-king they are demanding, of course, but a godly king, and so ultimately God gives them one in David.

David built the military and cultural power of the nation and directed it toward the worship of the true God. He ruled through the law of God as if it were his own law. At this point in the narrative, Israel achieves a sort of completion: they have priests, they have a king, they have prophets, and so finally God gives them permission to build a permanent temple. They will become a temple-state, like the nations, but really as an inversion of the nations, with a true priesthood and a true kingship worshiping the true God through a true law. We ought to see here, again, God moving to retain the primordial mission of man. Mankind was made to be kings, priests, and prophets to order the world into a temple for the worship of God. This mission was severely compromised in the Fall. Here, with the establishment of the Davidic monarchy, all these pieces come together again, but they did so at a much lower level than had been the case in Eden. They did so at a remedial level, full of law and mediation. They did so in a manner that bore within it the scars of the Fall and which resembled the idolatrous nations that surrounded Israel. We might think of the Davidic kingdom as a little outpost of the City of God, a little foothold, a beachhead, within the nearly omnipresent City of Man.

With the establishment of the Davidic kingdom, the truly universal nature of salvation history again becomes apparent. The kingdom's Wisdom Literature propounded a philosophy and theology that began to understand the Law as truly a universal law. It began to understand that all humanity was called ultimately to the kingdom of God, to the City of God. But this aspiration to universal wisdom remained, as before, unrealizable. David's kingdom was an anticipation of the coming Kingdom of God, but it was not yet it. It remained primarily external, primarily oriented toward certain practices and certain intellectual formulations rather than toward the conversion of hearts to charity. Under the Davidic kingdom, Israel came to understand the call to charity. This is clear. But they were not given the grace that answering the call required.

And so, they again fell. Having been given so much, the monarchy's fall into depravity was even more grievous than Israel's previous failures. Again, we see how slavery is tied to vice. Falling away from the true law is a falling into slavery, not merely some sort of spiritual slavery, but real, political slavery. This is the central theme of the preaching of the major prophets: the turning away from God was a turning toward war, famine, and pestilence. Both spiritual and physical suffering and slavery follow from disobedience. As the kingdom fell into depravity, it suffered more and more. Finally, the fall of the monarchy into idolatry and sin led to God taking it all away. The Temple, the land, the monarchy—it was all swept away as the people were carried off into exile in Babylon. In exile, all Israel had left was faith in the Lord. They returned to Jerusalem a couple generations later a humbled people.

Why did all this happen? What is the purpose of this history? Many Christians find it confusing and even bizarre. The tradition, though, has always maintained that all of this happened for a reason. St. Thomas Aquinas, for example, argued that the events of the Old Testament were appropriate for the "conquering of men's pride." Man, Thomas tells us, is prideful on account of his knowledge and his power. This is what we saw in the Garden. After the Fall, God left man to his own devices, left him thinking that his own "natural reason" could "suffice for his salvation," that he could find peace, find the happiness of the three loves, through his own resources. This was the Age of Nature, and during it, man learned the deficiencies of his own reason as he fell into "idolatry and into the most shameful vices." God, then, gave mankind the written law as a "remedy for human ignorance." During the Age of Law, man was instructed in what was true. This knowledge led to the conquering of his pride with regards to his power because he now knew the truth and yet lacked the ability to fulfill it. Try as he might, he constantly failed to live the truth that he knew.[8] What St. Thomas is telling us is that the Age of Nature and the Age of Law showed man the weakness and fallenness of his intellect and his will. He could not find salvation on his own. He could not even live according to his own nature. Adam and Eve's bid to become like gods was exposed as folly through the long centuries of trying, often desperately, to bring it to fruition. Man was not a god. He could not build a world of justice or peace if that world remained oriented down, closed in on itself. He could not find happiness. He was weak. He needed a savior.

The Old Testament prepared a particular people for the coming of Christ. But this preparation was not merely for them, so that they could be saved. If this were all the Old Testament was about, it would be confusing why the nations do not all have to go through a similar experience in order to receive Christ. Israel's preparation, rather, always included the nations. Israel was prepared to be an appropriate context for the savior's appearance in such a way as to be intelligible to the nations. Israel, as we have seen, was prepared as a mediator between God and the nations. Israel was incarnational in its divine, yet human, order. The actual Incarnation of Christ as the perfect mediator would fittingly appear in this nation, constituted as it was between man and God and yet humbled through its long centuries of experience. It was here, through the language and through the stories that Israel possessed, that Christ found it fitting to reveal to all the nations that he was what they were looking for. Mary, the mother of God, was a perfect Israelite, the product of Israel's history, and Christ was born into her family, taught her language and customs, instructed through her human law, and loved in her home. Is all of the Old Testament in the end about her? She articulates its major themes in her beautiful Magnificat. Did it all happen so she could be her, so that through her God could be Jesus? What is clear is that Christ was born into this particular social world for a reason.

---

[8] *ST* I-II, q. 98, a. 6.

4. The Age of Grace

The Incarnation of Jesus Christ is the central event of world history. All that came before it was leading to it, and all that comes after is a consequence of it and a response to it. The universe is a different place because God became a man. This is so not merely because we now have new information, because through the teachings of Christ we learn more truth, though we certainly do. Rather, the Incarnation opened a channel of grace that flows into human hearts. We are different. We know more, indeed, but we are also capable of more. The rules have changed.

The Old Testament, as we have seen, was about a temple, a place for God to dwell with man. The New Testament is about the same thing. The Incarnation is the definitive temple event. As the first chapter of John's Gospel makes clear, Christ was the Word of God through whom all the cosmos had been spoken into being. In the Incarnation, this Word of God came to "pitch his tabernacle," to dwell with us so that we could see him, touch him, and hear his teaching. He was "Emmanuel," God with us. He was truly one of us. Human beings are very complicated. We are born into cultures with long histories; we are born into families that live in those cultures; and we are taught our language, our mores, our ways of making sense of the world through these social realities. We are born into and initiated into a particular world, a particular social architecture that was built by those who came before us and which we cannot escape. When God became a man, he entered into our social embeddedness.

He was born into a family and grew up as a child. He was not some abstraction of a man. He was a first-century Jewish man from Galilee. He was a member of that people, there, then. In the Incarnation, God dwelled with them in their world. But, of course, this world had been long prepared through the history of the Old Testament. The Word of God became a particular man as a member of a particular nation with a particular social architecture that he had himself shaped through the long history of the Old Testament. Israel had been called out of the history of the nations for this event. Israel was literally made for him.

Christ was the fulfillment of Israel. As is the case with all hierarchical fulfillment, this was an elevation of Israel past all that it was capable of on its own, past all that it could even imagine. All the categories of the Old Covenant were fulfilled precisely in being surpassed beyond themselves. For example, Christ showed how the Law was fulfilled precisely by moving past the Law. He declares: "Do not think that I have come to abolish the law and the prophets; I have come not to abolish them but to fulfil them" (Matt 5:17). The Law, Christ teaches, will never pass away, and those who teach the Law "shall be called great in the kingdom of heaven" (Matt 5:19). Indeed, Christ demands not less but more dutiful obedience to the dictates of the Law, a virtue which the Bible calls righteousness. And yet, things are different: "You have heard that it was said to the men of old, 'You shall not kill; and whoever kills shall be liable to judgment.' But I say to you that everyone who is angry with his brother shall be liable to judgment" (Matt 5:21–22). And again: "You have heard that it was said, 'You shall not commit adultery.' But I say to you that every one who looks at a woman lustfully has already committed adultery with her in his heart" (Matt 5:27–28). Christ is deepening the Law. Christ is asserting that the Law is actually kept or broken through the movements of the heart rather than through external actions in response to commands. To hate is to murder more properly than to kill. To lust is to fornicate more properly than to commit adultery. The Law was given as a response to movements of the heart. The external Law, the commands, are, therefore, fulfilled not through mere obedience in works but through the heart. One is truly righteous only when the Law becomes written not on stone tablets but on the fleshy tablets of his heart. It is not enough to refrain from killing our enemy. We must not want to kill him; more, we must love him.

St. Thomas Aquinas explains that law is fulfilled not in the mere performance of the acts that it mandates but in the performance of these acts in a certain way. As we discussed earlier, the Old Law was a specification of the natural law. The Ten Commandments were basic statements of the natural moral law, and the judicial and ceremonial precepts were the particular application of that law to Israel. To obey the Law outwardly was, then, to *act* in a moral way. It was to perform the "acts of the virtues." But this is not the same as having virtue itself. Someone who has virtue obeys the law not because he is told to but because he is the type of person who knows that it is right and wants to do what it says without even having to be told.[9] So, for example, a man with the virtue of chastity remains faithful to his wife not because it is against the rules to cheat but because he simply doesn't want to. He

---

[9] See, for example, *ST* I-II, q. 107, a. 1.

loves his wife and simply wants to do the right thing as an aspect of who he is, as an aspect of his character or personality.

Such virtue, St. Thomas explains, is a type of second nature.[10] Virtuous men perform the acts of the virtues as if they were natural to them, like eating and drinking. To acquire the virtues is to "internalize" the law, to make the law a part of who you are. This is what is meant by the law being written on our hearts rather than written on stone. Instead of dictating what we should do, the law begins to describe who we are. Through virtue, the law is both perfectly obeyed and the law is, in a sense, done away with. A perfectly virtuous man is free from the law; the law does not compel him to do anything he does not already want to do. This is the fulfillment of the law that Christ is talking about. This is true righteousness wherein we are free from the law and yet "not an iota, not a dot, will pass from the law until all is accomplished" (Matt 5:18).

Can one coerce virtue? Can one demand that an action be performed with a certain internal orientation? Can one force love? The answer is clearly no. Real virtue cannot be commanded. This fact points to the radical nature of Christ's fulfillment of the law. The law, St. Thomas Aquinas explains, instructs us in what is just. But this instruction is not enough for us to actually be just. After the Fall, our hearts were turned to sin, and we accumulated terrible vices, the very opposite of virtue. The presence of these orientations toward evil—the presence of concupiscence, ignorance, weakness, cowardice—made the formation of true virtue impossible. We could obey out of fear. That is clear. We could even obey out of the type of love that a man has for his commanding officer in an army or out of the kind of love that a slave might develop for his master. But, because of the ever-present effects of sin, we could not shift from submission to the true obedience that flows only from true righteousness. This gap was too great. The New Testament, then, brought a New Law as a fulfillment of the Old Law, and this New Law did not merely instruct; it also assisted. It did not just tell us what to do; it gave us the power to do it. The New Law was not merely a law; it was grace itself. Grace is unmerited and totally disproportionate help from God. "Grace" means "free" or "gift," and that is just what it is, a free gift from God that penetrates our very hearts and gives us a second nature that allows us to fulfill the law in virtue.

---

[10] See, for example, *ST* I-II, q. 58, a. 1, 4; *ST* I-II, q. 71, a. 2, ad 1; *ST* II-II, q. 18, a. 4, resp.

This is an at least partial return to the situation in Eden. For example, Christ preached that divorce was wrong and that any man who divorced his wife and married another committed adultery. This shocked his listeners because the Old Law had allowed for divorce. Christ responded that it was only because of their "hardness of heart" (Matt 19:8)—that is to say, only because of their inability to achieve true virtue—that divorce has been allowed, but that had not been the way of things in the beginning, and now that grace was restored, it would not be the way of things going forward. Through Christ, our hearts again became capable of true fidelity in marriage. Through the grace of Christ, the fundamental horizontal relationship between people, the relationship between husband and wife and, by extension, between them and their children, was restored. The love of neighbor no longer lay out of reach.

Grace fulfilled the law by elevating it over an infinite gap. No amount of law or law abiding ever transitioned to grace and the true virtue it makes possible. Grace was categorically different. The New Law was really a new law, and yet because of the way hierarchies work, it included within it the perfection of the Old Law. The Old Law was to the New Law as the imperfect was to the perfect: two laws that were really, finally, one Divine Law. The New Law was lived through the virtues of Faith, Hope, and Charity. These virtues were divinely infused, which means that they are gifts from God. When men accept these gifts, they are capable of acquiring all the particular virtues demanded by the law. Through Faith, one came to know and understand the truth about God and man. Faith perfected the intellect to see and understand what was truly good. Through Charity, man came to desire this good perfectly. Faith working through Charity, or love, is to know and desire the true and the good. It is to be restored to our nature through being elevated past our nature. Understanding this allows us to understand what St. Paul means when he says that "faith is reckoned . . . as righteousness" (Rom 4:22). In the Old Law, righteousness was thought to be perfection. In the New Law, this perfection is revealed to be found only in Faith working in Love. Faith is perfect righteousness, but it is not merely righteousness. It surpasses righteousness. A man with Faith is righteous, even though he is free from the Law. This is a paradox that becomes coherent only through Christ.

A grace-filled man is a man of perfection. This is what Christ calls us to: "You, therefore, must be perfect, as your heavenly Father is perfect" (Matt 5:48). Such a thing becomes possible only because God comes to us. God became a man so that, as men, we might become godlike. This sounds really abstract, and it is. It is mysterious, in fact. But it can be at least partially understood. The Fall closed us in on ourselves. We retreated into human history to build our own kingdoms with our own idols, made of human hands. When we did this, and as we sunk lower into this "earthiness," our connection with what was above was weakened almost to the point of breaking. In the Incarnation, God came into that fallen world. We could no longer reach up to him, and so he came down to us. We could no longer find communion in prayer; we no longer walked with God in the garden, and so God came down to talk to us in human language and to walk with us through our own fallen temple-kingdoms. He entered into the City of Man.

There is a perhaps strange irony in this. Human beings had placed themselves at the top of the hierarchy of being. In our pride and our desire to be gods, we had usurped God's rightful place and constructed a world in which man was supreme. God does not merely "shove" us back into our rightful place, as he would have certainly been justified in doing. He does not come as a terrifying god of power to force us in our fallenness to cower in fear and so acknowledge our inferiority. Rather, through the Incarnation, he makes our grave error in a sense correct, renders it true, though in a totally unexpected way. Through the Incarnation, God, who is infinitely above all creation, who is the top of the hierarchy in a manner so extreme that it explodes the very notion of hierarchy, becomes a man. *God becomes man.* In the face of our false kings who claimed to be man-gods, He becomes our true King as a true God-man. Through the Incarnation, human nature really is elevated to the very top of the hierarchy of being. God reaches down to where we are, enters into our world, and elevates it to his place, the very place that we tried to claim for ourselves in the Fall. He undoes the City of Man not by destroying it with a flood or with fire from heaven, but by sanctifying it. Rather than merely humbling us, he humbles himself. Such is love. Through this love, the redemption of our sin becomes an elevation past what even Adam in his original justice experienced; we become deified. We had been only "for a little while lower than the angels" (Heb 2:7). Now, ironically, through our sin and God's reaction to it in the Incarnation, our nature was joined to the divine nature above even the angels. "Oh, Happy Fault!" the liturgy sings of Adam's fall.[11]

Through this entering into our world, Christ brings his grace. God becomes intelligible to us in terms of our world, in terms even of our superstitions and cults. He talks to us about himself in language so clearly incapable of capturing his essence as to be absurd. And yet, this world of rituals, sacrifices, laws, and kingdoms was the temple-world we had built after the Fall and the world that he had already been bending in his direction through the Old Testament. He does not sweep this world away but elevates it. The ceremonies of the Old Law become the sacraments of the New. Ritual remains, the things, sounds, smells, and bodily motions remain, but now they are more than mere symbols of Christ as they had been in the Old. Now, they actually bear him within them. They are no longer merely symbols that instruct; they are the thing itself that acts, that assists. They actually give the grace that they signify. Purified in Faith and Charity, the Christian no longer experiences in these rites even the vestiges of the idolatry from which they emerged. He experiences, rather, Christ himself. Not a man-made god, but God made man. This is the wholly unexpected surprise of the Incarnation.

Through Christ, communion becomes again possible. Because the Son of God became one of us, we became capable of friendship with God. But it's more than friendship. The New Testament makes it very clear that we can become one with Christ, that through Faith and Charity, we can experience a true unity with Christ. We become, together, the body of which he is the head. Here our horizontal and our vertical relationality are united through one person. We are united together as a body and united with God as the head of that body. We become one organism that is given its life through the grace that flows through the Incarnation and the preaching and sacraments that follow. Christ is the vine and we are the branches, different pieces of one living thing. Christ is the bridegroom and we are the bride, different persons who become "one flesh" in a real union. We are the adopted brothers of Christ and so heirs to the kingdom of God, one family, divine and yet human. The love of neighbor as ourselves becomes possible through the shared love of God.

This is the ultimate temple-event. Here, in the union that is the Church, God dwells with us as one of us. In the Old Testament, God dwelled in the temple. It was a particular building that people visited

---

[11] Exsultet, Easter Vigil.

to worship at discrete times and in particular ways. God was there, but he was external to us, as the Law was external to us. In the New Law, we become the stones of the temple. The temple is our life in a world that we creatively build, as it was in the beginning. As we have seen, in the New Law, the law, the Word of God, is not merely external to us; it becomes internalized through grace, and we are conformed to it. He dwells in us. We are transformed into temples for God, and we are assembled as living stones into the great temple which is the Church itself, redeemed humanity. And along with humanity, all of creation is redeemed. We are returned to the primordial mission. Our world is the temple of God, and our mission is to expand from this Eden, to multiply, to subdue and have dominion, to use our reason and creativity to construct the entire cosmos as this temple-world, which means to convert it to Faith and Charity through grace. God becomes one of us so that we can again become ourselves. We are restored as kings, priests, and prophets and rescued from our bondage to false gods and the corrupt societies that served them.

This is a great undoing of the temple-states and the god-kings of the ancient world. A central piece of Christ's teaching concerned the coming of the kingdom of God. The kingdom of God was at hand. As in every other transition from the Old to the New, in the New Testament Christ's kingdom is revealed to be profoundly different and yet a perfect fulfillment of the kingdoms of the world. Egypt is undone, ironically, by becoming in a sense true. In Christ, we gain a king who is, in fact, a god-man.

As we have seen, the idolatrous kingdoms of the City of Man were never totally depraved. They were, rather, perversions of man's natural and inescapable drive to order the world in a hierarchy that descends from perfect power, from God. In sin and pride, we made a man god and provided society with idols, priests, and temples in order for his power to descend into all aspects of our lives, to order us as slaves to his will in a desperate attempt to find some measure of peace. We attempted to satisfy our natures without ever looking up, without ever humbling ourselves. This, of course, can't but fail. Nevertheless, before the coming of Christ, mankind continued the project with a sort of frantic despair. This project reached a culmination with the Roman Empire. Caesar Augustus, the first emperor, was acclaimed as divine. This was not an especially unusual thing for the Romans. Powerful men often developed a cult, and many of the gods were understood to have been men at one time. Even fathers were sometimes considered gods by their wives, children, and slaves. Augustus was just a particularly powerful man, and so his divinity seemed clearer and of more widespread importance. The peace of the empire that, in fact, rested on the devastating effectiveness of its legions and the terror inspired by its raw power was thought to flow from him. Treating him as a god just made sense. His overwhelming power was the source of the "peace" of the empire. This was not a meaningless peace. One really could travel across the Mediterranean world freely and safely. One really could grow crops and bring them to market without fear of foraging armies or thieving brigands. Such peace offered through god-kings is why men continuously created them. This peace, though, was a merely external peace in keeping with a merely external law dictated through a merely external idol and resting, ultimately, on extreme violence.

There was a sort of virtue in the Romans that made their empire possible. They disciplined themselves, trained themselves, sacrificed superficial pleasures, and dedicated their lives to something bigger than any one of them; but this thing, this love to which they were devoted, was nothing more than glory, nothing more than the intoxicating exultation of power. This was their real god: power itself. The insincerity that historians sometimes sense in the emperor cult or the cynicism that Roman intellectuals sometimes displayed toward the pantheon of gods that the people worshiped is rooted in this simple principle. Power was divine, and he who wielded power was a god, or at least the son of a god. The emperor was not a god because of some magical ceremony or because he had some secret knowledge. He was a god because he could marshal the force to destroy nations. He held life and death in his hands and meted it out according to his will. This, to the Romans, was divinity.

Christ was born into a Jewish culture that was subject to this Roman Empire, and his declaration that the kingdom of God was at hand and that he was, in fact, the Son of God must be read directly in this context. It was radically subversive, and it is why the Romans killed him and martyred so many of his disciples. Christ, for example, told a parable about the kingdom of heaven. The kingdom of heaven, he said, was like a king who was holding a marriage feast for his son. He sent out servants to invite the guests to the dinner. Instead of coming, the invited guests abused his servants and even killed them. This made this king angry, and he destroyed the guests with his army and sent his servants out to invite strangers (see Matt 22:1–14). Now, the meaning of this parable is about as simple as can be. God was the king and Christ was his son. The Jews had been invited to the king's feast and had rejected him. God would therefore destroy them and move on to another people. This was a direct threat to the survival of the status quo.

This threat was not some sort of spiritualized story with no immediate "political" consequences. The Pharisees recognized this immediately and so responded to Christ's parable by asking him if it was lawful to pay taxes to Caesar. Jesus responds, "Why put me to the test, you hypocrites? Show me the money for the tax." They brought him a tribute penny, and he continued, "Whose likeness and inscription is this?" They replied that it was Caesar's, and Christ responded, "Render therefore to Caesar the things that are Caesar's, and to God the things that are God's" (see Matt 22:18–21). We have to take a moment to understand what is going on here. On its obverse, the tribute penny bore the image of Tiberius, the current emperor, with the inscription "Caesar Augustus Tiberius, son of the Divine Augustus," and on its reverse, it had an image of the queen mother as the goddess Peace. The coin was struck for the very purpose of maintaining the power of a god-king. It was itself an idol, and its dutiful payment was a form of submission, even worship. The money was paid because the emperor was a god of power. Christ attacks this directly. He looks at the penny and sees it for what it is: merely the mechanism, the property, of the man called Caesar. Like all idols, it is merely the work of human hands, fashioned of silver and cast by men. There is nothing divine about Caesar's power. The coin is an empty boast. Give it, therefore, back to its owner, but do so not with the worship for which it was made, but rather as a sort of pitiful nothing. Give worship to the true God, the true king. Give to the true king what is his. And what is his? A couple lines later, Christ tells us: "You shall love the Lord your God with all your heart, and with all your soul, and with all your mind. This is the great and first commandment. And a second is like it, You shall love your neighbor as yourself" (Matt 22:37–39). What is left for Caesar? His worthless little coin and his absurd claim to be a god.

This was more or less treason. Christ's assertion to be a son of God, who had come to establish a kingdom, was clearly rebellious. Such treason formed the basis of Christ's trial. The Jews brought Christ before Pilate with the charge that he asserted himself to be the king of the Jews and the Son of God. In the political-theological world in which they lived, these claims amounted to the same thing. So, Pilate asks Christ, "Are you the king of the Jews?"

> Jesus answered, "My kingship is not of this world; if my kingship were of this world, my servants would fight, that I might not be handed over to the Jews; but my kingship is not from the world." Pilate said to him, "So you are a king?" Jesus answered, "You say that I am a king. For this I was born, and for this I have come into the world, to bear witness to the truth. Every one who is of the truth hears my voice." Pilate said to him, "What is truth?" (John 18:36–38)

Christ confused Pilate. To Pilate, kingship simply was worldly power. To not have an army was to be no king at all. Christ's assertion that he is a king and that he does not fight for worldly power because his kingship is not from the world, not from below but from above, was a sort of nonsense. Christ explains that his power is based in truth. This brings us back to our discussion above on the difference between external law and internal virtue. To be virtuous is to live in the truth, the truth of human nature, of the cosmos, and of God himself. We have already seen how this is the fulfillment of the law. The law is external and coercive and is necessary because of sin. Its power comes, in a sense, from below, from the world. Christ brings grace and the internal conversion of hearts. His power is from above. However, this does not leave the power of the world alone. As we saw with Christ's discussion of the tribute penny, it pulls the rug out from under it. The power of the god-king is the power of the liar: His claim is that peace comes only through violence, from below. Christ reveals that men restored to truth through grace, however, are not subject to this power of lies. They can have peace without Caesar. This is a more radical rebellion than any army could have mounted. However, it doesn't make sense to Pilate because he does not have a concept of truth that is distinct from power. He is a Roman through and through. Power is truth. Truth is nothing more than power. So, for Pilate, Christ seems insane.

He and his soldiers, therefore, mock him, saying, "Hail, King of the Jews!" and put a crown of thorns on his head and clothe him in a purple robe. Pilate then tries to give him back to the Jews because he doesn't see a threat in him. They answer, "We have a law, and by that law he ought to die, because he has made himself the Son of God"

(John 19:7). This frightens Pilate. Sons of gods were, after all, kings. That is what it meant to be a son of god. Nevertheless, Pilate sees no actual power in Christ and so tries again to release him. The Jews cry out, "If you release this man, you are not Caesar's friend; every one who makes himself a king sets himself against Caesar" (John 19:12). This is the decisive charge. They connect the dots in no uncertain terms: Caesar's power is as a son of god. This man claims to be the son of the god of the Jews. Therefore, this man claims to be a rival king. What is more, Pilate now sees that he is more than merely a crazy claimant. As the mob makes clear, he does, in fact, seem to have power, even if it is a strange, confusing, and unconventional power. He must, therefore, be the son of the Jewish god. He must be the King of the Jews. "Pilate said to them, 'Shall I crucify your King?' The chief priests answered, 'We have no king but Caesar.' Then he handed him over to them to be crucified" (John 19:15–16).

The chief priests and the Pharisees were committing an extreme form of idolatry, the most extreme in the Bible. They were the custodians of the Divine Law, of the very Law of God that he had given them as their king. Its content was Christ himself, but it was an external law, and so it was similar in form to the external commands of the pagan god-kings. This was what Christ had come to change through grace, to elevate this law into the New Law of the heart, to open it up to what was above, exploding its boundaries through its fulfillment. The Pharisees recognize throughout Christ's mission that he was a threat to the self-enclosed nature of their law. They had come to pervert the Divine Law in such a way that it no longer attempted to reach beyond its own confines, to make contact with its creator. In contrast to the law of the Psalms (the law of the Davidic Kingdom), which was constantly, yet hesitantly, pointing beyond itself into the mystery of God the true king, the law of the Pharisees had become a self-enclosed mechanism of social control that was operated by the elites and the chief priests. It had become a mechanism of power. It had become no different, ultimately, from the law of Pharaoh or the law of Caesar. The final apostasy was to assert that the breaking of the Divine Law was identical to the breaking of the law of Caesar, that it was his law, that he was the divine lawgiver, the true king, that rendering to God what was God's and rendering to Caesar what was Caesar's was the same thing. This is exactly what the chief priests do. In order to defend their own power, the Jewish authorities essentially made themselves slaves to other men. They made Caesar their god. This is the tragic paradox of sin. Slavery to the drive to amass power always leads, ironically, to slavery to other men. The Romans crucified Christ as the king of the Jews. This is what Pilate wrote on his cross. It was the justification for the execution. In killing Christ, Pilate sought to destroy the independence of Israel and absorb them into the Roman world definitively. In order to have Christ killed, the Pharisees and priests gave Pilate what he wanted. They acknowledged Caesar as son of god and king of kings. Vice equals slavery.

In the crucifixion, the Romans unleashed all the power that they had. They tortured and killed Christ. The kings of the world only have such violence, such external power. Had Pilate and Christ's accusers been right about the world, this would have worked. If raw physical power is what characterizes the sons of gods, in his crucifixion, Christ would have been robbed of this status. Death is the ultimate moment of powerlessness, the ultimate moment of defeat. The onlookers understood this, saying "You who would destroy the temple and build it in three days, save yourself! If you are the Son of God, come down from the cross. . . . He is the King of Israel; let him come down now from the cross, and we will believe in him. . . . Let God deliver him now, if he desires him; for he said, 'I am the Son of God'" (Matt 27:40–43). But rather, Christ dies. Christ defeats the power of the kings in a totally unexpected way. Christ defeats this power by passing through it, by dying and being resurrected. When he rose from the dead, he was not a ghost, not merely a spirit that the forces of the world could safely ignore. Instead, his body was raised. The thing that the lords of the world dominated escaped their grasp. The suffering that love endures in the world conquers suffering through resurrection. The Resurrection is the final undoing of the power of fear.

This was the Good News. It was the establishment of the Kingdom of God on Earth, the Church. This kingdom and its New Law were universal. As St. Thomas explains, the Old Law, like human law in the nations, was particular to a certain people at a certain time and place. But the New Law, because it was in the heart, was not tied to a certain time and place. Rather, all cultures, all times and places, can live by the New Law through their particular human laws.[12] The universal is in the particular, and the particular reaches out to and is fulfilled in the universal. The New Law is universal, which is what the word "catholic" means, and yet we live it in our concrete histories. Just

---

[12] *ST* I-II, qq. 107–108.

human law is a participation in the Divine Law.

The kingdom that Christ established, the Church, is both temporal, existing in history and governed by external laws, and spiritual, animated through grace and united with the Kingdom of God in heaven. We might have expected God to establish his kingdom in a purely temporal way; many of the people of Jesus's time did. They expected Christ to establish a powerful monarchy capable of casting off Israel's enemies through military might. Conversely, we might have expected God to establish a purely spiritual kingdom made up of an invisible communion of believers, united spiritually with the saints in heaven and indifferent to the power of the world. The Church that Christ did establish, however, was both temporal and spiritual. It is a temporal society that moves through history and so has a governmental structure: it has rituals, buildings, laws, priests, and kings. But it is a society that is bound together not simply through these things, as is a merely temporal kingdom, but also through the spiritual which comes from beyond it, through the faith and charity that grace makes possible. This society is united with the Kingdom of God in heaven; it is aloof and yet it concerns itself with the minutia of the temporal. It is truly the City of God: a real city that stretches from earth to heaven itself.

Christ gave us an ecclesial structure that is based on the fulfillment of the structure of Israel. Israel had been organized through twelve tribes. Christ called twelve Apostles to lead his Church. He bestowed special graces upon these twelve, establishing them as the first bishops of the Church. They were called to preach the Gospel with authority, as Christ had. They were also given the fullness of sacramental powers. The sacraments of the New Law, like the Incarnation itself, bring together the world of men and the world of God, the particular and the universal, the temporal and the eternal. God does not sweep away what makes us human; he elevates it to the divine through his humble assumption of our humanity. He comes down to meet us, and in so doing brings the unscalable heights of his nature within our reach. Through our world of things and words, God's grace flows into our hearts. The Apostles were given power over these sacraments. What they bound on earth would be bound in heaven; what sins they forgave would be forgiven (see Matt 16:19). What a shocking display of divine humility, and what an unexpected demonstration of human dignity. This basic structure, through which Christ's teaching and his grace are perpetuated through the Church, was established by Christ himself and is evident in the books of the New Testament.

This structure was like a little Eden for redeemed humanity to again set out to transform the world into a temple for God, to convert the City of Man by absorbing it into itself.

Christ revealed through his life, death, and resurrection that his kingdom was dramatically different from the kingdoms of the world. As Christ said:

> You know that the rulers of the Gentiles lord it over them, and their great men exercise authority over them. It shall not be so among you; but whoever would be great among you must be your servant, and whoever would be first among you must be your slave; even as the Son of man came not to be served but to serve, and to give his life as a ransom for many. (Matt 20:25–28)

Christ was explaining how a hierarchy of service and love works. Christ is the king of the cosmos, and yet he comes not to dominate but to serve. His power is for those below him, those under his care. This, Christ instructs the Apostles, is how the Church will function. It will have structures of authority. It is made of men and so it must. But such authority must exist for those under it. People with authority must wield it as servants. This is a radical inversion of the kingship of the nations. It is, rather, the type of authority wielded by good fathers and mothers. A good father has power over his children, but he has this power so he can lead them deeper into their own good. We might say that through the power of a good father, the child becomes powerful. But what we are really seeing is the undoing of the worldly notion of power as the ability to satisfy one's own desire. When a father puts his power at the service of his child, neither merely his desires nor the child's desires direct its use—the father is humbled even as the child is elevated. On the other hand, a wicked father is precisely a father who uses his power for himself, who abuses his family for his own gain, who embraces his power as at his disposal. Christ revealed that all true authority would be the authority of a good father. Christ emptied himself for mankind, all the way to the cross. He revealed that all power, if it is just, will have an element of the cross in it. All good fathers and mothers suffer in their love for their children. All good bishops and priests suffer in their care of their flocks, and all good kings suffer in their care for their subjects. This suffering is the mark of self-emptying. Love, and so true power, in a world still rent by sin, hurts.

Christ, however, shows that this suffering is not the final word. The cross is not the end of the story. The Resurrection is the end of the story. The suffering that love endures in the world conquers suffering through resurrection. The Church, then, makes sense as a suffering Church of servants only in reference to the final resurrection. The Church endures suffering in her faith and in her charity because of her hope, and in her hope, the suffering is translated into joy. A virtuous mother feels joy in her heart as she rocks her crying baby to sleep at three in the morning because her love for the child spills out of the present moment of suffering, and through hope, she feels the goodness of her love in her pain. The Church suffers in joy through history because the Church knows that Christ is the Lord of history and that the final victory is already won.

As the end of Jesus's earthly life approached, he made a promise to his disciples: "But the Counselor, the Holy Spirit, whom the Father will send in my name, he will teach you all things, and bring to your remembrance all that I have said to you" (John 14:26). Ten days after Jesus's Ascension into heaven, the Apostles were gathered together with Mary in the "Upper Room," perhaps the same room where Jesus celebrated the Last Supper. There, the Holy Spirit finally came to them:

> When the day of Pentecost had come, they were all together in one place. And suddenly a sound came from heaven like the rush of a mighty wind, and it filled all the house where they were sitting. And there appeared to them tongues as of fire, distributed and resting on each one of them. And they were all filled with the Holy Spirit and began to speak in other tongues, as the Spirit gave them utterance. (Acts 2:1–4)

Most of us are familiar with Pentecost. It is one of the great feasts of the Church. We celebrate it every spring, fifty days after Easter Sunday. Long before the Incarnation, however, Pentecost was a Jewish feast, celebrated in commemoration of God giving the Law to Moses at Sinai. For this feast, Jews traveled to Jerusalem from across the known world. So, on the day when the Holy Spirit came to the Apostles in the Upper Room, thousands of people, all speaking different languages, were crowded outside in the streets.

That language difference, however, posed no barrier to the Apostles. Immediately, they went out and began preaching the Kingdom.

Because the Holy Spirit allowed them to preach in different tongues, all the people understood them. They heard about Christ and about God's plan for our salvation. And they heard the call to be baptized. On that day, the Holy Spirit made the Church known to the world. This is why Pentecost is sometimes considered the birthday of the Church. Pentecost is considered the Church's birthday for another reason as well. The Jewish people celebrated Pentecost in remembrance of when God gave them the Law, which took place on Mount Sinai, fifty days after the first Passover, when God delivered the Israelites from slavery in Egypt. That first Passover, however, pointed forward to the definitive Passover of Christ's death and Resurrection, through which the people of God would be definitively freed from slavery. Likewise, the giving of the Law on Mount Sinai also pointed forward to the giving of the New Law, which, as St. Thomas Aquinas tells us, "is in the first instance the very grace of the Holy Spirit that is given to those who believe in Christ."[13]

In other words, the Jewish feast of Pentecost, like the Jewish feast of Passover, was fulfilled in Christ. When the Holy Spirit came on Pentecost, people received the grace to live as Christ's followers. They received the New Law, which is the law of Love. "This is my commandment," Jesus said, "that you love one another as I have loved you" (John 15:12). The City of God, the Church, is known because it is constituted by people who live according to this universal law of love, through the continuous action of the Holy Spirit, who makes Jesus ever present to us.

Pentecost was unexpected. Humanity had been divided up into nations with different languages in the story of the Tower of Babel. Humanity, at first, shared a language and a culture. This humanity organized itself in order to build a giant false temple to themselves as gods. God sees this, sees the great sin they are trying to commit, and stops them by dispersing them through the world and giving each group a different language, a different culture. We might think, then, that when the Holy Spirit brought redemption, he would undo Babel by making all humanity again one nation, one culture, with one language. But this is not what he does. Rather, the fall at Babel is revealed as another *felix culpa*, another "happy fault," where human sin makes possible a healing that elevates humans past where we had been. At Pentecost, our division into different languages and different cul-

---

[13] *ST*, I-II, q. 106

tures, with different laws, would no longer be a barrier to our more fundamental unity because this unity came not from below but from above. Because of the grace flowing through the Church, the New Law could be preached and so instituted *within* every language and every culture. Our particular diversity happens within our universal unity, our Catholicity. As St. Augustine would write four hundred years later:

> While the Heavenly City is on a pilgrimage in this world, she calls out citizens from all nations and so collects a society of aliens, speaking all languages. She takes no account of any differences in laws, customs, and institutions, by which earthly peace is achieved and preserved—not that she annuls or abolishes any of these, rather she maintains them (for whatever divergences there are among the diverse nations, those institutions have one aim—earthly peace), provided that no hindrance is presented thereby to the religion which teaches that the one and true God is to be worshipped.[14]

But nevertheless, the unity of the universal Church, of the City of God, is real, here, in history. After Pentecost, the diversity of the nations and the unity of the real, concrete Church are not in competition with each other. Through grace and the New Law written on the hearts of men, diverse human laws can all be elevated to participation in a single society that operates with its own structure and its own laws. A hierarchy of service makes this possible. The higher unity reaches down into the lower unities and enters into them, not to destroy them or force them to work in its service but to lead them deeper into their own good, like a father or mother and their children. Through the Holy Spirit, the universal Church reaches down and into every people. She is the mother of the nations, the light of the nations, showing them the way. The City of God was a proper city, with a proper hierarchy, which is an inversion of the hierarchy of the City of Man. This proper hierarchy reaches up, with each level lacking self-sufficiency and so demanding humility. This was the restoration of freedom, the freedom that operates only within such order.

With the coming of the Holy Spirit, the architectonic office of man was restored. Man was restored as a legislator, as a maker of just human law, as a builder of worlds. Such human law was the way that

---

[14] Augustine, *The City of God*, 19.17.

the particular, the way of life of a certain people in a certain time and place, was connected to the universal, to the natural law elevated through grace to the New Law. This is why, St. Thomas explains, the New Law has so few positive mandates.[15] The particular specification of the law of God was, for the most part, restored to the redeemed creative rationality of the baptized. Remember, the Mosaic Law had been divided into the judicial and the ceremonial precepts. The single Divine Law governed both man's horizontal and his vertical relationality. This continued into the New Law. To the laity, to the temporal power, was restored the legislative office with regards to the judicial, earthly realm of things and bodies. To the clergy, to the spiritual power, was restored the legislative office with regards to the ceremonial, supernatural realm of truth and grace. Together, the temporal and spiritual powers, if living truly in the New Law, could creatively specify for their peoples the natural law, both those aspects concerning love of neighbor and those aspects concerning the love of God. The New Law was a law of freedom, St. Thomas tells us, not only because through grace we can achieve the virtue that frees us from the law but because through grace we were restored as the architects of our own worlds.[16]

Human law, though, unlike in the Garden of Eden, now had a coercive component. In innocence, people had obeyed human law through charity, because they loved the lawgivers and believed in the social project under construction. As we have seen, after the Fall, human law became increasingly corrupted into false law that was made and enforced for the benefit of those in power. People obeyed this "law" mostly out of fear. In contrast to the "laws" of the nations, the Old Law was perfectly just; nevertheless, its power was, in the first instance, rooted likewise in fear. This was so because Israel was not immune from the consequences of the Fall; they too had fallen into the vice that leads always to some form of slavery. The Law, then, relied upon the fear that animated such fallen people in order to lead them to act in a virtuous manner. The Old Law remained, St. Thomas tells us, a servile law, even if it pointed beyond fear to true obedience, true righteousness. The New Law, as we have seen, fulfilled the Old Law, and this meant that it contained within it all the "functions" of the Old Law. It contained within it the mechanisms of fear through

---

[15] *ST* I-II, q. 108, aa. 1–2.
[16] *ST* I-II, q. 108, a. 1.

punishment that the Old Law had relied upon.

This was necessary because the New Law was given to govern a humanity that was still born into the State of Nature, was still born into original sin and into social structures that everywhere bore the scars of this sin and which attempted to lead people deeper into depravity. The New Law, therefore, had to have coercive punishments to lead people out of the Age of Nature, through the Age of Law, and into the Age of Grace. These were the very steps of the spiritual life. For those in vice, the first step was submission through fear, a submission that, through grace, could transition away from fear and into true obedience, into the Faith, and that could from there transition to Charity, which was the final internalization of the law in virtue. The New Law, then, remained a pedagogue, a teacher. But it was a perfect pedagogue that had within it the ability to surpass itself through fulfillment. The restored human law within the New Law, therefore, bore the sword, but unlike the nations, it did not bear this sword in vain. The sword was necessary, but the sword was always remedial, always being surpassed through the redemption that the New Law made possible. The establishment of the Church, then, was the reestablishment of the possibility of true politics precisely in the surpassing of worldly politics. The City of God fulfilled the ambitions of the City of Man. This is what makes it universal, what makes it capable of being instantiated in the life of the nations, not through destroying their worlds but through redeeming them, even their coercive law. This is what Pentecost is about.

At first, the Apostles' efforts focused on their own people, and many Jews were baptized. As they began proclaiming the Gospel, however, the Apostles and other disciples encountered resistance from both the Jewish and Roman authorities, who had, of course, just crucified Jesus. It didn't take long for that resistance to turn fatal. In the Book of Acts, we hear about the martyrdom of St. Stephen, who was one of the first deacons and "a man full of faith and of the Holy Spirit" (Acts 6:5). When he was dragged before the Jewish court on charges of blasphemy, he testified boldly that Jesus Christ was the culmination of the entire story of Israel and those who had killed Jesus were just like the unfaithful members of Israel who had rejected the prophets of the Old Testament. When the authorities became enraged and began to stone him, he faced his death bravely, asking God to forgive them for their sins.

The power the Holy Spirit gives to Christians suffering for Christ is made particularly clear when we compare the bravery of the first Christians before and after Pentecost. On the night that Jesus was arrested, the Apostles weren't willing to give their lives for Jesus. Instead, they ran away. Peter, the leader of the Apostles, even denied that he knew Jesus. Of the twelve, only St. John was at the foot of the cross. They remained in hiding, even after they knew that Jesus had risen from the dead, "for fear of the Jews" (John 20:19). On the day of Pentecost itself, the Apostles were together in "one place" (Acts 2:1), likely still in hiding. But immediately after the descent of the Holy Spirit, they came forth, preaching to the crowds, willingly facing persecution and even death. The Holy Spirit changed them. He gave them the power to bravely face the world.

We can see the dramatic effect of the action of the Holy Spirit in the conversion of St. Paul. Before he became a Christian, Paul (Saul) was one of the Jewish authorities who persecuted the first followers of Christ. He was present at the stoning of St. Stephen, "laid waste" the Church, and "dragged off men and women and committed them to prison" (Acts 8:3). One day, however, when he was traveling to Damascus in order to hunt down Christians, he saw a "light from heaven" flashing around him, and he fell to the ground. Then, Jesus spoke to him, asking him, "Saul, Saul, why do you persecute me?" (Acts 9:3–4).

Saul, blinded by the light, was led into the city by his companions. There, God sent Ananias, one of the leaders of the Christians, to find Saul: "And laying his hands on him he said, 'Brother Saul, the Lord Jesus who appeared to you on the road by which you came, has sent me that you may regain your sight and be filled with the Holy Spirit'" (Acts 9:17). After this, Saul could see again. But more importantly, he was filled with the Holy Spirit. He believed completely in Jesus, was baptized, and started preaching the Gospel. Like the other apostles and disciples, he also endured persecution, which he faced boldly. Through the Holy Spirit, he began an aggressive missionary campaign to the Gentiles. Paul's mission to the Gentiles opened the universal Church to all nations.

St. Paul made three missionary journeys throughout the eastern Mediterranean. He preached Christ crucified everywhere and made thousands of converts among the Gentiles. He also wrote letters of profound theological and spiritual insight. These letters, of course, made their way into the New Testament and form the bedrock for all later theology. Paul's mission to the Gentiles was successful, but it was also profoundly painful. St. Paul himself wrote:

> Five times I have received at the hands of the Jews the forty lashes less one. Three times I have been beaten with rods; once I was stoned. Three times I have been shipwrecked; a night and a day I have been adrift at sea; on frequent journeys, in danger from rivers, danger from robbers, danger from my own people, danger from Gentiles, danger in the city, danger in the wilderness, danger at sea, danger from false brethren; in toil and hardship, through many a sleepless night, in hunger and thirst, often without food, in cold and exposure. And, apart from other things, there is the daily pressure upon me of my anxiety for all the churches. Who is weak, and I am not weak? Who is made to fall, and I am not indignant? (2 Cor 11:24–29)

It might seem obvious to us that Christianity is for all human beings regardless of nationality, but this was not clear immediately after the death and resurrection of Christ. As we have seen, the Old Testament was about the Israelites, a particular nation among a multitude of human nations. Christ was the fulfillment of their scriptures, of their law. It was not at first clear that the salvation that he offered was offered to all men. It was also not clear how much of the Jewish law should be retained among the followers of Christ. The law, for example, forbade a Jew from eating with or entering the home of a foreigner. The law also forbade Jews from eating a wide variety of foods that were common among non-Jews. Christ was the Jewish messiah; his followers knew this, but did this mean that all of Christ's disciples must be practicing Jews? This was unclear. We can see clearly in the Acts of the Apostles how the Holy Spirit guided the early Church through this problem to the realization that the Age of Law was over.

There was a Roman army officer named Cornelius who had come to believe that the God of the Jews was, in fact, the true God. God sent an angel to Cornelius, telling him that God had seen his faith and his good works and instructing him to call for the apostle Peter. At the same time, God gave Peter a vision of "all kinds of animals and reptiles and birds of the air. And there came a voice to him, 'Rise, Peter; kill and eat.'" Peter protested that it would be against Jewish law to eat such unclean or common animals, but the voice responded, "What God has cleansed, you must not call common" (Acts 10:12–13, 15). The meaning of the vision was, of course, that followers of Christ no longer had to keep the Jewish dietary laws, and by extension that they no longer had to be Jewish. Right after the vision, Cornelius's messengers arrived summoning Peter, and he followed them into Cornelius's home, the home of a Gentile. Peter proclaimed, "Truly I perceive that God shows no partiality, but in every nation anyone who fears him and does what is right is acceptable to him" (Acts 10:34–35). He proceeded to preach the life, death, and resurrection of Christ. The Holy Spirit descended on Cornelius's household, and Peter commanded them to be baptized (see Acts 10). Peter returned to Jerusalem and explained to the suspicious Apostles what had happened. Their suspicions evaporated, "and they glorified God, saying, 'Then to the Gentiles also God has granted repentance unto life'" (Acts 11:18).

The controversy among the early Christians concerning the Gentiles was not yet over. Some Christians started preaching that Gentiles who converted had to be circumcised and obey the Mosaic law. Basically, they were arguing that in order to be Christian, you had to be Jewish and that Jewish law was still in full effect. This was a debate of profound significance. It was really over the universal nature of the Church. Was the Church a gathering of nations, or was the Church only the fulfillment of Israel in such a way that to convert to Christianity meant leaving behind one's own people to join the Jewish nation? Would the unity offered by the Church be of a different order than that offered by nations, or would it merely be that national order would be extended to include all the world? In order to address this problem, the Apostles called a council in Jerusalem around AD 50. This was the first instance of such a gathering, and it became the prototype for how the Church would solve major disputes throughout its history.

St. Paul traveled to the council and made his case against the "circumcision party." The Apostles and the elders of the Church listened to the arguments and considered them. Then St. Peter, the first pope, rose and spoke in favor of St. Paul. The Gentiles were not to be burdened with the Mosaic law. James spoke in support of Peter, and the council determined against the proposition that Gentile converts had to keep the Old Law. The council then drafted and distributed a letter with its determination. We can see here the first example of how the Holy Spirit guides the Church in history as it wrestles with doctrinal and disciplinary problems. The Church does not always immediately know what is true and what is right. History is a confusing muddle with many moving parts and many conflicting points of view. The Church makes her way through this uncertainty guided in prayer by the Holy Spirit. This is how the Council of Jerusalem settled the question of the Mosaic Law, and it is how, as we will see, the Church has settled one profound question after another.

St. Augustine described humanity after the Fall as being divided into two Cities: the City of Man and the City of God. Through the Age of Nature and the Age of Law, the City of Man reigned. It is not that the City of God was extinct. That is impossible. To the extent that man is always bound to the natural law, to the extent that he is always oriented toward peace and justice, to the extent that at some deep level he seeks the love of God and the love of neighbor, to that extent the City of God is always present. But through the Age of Nature and, to a lesser extent, the Age of Law, the City of God was, in a sense, found *within* the City of Man. Israel was the City of God in anticipation. It was the City of God in immaturity, we might say. So, within the dominant City of Man, there were movements toward God, promises in the direction of God, graces that worked in an extraordinary way to anticipate the City of God. In this way, the New Law, St. Thomas tells us, was present during the Old Law wherever God had elevated men past that Law and into charity, an elevation that always surpassed what the Law itself was capable of.[17] The Law itself, as law, was always earthly.

However, with the Incarnation, the Resurrection, and the coming of the Holy Spirit, the situation has been exactly reversed. The Fall is turned upside down. The Church is holy in her essence. Her life in Faith and Charity is fundamental to who she is. She *is* the City of God. However, the Old Law, the City of God in anticipation within the City of Man, exists within her wherever men have not yet achieved perfect virtue. But this lingering City of Man within the City of God is exactly what is being undermined and reformed, being transitioned into the fullness of the City of God. This is the action of salvation, which is an action of continuous reform. This is why the visible Church in history is never perfect, why it has within it sin, why it has within it the temptation to return to the world, why it is often drawn back toward the earthly City of Man. This lingering City of Man is not merely an imperfection; it is also, we might say, how the Church is opened to the nations. The visible Church reaches out into the fallen nations, into sinful humanity, and pulls them into her essential perfection through the truth and grace that she makes possible. The

---

[17] *ST* I-II, q. 107, a. 2, ad 2.

goodness that is in the nations is a participation in the perfect goodness of the Church. She penetrates into them through these strands of goodness. At the same time, their error, their sin, tragically extends its tentacles into her, wounding her. She, we might say, bears the sins of the world within herself, as Christ bore the sins of the world, and those sins hurt her as she does the penance and receives the grace necessary to surpass them. As we will see throughout the rest of this history, like Israel before her, the Church lives in a series of cycles of corruption and reform. This is her personality, her working in history, not because her corruption is ever good or a part of the plan, but because this cycle is what saving mankind looks like. It is the Passover and Exodus fulfilled. The Church, then, is in her essence not only Faith and Charity but also Hope. The Old Law remains within the New Law, and the Church not only retains Israel's function as a mediator between the nations and God but perfects it. She retains, as she must, a disciplinary and pedagogical law, but this law would be merely more of the "written code [that] kills" were it not for the "Spirit [that] gives life" (2 Cor 3:6).

II

The Ancient Church

1. Growth and Persecution

First-century Palestine was part of the Roman Empire. At its peak, the empire stretched from Cairo to Scotland and included the entire Mediterranean world. Christianity arose during what is often called the *Pax Romana*, the Roman Peace, which was a period of political stability and unity in the empire that started around 40 BC and lasted to around AD 180. During this period, one could travel from one end of the empire to the other on decent roads and without encountering tolls or needing a passport or fearing brigands. This situation, of course, aided the spread of the new faith, and the early Christians saw clearly the work of providence in Christ's birth at just that time in history.

The empire's power was based on its massive army, numbering around one hundred thousand free men at the time of Christ's birth. This military machine was animated by a deep civic patriotism, by a profound love of Rome, and a willingness to suffer and sacrifice for its glory and for its dominance over other peoples. In the first century, this military was made up almost entirely of men from the city of Rome or from the Italian peninsula. It was a committed and well-trained military force that was the locus of unity for the huge empire. Because unity was focused on the military, the early empire had a fairly decentralized political organization. It was really a coalition of self-governing city-states that were organized under the city of Rome through the army. These cities paid tribute to Rome and enjoyed the protection of its military, but the imperial government itself was rather small and didn't deal with the day-to-day affairs of local peoples. This was an ideal situation for the spread of Christianity, especially among the Jewish communities that were scattered throughout the empire.

Christianity spread quickly. Estimates of its rate of growth are incredibly difficult to make given the distance in time and paucity of detailed records. However, it seems that by the year 250, about 2 percent of the population was Christian. This might not sound like a lot, but it was actually around 3.5 million Christians. Fifty years later, 11 percent of the population was Christian. By the year 350, that number was 57 percent. In one hundred years, Christianity went from a small sect to a faith that could claim the majority of the empire as members. Why? How?

Sometimes modern historians bemoan the conversion of the empire, as if Christianity was some foreign force that had come from without and destroyed a vibrant, tolerant, and beautiful civilization, replacing it with ignorance and superstition. In this telling, conversion to Christianity was a sort of fraud or ruse through which a civilization that had once been happy, joyful, and truly alive was tricked or coerced into misery, into replacing its dancing with judgmental and rigid morality, into surrendering philosophical curiosity and rigor to close-minded dogmatism. This telling is profoundly wrong. It is mistaken in its very framing. Christianity was not a foreign force that invaded and conquered Roman paganism. Christianity arose *within* the empire and it spread through the empire as pagans converted by the millions. Christianity was something the people of the Roman empire did, not something that happened to them. It was as a Roman movement that Christianity became a movement of world historical significance. So, the question is: why did the Romans become Christians?

The Roman Empire was stable, but it was cruel and harsh. About a third of the population were slaves, literally conquered people who lived under continuous military domination. The empire was organized through a rigid social and political hierarchy that did not hesitate to use violence. In addition to the slaves, women, half the population, were in particular terribly treated. Their husbands had near-complete control over their lives, and they had little legal or social protection. While the government ruled through law, the law was harsh and brutal in application. It was more a mechanism for the maintenance of power and stability than it was a mechanism for justice for the weak. Indeed, power in the Roman Empire was felt immediately and used unhesitatingly. It was, in fact, understood as divine.

Power, more than anything else, was what mattered to the Romans. This love underwrote their political order and perhaps more importantly their conception of cosmic order.

Throughout the empire, hundreds of gods were worshiped. Most of these were local, of concern only to the inhabitants of a particular region. Some, such as Jupiter, were a part of the official cult of the empire as a whole. It is important, though, that we do not mistake their gods for smaller versions of God himself. The pagan gods were power. If the weather had power, it was a god. If the river had power, it was a god. The people understood the power that everywhere affected their lives, demanding their submission, to be aspects of the divine. They worshiped these instances of power. But it was not the worship of adoration and thanksgiving that Christians have grown accustomed to. It was more likely to be attempts at placating the divine power, of seeking its favor and mitigating its wrath. It was for this reason that it seemed obvious to the Romans that the emperor was divine. He had immense power, and power was what it meant to be godlike. There was an empire-wide cult, then, of the emperor himself. This cult will become very important later, when we discuss Roman persecution of Christians. For now, though, what we need to see is that residents of the Roman Empire lived under the power of others, men and gods, to whom they were expected to submit or suffer the swift and pitiless consequences. This produced a certain fatalism, the belief that the course of one's life is out of one's hands and is the result of the arbitrary will of others, which leads to despair and fear. People were scared, and fear produces the desire for power, the drive to amass for one's self the ability to determine fates, to steal from the gods, to become godlike to others, to achieve glory. This was the circular source of Rome's ambition for power, what St. Augustine called its *libido dominandi*, its lust for domination.

Christianity proposed a different way. Rather than a cosmos of chaos that is put in order by violent power, Christianity proposed that the universe was the creation a single loving God and that it had been made for peace and harmony and subsisted in this peace, that it only really *was* to the extent that it enjoyed what St. Augustine called the "tranquility of order." It was not violent power that provided order in this universe but love and forgiveness. Violence was what tore this harmony apart. Rather than the source of order, violence was the source of disorder. This was a radical inversion of the pagan understanding that nevertheless comprehended the pagan conceptual world. It was capable of explaining paganism to itself as a piece of showing the pagans another way.

Christianity taught that Christ made it possible for the primordial order of love to re-penetrate human society, reordering it according to its own deep nature. The early Christians enacted this reordering immediately among themselves. They lived in common, sharing all things. The weak and needy were given more, and the strong and prosperous gave more. They lived as if they were one body, feeling directly each other's joys and pains.[1] They believed that all people were called to this life and that all people, even women and slaves, were capable of achieving true freedom through virtue through grace. The contrast with pagan society could not have been starker. Christians became known by their love, as Christ had commanded them. The *Didache*, an important Christian document from around the year 100, exhorts the early Christians: "Do not hate anyone—but reprove some, pray for others, and love still others more than yourself."[2] Their love was the cause of their profound unity. To the early Christians, nothing was as abhorrent as division.[3] Unity in faith and charity was the antidote to the suffering of pagan society. St. Ignatius of Antioch wrote of faith and love: "This is the beginning and end of life: faith is the beginning, love is the end. And the two together in unity are God; all other things that lead to nobility of character follow."[4]

The Church was a place of unity, of peace. And little caused more division, the early Christians thought, than devotion to money and wealth. The Christians insisted that one's wealth was not one's own but was for service to the community, service to the weak. The world of money, the early Christians taught, was the world of "adultery, depravity, avarice, and deceit."[5] Wealth was about power, and the lust for power was the root of human suffering. This is why so many of the Christians lived in community, sharing all property, and why they shocked the pagans with their charity to the poor.

To a world of fear, Christianity offered salvation. This was a salvation that not merely awaited one in heaven, but a salvation that started in this life, in the society of peace called the Church. This

---

[1] 1 Clement 46.
[2] *Didache* 2.7.
[3] 1 Clement 2:6.
[4] Ignatius of Antioch, *Epistle to the Ephesians*, 14.
[5] 2 Clement 6.

salvation flowed into the Church through Christ in his sacraments, especially the Eucharist.[6] As Ignatius of Antioch wrote, "For when you frequently gather as a congregation, the powers of Satan are destroyed, and his destructive force is vanquished by the harmony of your faith. Nothing is better than peace, by which every battle is abolished, whether waged by those in heaven or by those on earth."[7] While the liturgy has obviously developed over the history of the Church, it is startling how familiar the worship of these earliest Christians is. They gathered on Sunday, they sang hymns and psalms, they read from the Scriptures, they blessed the bread and wine and shared it as the Body and Blood of Christ himself. They gave the sign of peace and recited the Lord's Prayer. They had the Mass. You can already see this, of course, in the texts of the New Testament, but the non-biblical writings of the early Christians are especially clear in their descriptions.[8]

The grace of peace flowed through the Eucharist, and there existed from the beginning both a particular liturgical form and a hierarchy to perform and oversee it.[9] This hierarchy began, as we have already discussed, with the Apostles, but it continued in the order of bishops. The earliest Church understood apostolic succession as well as we do, probably better. The bishops were essential to the unity of the Church.[10] They taught the faith that united the minds of Christians, and they governed the sacraments that enabled their love. St. Ignatius of Antioch was particularly outspoken on the importance of the bishops. He taught that unity with the bishop was the same unity as that of Christ with the Church and, through him, with the Father.[11] Indeed, the bishop should be looked upon as the Lord himself, as the shepherd who guides his sheep.[12] The bishop was assisted by the priests and deacons and organized in a hierarchy of service.[13] As Ignatius wrote: "I urge you to hasten to do all things in the harmony of God, with the bishop presiding in the place of God and the presbyters in the place of the council of the Apostles, and the deacons, who are especially dear to me, entrusted with the ministry of Jesus Christ, who was with the

---

[6] *Didache* 9.4.
[7] Ignatius, *Ephesians*, 13.
[8] Justin Martyr, *First Apology*, 65–67; *Didache* 9, 14.
[9] 1 Clement 40.
[10] Ignatius of Antioch, *Epistle to the Trallians*, 15.
[11] Ignatius, *Ephesians*, 4–5.
[12] Ignatius, *Ephesians*, 6; *Epistle to the Magnesians*, 2–3; Rom 2.
[13] Ignatius, *Magnesians*, 6; 1 Clement 37–38, 60–61.

Father before the ages and has been manifest at the end."[14] The unity that this hierarchy provided was the same unity that was made possible through the Eucharist. Again, Ignatius said: "And so be eager to celebrate just one Eucharist. For there is one flesh of our Lord Jesus Christ and one cup that brings the unity of his blood, and one altar, as there is one bishop together with the presbytery and the deacons, my fellow slaves."[15]

The Church offered the pagans something very different from Roman society. The Romans were organized through force and worshiped frightening gods in temples that were also centers of power. The Church presented itself as a new temple, made not of stones but of human beings.[16] It provided a stable, peaceful society of order and unity that was a near inversion of the pagan understanding. And yet, it held together—it worked. This is what drew the attention of the Romans because it seemed impossible. In Christ, things had changed. Through Christ, real peace was possible because through Christ, God dwelled with us, and "where there is division and anger, God does not dwell."[17] This is what attracted the millions of converts to Christianity.

Roman paganism was a strange mixture of extreme superstition and often cynical skepticism. As we have already discussed, the gods were everywhere. Every home had its own gods of the hearth. Every field, every river, every town, every trade, every human activity had its own gods. These gods had power and had to be placated. Humans had to keep them happy through sacrifice and ritual, or they might turn against them and take away good fortune. The will of the gods could be ascertained through auguries, such as cutting open an animal and seeing how its entrails spilled out or watching the flight of birds and seeing which direction they darted. It could also be ascertained by consulting oracles, who were men and women set apart to read the will of the gods and convey it, often in riddles, to men who asked questions. For the Romans, their paganism and their politics and economics were all different aspects of the same thing. The governmental and economic centers of the cities were also the temples. This religion was, at heart, a decentralized and fragmented religion, lacking any real transcendent unity. The many gods lived and operated within

---

[14] Ignatius, *Magnesians*, 6.
[15] Ignatius of Antioch, *Epistle to the Philadelphians*, 4.
[16] Ignatius, *Ephesians*, 9.
[17] Ignatius, *Philadelphians*, 8.

the same world as men, simply with more power. Because Roman paganism acknowledged a pantheon of gods that were tied to particular places or activities, the incorporation of new peoples with new gods was not a problem. As the Romans conquered, the gods of the conquered peoples were merely added to the total pagan cosmos. The conquered cities, with their governments, their economies, and their religions, were just incorporated into the empire as yet another little corner of the massive pagan world. They paid tribute to the Romans and accepted the Roman gods as superior. This was just paganism in action. This paganism, though, was an anxious religion. The gods, like the kings of men, were fickle and easily offended, and they often demanded severe sacrifices. The gladiatorial games, for example, where thousands of slaves were forced to fight to the death or were fed to wild animals before cheering crowds, were not mere entertainment. They were religious rituals of human sacrifice on a grand scale. The gladiators' tormented deaths kept the Roman gods happy. To the Roman way of thinking, the empire had grown and was powerful because it had pleased these gods.

This popular religion was complemented by a more intellectual skepticism. Rome had many schools of philosophy, which disagreed on how the popular beliefs and practices corresponded to the reality of the divine. Some argued that popular religion and myths had to be interpreted allegorically in order to arrive at the true wisdom of philosophy. To these men, it was not that the popular religion was false. Rather, it was that it was symbolic and pointed to more fundamental truths about the gods and the universe they governed. Some of these thinkers even proposed a sort of monotheism in which all the gods were really aspects of a single divine being. However, few questioned the importance of the popular religion or sought to undermine its practices. The gods may not really be in the form of their idols nor have the names that the people applied to them, but they did demand the people's obedience, and the strength of Rome depended upon this obedience.

Generally speaking, then, the Romans left local religions alone. They did, however, demand that the conquered people incorporate into their devotions the central gods of Rome and especially devotion to the emperor as a son of god, if not a god himself. For most of the pagan peoples of the world, this was no great imposition. They had their gods of power; why couldn't the Romans have theirs? The Romans were powerful, so it stood to reason that their gods were powerful. It was probably a good idea, therefore, to seek their good pleasure. The Jews were an exception. Obviously, Jewish monotheism forbade any idolatry and denied emphatically any justification for polytheistic worship. This made the Jews suspicious in the eyes of the Romans. The Romans, however, had great respect for antiquity. They appreciated very old things and were hesitant to disrupt them. They knew the great age of the Jewish people and their God and so made an exception in their case, allowing them to remain in the empire, but without sacrificing to the Roman gods. Nevertheless, as the execution of Christ himself makes clear, Roman tolerance of Jewish religious independence had clear limits.

At first, the Christians were lumped in with the Jews and shared in their legal protection. This changed under the emperor Nero. In the year 64, there was a massive fire in Rome that destroyed most of the city. To the Roman populace, it was clear that the gods had somehow been offended and that some massive sacrifice had to be made to appease them. Nero, frightened that the mob might turn against him, diverted its attention to the Christians. They were something new in the empire. They did not perform the sacrifices. They lived impious lives and were, no doubt, the reason for the gods' anger. The pagans of Rome, therefore, rounded up thousands of Christians and killed them in terrible ways as a form of human sacrifice. St. Peter and St. Paul were probably among them.

Over the next hundred years, the Christians grew in numbers and became increasingly obnoxious to the pagans. The Christians were not merely passive recipients of irrational pagan anger, however. The pagans may have been mistaken about the details of Christianity, but they were right to see Christianity as a threat to their order. Christianity really did undermine paganism and the political and economic systems that were integral to it. The Christians did not teach that the pagan gods weren't real. They taught that they were wicked demons, whose real power was present everywhere there was violence and suffering.[18] Christians would not worship the gods, not because they were fake but because they were devils. The Christians taught that God was the creator of all and that all that was good and true, even in paganism, was fulfilled only in Christianity. Nothing that was good was really "pagan." As St. Justin Martyr remarked, "Whatever things

---

[18] Justin Martyr, *First Apology*, 5–6.

were rightly said among all men, are the property of us Christians."[19] Paganism was, then, in a sense true. The gods really did have power, and this power really did rule through violence; however, only the violence, only the disorder was distinctly pagan. All the truth and all the goodness of Roman life was fulfilled in Christianity. Christianity gave a way out of the plight of the pagan world from the inside. This was very aggressive.

But even more aggressive was the Christian assertion that Jesus Christ was the only Son of God, a title claimed by the emperor. The Christians insisted that Christ was their king, that he was, in fact, the true king of all men, whether they liked it or not. They refused to worship the emperor because they were already worshiping the true God-king. As one Christian responded under interrogation, "I do not recognize the empire of this world; but rather I serve that God, whom no man has seen nor can see . . . I recognize my Lord, the King of kings and Emperor of all peoples."[20] This was not only atheism in the eyes of the pagans; it was simple treason. It was also very confusing to the pagans. In an account of the martyrdom of St. Polycarp, as the pagans lead him to his death, they repeatedly plead with him to offer sacrifice to the emperor, to merely acknowledge him as divine, as Lord. Why won't he do such a small thing? He responds by insisting that only Jesus Christ is his God and his king.[21] This was baffling. As we have seen, to the pagans, power was divine, and the emperor was obviously powerful. To the pagans, as the emperor killed the Christians, he was at the same time proving them wrong about the kingship of Christ; he was proving that he was powerful and that their god was weak, that he was divine and that their god was nothing. Martyrdom appeared, therefore, insane. This was, of course, a continuation of the dynamics of the encounter between Pilate and Christ.

The early Christians' arguments with the pagans were often genius in their subversive logic. Tertullian, for example, argued that sacrificing to the gods for the success and prosperity of Caesar didn't make any sense, because Caesar was clearly the one with real power in paganism. Even the dutiful pagans were more afraid of Caesar than they were of the gods. What is more, the gods themselves depended

---

[19] Justin Martyr, *Second Apology*, 13.
[20] *The Martyrs of Scilli in Africa Proconsularis*, in *A New Eusebius: Documents Illustrating the History of the Church to A.D. 337*, ed. James Stevenson (London: SPCK, 1987), 44.
[21] *The Martyrdom of Polycarp*, 8–10.

upon Caesar's power. Caesar built their temples, constructed their statues, compelled their liturgies. The gods, Tertullian argued, were less powerful than Caesar. They were below Caesar, under his dominion; ultimately, they were his property. Here, Tertullian was exposing the very heart of the political theology of pagan god-kingship and the idols that were the mechanisms of pagan power. He seemed to be flattering Caesar, but of course what he was really doing was undermining the pretensions of Caesar's power and exposing the mechanisms of fear and control through which he maintained it. In a move of subtle genius, Tertullian asserted that Christians prayed to God for the emperor and that they respected him as the highest man, whose authority was given him by the one true God. He was offering Caesar an office. But it was an office now positioned below the divine and not above it. Rather than the divine being under the dominion of Caesar, if Caesar were to have the Christians' loyalty, he would have to come to understand that things were the other way around, that he was under the dominion of the one true God. Caesar's authority could be real, but he could never have the power of a god-king.[22] This was clearly a development of Christ's juxtaposition between rendering to Caesar and rendering to God, and Tertullian took up this passage, arguing that to Caesar was owed what bore his image and likeness, the coin, and to God was owed what bore his image and likeness, humanity itself.[23]

We can see, then, why the Roman elites, who had a pretty good sense of how paganism worked, viewed Christians correctly as a threat to the order of the empire. The subtle and in no way naive elites believed that the world was a world of violence and disorder and that it was only the power of the empire that held chaos at bay. One such member of the elite, Celsus, defended the divinity of the emperor, arguing against the Christians, "If you overthrow this doctrine, it is probable that the emperor will punish you. If everyone were to do the same as you, there would be nothing to prevent him from being abandoned, alone and deserted, while earthly things would come into the power of the most lawless and savage barbarians, and nothing more would be heard among men either of your worship or of the true wisdom."[24] Jewish and Christian powerlessness was, for Celsus,

---

[22] Tertullian, *The Apology*, chap. 29–33.
[23] Tertullian, *The Five Books against Marcion*, 4.38.
[24] Origen, *Against Celsus*, in Stevenson, *A New Eusebius*, 152.

proof that their religion was false and ultimately self-destructive. He was arguing that the Christians themselves relied upon the power of Caesar. In a world of god-kings, only a god-king could protect order, the very order that allowed the space for Christianity to exist.

Within the fallen world of the Age of Nature, of course, this is not wrong. In the City of Man, it is true that power rules. Falling back into this belief was the constant temptation of Israel in the Old Testament. Falling back upon the safety of power is why they exclaimed in 1 Samuel, "No! but we will have a king over us, that we also may be like all the nations, and that our king may govern us and go out before us and fight our battles" (1 Sam 8:19–20). But as we have seen, it was this very reality that Christianity undid. The pagans were not wrong about Christianity's threat to their world. They were not wrong when they perceived martyrs such as St. Polycarp to be "the destroyer of our own gods."[25] What those who remained pagan were wrong about was the conviction that their world was the only possible world. From within their fallen world, the pagans understandably asked of the martyrs, "Where is their god? What profit has their religion brought them, which they have preferred to their own life?"[26] The answer, of course, could not be provided within the pagan framework, within the pagan architecture. The acceptance of martyrdom was the demonstration that the Christian had moved into a world that was governed by different rules, that was governed by the logic of the Resurrection, that he was a citizen of a City of God that now longer needed the power of the god-kings

Justin Martyr wrote to the emperor in defense of Christians. He asserted that Christians "more than all other men are your helpers and allies in promoting peace" because "those [criminals] who endeavor to escape detection when they offend [your laws] . . . , if they learned and were convinced that nothing . . . can escape the knowledge of God, would by all means live decently . . . But," he pointedly suggests to the emperor, "you seem to fear lest all men become so righteous, and you no longer have anyone left to punish." He finishes by chiding the emperor, "Such is the concern of a public executioner, but not of a good prince."[27] The Christians understood that the structures of Caesar's power rested on sin. To undo sin was to undo Caesar as a

---

[25] *The Martyrdom of Polycarp*, 12.
[26] *Martyrdom of Justin and His Companions*, in Stevenson, *A New Eusebius*, 42.
[27] Justin Martyr, *First Apology*, 12.

god-king, to undo the pagan order. Many of the pagans, in their own backward way, understood this as well.

Christianity was not the only new religion that was spreading in the empire. It was accompanied by many "mystery religions," as they are often called. These movements were normally highly mystical and based on dualist conceptions of the cosmos. They thought that the material world was evil and ruled by an evil god, while the spiritual world was good and was ruled by a higher, good god. These sects normally proposed some sort of secret knowledge, or gnosis, through which a person's soul could escape the prison of material reality. Some of these Gnostic sects adopted language and concepts from Christianity, and the orthodox Church was continuously arguing with them and warning the faithful to beware of their errors.

The leader of one such group was named Marcion. Marcion was a member of the Christian community in Rome around the year 135. He was expelled from communion because he began to teach a deviant doctrine. He promptly started his own sect, which became a true rival to the orthodox Church. Marcion taught that Christianity was a total break from the Old Testament. Christ had revealed a new and unknown God, who taught a message of faith and love. This God was not the God of the Old Testament, who was the creator of the material world and was legalistic and strictly just. Christ's God was wholly new and perfectly merciful. Marcion taught disdain for the material world. Christ, therefore, could not have been truly the incarnate God but, rather, merely appeared to be a real man. This error become known as Docetism. Unsurprisingly, Marcion denied the importance of the Old Testament altogether and taught that only Luke and the Pauline letters were authentic Scripture. Marcion was a talented Scripture scholar, and the Church took him very seriously.

To counter him and similar heretics, the orthodox bishops and theologians had to explain the true meaning of the Incarnation and think seriously about which books constituted true Scripture and which did not. This contributed to the establishment of the biblical canon. Such conflicts also helped accelerate the formation of the clerical hierarchy in the Church. Who had authority? How do we maintain unity when there is such profound disagreement? Thinkers such as St. Irenaeus, in his work *Adversus Haereses* (ca. 180), for example, not only articulated the importance and reality of apostolic succession among the bishops but also singled out Rome as the center of authority. In order to demonstrate his point, he listed the twelve popes reaching from his own time back to Peter himself.

Orthodox Christianity emerged as a social force, both doctrinally and institutionally, as it struggled both internally against its own temptations toward error and externally against pagan and Gnostic forces. It formed the bottomless truths of Revelation into the specific form of Roman Christianity in response to these struggles and so this form was capable of reaching out into these rival social orders, of speaking their language, of absorbing them into itself. Another way of saying this is that Roman Christianity formed as the conversion of the Romans and not over and against them.

In the second century, the Roman Empire was transitioning from a decentralized coalition of cities into a centralized monarchy. Part of this centralization was an increase in the intensity of emperor worship. Simultaneously, Christianity was rapidly spreading. During the second century, then, we start to see sustained persecutions of Christians in the outlying provinces that were being "Romanized." In an effort to integrate the provinces more tightly to the center, Roman officials displayed little patience for Christian scruples concerning pagan worship. In many parts of the empire, simply acknowledging that one was a Christian was grounds for execution. Pagan conviction that Christians could not be tolerated grew over the century, and by the third century, the imperial government took the lead in their attempted suppression and the persecutions became more organized, targeting the Church's leadership. By some counts, as many as eight popes were martyred in the second century.

In the third century, these persecutions intensified, and Christianity continued to spread, driven on by the shocking witness of the martyrs. As Tertullian remarked, "the blood of the martyrs is the seed of the Church."[28] During this period, Christianity started to spread more consistently among the upper classes of Roman society, diverting more and more commitment of the governing class away from the prosperity of the pagan regime. This was rightly understood as a threat to the stability of that regime. At the same time, barbarian tribes were attacking the borders and there were multiple peasant rebellions. But most significantly, the empire was rocked by incessant civil war. The Roman army had turned on itself, fighting for control of the imperial throne. One section of the army would succeed in placing one of their own on the throne, only to be shortly overthrown by

---

[28] Tertullian, *The Apology*, 50.

another faction. Between 235 and 284, a fifty-year period, there were twenty-six different emperors. For the Roman elites, imperial unity was a top priority.

Therefore, in 249, the emperor Decius ordered all citizens to sacrifice to the Roman gods. He was desperately trying to unify all the empire under a single religious system, which meant, of course, a single political and economic system. Decius was not particularly concerned about Christianity. In 249, only about 2 percent of the population was Christian. Decius was more worried about the decline in paganism itself. It seems that through the second century, and accelerating in the third century, traditional pagan practices were on the wane. This decline in paganism was matched with a decline in the civic patriotism that had made the empire strong. Fewer and fewer people were willing to sacrifice for the good of the empire as a whole. Decius sought to turn this around by building a strong centralized cult to match the universal citizenship that had been granted to all males in the empire a few decades before. This was an effort to turn the empire into a single temple-nation rather than a coalition of temple-cities with waning devotion. Even if not aimed specifically at them, the universal order to sacrifice hit the Christians very hard. In Rome, Pope Fabian refused and was immediately executed. Thousands followed him to their deaths.

However, thousands of other Christians gave in and offered sacrifice to the gods rather than die. The Decian persecution was short-lived, lasting for only a couple of years. But it had a lasting impact on the Church. The Church was faced with a situation of both mass martyrdom, the ultimate act of sanctity, and mass apostasy, the ultimate act of wickedness. As the intensity of persecution waned, many of these apostates sought reentry to the Church. Under what terms should they be allowed back into communion? Was forgiveness for such a grievous sin possible? The debates surrounding this issue threatened schism. This threat led to a further strengthening of the authority of the bishops. An empire-wide organization of bishops emerged, with each bishop presiding over a particular territory while remaining in constant contact with the other bishops. These bishops were organized under regional metropolitans (what we call archbishops) with more authority. These bishops were capable of avoiding schism by working through problems together and by recognizing the overarching authority of the bishop of Rome. St. Cyprian, for example, articulated a theory of the Church that was based on the profound unity of the body of bishops, a unity that was symbolized in Peter and

Christ's particular commission to him. Rather than destroying Christianity, Decius strengthened the early Church.

In fact, the years 250–300 were a period of dramatic Christian expansion, from 2 percent of the population to over 10 percent. The empire's troubles continued. Finally, in 284, a man of power and ability, Diocletian, came to the imperial throne. He was committed to restoring order and the past glory of Rome. He passed sweeping reforms that centralized the empire into a single monarchical state. He divided this state into manageable units that came to be known as dioceses and which the Church would eventually inherit. He also divided the empire into eastern and western halves, each with their own administration and their own emperor. Shoring up the pagan cult was a key aspect of Diocletian's policy of centralization. He was dismayed by the decrease in pagan practice and sought to stem it by emphasizing the empire-wide gods, especially Jupiter and Hercules, at the expense of the local ones. He wanted Roman piety, like Roman politics and Roman economics, to look to Rome as its center. Under Diocletian, the divinity of the emperor was emphasized as the chief conduit through which the will of the gods governed mankind. He went so far, in fact, as to assert that he was Jupiter himself on the throne, incarnated in a man. He demanded to be adored as a god as he adorned himself in gold and jewels. Diocletian sought unity in the empire through establishing himself as a man-god above all other gods. Obviously, Christianity was a huge obstacle.

In 298, sacrifices were offered to the gods in thanksgiving for the successful conclusion of the emperor's war with Persia. Apparently, when the animals were opened, there was a disturbing augury in the entrails. The Christians were blamed, and what has become known as the Great Persecution began. First, Christians were removed from the army and the civil service and persecuted through legal impediments. This non-violent persecution quickly escalated. Christians were rounded up by the thousands and sent to the mines or galleys as slaves. Many more were killed. One eyewitness, the famous historian Eusebius, witnessed an assembly line of decapitation, writing, "the murderous axe was dulled, and worn out, and was broken in pieces while the executioners grew weary and took it in turns to succeed one another."[29]

---

[29] Quoted in Margaret M. Mitchell, Frances M. Young, K. Scott Bowie, eds., *Origins to Constantine*, vol. 1, *The Cambridge History of Christianity*, (Cambridge: Cambridge University Press, 2006), 521.

The persecution wore on for seven years. During this time, countless churches were burned, Bibles confiscated, and men, women, and children killed. In addition, large numbers of Christians gave in to torture and offered sacrifice to the gods. The pagan empire had done its worst in a last-ditch effort to eradicate the upstart religion and reestablish the power of the empire. And it failed, again, like Pilate. In 305, Diocletian abdicated the imperial throne and retired. Shortly after, the persecution came to an end. Christianity, however, emerged stronger than ever, and in seven short years, there would be a Christian emperor.

The period of persecution had several important consequences for the history of the Church. It established martyrdom as the ultimate display of devotion to Christ. To give up one's life in imitation of Christ was the supreme display of faith and charity. It led to the formation of the doctrine of penance. Could Christians who had committed the horrendous sin of apostasy and idolatry be readmitted to the Church? The answer was, of course, yes. The sacrament of penance had no limits. But sorting this out led to a long-lasting division in the Church between rigorists and those inclined to a more lenient position. The period of persecution led the Church to organize into a more formal system of bishops in communion with each other and centered on the bishop of Rome as their head. It also led to the development of the theology of the episcopate as the locus of Church unity. Perhaps most fundamentally, however, the period of persecution resulted in the turning of the tide against paganism. Christianity withstood its assault and spread in spite of it. The pagan emperors declared themselves to be the "son of god." Christianity put in their place the actual Son of God, Jesus Christ, King of kings, and Christianity won.

2. The Christian Empire

Christianization of the Empire

Less than seven years after the end of Diocletian's persecution, the imperial throne was again being fought over by rival generals. One of these men, Constantine, was on the cusp of defeating his rival. In 312, he was outside Rome, preparing to face him in a final battle. Before the battle began, Constantine had a vision from God. There are different versions of what happened, but the most popular is that Constantine was given a vision of the Chi Rho symbol, which was a common abbreviation for the word "Christ," and was instructed to fight under it. He had the symbol painted on the shields of his men and proceeded to destroy his enemy at the battle of Milvian Bridge. With this victory, Constantine became the emperor of the western half of the empire. He quickly issued the Edict of Milan, which made Christianity a legal religion in the empire. In only a few years, Christians went from being thrown to the lions to counting the emperor himself as one of their own and enjoying a privileged position in the empire. This position was strengthened even further when, in 324, Constantine defeated his eastern imperial rival and became the sole emperor over the entire empire.

The conversion of Constantine directly on the heels of the rule of Diocletian is revealing of the way in which the strength of Christianity had grown within Roman society even as that society simultaneously developed in the direction of more militant pagan centralization. These two movements were not unconnected. Rather, this single society was seeking to solve the "problem" of fallen man in two directions: one direction sought to overwhelm violence with more violence, the other sought to displace violence through the unity that revelation and grace made possible. They were two diametrically opposed solutions that emerged within a single, struggling cultural world. The movement from one to the other was not, therefore, as far as we might be tempted to think. Desperation for peace, exhausted in the Diocletian project, was the fuel for the spread of Christianity, and the increasingly obvious failure of the pagan project shifted quickly to support for its rival.

Under Constantine, however, Christianity was not made the official religion of the empire. Rather, it was fully legalized and so made equal with the paganism that the vast majority of Romans continued to practice. In fact, only about 10 percent of the population was Christian in 312. This began to change very quickly, however, and by 350, Christians were in the majority. Constantine favored Christianity heavily. One of the things that he did, for example, was launch a massive church-building campaign. When Christianity was illegal, churches were small, if communities had them at all. Most congregations still met in their members' homes. Constantine, though, changed this. He and his allies built massive, architecturally amazing churches throughout the empire. He donated, for example, St. John Lateran to the Church and built the old St. Peter's in Rome. He also built a whole new city in the eastern half of the empire called Constantinople. Constantinople was Christian top to bottom.

These construction projects were important. Not only was the diversion of imperial patronage to Christianity important in its own right, but it also provided an example for other wealthy families to follow. Traditionally, the Roman elites had gained prestige in service to their cities. This service included using their wealth for public works: temples, bridges, roads, baths, and so on. During the last decades of the third century, however, as Diocletian had worked to centralize Roman government, this practice declined sharply. It was revived under Constantine and his Christian successors, only now it was directed primarily at the Church. As more and more Romans converted to Christianity, they increasingly directed their patronage toward the Church. They built churches, hospitals, almshouses, and orphanages. The Romans had not traditionally been too concerned with the weak and powerless. Theirs was an empire built on slavery, after all. Human life was cheap. This changed as more and more people converted to Christianity. The Church emerged as a major institution of what we would today call social services. Because such social concern was new and profoundly Christian, it made sense that it was pursued outside the imperial government and through the construction of the institutions of the clerical Church.

As more Roman elites converted, the wealth at the disposal of the ecclesiastical hierarchy increased. The bishops did not personally own the wealth of their sees. Rather, they acted as trustees. They were elected and assumed control of the property of their churches, but it was not theirs and they could not leave it to their heirs. What this means is that over time the dioceses became wealthier and were capable of an ever-increasing amount of social action. The importance of their role in their cities grew steadily.

During the fourth century, the office of bishop became increasingly prestigious. Bishops' primary functions were preaching and performance of the liturgy, but during this period, they also became important local officials who controlled a vast amount of wealth and power. Being a bishop became a very respectable career for members of the traditional ruling class of the empire. In fact, bishops became an aspect of the government of the empire, with the emperors often commissioning them to serve as local judges. In many towns, the bishop became the most important and powerful person. But this was a different kind of power than had been wielded under united paganism. For example, in acting as judges, the bishops often exhorted people in conflict to come to terms through mutual forgiveness and mercy rather than through the strictures of Roman law. They ruled based on biblical principles as often as they did on legal ones. They sought to minimize the need for the coercive apparatus of the imperial state in favor of local cooperation and friendship. This was just the application of Christianity, of course, but it had the consequence of weakening the importance of the central government.

The bishops constructed an organization that was, in many ways, parallel to the imperial administration. Nearly every city had a bishop, and they were organized along the same lines as the imperial provinces and under archbishops who resided in the provincial capitals. The episcopal hierarchy operated differently, however, than the imperial hierarchy. In the imperial hierarchy, men started out at the lower rungs of the ladder and then steadily climbed higher. They sought advancement and an increase in their wealth and power. Each advancement brought them closer to the center of power, the emperor himself. The bishops, on the other hand, could not be promoted. The bishops operated instead always at the local level, concerned first with their own city. In modern times, we are used to bishops being moved from diocese to diocese. But that was not the case in the early Church. Rather, bishops were thought of as having married their churches, and they had to remain faithful for life. This fact seriously mitigated any ambition among the episcopal ranks. The bishops were important local leaders, and as the patronage of the wealthy classes shifted in their direction, that meant that more and more of the wealth of society was focused locally. The bishops rose in stature not by climbing away from their city but by using the resources of the city for the good of its citizens. This is how the Christianization of the empire was also the decentralizing of its government, at least in the West. The unity of the Christian empire became increasingly the unity of the bishops in faith and charity, the unity of the Church, and less the unity that can be built through coercive power.

The period after the conversion of Constantine was a period of amazing intellectual production. Many of the greatest minds that the Church would ever see lived and worked during the fourth and fifth centuries. They laid the groundwork for theology and Scripture study upon which we are still building. Some of these fathers include St. Basil (d. 379), St. Gregory Nazianzen (d. 390), St. John Chrysostom (d. 407), St. Athanasius (d. 373), St. Ephrem (d. 373), St. Ambrose (d. 397), St. Jerome (d. 420), and St. Augustine (d. 430). One of the reasons that this was a period of so much intellectual activity is precisely because so much of Catholic doctrine remained unclear. What was the relationship between the Old Testament and the New Testament? What happens after we die? What was the proper relationship between the clergy and the laity? What was the Church and what were her sacraments? Who was Mary? What exactly was the Incarnation? What was the nature of the Trinity? These were fundamental questions. The answers, of course, were to be found in Scripture, in the apostolic tradition, and in the lived experience of the saints. But they still had to be found; they had to be looked for and uncovered and thought through and expounded. This was what the Church Fathers were doing.

They weren't doing it, however, because of curiosity. Rather, it really mattered. First, they had to defend Christianity from pagan attacks. Paganism had developed an extremely complex philosophy of great subtlety. In its popular forms, paganism may have been saturated with superstition, but its elite form was profoundly intelligent. The Church Fathers had to think through Christianity and articulate it in a way that stood up to this intellectual power. Second, the Christian Church itself was divided over doctrine. The Church Fathers sought to bring clarity to doctrine in order to bring unity to the Church. They had to determine what was orthodox and why, what was heterodox, and exactly what the heretics were getting wrong. Their work, then, was driven first and foremost out of pastoral necessity. Appropriately, most of the Church Fathers were bishops, and a great deal of their writings were first sermons or lessons on the Bible. These were not academics engaged in flights of speculative fancy. They were pastors, men in the trenches, who knew what was troubling their flocks and sought, through the guidance of the Holy Spirit, to bring the people ever deeper into the truth. They were not just intellectuals; they were saints.

The unsettled nature of Christian teaching became clear as soon as Constantine converted and the Church emerged into social prominence. Constantine himself was distressed to learn that something as fundamental as the divinity of Christ was a matter of debate. Some bishops were teaching that Christ was not actually divine. How could it be, they asked, that the transcendent God, the very Logos, the supreme reason of the cosmos and the creator of all things, became a man? One bishop named Arius proposed that Christ was not actually God. He was, rather, God's most glorious creation. He was a creature, Arius argued, though the most exalted creature. Arianism, as this position has been named, made sense to many well-meaning Christians, and Arius quickly amassed a large following. Arius was wrong. The orthodox fathers knew him to be wrong. But they had to demonstrate why.

To resolve this controversy, Constantine called together a massive gathering of bishops in 325 at Nicaea. Arius himself attended. The result of this first ecumenical council since the Council of Jerusalem was the promulgation of the Nicene Creed, which declared the Son to be "consubstantial" with the Father. This was a direct repudiation of Arianism. Consubstantial means "of the same substance;" it means that the Son is fully divine, as divine as the Father. The First Council of Nicaea had declared against Arius, but this was not the end of the doctrinal troubles. Many Christians did not accept the council's doctrine and slid into schism. Even many members of the imperial family, including Constantine's son, became very sympathetic to the Arian position, and many pro-imperial bishops, especially in the East, held to an Arian or semi-Arian Christology even after the council. After Nicaea, those who opposed imperial absolutism gravitated to the orthodox party, and those who championed maximal imperial power gravitated to the Arian position. In the decades after 325, therefore, the Arian conflict accelerated and came to involve the very "constitution" of the empire itself.

It is not too hard to see why this might be the case. If Christ was merely a highly exalted creature and not God himself, then the gap between earth and heaven remained unbridged. God the creator remained distant, and the material world remained closed in on itself. If Christ is "divine-like" but not God himself, then he is essentially a pagan god, even if he is the one true pagan god. The material world, the world that the emperors governed directly, remained self-contained and capable of being dominated from within. Such a Christology left intact the imperial dream, the dream of a unitary political order under a Caesar who alone mediated the divine to the world. Orthodox Christology, on the other hand, undermined such a political theology. If God really became a man and so interpenetrated directly the world of human social experience, then that experience could never be "closed," could never be dominated by a mere man, because it always reached beyond itself to the divine. Christ bridges the gap between the transcendent and the immanent, between the divine and the human, but he does so in a way that does not "confuse" or "collapse" them into each other. The world is revealed as what it really is—*as the world of creation*—only by reaching past itself through Christ and through the sacraments of the Church to a participation in the life of the creator.

A just and peaceful world, a world that was truly itself, could, therefore, only be achieved through the combination of law and grace, through the incarnational cooperation of the imperial and priestly powers. In such a vision, the power of a Christian Caesar, the power of a just and righteous emperor, could come into being only through his incorporation into the sacramental order of the Church, a Church which necessarily transcended his power. The Arians tended to see the Christian emperors as representing God the Father directly. The orthodox tended to see him as a new Davidic king, and Davidic kingship did not have the resources to sustain itself but was only fulfilled in its elevation in the Incarnate Christ. It makes perfect sense, then, that many partisans of imperial power found themselves supporting Arianism and why many of the barbarian tribes, coming straight from primitive paganism, found converting to Arianism to be less disruptive and so more attractive than converting to orthodoxy. It is also why the defenders of orthodoxy, such as St. Athanasius of Alexandria, were often compelled to oppose the emperors directly.

Such opposition to the emperors' Arianism was not merely a stubborn statement of the orthodox Christological position; it was the enactment of that orthodoxy. If the orthodox were right about Christ, then the emperor could not claim total power, and disobedience to him when he erred in matters of faith, morals, and sacraments was not only justified but demanded. The converse was also true: when Constantine's Arian son, the emperor Constantius II, declared against the orthodox, "What I will is the law of the Church," he was demonstrating the implications of Arianism. If the Arians were right, then the emperor's power was complete, and his will was the Divine Law. As Athanasius relates:

> When the Bishops heard [the emperor's claim that his will was law] they were utterly amazed, and stretching forth their hands to God, they used great boldness of speech against him, teaching him that the kingdom was not his, but God's, who had given it to him, Whom also they bid him fear, lest He should suddenly take it away from him. And they threatened him with the day of judgment, and warned him against infringing Ecclesiastical order, and mingling Roman sovereignty with the constitution of the Church,

and against introducing the Arian heresy into the Church of God.[30]

It would be a terrible mistake to see in this conflict a movement toward the separation of Church and State or some other modern conception of distinct "secular" and "religious" spaces. Rather, the conflict was directly theological, dealing with the most fundamental doctrines of who God was and what the Incarnation meant, dealing with the very structure of the cosmos and man's place within it. But it was, for all this, no less political, dealing directly with the power of the emperor and the power of the priesthood. What we are seeing is how profoundly united the "religious" and the "political" were. This should be obvious and not shocking.

As we have seen from the beginning of this book, Christianity is about the salvation of mankind, and mankind is essentially social. The redemption of men through the Incarnation was the redemption of mankind as a political being. Because they understood this, the orthodox were arguing that a proper worship of the true God through his Incarnate Son meant that society could not continue in its late pagan form. Things were different under Christianity. Power was now sacramental, and the sacraments were the efficacious ordering of the temporal in and through the spiritual. The redeemed temporal was not divorced from the spiritual; it was completely dependent upon it, even as the spiritual was efficacious and manifested always through the temporal. The Arian controversy was integral to the particular historical circumstances of the fourth century, even if the doctrine under debate transcended those circumstances.

Christianity had spread the furthest and fastest among the poorer classes of the empire. After the conversion of Constantine, the upper classes started converting in increasing numbers, but for most of the fourth century, the majority of aristocrats remained pagan. As Christianity spread, the hostility of these aristocrats increased. The attempt to establish Arianism as the standard form of imperial Christianity can be seen as an attempt at meeting these pagan elites halfway. Arianism offered a way of being Christian that did not fundamentally challenge the Diocletian ordering of the empire. The Arians proposed that the emperor was the "bishop of bishops," that he was, as he had been under the pagans, the *pontifex maximus*, the high priest. The orthodox,

---

[30] Athanasius of Alexandria, "History of the Arians," in *Nicene and Post-Nicene Fathers II*, ed. Philip Schaff, vol. 4 (Peabody, MA: Hendrickson, 1994 [reprint]), no. 33.

however, resisted with all their might and slowly wore the Arian party down.

When Constantius died in 361, his Arian policy collapsed, not through the victory of the orthodox but rather through the return of a type of paganism. Constantius was succeeded by Constantine's nephew, Julian. Julian renounced Christianity and returned to paganism and so is known to history as Julian the Apostate. With the failure of Arianism, it had become clear to Julian and his supporters that Christianity was not compatible with imperial ideology. They opted, then, to attempt to suppress it and especially to stop the conversion of the upper classes. Julian forbade Christians from teaching, took away government support for the clergy, restored pagan temples, set up a pagan priesthood supported by the state, and restored the pagan feasts, among other initiatives. These policies had few long-term consequences. Christianity had already sunk deep roots, and its inertia was significant. Julian died in battle in the eastern reaches of the empire in 363, and his pagan efforts died with him. He was the last non-Christian emperor.

After Julian, the spread of orthodox Christianity accelerated. In 382, the emperor Gratian shifted imperial policy away from merely favoring Christianity and toward the active suppression of paganism. He forbade many pagan practices and even removed the Altar of Victory from the Roman senate house. This was the religious heart of the oldest Roman aristocratic families, many of whom were still pagan. The Senate, the ancient government of Rome, was now no longer pagan. This was of major symbolic significance. It was Theodosius (r. 379–395), however, who finally made Catholic Christianity the official religion of the Roman Empire. By this time, the majority of people had already converted, and the back of Arianism had been broken. Theodosius, then, sought to unify the empire under Christian orthodoxy. He faced, however, new heresy.

Arianism largely concerned the divinity of the Son. But what about the Holy Spirit? A vocal group of Christians asserted that the Holy Spirit was not fully God. At the same time, a doctrine arose in reaction to Arianism that maintained that Christ did not really have a human nature but was, rather, God inhabiting a human body. In 381, Theodosius sought to bring unity to the feuding Church by calling another council, this one to meet in Constantinople. The First Council of Constantinople gathered, debated, and issued a revised version of the Nicene Creed. This is the version that most modern Christians still recite. It reads:

I believe in one God,
the Father almighty,
maker of heaven and earth,
of all things visible and invisible.
I believe in one Lord Jesus Christ,
the Only Begotten Son of God,
born of the Father before all ages.
God from God,
Light from Light,
true God from true God,
begotten, not made, consubstantial with the Father;
through him all things were made.
For us men and for our salvation he came down from heaven,
and by the Holy Spirit was incarnate of the Virgin Mary,
and became man.
For our sake he was crucified under Pontius Pilate,
he suffered death and was buried,
and rose again on the third day
in accordance with the Scriptures.
He ascended into heaven
and is seated at the right hand of the Father.
He will come again in glory
to judge the living and the dead
and his kingdom will have no end.
I believe in the Holy Spirit, the Lord, the giver of life,
who proceeds from the Father [and the Son],[31]
who with the Father and the Son is adored and glorified,
who has spoken through the prophets.
I believe in one, holy, catholic and apostolic Church.
I confess one Baptism for the forgiveness of sins
and I look forward to the resurrection of the dead
and the life of the world to come. Amen.

Here we would seem to have a final declaration on the divinity of both the Son and the Holy Spirit as well as the nature of the Incarnation. But that was not to be. The mystery of the Trinity and the mystery of the Incarnation are the most fundamental mysteries in Chris-

---

[31] The phrase "and the Son" was added to the creed in the Western, Latin half of the empire during the Middle Ages.

tianity. They concern God directly, and God cannot be captured in tidy philosophical formulas. This is why it was so hard for the Church to come to agreement on how to understand and express these mysteries. It was easy to be misled into error, even in good faith.

For example, Nestorius was the patriarch of Constantinople, the second-most important bishopric in the Church after Rome. He began teaching that the human nature and the divine nature in Christ were separate and that we should conceptualize them as distinct, even in Christ. So, for example, Nestorius thought that it would be appropriate to refer to Mary as Mother of Christ because she gave birth to the human Christ, but it would be inappropriate to refer to her as Mother of God because she did not give birth to the divine in Christ. This heresy, like Arianism, removed history from salvation. It was an attempt at a reassertion of the independence of the material from the spiritual. In 431, the emperor Theodosius II called a council at Ephesus to deal with this conflict. The over two hundred bishops who assembled condemned the doctrine of Nestorius, or Nestorianism as it became known. Mary was, indeed, the Mother of God. Christ was one in his humanity and in his divinity. Nestorius was removed from his see and retired to a monastery where he soon died. This condemnation led to a schism in the Church, with many eastern communities adopting a Nestorian Christology. There remain to this day Nestorian communities.

The Council of Ephesus did not definitively resolve these debates, however. In reaction to the Nestorian division of the two natures of Christ, some Christians asserted that Christ had only one nature that was both fully divine and fully human. This position became known as Monophysitism. This was an overcorrection. It tended to deny the integrity of the historical, material world altogether, opting instead for what amounted to a form of pantheism. Pope Leo I wrote a lengthy treatise on the Incarnation that became known as *Leo's Tome*. In this work, the pope asserted against both the Nestorians and the Monophysites that Christ did indeed have two natures, a human and a divine, but that these natures with definitively united in one person. Leo wrote:

> So the proper character of both natures was maintained and came together in a single person. Lowliness was taken up by majesty, weakness by strength, mortality by eternity. To pay off the debt of our state, invulnerable nature was united to a nature that

could suffer; so that in a way that corresponded to the remedies we needed, one and the same mediator between God and humanity, the man Christ Jesus, could both on the one hand die and on the other be incapable of death. Thus was true God born in the undiminished and perfect nature of a true man, complete in what is his and complete in what is ours.[32]

The debate raged on and finally, in 451, the emperor summoned the bishops to Chalcedon to resolve the dispute. Over five hundred bishops came. The discussions were intense, but the assembled bishops eventually came to accept Pope Leo's explanation of the Incarnation and issued what has come to be known as the Chalcedonian Definition. It reads:

> So, following the saintly fathers, we all with one voice teach the confession of one and the same Son, our Lord Jesus Christ: the same perfect in divinity and perfect in humanity, the same truly God and truly man, of a rational soul and a body; consubstantial with the Father as regards his divinity, and the same consubstantial with us as regards his humanity; like us in all respects except for sin; begotten before the ages from the father as regards his divinity, and in the last days the same for us and for our salvation from Mary, the virgin God-bearer [Theotokos], as regards his humanity; one and the same Christ, Son, Lord, only-begotten, acknowledged in two natures which undergo no confusion, no change, no division, no separation; at no point was the difference between the natures taken away through the union, but rather the property of both natures is preserved and comes together into a single person and a single subsistent being; he is not parted or divided into two persons, but is one and the same only begotten Son, God, Word, Lord Jesus Christ, just as the prophets taught from the beginning about him, and as the Lord Jesus Christ himself instructed us, and as the creed of the fathers handed it down to us.[33]

Here, finally, was a definitive statement on who Christ was, on what really happened at the Incarnation. It had taken over four hun-

---

[32] Norman P. Tanner, ed., *Decrees of the Ecumenical Councils*, (Washington, D.C.: Georgetown University Press, 1990), 1:78.

[33] Tanner, *Decrees of the Ecumenical Councils*, 86–87.

dred and fifty years and the concerted efforts of Christianity's greatest minds to come to this definition. That is how difficult the problem was. The problem was not merely speculative, however. As we have seen, it bore directly on the social order of the now-Christian empire. The conversion of the empire away from paganism in both doctrine and "political" form was a part of the process of coming to understand the full meaning of the Incarnation. The rejection of Arianism was the rejection of the superiority of the temporal and material. The rejection of Nestorianism was the rejection of the idea that the temporal and the spiritual were entirely separate, operating in independent realms. The rejection of Monophysitism was the refusal of the possibility of the spiritual entirely absorbing the temporal into itself. Sorting out Trinitarian and Incarnational orthodoxy was, at the same time, the sorting out of the relationship between what would eventually become known as the temporal and spiritual powers, the powers of the laity and of the priesthood, within a united Church that was a polity. Political theology was integral to fundamental dogmatic theology.

The Christianization of the empire transformed it. Under Diocletian, the empire had become a centralized monarchical state whose emperor wielded absolute power as a god. The religious authority and the political authority were one in the emperor himself. This was an appropriate ideology for the essentially tyrannical state that he was building. The conversion of the empire made this sort of regime impossible. In Christian thought, the emperors were essential to the well-being of mankind. Christianity did not challenge the authority of political power. What it did do, however, was insist that such authority had to be used in the service of ultimately spiritual ends. The emperors had to use their power in order to help Christians live in peace and, ultimately, enter heaven. They did this by defending them from attack, by punishing wrongdoing and encouraging virtue, and by organizing the productive forces of their society in order to achieve the necessities of life. All of these activities were not just essential; they were themselves Christian, religious, as we would now say. When an emperor used his power justly, he was obeying the will of God. However, his power was limited by and, in a sense, dependent upon the power of the bishops and their priests. In order to be a good emperor, he relied upon the grace that the priesthood made available to him. The emperor was himself a Christian in pursuit of virtue, and he needed the preaching of the Gospel and the grace of the sacraments in order to achieve progress. At the same time, he needed the people to be moving into virtue through the same teaching and grace, virtue that would manifest partially in obedience to his just authority. He had to use his power justly and in pursuit of the common good of society so that the people would be ready to receive the preaching and the grace that came from the clergy, making his power ever more authoritative. He needed the power of the priesthood in order for his own power to come fully into being as authority, as a mediation of the power of God. If he acted otherwise, if he was violent or unjust, the emperor betrayed his office, and the bishops had both the right and the obligation to correct him.

In a Christian empire, the material, the things of the world, were good and right and necessary, but they were always oriented toward and ordered by salvation itself, which came only through grace and so the clergy. This meant that the power of the emperor was limited. He was not a god-king. He was a king, hopefully a godly king. However, this also meant that the power of the priesthood was limited. Diocletian had been a priest. Under the god-kings, the power of the priesthood was the power of the emperor. Under the Christian emperors, on the other hand, the priests could not command armies or build cities. With its emphasis on the unity of the body and the soul, on the unity of the divine and the human in Christ, on the ultimate unity of the earthly and the heavenly, Christianity had within it a duality within a unity that denied the possibility of absolute rule because the particular was always pointing beyond itself to the universal, even as the universal was only encountered through the particular. The power of the king mediated the power of God, but it could never be mistaken for it. Likewise, the power of the priesthood mediated the grace of God, but it could never be mistaken for its source. Christianity tied human power always beyond its immediate manifestation to a source and standard that it did not control. Only God, ultimately, had perfect power.

An episode that occurred in 390 demonstrates this new reality. The emperor Theodosius, whom no one doubted to be a pious Christian, suppressed a rebellion in Thessalonica, massacring thousands of people. He returned to Milan where he lived and attempted to enter the cathedral for Mass. He was met at the door by the bishop, St. Ambrose. Ambrose refused him entry, stating that his great sin forbade him from participating in the sacraments. The emperor was excommunicated. Ambrose was asserting the power of the episcopate over the flow of grace through the sacraments. The emperor had to do penance. Ambrose pleaded with the emperor:

> You are a man, you have met temptation—conquer it. Sin is not removed except by tears and penance. No angel or archangel can remove it; it is God Himself who alone can say: "I am with you"; if we have sinned, He does not forgive us unless we do penance. I urge, I ask, I beg, I warn, for my grief is that you, who were a model of unheard-of piety, who had reached the apex of clemency, who would not allow the guilty to be in peril, are not now mourning that so many guiltless have perished. Although you waged battles most successfully, and were praiseworthy also in other respects, the apex of your deeds was always your piety. The Devil envied you this, your most outstanding possession. Conquer him while you still have the means of doing so.[34]

Theodosius left, heartbroken, and in time returned, ready to submit to the bishop and to do penance for his sins. This was a new reality. It was not that the bishop was king. Ambrose could not order Theodosius's armies into the field. The bishops and the emperor needed each other, and the Christian people needed both. Power was dispersed and yet more fundamentally unified.

Both the royal and the priestly power came directly from God; they were both manifestations of his power and so fundamentally united, and yet like the body and the soul, they were distinct. Only together were they the Church, the City of God. Pope Gelasius (r. 492–496) articulated this understanding when he wrote:

> It happened before the coming of Christ that certain men, though still emerged in carnal activities, were symbolically both kings and priests, and sacred history tells us that Melchizedek was such a one. The devil also imitated this among his own people, for he always thrives in a spirit of tyranny to claim for himself what pertains to divine worship, and so pagan emperors were called supreme pontiffs. But when he came who was true King and true Priest, the emperor no longer assumed the title of priest, nor did the priest claim the royal dignity—though the members of him who was true King and true Priest, through participation in his nature, may be said to have received both qualities in their sacred nobility so that

---

[34] Ambrose of Milan, *Saint Ambrose: Letters*, in *The Fathers of the Church*, ed. Roy Joseph Deferrari, trans. Mary Melchior Beyenka (Washington, D.C.: Catholic University of America Press, 1954), 26:24.

they constitute a race at once royal and priestly. For Christ, mindful of human frailty, regulated with an excellent disposition what pertained to the salvation of his people. Thus he distinguished between the offices of both powers according to their own proper activities and separate dignities, wanting his people to be saved by healthful humility and nor carried away again by human pride, so that Christian emperors would need priests for attaining eternal life, and princes would avail themselves of imperial regulation in the conduct of temporal affairs.... Thus the humility of each order would be preserved, neither being exalted by the subservience of the other.[35]

The fourth and fifth centuries, the Age of the Church Fathers, was a period of remarkable vitality and growth. Christianity went from a tiny, persecuted minority to the official religion of the Roman Empire. The empire transitioned from Diocletian to Theodosius, from a god-emperor whom the pagan priests served as little more than slaves to a god-fearing emperor who submitted to the bishops in spiritual matters and who acknowledged himself to be another sinner. Bishops transitioned from being scattered pastors operating out of homes to being some of the most powerful and important men in the empire, and the Church was built as a large and complex organization, with Rome and the papacy at its center. Doctrinally, the Church tackled the most fundamental mysteries concerning Christ and the Trinity and came to definitions of deep profundity and lasting influence. All these developments were remarkably important. But just as important, if not as noticeable, was the development of monasticism.

Monasticism

The earliest Christian communities, as we have seen, lived in common. Their property was the property of the community, and their lives revolved around communal worship in the liturgy and service to the poor. As time went by, however, and as more and more of society converted, membership in the Church expanded to include all types, from the pious to the lukewarm, and to include the complexities of social

---

[35] Gelasius, *The Fourth Tract on the Bond of Anathema*, chap. 2., in Hugo Rahner, *Church and State in Early Christianity* (San Francisco, CA: Ignatius Press, 1992), 173–78.

and political life. The Church developed a sort of scale or hierarchy of sanctity, from beginner to living saint. The holiest people in the third and fourth centuries were the hermits. These were people, mostly in the Eastern deserts, who fled civilization to live lives of extreme mortification and contemplation. The most famous of these hermits was St. Anthony of Egypt. Their lives were committed to achieving perfection in charity and faith and so to experience in anticipation the glory of heaven. The hermits were famous, and many Christians went out to the wilderness to see them, to hear their preaching, and to be blessed by them. Along with the hermits, the heights of sanctity were achieved by the martyrs. There was a similarity here. Both the hermits and the martyrs gave up their lives for Christ and received graces untold.

After the conversion of Constantine, martyrdom faded from the experience of the Church, and the life of extreme asceticism rose in its place. The lives of the hermits were a sort of living martyrdom. It was an extreme form of asceticism and was possible only for certain people of certain dispositions. However, early in the fourth century, St. Pachomius founded the first cenobitic community. Cenobitic means "pertaining to a common life." These monks lived together; they worked together; they prayed together. While the life of a hermit has remained in the Church as perhaps the most spiritually advanced, it was the common life that became what we tend to think of as monasticism. This way of life spread rapidly. It moved from East to West through monks such as St. John Cassian, who established a monastery in France in the early fifth century and who wrote extensively on the monastic way of life.

Monasticism developed as a way of pursuing perfection in the Christian life. It combined intellectual development with manual labor, the cultivation of virtue, and devotion to liturgical and contemplative prayer. It was a Christian ideal. Not surprisingly, then, many of the Church Fathers were either monks themselves or directly supported monasticism. For example, St. Basil was a monk and wrote an important rule of life for his community. St. Ambrose and St. Augustine organized monastic communities. St. Jerome started monasteries in the Holy Land. As we have already seen, for the Church Fathers, Christianity was not merely a set of ideas; it was a way of life. It was communion and peace, not only horizontally between men but vertically between men and God. This is precisely what monasticism sought. Monasticism spread rapidly through the fifth century.

The most important monk in the West was St. Benedict. St. Benedict lived from 480 to 547. Benedict started out as a hermit of great sanctity. But, like many such hermits, he attracted students and so decided to start a community. Benedict is famous for the rule that he wrote for these monks to live by. The Benedictine Rule is a masterpiece of Roman prudence and moderation. St. Benedict had a deep understanding of the pitfalls and struggles of the monastic life, and he understood where to be severe and where to be lenient so as to most effectively lead the community deeper into sanctity. The Rule emphasized poverty, chastity, and obedience, and it combined liturgical prayer with work, either in the fields or through copying texts. The Benedictine monk lived a life of quiet and peaceful simplicity. It was not a life of extreme mortification but of consistent, steady, and intentional growth into holiness. In his own lifetime, St. Benedict's rule and the life it regulated did not spread much beyond the walls of his own monastery. But, as we will see in Part III of this book, it had a major and long-term impact on the Church.

By the end of the fifth century, the Catholic Church had taken on the form not merely of a religion among religions. It had, rather, taken on the form of a civilization. The Church had a place for everyone, from the emperor himself to the powerful bishops to the simple priests and laypeople to the spiritual experts, the monks. The Church was the redemption of mankind as a whole, and there was no aspect of man's life in this world that was not properly a part of it. Of this fact the Church of the Christian empire was convinced. But it had more to learn. This became clear as the empire began to crumble around it.

The Fall of the Western Roman Empire

The Western Empire never really recovered from the intense disorder of the third century, and the fourth-century attempt at centralization was never very effective. The empire had always relied upon the strength of its armies, and we can see the nature of its struggles by looking at the composition of the legions. In the first century, the Roman army was made up primarily of Italian free men. In the second century, the empire began to recruit from the provinces and from the ranks of defeated peoples. In the third century, the army was increasingly not a Roman army at all. Rather, the government began bringing in whole tribes of barbarians from outside the empire to serve as self-sufficient military units. The chiefs of these tribes were made Roman generals, and their people were often given land to settle within the empire. Over the late fourth and into the fifth centuries, the government in Rome became weaker and weaker. It relied more and more on barbarians for security. Unable to pay these tribes, the emperors began settling them in the empire and giving them the right to tax the local populations directly. This, unsurprisingly, accelerated the decline of Roman power. The barbarian forces were, of course, loyal to their own commanders and not to the emperor. What is more, given the ability to tax directly, they no longer relied on the central administration for payment.

The Western Empire found itself in a situation where much of it was now effectively governed by non-Romans. These barbarians were normally either heretical Christians, such as Arians, or still practiced their pagan religions. Throughout much of the empire, therefore, there was a settled population of Roman Catholics that was being governed and protected by barbarian non-Catholics, who were more or less independent from the central government. We have already seen how the growing strength and importance of bishops helped decentralize the empire as the Christian populations, including the most wealthy and powerful members of society, focused more of their attention and resources locally. These dynamics combined to dramatically decentralize the empire as it fractured into increasingly self-reliant regions. During the fifth century, the emperor in Italy became largely powerless as barbarian generals took charge.

This new order became shockingly obvious when, in the year 410, a Visigoth army that had been a part of the Roman army rebelled against the empire and successfully sacked the city of Rome itself. Even though the Visigoths eventually withdrew, this event shocked the Roman world. Many people thought the end of the world must be near. It was clearly the case that the Western Roman Empire was on the brink of falling. The lingering Roman pagans asserted that the empire was teetering on the edge of destruction because the people had abandoned the traditional gods for Christianity. Many Christians, for their part, had so tightly bound the empire and Christianity together in their minds that the fall of the empire seemed to them to be the fall of Christianity itself. The Christian empire was in crisis.

It was in response to this crisis that the greatest of the Latin Church Fathers, St. Augustine, wrote *The City of God*, which we have already had an opportunity to discuss. *The City of God* is one of the most important works of theology in the history of the Church. St. Augustine explained that Christianity was not bound to any particular polity. Rather, Christianity was a vast polity that transcended all particular times and places even as it was directly present in them. The City of God, the Church, was in the world, but it was not merely of the world. It reached always beyond human history to heaven itself. As we discussed in the first part of this book, the City of God was engaged in a cosmic battle with the Earthly City, the City of Man. This was the city of fallen men and demons. It, too, was bound to no particular political organization. These two cities moved through history engaged in constant combat within the human organizations of governments, economics, and even the ecclesiastical structure itself. The Earthly City sought to drive all creation into depravity and ultimately to hell, while the City of God sought to convert all of creation to justice through the grace of Christ and to ascend to the angels and saints in heaven. The Roman Empire was not essential to the City of God. Far from it. As we have seen, it had first been dominated by the Earthly City and had been a force for evil in the world. With its conversion, it had shifted to being more dominated by the City of God—this was true—but the City of God did not need the empire. It is destined for glory while all empires are destined to fall.

St. Augustine provided the Church with a theory of history. According to this understanding, history was not the story of the rise and fall of nations. This was merely the surface data of what happened. History was really the story of the fall and redemption of man. For St. Augustine, political organization was important in this story. The City of God was really in the world, and it really sought to build societies of justice and peace. Likewise, the Earthly City really sought to build societies of power and greed. Their battle in history was precisely over control of real societies, of real people bound together in polities. The stakes were high. St. Augustine was not advocating for some sort of Christian withdrawal from concern for the world. Far, far from it. What St. Augustine was arguing was that Christians were engaged in a far larger drama than the drama of national or imperial histories. They were engaged in the drama of salvation history that started with the fall of Adam and would end with the Second Coming of Christ and the creation of a New Heavens and a New Earth. In this drama, the City of God would have to fight tooth and nail against the Earthly City. This fight was nothing more than the fight against sin itself. But the victory through grace was assured. This vision of

Christianity as being not merely the religion of an empire but the lens through which all of human history is viewed would become the vision that has dominated Roman Catholicism ever since. It is the view that guides this book.

The decline of the Western Empire continued. Finally, in 476, a barbarian general deposed the emperor and didn't bother to place another puppet on the throne. This is normally the date given for the fall of the Western Empire, and it is as good as any other. It is certainly the case that, starting about the year 500, we can start talking about the Middle Ages and the next chapter in the history of the Church.

III

The Medieval Church

1. The Early Middle Ages

After 476, there were no longer Western emperors. There remained, however, an emperor in Constantinople, in the Greek half of the Roman Empire. After the year 500 or so, we normally refer to this half of the empire as the Byzantine Empire; however, the people at the time continued to call it the Roman Empire and to think of themselves as Romans. The barbarian kingdoms that divided up the western half of the empire mostly recognized the Eastern emperor as having nominal lordship over the West. Indeed, most people continued to think of the western half of the empire as solidly a part of the still-standing empire. To people of the time, the West had become weak and decentralized, and it was being governed by barbarians that were in various degrees of rebellion. However, it was still part of the empire, and the barbarians were still, for the most part, technically branches of the Roman army. The Greek-speaking Church in the East and the Latin-speaking Church in the West were still united, and everyone looked to Constantinople for leadership.

In the middle decades of the sixth century, the Eastern Emperor Justinian set out to reunite the entire Roman Empire. He conquered North Africa and Spain from the barbarians who had held them and retook the Italian peninsula from the Ostrogothic kings who had ruled there for about fifty years. With Justinian's conquests, the Roman Church was again definitively a part of the imperial Church. This made perfect sense to the popes. The bishops of Rome understood themselves as occupying a special place within an imperial system. The pope was the patriarch of Rome, but there were also patriarchs in Constantinople, Antioch, Alexandria, and Jerusalem. Each patriarch ruled his own region through his bishops, and they all came together under the emperor for councils when necessary. This system was known as the pentarchy. The papacy had special authority to ensure orthodoxy within this system, though this authority was not always recognized by the other patriarchs. Obviously, when Italy had lain under barbarian rule, this system was strained, but Justinian definitively reestablished it. However, Justinian did not reconquer all of the Western Empire. Most of western Europe remained under the rule of barbarian kingdoms.

Justinian's reunion of the empire was almost immediately put under enormous strain. First, there was a terrible plague that ravaged the empire and severely weakened its ability to project military power. Then, a tribe called the Lombards successfully invaded Italy in 568 and ruled most of it for the next two hundred years. The Lombards, however, did not control the area directly around Rome. This territory remained within the empire ruled from Constantinople. Over the six and seventh centuries, even in Rome itself, imperial rule grew weaker and weaker, and, in effect, the pope became the ruler of this territory.

The next major threat to imperial power came from the Arabian Peninsula. Sometime in the 630s, Muhammed united the various tribes of the region into a vast military machine. He claimed to be a prophet sent from God. This was the founding of Islam. More than just a religion, Islam was a political and military powerhouse. Quickly, the Islamic forces swept through the Middle East and conquered North Africa, which was at the time Christian and still a part of the Roman Empire centered on Constantinople. The Muslim armies crossed at the Strait of Gibraltar and conquered most of Spain. In fact, they penetrated deep into France and were finally turned around at the Battle of Tours in 732, only about 150 miles away from Paris. The rise of Islam had major consequences for the Roman Catholic Church, as we will see later in this history. However, the first consequence was that the Eastern emperors became almost totally consumed with fighting the Islamic forces in the East. The Byzantine Empire had been reduced to the area directly around Greece and Asia Minor, modern-day Turkey, and this territory was under constant threat. Fighting in the East meant that imperial lands in the West, including Rome, were largely abandoned. As the empire became less and less capable of defending the territory around Rome, the papacy stepped in to fill the power vacuum.

One of the most important popes of this general period was Pope

Gregory the Great (r. 590–604). Gregory strengthened the papacy as an institution, reformed the liturgy, and is recognized as a Doctor of the Church for his vast theological writings. However, perhaps the most important thing he did was send missionaries from Rome to the barbarian tribes of the West, most famously to England. Most of the barbarian kingdoms were either still pagan or practiced Arian Christianity. Gregory's missionaries and the priests and monks who followed them, however, were largely successful in converting these tribes to Catholic orthodoxy.

The most important of these tribes was the Franks. The Frankish kingdom stretched across much of western Europe, including modern France, Belgium, the Netherlands, Switzerland, and parts of Germany. The Franks had technically converted to Roman orthodoxy very early in the sixth century under King Clovis. However, during the seventh century, missionaries from the British Isles, led by men such as St. Boniface, built an episcopal hierarchy and a network of monasteries in the vast Frankish domains. These missionaries were the direct descendants of the missionaries that Gregory the Great had commissioned, and so they taught a very Rome-centered form of Catholicism. This focus on Rome is called *Romanitas*, which means something like "Roman-ness." As the Franks strengthened their kingdom, they internalized this notion of *Romanitas*. They saw themselves as building a truly Christian kingdom and understood that this meant they had to be united with the bishop in Rome. The problem, of course, was that Rome was still a part of the Byzantine Empire, even if that empire had grown weaker in the face of Islam, and the papacy wasn't too concerned about what was happening far out in the West and North, in the old lost provinces of the empire. The Christian world was, therefore, divided into two. There was the imperial Church that was still governed by the emperor in Constantinople, which largely spoke Greek and, in the seventh century, included the papacy and Rome. Then, there was the barbarian Church that fell outside the imperial system. These barbarians, however, tended to look to Rome and not Constantinople for ecclesial leadership.

Things changed in the eighth century. The Byzantine Empire had evolved a form of Church governance and politics that is sometimes referred to as Caesaropapism. Caesaropapism just means that the emperor was also effectively the head of the clerical hierarchy, that the political organization and the ecclesial organization were the same organization, headed by the emperor. The emperors ever since

Constantine had been involved in ecclesial affairs. But, with Justinian, this involvement transformed into direct governmental control, and by the eighth century, this control crossed over into doctrinal issues. In 726, Emperor Leo III launched an iconoclastic policy. Iconoclasm was the belief that the veneration of all images was a sin. The iconoclasts destroyed as many images as they could, and the emperor launched a persecution of orthodox Christians. Pope St. Gregory II condemned iconoclasm and the whole principle of emperors making doctrinal pronouncements. The emperor attempted to take control of Rome but lacked the local power, demonstrating that the real power in the city lay with the papacy. Instead, he confiscated all the papal lands that were under his control and transferred them to Constantinople's ecclesiastical jurisdiction, effectively ejecting the pope from the imperial Church. The iconoclasm controversies raged on and off for the next century, ensuring that the papacy was not reintegrated into the Byzantine Church.

The papacy was on its own. And it was in danger. All around it lay the Lombard kingdom that had long wanted control of Rome and the surrounding countryside. The papacy needed protection, and it found it far to the north with the Franks, whose power was rising and who were imbued with *Romanitas*. In 751, Pope Zachary transferred the Frankish crown from the ineffectual Merovingian dynasty to the Carolingians, who had long held most of the power in the kingdom. The papacy and the new Frankish kings developed a very special relationship. The papacy needed them for protection, and they needed the papacy in order to realize their own understanding of Christian kingship. In 755, the Carolingian king, Pepin, invaded Italy to protect the pope from the Lombards, restoring the papal lands to him. Pepin's son, Charles, invaded again in 773, only this time he destroyed the Lombards and made himself their king. The Franks and the papacy were engaged in constructing a new ecclesiastical and political world, totally outside the Byzantine Empire.

As Frankish and Roman interests converged, Roman liturgical norms and practices were promulgated throughout the Frankish realm, and the Carolingians, with a conception of kingship heavily laden with Roman and biblical images, began to understand themselves as the protectors of the high priesthood of the pope. This movement reached its culmination on Christmas day in the year 800, when Pope St. Leo III crowned Charles, known as Charlemagne (Charles the Great), emperor of the Romans. Everyone still thought in terms of the Roman Empire. With the Eastern Empire wallowing in heresy and with a Church dominated by the emperors, the papacy in Rome reestablished the Western Empire.

Carolingian kingship was profoundly Christian. The king was a Christological David who was tasked with leading the Christian people into true peace and finally to salvation. *Romanitas*, Roman Catholicism and so the papacy, was integral to the Carolingian understanding of their own power. Charlemagne himself wrote to Pope Leo III:

> For it is our task, with the aid of divine goodness, to defend the holy church of Christ everywhere from the attacks of pagans without and to strengthen it within through the knowledge of the Catholic faith. And it is your duty, O Holy Father, with your hands raised high to God, after the manner of Moses, to aid our armies so that by your intercession with God, our leader and benefactor, the Christian people may always and everywhere be victorious over the enemies of His Holy Name and the name of Our Lord Jesus Christ be proclaimed throughout the world.[1]

It was not so much that the Franks were making an alliance with the papacy. It was rather that the Franks were merging the papacy into their own society, a society that had been built as Christian from top to bottom.

Nothing that contributed to this mission lay outside the king's potential authority. Charlemagne sent representatives called *Missi* throughout his empire, tasked with making the Carolingian vision a reality. The commissioning document reads:

> And let no one, through his cleverness or astuteness, dare to oppose or thwart the written law, as many are wont to do, or the judicial sentence passed upon him, or to do injury to the churches of God or the poor or the widows or the wards or any Christian. But all shall live entirely in accordance with God's precept, justly and under a just rule, and each one shall be admonished to live in harmony with his fellows in his business or profession; the canonical clergy ought to observe in every respect a canonical life without heeding base gain, nuns ought to keep diligent watch over their lives, laymen

---

[1] Letter from Charlemagne to Pope Leo III, in Marshall W. Baldwin, ed., *Christianity through the Thirteenth Century* (New York: Macmillan, 1970), 119.

and the secular clergy ought rightly to observe their laws without malicious fraud, and all ought to live in mutual charity and perfect peace. And let the *missi* themselves make a diligent investigation whenever any man claims that an injustice has been done to him by any one, just as they desire to deserve the grace of omnipotent God and to keep their fidelity promised to Him, so that entirely in all cases everywhere, in accordance with the will and fear of God, they shall administer the law fully and justly in the case of the holy churches of God and of the poor, of wards and widows and of the whole people. And if there shall be anything of such a nature that they, together with the provincial counts, are not able of themselves to correct it and to do justice concerning it, they shall, without any ambiguity, refer this, together with their reports, to the judgment of the emperor; and the straight path of justice shall not be impeded by any one on account of flattery or gifts from any one, or on account of any relationship, or from fear of the powerful.[2]

This was the program for the building of a civilization. It was the reestablishment of the Roman Empire on an entirely new foundation. Christianity is not here added to an imperial organization. Rather, the formation of a Roman Catholic society was the empire's very *raison d'etre*.

In the Carolingian Empire, *Romanitas* merged with Germanic culture. And as Charlemagne's empire grew, conquering one barbarian kingdom after the next, *Romanitas* spread. This *Romanitas* was, perhaps, most marked in the spread of Benedictine monasticism. As we have already discussed, St. Benedict wrote his rule early in the sixth century and had established a monastery in Italy. The rule was profoundly Roman in disposition, emphasizing moderation and order. Nevertheless, medieval Benedictine monasticism was not an Italian phenomenon. In fact, St. Benedict's monastery had been destroyed by the Lombards, and there is no evidence of any Roman monastery following his rule until the tenth century. Rather, the Rule of St. Benedict survived mostly in England as an aspect of British *Romanitas*. The British missionaries to the Franks brought it with

---

[2] General Capitulary of the Missi, 1, in Merrick Whitcomb, John Bach McMaster, Arthur C. Howland, William Fairley, and Dana Carleton Munro, eds., *Translations and Reprints from the Original Sources of European History* (Philadelphia: University of Pennsylvania Press, 1900), 4:16–18.

them and spread it throughout the kingdom. Under the Carolingians, the Benedictine Rule became the standard monastic rule of the Latin Church.

The Carolingians understood their kingship as directly tied to the favor of God, and the establishment and reform of monasteries were rooted in the idea of vicarious merit and the efficacy of prayer. The liturgical prayer of the monks and the merit earned by their penitential lives was as important to the strength of the Carolingian Empire as its armies. Indeed, Charlemagne understood himself to have two vast armies: one was material, armed with the iron sword, and the other was spiritual, armed with the sword of prayer. He needed both to expand his Christian kingdom and to spread Roman Catholicism in the process. Charlemagne, then, sought the perfection of monastic observance. To this end, he launched what is sometimes referred to as the Carolingian Renaissance.

The Carolingian Renaissance was a reform movement aimed at restoring the intellectual patrimony of the West that had been largely lost after the fall of the Western Roman Empire. However, the Carolingians did not care about literacy or textual accuracy for their own sakes. Rather, they cared that the monks pray correctly, that they sing the right words and meditate on the correct Scripture. There is a commonly made argument that there was nothing new or creative in the Carolingian Renaissance, but this misses a fundamental point. The lives of the monks themselves were the original creation of Carolingian culture. It was a mentality focused on experience, on lived truth, and so, appropriately, it was not a period of great theological speculation but one of liturgical development and standardization. The liturgy was the center of it all. In the liturgy, the classical, the Christian, and the Germanic merged. The classical seven liberal arts were divided into the trivium—grammar, rhetoric, and logic—that the monks might read and correct the sacred texts, and the quadrivium—arithmetic, geometry, astronomy, and music—that the monks might perfectly perform the liturgy and calculate the movable feasts. Following the classical Benedictine rule, the monks offered a redefinition of the classical tradition within the context of the Christian liturgy. But it was also Germanic. Indeed, the monks were men of action through prayer, and they were integral to the well-being of their kingdom; they were crucial to the strength of the king and his army. They fought a combat within the cloister that was parallel to that of their brothers in the world. Just as the political ideas of the Roman Empire were merged with those of the Franks in the person of Charlemagne to produce something new, so the religion and culture of Rome was fused with that of the Franks in the persons of the monks to produce something new. This merger of the Roman with the Germanic was exported to Rome itself.

Indeed, the Roman Liturgy as we think of it was, in many ways, a production of the Frankish monks, and the strongest formulations of papal power of the period were advanced by Franks. Rome had sent missionaries north; they had converted the nations to a *Romanitas*-imbued Catholicism, and then those nations brought *Romanitas* back to Rome, a Rome that had spent centuries immersed in the Greek Church and which had largely become Greek in its thought and practice. The merger of the Frankish with the Roman in the Carolingian Empire was something new, and it was the foundation of Western culture and politics. Some historians have said it was the creation of Europe. And this is, in a sense, very true. The Roman world had been a Mediterranean world. The heart of Roman civilization was the coastline all the way around the Mediterranean Sea, and the vast stretches of wild forest to the north were the peripheries, the provinces. This had now changed. Islam had ripped the Mediterranean civilization in two. More than half of the old empire now lay under Islamic rule. The Byzantine Empire became a truly Eastern empire, based in Greece and oriented toward the East in order to hold back the Islamic forces. In the West, the papacy turned north in its orientation, toward the wilds, and built with the Franks a new Roman Catholic civilization there. This shift can be seen in the nationalities of the men who were called to the papacy. In the years between 685 and 752, all but one pope were either Greek or Syrian. In the years between 752 and 844, all but two were Romans. This was the formation of Europe as a distinct cultural unit. The formation of Europe, however, was inseparable from the formation of Roman Catholicism as a distinct form of orthodoxy. Indeed, what was really formed in these centuries was Christendom: the Catholic civilization of the Middle Ages. Christendom was formed by the gradual unification of the Germanic barbarians and the Romans.

The Carolingian Empire did not last long. The empire was divided between Charlemagne's three grandsons into the kingdoms that would eventually become France, Germany, and Italy, and they quickly began fighting each other. The imperial title eventually became tied to the Germanic lands. France developed its own weak line of kings, and Italy decentralized into many small principalities with a nominal relationship to the emperor. Civil war led to civil unrest and destabilization. At the same time, in the ninth and tenth centuries, the Vikings came from the north, from Scandinavia, raiding deep into the empire. From the south, Islamic raiders preyed upon Christian settlements, stealing their wealth and their populations for slaves. In the year 846, Rome itself was raided. In the East, Hungarian tribes attacked, penetrating deep into the interior of the empire. The empire that the Carolingians had built could not withstand the onslaught.

The central government faded away in favor of local organization. The Carolingian army had been based upon mustering the freemen from the vast kingdom in order to form the host for a campaign season. The problem now, however, was that the new enemies were unpredictable and fast. They appeared as if out of nowhere, raided, and left. There wasn't time to call together the host, and there was no established enemy territory to attack. The solution was decentralization. The military would become local, based in castles scattered across the countryside and dependent only on local resources. The core of this fighting force would become what we think of as knights: petty nobles who controlled enough land and wealth to deploy themselves, and normally a small force of cavalry and infantry with them, at a moment's notice. They taxed the populations of their lands directly. Over time, these men came to take over most of the functioning of the imperial government. To the local populations, they effectively were the government. These knights themselves often owed fealty to more powerful nobles such as dukes. Fealty was a promise of loyalty and an oath to fight for the lord if summoned. These powerful nobles, in turn, often owed fealty to the king or emperor. This arrangement is often called feudalism. Feudalism wasn't a formal system, and many historians have rightly questioned any treatment of this society that gives the impression that it was organized in any sort of standard or "constitutional" manner. In fact, arrangements between knights, lords, bishops, abbots, and kings varied dramatically from region to region and from time to time. The word "feudalism" is salvageable, however, if we limit what we mean by it. All I mean here by a feudal society is a society that was highly decentralized and wherein local mechanisms of power were held personally and were united into larger units only through personal relationships of family, friendships, honor, or oaths and not through standing juridical institutions.

The clergy and monasteries of Europe were slowly integrated into this feudal society. Cathedrals, with their bishops and priests, and monasteries became parts of the local property and institutions which were controlled by knights and other nobles. It was not uncommon at all for a noble to think of himself as owning a certain bishopric and appointing his relatives or friends to be bishop. Likewise, the monasteries became often directly controlled by the nobles, leading often to corruption and lapsed monastic practice. Many monasteries were abandoned. What is more, while decentralization helped in fighting the invaders, it also lent itself to local warfare. Knights often fought each other in local disputes. Warfare, therefore, became both more common and less destructive. Violence became ubiquitous. During this same period, the papacy in Rome reached a low point, both morally and with regard to ecclesiastical and political power. Without connection to a strong imperial power, the papacy become embroiled in local Roman politics and rival Roman families vied for control of the office. This, not surprisingly, led to corruption. This was the reassertion of the worldly element within the Church. The Church, meaning the full body of the baptized, clergy and laity alike, was sliding into worldliness; the City of Man gained ground within the City of God. As the particular was asserted, the universal aspect of the Church was pushed aside and minimized. Peace, the ultimate unifying principle, gave way increasingly to violence, the ultimate principle of division. The Church was falling into corruption.

2. The High Middle Ages

The Reform Movement

The post-Carolingian world may have been violent and disorganized, but it was profoundly Christ haunted. The warrior class was guilt ridden because of its way of life. The knights knew that violence was wrong and that their way of life demanded penance. As the invasions subsided, therefore, this knightly class turned its attention to reforming and expanding monasticism. The monks were drawn from the same class as the knights. They were literally their brothers. The life of the knights was harsh and violent, and so their brother monks prayed for their souls and did penance for their sins. Powerful nobles established new monasteries or insisted that old monasteries be reformed and follow a purer observance. The nobles knew that lay ownership of the monasteries and of the Church in general was not conducive to such spiritual rigor, and so there emerged the practice of endowing reformed monasteries and bishoprics with lands and revenues, of essentially donating back to the monks and clergy the property that feudalism had defused through society. There were two main centers of monastic reform: one was in northern Germany and the other was in France. The German reform movement was championed by the emperors, the descendants of Charlemagne. The reform movement in France was more independent and focused on the monastery of Cluny. Reformed and new monasteries exploded across Europe in the late tenth and through the eleventh centuries. There were thousands of them.

This monastic reform movement spread through Europe and led to the reform of the whole civilization. The monks viewed their lives as the pursuit of perfection, and while everyone knew that the external world of work and politics was never going to be as perfect as the world of the monastery, they thought it could get closer. They believed that through God's grace, poured into society through the sacraments, there was no reason why all of Christian society couldn't share in holiness and achieve a degree of perfection. This was a weakening of the idea that life in the world was simply sinful and that one's only hope was the vicarious merit and penance of the monks—an idea that helped launch the reform movement. Now, the idea that everyone was called to a degree of holiness gained ground. More and more people came to believe that it was possible for the peace found in the monastery to be extended into society as a whole, that justice was realizable, that charity was a real force in the world. The drive to "expand" the walls of the monastery to include more and more of the world within its sacramental perfection was the central dynamism of the reform movement of the High Middle Ages. The monks wanted perfection for all the baptized, and the baptized laity wanted to participate in the perfection of the monks. The reform movement was a movement of the whole society, lay and clerical.

The emperors in Germany seized upon this movement in their lands and became its champions. They sought to reunite the fractured empire under their rule through sanctifying it as a truly holy empire. They understood the clergy and the religious to function within offices that were a part of the imperial structure itself, and they sought to isolate the religious and clergy from local politics by extending their imperial power to include them. What this meant

The Medieval Church

was that the emperors tended to view themselves as the governmental head of the Church in their lands, even as they genuinely supported the reform of that Church. The reform movement in France and other parts of Europe was different. These parts of Europe effectively lay outside the control of the German emperors and were controlled by a decentralized feudal system under weak kings. The reform monasteries, therefore, looked not to the emperor or to a king for protection and support but to the papacy. This reform movement clamored for the papacy to extend its power to include them so that they might be protected from local, feudal politics.

The papacy, however, was corrupt. The papacy reached its low point under Pope Benedict IX. A member of a powerful Roman family, Benedict was placed on the papal throne in 1032 through bribery. He was young—twenty or so. While orthodox in his teaching, such as it was, Benedict led a very immoral life. The Roman people finally grew tired of his debauchery and forced him to flee the city. They then elected a new pope, Sylvester. Benedict rallied his forces and drove out Sylvester, retaking the papal throne. Under pressure, he then sold the papacy to his uncle, who took the name of Gregory VI. Benedict, however, had second thoughts and attempted to drive Gregory from the throne. This was more than anyone could take, and prominent members of Roman society appealed to Emperor Henry III to do something. Henry was a supporter of the reform movement in his lands, and he saw here an opportunity to extend it to the papacy. He, therefore, called a synod at Sutri in 1046 which deposed all three papal claimants and put a German reformer on the throne as Clement II. Clement, who was committed to the reform movement, unfortunately died shortly after taking office. Benedict IX took this opportunity to retake the papal throne again . . . his *third* time as pope. The emperor again intervened, and Benedict went into exile, this time for good. The emperor had Damasus II elected, but he died almost immediately. He was followed in 1049 by Leo IX, a German committed to the ideals of reform.

The papacy of St. Leo IX marks the true beginning of the papal reform movement. Leo brought reforming zeal and an entourage of like-minded clerics, one of whom would become Pope Gregory VII. The papal reform movement is often called the Gregorian Reform after Gregory VII. The reformers took immediate action. Leo's reforming work focused on simony and clerical marriage. Simony was the practice of buying and selling Church offices, such as bishoprics or abbacies. Celibacy for priests had been widely practiced and had been the ideal since the Church Fathers. However, during the centuries of disorder after Charlemagne, it had become fairly common for priests to marry or at least to live with a woman and have children with her. As one reformer wrote:

> The whole world was placed in wickedness, sanctity had failed, justice had perished, and truth lay buried. Iniquity was king, avarice was lord, Simon magus held the Church, bishops and priests were given over to pleasure and fornication. Priests were not ashamed to take wives, they held their weddings openly ... But what is even worse than all this—hardly anyone was found who either was not a simoniac or had not been ordained by simoniacs.[3]

Both simony and marriage were part of the way in which the clerical Church had been integrated into the corrupt feudal society of the laity. Breaking the clergy free from this society was a central aspect of the reform movement in general. Simony and clerical marriage were great sins, and the reformers believed that the sanctification of all of Christendom could only be achieved if first the clergy were reformed. A holy clergy could preach the Gospel with conviction and distribute the sacraments worthily and, in so doing, lead all the baptized out of corruption and into holiness. The newly established reforming papacy, therefore, focused its attention on the clergy, but it did so as a means of reforming the entire Church.

The reform papacy was, first and foremost, a monastic papacy. The reformers sought the extension of the perfection of the monastic liturgical life and the isolation of larger and larger portions of the Church from the corruptions of the world. What they sought was the turning of all of society into one ideal liturgical act of worship, into one properly ordered monastery. The mentality of monasticism, therefore, animated the reform papacy. It was convinced that holiness was possible, and it was committed to using the power of the papacy to lead Christendom into it.

They were also concerned about the papacy itself. Popes had been elected for centuries by the people and clergy of Rome in what amounted to a process of acclamation. Candidates were presented to

---

[3] Bruno of Segni, *On Simoniacs*, I, in the edition of E. Sackur in MGH Libelli de Lite II, trans. W. L. North (Hannover, 1892), 546–562.

the crowds, and they acclaimed whom they wanted. Vestiges of this remain today when the new pope is presented to the waiting crowds after his election. This system was easily corrupted by simony and the influence of local politics. In the eleventh century, the system was profoundly corrupted "by the traffickers in simoniacal heresy."[4] In order to isolate the papacy from the influence of local corruption and venality, Leo and the reforming popes who followed him instituted the practice of the principal clergy of the city of Rome, the cardinals, electing the pope directly. Removing the papacy from Roman politics was a prerequisite to it assuming leadership over the reform of the universal Church. The papacy could not be merely another aspect of the feudal world. It had to be positioned above that world, capable of judging it and leading it deeper into reform. Establishing the College of Cardinals as the papal electors was a decisive step in this direction.

The reforming papacy was embraced by both the German and the French wings of the monastic reform movement. It was also extremely popular with normal Christian laymen who wanted holy clergy and who were increasingly seeking holiness themselves. However, it encountered considerable resistance. Feudal power was hard to break. For many noble families, control of the Church in their lands was a bedrock of their power. They often resisted reform efforts. Nevertheless, the reform generally gained ground.

The reforming papacy also encountered resistance from the Eastern Church. Since Charlemagne, relations with the eastern half of the Church had been strained. In effect, the Church had been divided with the reestablishment of the western half of the empire. In the two and a half centuries after 800, East-West relations had gotten steadily worse. The Roman Church had inserted the "filioque" into the Nicene Creed. This means "and the Son" and was the assertion that the Holy Spirit proceeded from both of the other persons of the Trinity. The Greek Church rejected this change to the creed. They also rejected the Latin Church's use of unleavened bread for the Eucharist and papal claims to jurisdictional primacy. The Latin and Greek Churches had also been competing in missionary endeavors to eastern Europe. However, the two halves were not in actual schism and remained in communication with each other. The renewed power of the papacy in the eleventh century brought these tensions to the fore and began

---

[4] Decree of 1059 Concerning Papal Elections, in Ernest F. Henderson, trans., *Select Historical Documents of the Middle Ages* (London: George Bell and Sons, 1910), 361–364.

to further aggravate them. In 1054, there was a relatively minor fight between the papal legate in Constantinople and the patriarch of the city. This resulted in mutual excommunications. This event is often given as the official date for the start of the Great Schism between the Roman Catholic and the Greek Orthodox Churches. While it is true that mutual excommunications were issued, the separation of the two parts of Christendom had, in fact, been steadily increasing over the previous centuries, and no one immediately recognized them as in schism after 1054. Rather, the two Churches continued to grow apart until schism was just a reality. When they then looked back at the history of how this tragic reality had come to be, 1054 stood out as an important milestone.

The Investiture Contest

The reforming papacy and the reforming empire eventually came to blows. The emperors of the eleventh century had managed to counter much of the chaos of the feudal period and had built a fairly organized imperial regime. This government was animated by Christian zeal for reform and rested on the "Liberty of the Church." What this meant in a German context was the liberty of the clergy from the local nobility through their integration into the imperial government. The imperial reform tended to think of the imperial hierarchy and the clerical hierarchy as two aspects of the same social reality, and the purification of one was the purification of the other. The emperors saw their empire as ideally a type of large monastery, with them as the abbot. In the early phases of imperial reform, the papacy had been weak and minimally involved. It was mired in its own problems. However, with the rise of the Gregorian Reform, this changed. All of a sudden, the papacy became a real force throughout Christendom. Nevertheless, the imperial and papal movements seemed to complement each other. Both sought the elimination of simony and clerical marriage; both sought monastic and liturgical reform; both sought the organization of society under principles of charity and justice; both sought the "Liberty of the Church."

Through the reign of Emperor Henry III (r. 1046–1056) and through the childhood reign of his son Henry IV, the empire and the papacy continued to work together. As the reform movement strengthened, however, this cooperation broke down. The emperors had fully incorporated reformed bishops into their powerbase and had developed the practice of "investing" them with their offices. Bishops held expansive lands and wielded often immense temporal power. They were important officials in the emperor's government. Among some of the more zealous reformers, this began to look an awful lot like simony. Finally, conflict erupted when two competing bishops were elected and invested in Milan. One was the imperial candidate, supported by much of the upper class; the other was the papal candidate, supported by the radical reforming population. This conflict escalated. Pope Gregory VII excommunicated Henry IV and his many, many episcopal supporters. In response, in 1076, the German bishops renounced their obedience to the pope in favor of their monarch. The papacy claimed to have authority over all bishops and asserted that no temporal power could invest a bishop with his office. What is more, the pope asserted that "it may be permitted to him to depose emperors," that "he may absolve subjects from their fealty to wicked men," that "of the pope alone all princes shall kiss the feet," that "he alone can depose or reinstate bishops," that "he himself may be judged by no one," and that "the Roman church has never erred; nor will it err to all eternity, the Scripture bearing witness."[5] Unsurprisingly, the emperors viewed these claims as a direct assault on their authority. Both sides believed they were fighting for the "Liberty of the Church."

The Investiture Contest raged for the next fifty years, sometimes breaking out in actual warfare. The technical issue was over who invested bishops with their offices, but the real fight was over competing visions of the reforming Church. Would it take a shape similar to that in Byzantium, where the emperor was the head of the Church and the judicial mechanisms of his authority were the same as that of the bishops? Would the Western Church go down the Caesaropapism road? Or would the vision of St. Ambrose and St. Augustine win? In this vision, the Church was governed by two powers, the temporal and the spiritual. The temporal power was wielded by laymen, and the spiritual power was wielded by the clergy. They were different, but they were not divided. In this vision, Christendom absolutely needed both powers and both powers came from God, but they were distinct. Society needed the order and discipline of the temporal power, but that order could only be sanctified and so fulfill its function through

---

[5] Gregory VII, *Dictatus Papae*, in Henderson, *Select Historical Documents of the Middle Ages*, 366–367.

the grace that poured through the spiritual power. To the papal party, the temporal and spiritual powers formed a single living organism, like a man with both a soul and a body.[6] Both sides in this conflict believed in the fundamentally sacral nature of society itself; both sides believed that holiness was the purpose of all government. Both sides, as we have seen, flowed out of Benedictine monasticism, which integrated rule, work, study, and prayer into a single, integral way of life. Both sides in the Investiture Contest believed this was how all of Christendom ought to be. But they disagreed fundamentally on how it was to be built, organized, and governed.

Finally, in 1122, a compromise was reached in a meeting at Worms. The emperor renounced the right to invest bishops with their ring and crosier, the signs of their office. The papacy conceded that the king or emperor had the right to invest new bishops, with their lands and temporal powers, using a scepter rather than a crosier. The Investiture Contest resulted in a clarification of the two powers in the Church. The bishops held both, in different respects. They were powerful temporal lords, and in this capacity, they had to be incorporated into the king's rule. They were also spiritual lords, and in this capacity, they had to be incorporated into the papal hierarchy. The kings, for their part, were definitively classified as laymen. They certainly had a God-given office in the Church—no one doubted that—but it was not to wield the Church's spiritual sword. The West was not to go the route of the Byzantine Empire.

Religious Movements and Lay Spirituality

As we have already discussed, over the eleventh century, the monastic reform movement captured the imagination of the entire Church, including the laity. The monks and reformed clergy were, of course, drawn from lay families and integrated into their social networks. This was one society, after all, and it was the laity who not only built but also populated the thousands of monasteries. Everyone agreed that holiness was a universal call. The Investiture Conflict was a fight that had emerged within this general movement. Over the twelfth and thirteenth centuries, all of Western Christendom was reconstructing itself as a truly Christian civilization.

---

[6] Hugh of Saint Victor, *On the Sacraments*, II.2.II–VII.

The reform movement, was, we might say, two sided. On one side, the monastic movement had basically taken control of the clerical hierarchy and sought to reform it into an institution of holy priests who preached the Word of God to the mostly illiterate laity and who brought them the sacraments, thus making holiness truly possible for all the baptized. And on the other side, the laity clamored for holiness and sought ways of life that were fundamentally compatible with spiritual perfection. We might think of these as compatible top-down and bottom-up movements. In this context, during the twelfth and thirteenth centuries, the university system was built. The universities were built in order to train preachers. The monasteries had focused on the holiness of the monks, and rightfully so. The universities were a modification of the monastic way of life in order to orient it toward the holiness of the common people. The monks practiced what was known as *lectio divina*, divine reading. This was a prayerful way of reading Scripture. The monks went from *lectio* (reading) to *meditatio* (meditation) to *oratio* (prayer) and finally achieved *contemplatio* (contemplation). In the universities, this became the process of *lectio* (reading), *disputatio* (disputation), *praedicatio* (preaching), and finally *contemplatio* (contemplation). The clergy in the universities sought holiness and learning so that they might preach the Gospel to the people and bring them to a share of the fruits of contemplation.

These scholars developed what we now call moral theology in order to understand how all Christians, from merchants to peasants, could live in a way pleasing to God. They developed canon law so that the Church could be organized and the sacraments delivered to the people in a way that was consistent and just. They sought to understand the great mysteries of the faith in order to explain them to normal people. These universities developed what became known as Scholasticism. Scholasticism was a way of doing philosophy and theology that brought together monastic wisdom with biblical and patristic studies and then combined them with the very best of ancient thought, Aristotle and Plato. Scholasticism reached a peak in the mid-thirteenth century with such giants as St. Thomas Aquinas and St. Bonaventure. It was profoundly speculative and profoundly deep in its investigations, but Scholasticism was always, ultimately, about preaching the Word of God so that the Church as a whole might move deeper into contemplation.

What we see in the twelfth and thirteenth centuries is the stabilization of the reform movement and its translation into a steady way of life, into a social architecture. This was the period in which the parish system was built. It was the period in which the sacrament of matrimony was elevated in importance and regulated by canon law. It was the period during which regular, private confession, which had been a monastic practice, became a normal part of lay devotion, and it was the period in which devotion to the Eucharist greatly intensified. The Church, including the laity, knew that it was through preaching and the sacraments that everyday Christians received the faith and charity that they needed to live lives of holiness in their lay vocations. This was a period of massive lay movements of penance and piety.

The religious orders that emerged during this period reflect this universal pursuit of holiness. During the twelfth century, many priests came together to live in community and according to a modified monastic rule. These communities became known as the Regular Canons. They sought personal holiness in order to preach more effectively and to confer the sacraments worthily. The Canons were essentially a new religious order, one that did not retreat from the world but, rather, lived right in the midst of it, in the cities. Their conviction, of course, was that the world was capable of holiness. The Cistercians were a reformed branch of Benedictine monasticism that was founded around 1100 but which grew dramatically over the twelfth century. They, as a sort of inversion of the Regular Canons, sought not to bring the monastery into the world but, rather, to bring the world into the monastery. They built self-sufficient monastic colonies, which included professed monks as well as vowed laity. These colonies included everyone from blacksmiths and peasants to the most highly educated noble priests. And the Cistercians were preaching specialists. In the Regular Canons and the Cistercians, we can see two attempts at realizing the same vision, making porous the division between the fallen world and the redeemed monastery.

These movements reached a culmination in the early thirteenth-century establishment of the Dominicans and Franciscans. The Franciscans emerged out of lay penitential movements. Following St. Francis's way of extreme poverty and charity, the Franciscans slowly became regularized, adopting a rule to live by, and eventually many of them were ordained to the priesthood so they could preach and give the sacraments. They were absolutely convinced that the Gospel could be lived in the world and was for the world. The Dominicans emerged out of the Regular Canon movement. Rather than being mostly laymen, they were mostly priests. They were founded first to preach, and they developed a life of extreme poverty and charity in order to be more effective in doing so. These two orders spread rapidly throughout the High Middle Ages. Both orders captured the spirit of the age, and both wanted to explode the monastic world to envelop all the Church. The Franciscans had come from the lay side of this movement and the Dominicans from the clerical, but they met in a way of life that was remarkably similar. They were known together as the Mendicant Orders, which means orders of beggars.

The Mendicants focused their efforts in the cities that had been growing throughout the twelfth and thirteenth centuries. These cities revolved around their cathedrals and the liturgical life that was based there. To be a citizen of a city was to be a child of the cathedral, having been baptized in its baptismal font. The daily life of the city moved to the rhythm of the cathedral bells, and the year moved along the liturgical calendar. The laity's trades were organized in guilds that were themselves liturgical clubs devoted to certain saints and feast days. By the mid-thirteenth century, the typical Catholic was certainly no scholar, but he could recite the prayers of the Mass and the creed, he attended Mass and went to confession, he followed the sermons of highly educated preachers, and he pursued a form of holiness that was appropriate to his calling in life. The reform movement that started in the cloisters of the Benedictine monks in the violent aftermath of the Carolingian Empire culminated with the vibrant Catholic civilization of the thirteenth century.

The Crusades and the Temporal Sword

The knights, the small-scale noble warriors who had formed the backbone of feudal society, were not left out of this reform movement. It should always be remembered that the monks who populated the thousands of monasteries were normally from the knightly class. The monks and the knights were literally brothers. The knightly families built the monasteries because they believed in the monastic ideal, in the pursuit of holiness. But what about the knights themselves? Could they fit into such a monastic Christendom? Was there a role for the sword in a society of peace and worship? The reforming Church answered with a definitive yes. There could be a properly Christian knighthood, but it would not be characterized by the glory-seeking petty warfare of the previous era. Rather, the knights could achieve

The Crusades and the Temporal Sword

holiness in their vocation by turning their swords to the pursuit of justice and peace.

This was possible because the world was fallen. There was sin and violence everywhere that had to be stopped. The Christian knight's vocation was to fight this sin. There developed an ethos that we call *chivalry*, which is simply the moral code of the Christian knight. They were to be honest, to keep their word; they were to sacrifice themselves for the cause of justice. They were to protect widows, orphans, and clergy—those who could not fight for themselves, the powerless of society—and they were to be pious. In this way, by aligning their use of the sword with the universal principles of Christian morality, they served the reforming Church. They warred against the physical forces of evil as their brothers the monks warred against the spiritual forces of evil. The theologian Alan of Lille (d. 1202) explained that just as man is made up of both body and spirit, so there are two swords with which to protect humanity: the material, which repels injury, and the spiritual, which repels molestations of the mind: "Externally let knights take up violence, therefore, for the reformation of peace in time; internally, though, with the sword of the word of God, let them seek the restoration of peace in their own hearts." True knights, according to Alan, protected the poor and defended the Church. Knights who oppressed the weak, he argued, were not knights at all "but robbers and plunderers; not defenders, but invaders" who thrust their swords "into the gut of Mother Church."[7] The exercise of knighthood, Alan tells us, was bound up with warfare against the devil himself, in both its spiritual and temporal dimensions. This was chivalry—the rule of holy knighthood, just as the monks had the rules of their religious orders. Chivalry reached its culmination in the Crusades.

The Crusades were a continuation of the war between Christians and Muslims that had been raging for centuries. You will recall that Islam began in the early seventh century in Arabia and spread quickly through conquest across North Africa and Spain to the West. In the East, the Roman Emperor in Constantinople was consumed with fighting the Muslim expansion, and throughout the entire Mediterranean Sea, Christian vessels fought constantly with Muslim pirates. By the 700s, most of the Eastern Empire was lost, leaving only modern-day Greece, the Balkans, and Turkey. Most of the conquered territory had been part of the old Roman Empire. In fact, by 800, two-thirds of

---

[7] Alan of Lille, *Summa de arte praedicatoria*, in *Patrologia Latina*, 210:185–87.

what were once Christian territories were under Muslim domination. The populations that Muslims had conquered were nearly all Christian, as were the armies that fought them.

In the centuries that followed, the fighting between the Christians and Muslims never stopped, and the Christians were generally on the losing side. The war in the East continued nonstop. The war in Spain was the same, and fighting on the sea was constant. The Muslims came to largely dominate the sea and launched relentless slave-harvesting raids against Christians. The Christian civilization of the Mediterranean was all but destroyed by the Muslim armies, with most of its population living under Muslim occupation and under heavy pressure to convert. Over the course of several centuries of occupation, this pressure worked on a massive scale, and Christianity became a minority religion throughout the region. This fighting went on for centuries. Finally, in the eleventh century, Islamic forces achieved a series of massive victories in the east against the Byzantine Empire, conquering Asia Minor, present-day Turkey. This was the heartland of the Byzantine Empire. When the territory was lost to the Muslims, it had been Christian for 700 years and had been a part of the Roman Empire for over 1100 years. The loss of Turkey sent shockwaves through Christendom. If it could fall, why not Greece itself? Why not Italy or even France? The emperor in the East appealed to his co-religionists in the West, sending multiple desperate letters to the pope begging for help. At the exact same time, the Muslim forces that controlled Palestine started harassing Christian pilgrims who were traveling to Jerusalem. Pilgrimages, which because of the inherent dangers were always considered the supreme act of penance, had, under the new Muslim anti-pilgrim policy, become almost suicidal.

In response, Pope Urban II in 1095 held a council at Clermont in France and called for a general expedition to the East to liberate the oppressed Christians of the Eastern Empire and the Holy Land. The pope exhorted the gathered crowds:

> From the confines of Jerusalem and the city of Constantinople a horrible tale has gone forth and very frequently has been brought to our ears, namely, that a race from the kingdom of the Persians, an accursed race, a race utterly alienated from God, a generation forsooth which has not directed its heart and has not entrusted its spirit to God, has invaded the lands of those Christians and has depopulated them by the sword, pillage and fire; it has led away a

part of the captives into its own country, and a part it has destroyed by cruel tortures; it has either entirely destroyed the churches of God or appropriated them for the rites of its own religion. They destroy the altars, after having defiled them with their uncleanness.... The kingdom of the Greeks is now dismembered by them and deprived of territory so vast in extent that it can not be traversed in a march of two months. On whom therefore is the labor of avenging these wrongs and of recovering this territory incumbent, if not upon you? You, upon whom above other nations God has conferred remarkable glory in arms, great courage, bodily activity, and strength to humble the hairy scalp of those who resist you ... Oh, most valiant soldiers and descendants of invincible ancestors, be not degenerate, but recall the valor of your progenitors.[8]

Urban offered what we would call today a plenary indulgence to all who joined the expedition. The response was incredible. Tens of thousands of knights in the West answered the call. But not just knights. Tens of thousands of peasants and other normal people rose up in the West as well and started the long march east to fight. The distance from Paris to Jerusalem was almost three thousand miles. As far as they were concerned, it was on the other side of the world. But they went. Tens of thousands, possibly as many as one hundred thousand, people left everything they knew, spent their fortunes, if they had them, and set out to an unknown land to fight a fierce enemy.

They marched across Europe to Constantinople and then crossed over into Turkey, which was enemy territory. They were immediately engaged in fighting. They fought their way through Turkey, into Syria and the Holy Land; finally in 1099, three years after they had set out, they drove the Muslim forces from Jerusalem and established a Christian kingdom in the Holy Land. Losses were horrific. Some historians have asserted that as few as 5 percent of those who had originally set out from Europe saw the conquest of Jerusalem.

This was the First Crusade, and it was a huge success. But the Christian foothold in the Holy Land was tenuous at best. The war never stopped. The Christian kingdom of Jerusalem needed constant reinforcements from the West. These came in large numbers. There

---

[8] Robert the Monk, *Urban II's Speech at Clermont*, in Dana C. Munro, "Urban and the Crusaders," *Translations and Reprints from the Original Sources of European History*, (Philadelphia, PA: University of Pennsylvania, 1895), 1:5–8.

was a constant stream of volunteers from Europe. And in addition, every generation or so—usually after the Christians had lost either a major battle or significant territory—another large expedition was launched. Whole armies left Europe on Crusade. These are the traditionally numbered Crusades: the Second in 1147, the Third in 1189, the Fourth in 1202, the Fifth in 1217, the Sixth in 1228, the Seventh in 1248, and the Eighth in 1270. For two centuries, crusading defined Christian knighthood. But no matter how hard the Christians fought, they could not maintain control of the Holy Land. Finally, in 1291, almost two hundred years after it had been established, the Christian Kingdom in the Holy Land fell to the Muslims.

This was the eastern front. There was also a western front in Spain. There, things went better, and reconquest of the Iberian Peninsula progressed steadily through the Middle Ages—which is, of course, why Spain is today a Christian nation and not a Muslim one. We should take a moment and consider that. What is the basis of the notion that the Crusades were colonial or aggressive in nature? One basis is certainly that we think of the Middle East as being Islamic and so we think of the Christians as attacking people in their home country. But what Spain reveals to us is that we only think that way because the Crusaders ultimately lost in the Middle East and so Islam put down deep roots over the centuries that passed after the Crusades. The Crusaders won in Spain, and we don't hesitate to think of Spain as a properly Christian country. This is the way Turkey, Palestine, and North Africa could have been if the Crusaders had been equally successful there.

Even with the fall of the Christian states in the Holy Land, which is often thought of as the end of the Crusades, the war between Christendom and Islam continued. In fact, the Muslim forces steadily won victory after victory as they pushed the Christian forces back. Through the fourteenth and fifteenth centuries, what was left of the Christian Roman Empire in the East was steadily conquered, with Constantinople itself finally falling to the Turks in the year 1453—this was the end of almost 1500 years of Roman Emperors, 1100 of which they had been Christian. Many people thought it was the end of the world. By 1600, all of North Africa, the Eastern Mediterranean, and Southeast Europe were a part of the Islamic world—with the Turks actually laying siege to Vienna itself, the capital of Austria, twice, in 1529 and 1683—both unsuccessfully.

It was only over the course of the modern period that the forces of Christian Europe, still under the leadership of the papacy, stopped the spread of Islam in the Mediterranean and in Europe and started to roll it back. People don't realize this, but even the great period of exploration in the fifteenth and sixteenth centuries, when Europe sent ships west to the Americas and south and east around the continent of Africa, was largely motivated by the imperative to find a way around the Muslim forces of the eastern Mediterranean and by the desperate hope that the Christians of Europe might find allies in distant lands to aid them in the centuries-long struggle.

This is the basic history of the Crusades, but in order to understand them, we must combine this history with the idea of chivalry. The Crusades were not merely a defensive war fought along just war principles. The Crusades were a holy war, and the Crusaders who fought and died were considered martyrs. The chivalry of Christian knighthood underwrote Crusade spirituality. These ideas were just forming when Pope Urban II called the First Crusade, and he appealed directly to them. He called on the knights of Europe to stop fighting each other over worldly matters. He exhorted them to make peace with each other and to devote themselves to fighting the true enemy, who was ultimately the devil himself, a force that manifested itself most dramatically in the onslaught of the Islamic armies against the Christians of the East and in the defilement of the Christian holy places, the very land where Christ had walked.

Urban II and the popes and Crusade preachers after him called on the knights to take up their crosses and to follow Christ, all the way to death, to a death as horrific as death on the cross. Remember, a crucial part of the monastic idea was that of penance. The notion was that the sins of the world were so great that only by devoting one's entire life to penance could one even begin to make amends to God, to make things somehow right. The monk's entire life became a pilgrimage. Unlike our notion of pilgrimages as a type of retreat-vacation, in the Middle Ages a pilgrimage was understood necessarily as being arduous and difficult, a journey filled with suffering, which, when turned to penance through devotion, atoned for sins. The monks' lives were a pilgrimage. In the world, laity went on pilgrimages; they left everything behind, taking only a staff and a small purse, and walked hundreds or even thousands of miles to visit the shrines of saints or even all the way to Jerusalem.

This idea was now transferred to the knights. They were to take up their crosses. This was the overriding theme of Crusade spirituality. The preachers would ask, "Who do the knights want to be?" Do they want to be the impenitent thief crucified to the left of Christ, the thief who hung on the cross of his own sins and yet remained arrogant and defiant in his sufferings? Or did they want to be the good thief, who also hung on the cross of his sins, but who united his sufferings to those of Christ, who asked for forgiveness, and who suffered all the penance that was required of him by sharing in Christ's own passion? Either way, there was a cross. The question was how one accepted this cross. Did he willingly take it up and follow Christ, or would it be imposed upon him in punishment for his sins? This interpretation of the two thieves had long been applied to the religious life of the monks and nuns, to how they accepted the rigors of their rules. It was now applied to the knights. They took up their crosses to go on Crusade, literally—they sewed large crosses onto their clothes as an outward sign of their inward intention. The word "Crusader" is derived from the Latin *cruce signatus*, which means "one who has been signed with the cross."

We can see here the logic of the plenary indulgence that was offered to them if they went on Crusade. The monks devoted their entire lives to penance and hoped to atone for their sins and those of their family by doing so; this was their cross and their total penance for sin. The knights did the same. They offered their entire lives to the Crusade. They sold their property, often driving their families into poverty, in order to pay for their expeditions. They set out on a military adventure that could take years and that would likely result in their deaths. This was their cross, and in taking it up in penance, they asked Christ, like the good thief, to "remember me when you come in your kingly power" (Luke 23:42). Like that of the good thief, the Crusaders' crosses were all the penance God asked in atonement for their sins, and if they died while carrying them, they would go straight to heaven.

We can see, then, the parallelism between the monks and the Crusaders. The monks were the *milites Christi*, the knights of Christ, in the spiritual realm. The Crusaders where the *milites Christi* in the world, in the temporal realm. The monks sacrificed their lives without reserve. So, too, did the Crusaders. The monks marched spiritually to the heavenly Jerusalem. The Crusaders marched physically to the temporal Jerusalem, but in doing so, achieved the heavenly Jerusalem. The Crusaders were a type of religious person, and like the monks, they took sacred vows. These were real vows and in canon law, the

The Crusades and the Temporal Sword

Crusaders were treated as ecclesiastical persons, like the professed religious.

The identification of Crusaders with monks was so pronounced that the two lives actually merged in the formation of the military orders, most famously the Knights of the Temple, often called the Templars. These were warrior monks: the *milites Christi* in both the spiritual and the temporal realm. The great preacher James of Vitry said of the Templars: "Going in time of war, returning in time of peace; going by means of action, returning by means of contemplation; going in war to fight, returning in peace to repose and devotion to prayer, so that they are like soldiers in battle and like monks in convent."[9] St. Bernard of Clairvaux was one of the famous and holy monks of the twelfth century. He wrote a book on the Templars. For Bernard they were

> a new kind of knighthood and one unknown in the ages past. It indefatigably wages a twofold combat, against flesh and blood and against a spiritual host of evil in the heavens. When someone bravely resists a physical foe, relying solely on physical strength, I find this hardly astounding, since this is not uncommon. And when war is waged by spiritual strength against vices or demons, this, too, is nothing remarkable, though I consider it praiseworthy, for the world is full of monks. But for a man powerfully to gird himself with both swords and nobly mark his belt—who would not consider this very worthy of great admiration, even more so since it has hitherto been unknown? Truly a fearless knight and secure on every side is he whose soul is protected by the armor of faith just as his body is protected by the armor of steel. Doubly armed, surely, he need fear neither demons nor men. Not that he fears death—no, he desires it. Why should he fear to live or to die when for him to live is Christ, but he would prefer to be dissolved and to be with Christ, by far the better thing. . . . How gloriously victors return from battle! How blessedly martyrs die in battle![10]

The Crusader, with the Templar as his exemplar, was the perfect

---

[9] James of Vitry, "Sermones vulgares," in *Analecta Novissima*, ed. J. B. Pitra, vol. 2 (Paris: Typis tuscalanis, 1888), 406.

[10] St. Bernard of Clairvaux, *In Praise of the New Knighthood*, trans. M. Conrad Greenia, OCSO, (Kalamazoo, MI: Cistercian Publications, 2000), 33–34.

example of the chivalric knight, of the good knight. The formation of chivalry was tied directly to this spirituality of Crusade. At the same time, back in Europe, these knights were building kingdoms based on the monastic reform ideals. The knights who went on Crusade were the knights who at home sought justice, who sought to stop the brigandage and petty warfare of the warrior class, who sought to protect the widows and orphans. They were the kings who built the court systems of Europe, who favored the poor over the powerful. They were the men who sought in the temporal sphere to form the kingdom of God on Earth, as the monks did in the monastery. They sought to sacrifice their entire lives to build a society of charity and faith: going on Crusade against the forces of Islam, forces that, as we have seen, would destroy the kingdom of God, was the ultimate manifestation of this drive. St. Louis IX of France (r. 1226–1270) is a clear example of the type. He pursued justice in all that he did, devoting his life to the protection of the poor and vulnerable, and he went on Crusade three times, dying on his final expedition. During this period, the power of the sword, the power of what we call the State, was integrated into the pursuit of holiness.

Ultimately, the idea is that the sword can be wielded without sin only if it is wielded always with the intention of peace, always with charity in one's heart. With such a heart, the use of force becomes Christ driving the money changers from the Temple, or that of a loving father disciplining his child, rather than violence for glory or gain. In such a way, the sword could be integrated into the City of God while it was still on pilgrimage in this imperfect world. But it had to be always integrated into a mission of building a better world for humanity as a whole, integrated into the salvation wrought by the Church.

This is the Christianization of the sword. This Christianization, however, is the scandal of the Crusades in the modern mind. But is it a scandal? What did the Christianization of the sword entail? It meant that the sword could not be wielded for gain, for the lust for power or wealth, or even for glory. It meant that the pursuit of territory or resources on their own was never sufficient to initiate armed conflict. It meant that force was properly deployed in society and against foreign enemies only in response to injustice and always with the purpose of reinstituting peace and of building a just society. It meant that one, ultimately, ought to love one's enemies, even if you are compelled to fight them to the death. It meant that the warrior had to sacrifice himself in charity. This was dramatically different from the ethos of war found in paganism and found throughout most of human history and in almost all human societies.

The Crusades gave us the notion that war ought not to be fanatical, suicidal, homicidal, or based on power and greed. They gave us the notion that a war ought only to be fought when it fits into a universal notion of right and wrong and so is directed always toward the good of all people. Wars ought to be fought not simply when one thinks one can win, or even when one thinks that a war might be justified, but rather, wars ought to be fought only when duty to what is right demands that the sword be taken up, and the people who fight in such wars should properly be doing so as an act of self-sacrifice, as a gift to others. This is the ethical legacy of the Crusades. Another way of saying this is that Crusaders gave us the notion that all wars ought to be, in a sense, *holy*—otherwise, they shouldn't be fought.

This is why, when Crusaders failed to live up to the ideal, when they gave into fanatical passion and did things like persecute Jewish communities or gave into greed and attacked Christian cities for gold, which they sometimes did, they were condemned by their fellow knights and excommunicated by the popes and bishops; for when they behaved this way, they were like the barbarians again, or like the pre-chivalric feudal knights. They were no different from the forces of evil that they were supposed to fight, having crossed over to the City of Man. This is the notion of war crimes, of morality in war.

The Civilization of the High Middle Ages

The civilization of the High Middle Ages, which spanned roughly from 1000 to 1300, was a civilization of remarkable creativity. It was defined by the conviction that through grace and in hope, a world of peace and charity was possible, that the City of God was a real place in which one could really live. It held a profoundly sacramental understanding of society. The spiritual was not merely some distant realm, the realm of angels and heaven. The spiritual was everywhere and always intermingled with the temporal, with the world of things and men. God had, after all, become a man. The monks, after all, did achieve a real anticipation of the perfection that would finally be found only in glory. Redemption was redemption of *this* world, even if it was completed only in the next. This was the understanding of St. Augustine's *The City of God*. History was a contest between those men who were seeking God, allied with his angels, and those who were seeking their own power, allied with the demons. There was no neutral ground: all of earth, like all of the cosmos, was implicated; all of history was salvation history, and the City of God would win.

The great council of Christendom was the Fourth Lateran Council, held in 1215 under Pope Innocent III. It was often known merely as "The Great Council," and it brought together four hundred-twelve bishops, seventy-one patriarchs and archbishops, eight hundred abbots, and thousands of lesser clergy and laypeople. It was the largest council that had ever gathered. Lateran IV was different from other councils because it was not chiefly concerned with a crisis. There were plenty of problems to be dealt with, for sure. For example, there was a heresy called Catharism that was spreading in parts of Europe that had to be countered, and the Christian kingdom in the Holy Land was in a bad position and a new expedition of Crusaders was desperately needed. Nevertheless, the council was primarily concerned not with a crisis but with pushing the reforming movement forward as a whole; it was primarily concerned with pressing the conversion of society, from top to bottom. Lateran IV promulgated the most extensive creed since the Nicene. This creed placed the Eucharist and the sacramental system at the very center of Christian doctrine and asserted that married people, normal lay people, were capable of holiness and salvation in their vocations. To this end, the council mandated that all people receive the Eucharist and the sacrament of penance at least once a year. Modern Catholics are so used to the idea that holiness and the sacraments are for everyone, that we all can achieve some degree of perfection, that the significance of these acts is often lost on us. But it was Lateran IV that created this new order that we've grown so accustomed to. Lateran IV taught with confidence that everyone was a part of the holiness that was the Church. Through her sacraments, grace flowed into all her members. Central to this understanding was the importance of preaching. The Gospel was not merely for the educated elite to contemplate. It had to be proclaimed so that all people could be converted through grace to faith. The council, therefore, demanded that the bishops appoint preachers and that they establish seminaries to train them. Again, we are used to this, but it was Lateran IV that made us so.

Lateran IV was the first official magisterial instance of the use of the term "transubstantiation" in reference to the Eucharist. It was not that the Church before this didn't believe that the Eucharist was the true Body and Blood of Christ; of course it did. Rather, by 1215, Christian thought had advanced to the point that we could start talking about this mystery with far greater precision. Similarly, Lateran IV clarified the idea of the analogy of being, which declared that while God is infinitely greater than his creation, creation nevertheless in some way images him. The metaphysics of analogy was a metaphysics that allowed for the fundamental order and harmony of creation and its union with God while simultaneously protecting God's transcendence. Communion with God was possible, and yet God was infinitely greater than anything we could imagine. But Lateran IV also dealt with humdrum matters of governance. It dealt with how the courts should function, how appeals should be made, how excommunications should be promulgated. It dealt with such minutia of governance because Lateran IV was the Church governing a society. It was a council for a unified Church that was, in a sense, "in charge." Lateran IV was optimistic. The council addressed many problems, but the hope that animated High Medieval civilization permeates its acts. Why couldn't Christians build a society of peace and charity? Lateran IV said that, through grace and in hope, Christians could.

Animated by this hope and confidence, the scholars of the High Middle Ages produced unbelievably ambitious works. St. Thomas Aquinas, for example, produced a synthesis of pagan philosophy with Scripture and the Church Fathers that is still the foundation of Catholic theology and philosophy. The idea was rather simple. All that is good in the world is really already Christian, and there is a great deal that is good in the world. The world is not a foreign place that we cannot understand. Rather, we can make sense of it. We were made to understand the world, and what is more, the world was made to be understood. We can come to understand truth, and through grace working on our natures, we can order our world accordingly, order it toward salvation. And this salvation is not something that merely awaits us after death. Rather, it is a salvation that begins here on earth in lives of virtue and peace. Salvation begins by redeeming nature and concludes in elevating it into supernatural perfection. This is the monastic vision that had become the vision for a whole civilization.

This vision was captured perfectly in the amazing architecture of the period. The Gothic cathedrals were built during this time. These structures took hundreds of years to build. Generations of communities worked on them, and the resources of whole kingdoms were poured into them. They were major undertakings that displayed in their very construction the ends to which High Medieval society was oriented. The cathedral was for the liturgy, for the sacraments, for the pursuit of holiness and salvation. Architecturally, the Gothic cathedral is characterized by extremely complex patterns of relatively simple elements. These patterns build vertically toward heaven. This is an architectural representation of the High Medieval world. The world was complicated, but it was not unintelligible. It made sense in its complexity as it mounted to God. The Gothic is also characterized by a parallelism between the inside of the structure and the outside and by large stained glass windows that flooded the interior with natural light. Here, we see the High Medieval notion that the world itself was properly the Church, the setting for the liturgy. There were no hard lines between inside the Church and outside. Rather, the Church was the place where holiness was found, and this place should, by rights, encompass the whole world.

The High Middle Ages was a time of prosperity. The climate had warmed, and agriculture was extremely fruitful, with long growing seasons and plenty of rain. Forests throughout Europe were cleared for farmland, and generally people were well fed and healthy. The cities that had largely fallen into ruins after the fall of the Roman Empire were slowly rebuilt and repopulated. It was a time of dramatically reduced warfare within Western Europe itself. Wars happened, of course, but Christian princes increasingly fought less amongst themselves and more against external enemies in the Crusades. Internally, they turned their attention to governing with justice, and they devised legal and institutional structures that would aid them in doing so. The monarchies of both England and France rose in importance during the period, establishing the institutions of governance, such as stable courts of appeal and fixed royal apparatuses for investigating and rooting out corruption, that were needed to pursue a society of peace and justice.

The papacy rose in importance during the High Middle Ages to become the leader of Christendom. Along with its episcopal allies, the papacy built the institutional Church as we know it, the Church of dioceses, parishes, religious orders, and lay organizations all united together through both the spiritual bonds of the sacraments and through the mechanisms of canon law. The papacy became the last court of appeal for all of Western Europe. A peasant in Scotland could appeal to the pope. So, too, could the king of Naples, or a bishop in Spain. There was a unity to Christendom that transcended language or custom or political organizations. This unity was the unity of the Roman Catholic Church, and it found its head in the pope.

The pope was not the king of Christendom. He did not rule it with the sword. Rather, he taught what was right and true, and he acted as a universal judge of what was sin. He could wield immense power if he declared a monarch to be in mortal sin and in rebellion against God. He could excommunicate such a man, pushing him outside Christendom. The other Christian powers would act toward such a wayward ruler as an enemy of their shared project, and he would often be brought to heel. But the pope was not a military force in his own right. The priesthood was powerful, but it wielded the spiritual sword, not the temporal sword of iron. The power of the pope was wedded, therefore, to the power of the Christian princes, and their power was wedded to his. His political efficacy was a product of their obedience, and their political legitimacy was a product of communion with his universality as the vicar of Christ. Together, they sought to rule Christendom and lead it ever deeper into its conversion, to push the long-running reform forward, to move it closer to the monastic ideal. It was a perpetual reform, of course, that would conclude only when the saints found perfect communion in the Church Triumphant.

This great reform encompassed all of society as it attempted to fulfill the promises of salvation history ever more completely. Society was divided into three orders: the laity, the clergy, and the religious. The laity worked in the world of men and things, of time and change, ordering it toward a realization of timeless perfection, of perfect peace. This perfection was modeled and anticipated on earth in the life of the religious, but it was mediated to the laity only through the preaching, example, and sacraments of the "secular" clergy, the men who had a foot, in a sense, in both worlds. These three orders mapped onto the three stages of salvation history. If the domain of the religious was Glory, that of the clergy was the New Testament, and that of the laity the Old. This is not to say that the laity lived in the Old Testament. Far, far from it. It is to say that to the extent that man remained subject to coercive law through fear, to that very extent the laity ruled through the temporal sword, through the law of fear, a rule forbidden explicitly to the clergy. In this lingering echo of the Old Testament, the laity became the anointed kings of Israel and the clergy became once again the prophets and priests of the Law, preaching repentance and obedience.

But, of course, this "Old" was not integral; it was shot through everywhere with its fulfillment, with the realized "New," with grace and its fruit, charity. Here, the clergy ruled. In this noncoercive realm of virtue, the truth poured from the clergy into the people that they might know justice, and grace poured through the sacraments that they might instantiate this justice in their order, in their restored human law. This is how the spiritual was superior to the temporal, and not through some boring notion of sovereign or martial hierarchy. This hierarchy was different than the pagan or the modern conception of hierarchy. Each of the orders reached down to those below and pulled them up, an action that was only possible through the aid of the order above. The temporal sword could only fulfill its function to chastise sinners with justice because its wielders had already been pulled above their station by the grace and preaching of the clergy, an elevation they could never have achieved on their own. And the whole social order, temporal as much as spiritual, was moving toward Glory, toward the perfection of contemplation that would only occur in heaven but which was anticipated in the monastic life.

The monastic life was superior to the life of the secular clergy and to that of the laity because it was, in a real sense, the fulfillment of both. The monasteries were full of both the ordained and non-ordained—clergy and laity—living an integral life of the elevation of the temporal ever deeper into the spiritual: work became worship and all of life became liturgy. In the imagery of the period, the monastery was the true temple of God only because each and every monk made himself the temple of God. In such a way, the religious formed the model for the forces of power in society. The vision of their order lay at the beginning of the work of the laity and the clergy; this work flowed out of the cloister. But it lay also at the end of this work: contemplation, the goal of the monastic life, was the fulfillment of human life itself in all its social complexity. And monasticism was also the means of this work. The prayers of the religious saturated every aspect, every nook and cranny, of society, and the efficacy of the monks' penance dragged the sinful world forward, or rather, upward. Monastic prayer and penance were integrated into politics, economics, family life, parochial and diocesan structures—it was the mysterious blood coursing through the veins of Christendom. The peaceful and spiritual economy of the monastery subtly penetrated and conformed the structures of medieval society into its likeness as those structures were reformed and rebuilt.

What this means is that the power of the kings could never be the power of the pagan kings, and the power of the priests could never approach the power of the pagan idols and their cults. Pagan power was always predicated on anxiety and fear and always tended toward its maximization. The god-kings and their priests attempted to establish themselves as the sources of all authority and order. The kings and priests of the High Middle Ages, however, did the opposite. Their power was never anything other than the mediated power of God himself. They were anointed. They could never "hold" this power as their own, and their objective (when true to their offices) was to replace their swords, their external power, with the law of charity, with the internalization of the Gospel in the hearts of their subjects and so the fulfillment of the law through its surpassing. They were the "source" of order, therefore, only where men remained in need of reform, only where men remained in sin and so in the Age of Nature or the Age of the Law. As society was converted, however, the architectonic capacity to rule themselves through human law was increasingly returned to local communities, now reformed by the Gospel. As conversion progressed, as true peace was established, the kings and priests shifted to being not the source of order but the judges of real, lived peace. The dynamic of this society was therefore the exact opposite of that of the pagan empires. Rather than the drive to centralize the power of violence into fewer and fewer hands, the drive to maximize force, this society was driven to decentralize governance, to reduce the purchase for force, as true peace was increasingly established.

Nevertheless, this drive toward peace and so away from "power" was, at the exact same time, a drive toward unity. This feels paradoxical, but that is only because we are used to thinking of unity as a product of coercive government, as did the pagans. For the Christians of the High Middle Ages, however, the most profound unity was found in faith and charity, not in law. Law was particular, temporal. Justice and truth, on the other hand, were universal, spiritual. This is why the profound diversity of Christendom was compatible with a profound unity. The pope emerged as the most powerful man in Europe, and yet at no point did he consolidate that power into an empire. For the two hundred years of crusading, for example, he called together immense armies, and yet they came freely and fought together without an empire and without establishing one. (The Holy Roman Empire was, of course, only an empire in name.) They had all the pieces of empire. They had agriculture; they had literacy; they had a shared religious and ideological system; they had advanced military technology; they had institutions that spanned the civilization. And yet, they did not build a pagan-style empire. This is a strange historical anomaly, and it points to the truth of Christendom. Christendom was an anti-empire.

The High Medieval reform, therefore, did not totally eliminate and replace the disunity and divisions of the corrupt feudal period that had proceeded it. Rather, this decentralization was retained as it was elevated; it was healed. Where the reform succeeded, the differentiation that underwrote war and hatred—the ultimate disunity—was replaced with the differentiation that underwrote friendship and charity—the ultimate unity. The reform did not do away, therefore, with peasants, knights, dukes, kings, abbots, or bishops, the externals of feudal society. It did not abolish the oath or eliminate the complicated personal bounds that held feudal society together. It, rather, elevated all these externals beyond themselves, fulfilling the goodness that had always lingered within them, even during the periods of profound corruption. Knighthood, for example, was not eliminated but perfected through chivalry. This is how the Church reforms from within.

In this society, in an inversion of the pagan, the highest office of unity was the least powerful in the sense of military might. The pope was the judge of the universal, of virtue and sin, and not a legislator of the particular, not a king of armies and economies. But this highest position was nevertheless the fulfillment of kingship. As the popes themselves explained, the pope was of the order of Melchizedek, priest and king, the order that had been replaced in the Age of Law by Israel's priesthood and monarchy and which was restored in Christ. He held the fullness of both temporal and spiritual power. But this office was the fulfillment of the Law, not the office which wielded the Law of Fear. That was to go back into the Old, to the kings. This lower royal office was necessary, as it had been in the Age of Law, but it was not definitive, and its task was to move past itself. This means that the authority of the papacy and the power of the kings were no more in competition with each other than were the Old and New Testaments. Both the spiritual and the temporal powers were necessary; the temporal was fulfilled in the spiritual, and both were fulfilled in the life of the religious orders: this was the movement of the Old into the New and on to Glory. The three were really one. It was Trinitarian. As the great thirteenth-century canonist Hostiensis explained:

> There are three types of men and through them the Trinity can be

perceived. The laity are similar to the Father through power, the secular clerics to the Son through wisdom, and the religious to the Holy Spirit on account of benevolence and grace. These three types, namely, the laity, the secular clergy, and the religious, are a trinity: but in the holy union of the Church and in the Catholic faith they are a unity. Likewise, the Persons of the Father and the Son and the Spirit are a Trinity, but in essence and divinity a unity.[11]

All the functions of society were Christian, from top to bottom. It was one city. It was one body. In an Easter sermon, Pope Innocent III stated that Mary Magdalene, Mary the Mother of James, and Salome represented the three lives: lay, regular, and clerical: "The lay life should anoint the feet of Jesus, the regular life the head, and the clerical life the body. For the feet of Christ are the poor, the head is the divinity, and the body is the church."[12] The laity supported the Church through the corporal works of mercy, the regulars through prayer, and the clergy through word and example.[13] They were united in the drive to transform society into one perpetual and extremely complex act of worship, one temple-society. As Innocent explained, the three orders of society were the same as the three types of people who participated in the Mass itself: the priests, those who served the priests, and the people. Together, they constituted the Body of Christ, and each was perfect in a different way. Their unity in Faith and Charity would only become complete in heaven, but it could be approached here and now, in history. No one was left out of this vision and no social function, even the use of violence, what we call politics, was understood as outside the Body of Christ. This was Christendom.

3. The Late Middle Ages

The Fragmentation of Christendom

The civilization of the High Middle Ages started to fail in the early fourteenth century. The rise and fall of civilizations are, of course,

---

[11] Henry of Susa, *Summa aurea* (Venice, 1574), 8.
[12] Innocent III, "Sermon for the Resurrection of the Lord," in John C. Moore, "The Sermons of Pope Innocent III," *Römische Historische Mitteilungen* 36 (1994): 138–142.
[13] See Innocent III, "Sermon for the Resurrection of the Lord," 81–142.

incredibly complex events. There are an infinite number of variables, and explaining these events in simple terms is always fraught with danger. However, certain trends in such transitional times do present themselves as especially important. In the Late Middle Ages, one of these trends is the trend toward fragmentation. As we have seen, High Medieval civilization was very complex. It was characterized by a sacramental union of the spiritual and the temporal. However, this union was manifested in many diverse ways in diverse times and places. It was one civilization, but it was not a centralized civilization and most certainly not an empire. We might imagine it as a rope made up of many strands. Each strand is a particular manifestation of the union of the spiritual and the temporal. One strand might be the French monarchy and its bishops, another might be the Dominicans and their relationship with the pope and kings, another might be the tanners' guild in Verona and its relationship with the city council, another might be the crusading orders, and another a simple Benedictine monastery in the Swiss mountains. All these strands together formed the rope that was this civilization, and the rope pulled in one direction, toward sanctification and so communion. A tight rope, of course, pulls its strands together ever more tightly without them losing their distinction. We might see the papacy and its allies among the bishops and kings as the leadership that kept the rope tight and pulling in the right direction. If a strand began to fray off the main rope, the pope or the monarchs would try to reconnect it, try to pull it again into line. This was the discipline that they offered. If the fray resisted long enough, they perhaps had to cut it off. This was the sword they wielded. But the main point is that all the strands that made up the rope of the High Middle Ages were aspects of the Church and so were sacramental, the merger of the material and temporal with the spiritual and eternal. There was no such thing as the secular.

What began to happen around 1300 is that the rope began to loosen. The various strands began to fray more often and even to start pulling in different directions. This was not a de-Christianization of civilization, let alone a secularization; it was rather a fragmentation, a fraying. For example, the kingdom of France was probably the heart of High Medieval civilization. It was there, more than anywhere else, that the vision of a sacramental society was realized in a union between the temporal and the spiritual powers. King Philip IV (r. 1285–1314) started to undo this. But he did it in a particularly medieval way. He did not assert his independence from the clergy. Rather,

The Fragmentation of Christendom

he asserted that the clergy of his kingdom were under his authority. He began to act as if the kingdom of France were its own church with him as its head. He launched a military campaign against neighboring Flanders, for example, and declared it to be a crusade, a holy war, and he did so without papal approval. This was an attempt to unravel a piece of the Christendom rope and pull it in another direction. This was the attempt to posit France as its own little Christendom at the expense of universal Christendom. Philip wanted his men to believe that fighting for the king and for France was fighting for God. Pope Boniface VIII defended a unified Christendom against Philip. In 1303, he published a famous bull known as *Unam Sanctam* in which he declared that there was no salvation outside the Church and asserted that the Church was under the Roman pontiff. He argued that Philip was trying to divide this single Church, trying to turn it into a two-headed monster. Rather, the pope argued, the particular kingdoms of Christendom had to be aligned together under the pope. This was the proper relationship between the temporal and the spiritual. The temporal was particular and divided; the spiritual was universal and unified. Together, they formed a sacramental society made up of particular kingdoms in a universal Church.

With the support of his bishops and his nobles, Philip IV went head-to-head with the pope and won. The conflict eventually ended with what is often called the Babylonian captivity of the papacy. In 1309, the papacy was moved to Avignon in France and did not move back to Rome until 1376. During this time, the papacy grew closer and closer to the French monarchy until it was less a force for Christian unity and more a pawn in France's political interest.

This was particularly important because Europe was divided into two warring camps from 1337 to 1453 in what is known as the Hundred Years' War. The Hundred Years' War was a massive conflict between France and England over the French throne. Most of the major powers of Europe allied themselves with one side or the other. Both sides believed themselves to be fighting for Christian truth against sinners and heretics. Both sides believed the other to be outside the Church and believed that their war was a crusade. The papacy should have been above the fray. The papacy should have been a force for unity, a force for correcting the exaggerated rhetoric of both sides and for bringing peace to Christendom. But the strands of the rope of medieval society had become too loose, too frayed. The power of the monarchies had grown immensely, and they followed Phillip

IV's lead in steadily taking control of the churches in their kingdoms. As the war progressed, the monarchies strengthened their positions. They built bigger and bigger armies; they built large governmental apparatuses in order to fund and supply the war effort, and they marshalled the ideological power of Christianity in order to motivate their people. As this went on, the papacy fell more and more under the sway of the kings of France.

Finally, in 1376, after sixty-seven years in France, Pope Gregory XI moved the papacy back to Rome. He did this largely on account of the pleas and even orders of St. Catherine of Siena. St. Catherine understood that the papacy had to be independent and free in order to bring peace to Europe. She understood that Rome was both a symbol of a unified Europe and the seat of its spiritual unity through its bishop, the pope. Through Catherine, Pope Gregory XI came to understand that it was imperative that the papacy return to Italy. Gregory, however, died in 1378, and the cardinals immediately began to fight. They elected Pope Urban VI, but he quickly fell into conflict with the French cardinals. These cardinals then claimed that Urban's election had been invalid. They met in a second conclave and elected another pope, who took the name Clement VII. Clement and the cardinals who supported him moved back to Avignon. This was the start of what is known as the Great Western Schism.

There were now two lines of popes. One was based in Rome, the other in Avignon. Unsurprisingly, the two sides in the Hundred Years' War disagreed over who was the true pope. The French and their allies supported the Avignon line while the English and their allies supported the Roman line. The temporal powers of Europe continued to war with each other, only now each side had their own pope. Now, the spiritual power was at war with itself. The schism was now an integral component of the Hundred Years' War, and the conflict dragged on decade after decade, pope after pope.

The schism had devastating consequences. The most important is probably the loss of papal prestige. The popes, even during the Avignon period, had maintained a certain moral high ground. Now, they fought each other like territorial princes. The princes used the popes in their fights with each other, and the popes tried to use the princes in their fight with each other. One of the consequences was that more and more people saw the papacy as just another type of political power, just another party contending for worldly power. The irony, however, is that during this time the actual power of the papacy declined dramatically. In their conflict with each other, the two papal lines needed the support of their respective princely allies. In order to get this support, they conceded to the princes more and more of the papacy's power over the ecclesiastical hierarchy. The English crown gained immense control over the Church in England. The same was true in France and in the many smaller kingdoms and principalities that made up Europe. By the year 1400, neither line of popes had much power left. Almost every bishop in Europe was appointed by a prince, and almost every prince used the wealth of the Church in his territories as if it were his own. The schism accelerated the fraying of the medieval rope. During the schism, we can start to talk about not just warring parties within Christendom, but with only a little exaggeration, of rival Christendoms, rival combinations of temporal and spiritual power. However, division is the hallmark of the temporal power, not the spiritual power. This means that a divided Christendom must be a Christendom dominated by temporal power, which is precisely what we have by the end of the fourteenth century.

Plague and Famine

As if war and religious division were not enough, the fourteenth century was a time of extreme natural disasters. The High Middle Ages had been a time of prosperity. Part of this was because the climate had warmed and so crops grew more abundantly. There was a lot to eat in the thirteenth century, and so the population exploded. However, the climate began to cool in the early fourteenth century. This meant less productive harvests, and this led to famine. The first terrible famine happened between 1315–1317. It became known as the Great Famine, and perhaps as much as 20 percent of the population of Northern Europe died. But the whole population was weakened, and many lesser famines followed throughout the century. In 1348, plague was added to war and famine. The Black Death swept through Europe, killing up to 50 percent of the population. Those who survived normally had some sort of immunity. However, their children often did not. This meant that the plague came back every twenty years or so to devastate the new generation.

Between war, famine, and plague, the fourteenth century was a time of great misery. There were spiritual consequences. Many of the most holy clergy died with their flocks, refusing to flee the plague or to take refuge during famine. They ministered to the dying and often died themselves. This had long-term consequences for the makeup of the priesthood, with often less scrupulous clergy surviving and so taking control of the institutions of the Church. Most people believed that all this suffering must have been a consequence of their sins, that it was the wrath of God. Therefore, there emerged movements of extreme penance. The Flagellants was one of these movements. The Flagellants proceeded through the countryside, from town to town, whipping themselves relentlessly to try to win God's favor.

There developed during this time a focus on death and suffering and on the futility of life. This was in marked contrast to the hopeful optimism of the previous era. In the High Middle Ages, the world itself had been easily seen as good and rational, as the dwelling place of God. Reform of the world into the City of God, a City that would transition into the triumphant City of Glory in heaven, seemed plausible. Now, that vision blurred. God and glory were pushed a little further away from the world. The world, as the fourteenth century tended to teach, was a place of suffering to be endured while heaven was distant, out of reach. After the fourteenth century, people became more inclined to believe that God was inscrutable, that his ways could not be understood. They were more inclined to believe that he acted arbitrarily according to his own reasons that had little to do with our own reason. Increasingly, God was imagined as a lawgiver, dictating from on high to a lowly and filthy world, rather than as a loving father who guided his good creation into its perfection in time. The fragmentation of Christendom included a fragmentation of the Church on earth from the Church in heaven. The fragmentation was both horizontal and vertical; gaps had opened up.

Conciliarism and the Councils

Largely in reaction to the papal schism, some theologians developed a new theory of the Church called conciliarism. Conciliarism maintained that the ultimate governing authority in the Church lay not with the pope but with the cardinals and bishops in a council. According to conciliarism, the pope was the head of the Church in its day-to-day affairs, but even he had to answer ultimately to a council. This theory was attractive for obvious reasons. There were, after all, two rival popes that were tearing the Church apart. If a group of bishops could get together and agree on which was the true pope, the schism could be ended. But this could only work if the council was superior to both popes. Conciliarism grew in strength over the course of the fourteenth century, and the popes, afraid of its power, traded even more of their authority away to the princes in exchange for the suppression of conciliarism in their kingdoms. The conciliar bishops, for their part, looked to their princes to support them in their attempt to bring unity back to the Church and so sought to align themselves more closely with their interests. The irony of conciliarism is that while it was devised to bring the Church together by undermining the principle of unity in the papacy, it actually increased the Church's fragmentation into rival, little Christendoms dominated by the various temporal powers.

Finally, in 1409, a council gathered at Pisa without the approval of either pope. Both papal lines had their own cardinals, but the majority of these cardinals abandoned their respective popes and gathered at Pisa. They declared both popes to be schismatics and heretics and therefore deposed. They then proceeded to hold a conclave and elect a new pope, who took the name Alexander V. Most of Europe declared its obedience to Alexander. Now there were three popes.

By 1414, most of the princes of Europe wanted the schism resolved, and by this point, they held most of the power in the Church. Therefore, the pope of the Pisan line convoked a council at Constance (in present-day Germany). He then resigned his claim to the papacy. The pope of the Roman line first reconvened the same council under his own authority, and then resigned the papacy. The council then deposed the pope of the Avignon line. There was now no pope. The council was run primarily by the princes. It was organized by nation, and when it came time to elect a new pope, this didn't change. In fact, in addition to the cardinals, each major power in Europe had votes in the conclave. The council waited for the Roman pope to pass away in 1417, and then elected a new pope, Martin V. The schism was over. The Church has since recognized the Roman line as having been the true line, but through the schism this was not clear to most people. There were saints (and villains) on all sides of the schism.

The schism did incalculable damage to Christendom. Not only did it soil the reputation of the papacy, robbing it of much of its moral authority, but it weakened it institutionally. In 1300, the papacy had been the most powerful institution in Christendom. By 1417, it was shockingly weak. Martin V quickly did what he could. He closed the

Council of Constance, which many people wanted to see as a permanent conciliar body of Church government. He tried to assert papal authority in France and England. But the papacy had traded most of its power away. Now, the churches of the great powers of Europe were run by their kings. They had become practically national churches, with primarily doctrinal connections to the papacy. The Europe of the fifteenth century was fractured into competing kingdoms that saw themselves as holy institutions without submitting in any substantial way to the universal in Christianity. This was a process that began with Philip IV and his conflict with Boniface VIII, but it was not completed until over a century later. The unity of Christendom was near breaking. Increasingly, people's loyalty was not to Christendom but to their particular kingdom. Crusading, for example, became a thing of the past, as fighting for one's nation took on the mantle of holy service and even martyrdom. Wars between Christians were becoming "holy wars" to the men who fought them.

With the Church fragmented into regional churches dominated by princes, the papacy found itself in a very tenuous position. It had emerged from the schism extremely weak, even in Rome itself. It was in danger of being subsumed into one kingdom or another. The papacy understood that it needed independence and that in a Europe of state-dominated churches, this meant that it had to be its own state. If the pope was not himself a king, some other king would assert control over the papacy. The papacy of the fifteenth century was therefore focused on Italian affairs. It was focused on building the papal state in central Italy as a small but real European kingdom. The papacy is often criticized for this construction, as if it sought worldly power for its own sake, which undoubtedly some popes of the Renaissance did. However, this criticism often fails to appreciate that it was only the papal state that ensured papal independence from the great princes of Europe. Regardless, the papacy of the fifteenth century was not a force of real consequence through most of Europe. Its institutional power was mostly limited to Italy, and its moral and doctrinal authority was only sporadically recognized throughout much of Europe.

Nominalism

This fragmentation of Christendom was accompanied by a revolution in philosophy and theology. The scholastic thinkers of the

High Middle Ages were, for the most part, what we call realists. At its simplest, what this means is that they believed that categories, or universals as they called them, are real things. So, for example, if I say, "Rover is a dog," "dog" is a real category, which is another way of saying that dogs have a nature. They are a certain kind of thing and are different from other kinds of things. When I assert Rover to be a dog, I am saying something real about him. This is very significant because realism means that our reasoning about the world around us is a participation in the reason that is actually embedded in that world. If I say, "Rover is a dog, and dogs like to play fetch; therefore, Rover likes to play fetch," as a realist, my chain of reasoning is about the actual world; it is an expression of how the actual world, in fact, operates in its own natures. To these realists, God was the creator of all things. He created all the natures and gave them to his creatures. He also gave man an intellect that was capable of perceiving truthfully these natures. This meant that our reasoning through the natures of things was a participation in the reasoning of God himself. Therefore, God was analogously accessible to us through his creation. Realism was a metaphysics that was particularly well suited for the high medieval project of uniting all of creation within one reformed movement toward heaven, of envisioning all of creation as a sacramental cosmos that could become ordered in a perpetual act of worship, as a temple. For the realist, all the pieces fit together, and they do so from within themselves. The pieces of the cosmos, in a sense, *want* to fit together and *want* to be known by rational minds because of what they are. Sin was what was keeping them apart, and so reform into virtue and the pursuit of perfection was synonymous with the project of bringing right order to all of God's creation. The moral life, the intellectual life, the social life, and even the ecological life were one dynamic movement.

Late medieval nominalism challenged all of this. Nominalism is normally associated with the work of William of Ockham (1287–1347), but as a movement, it went far beyond his work. Nominalism stressed God's omnipotence. It maintained that everything exists as a result of God's disposing will. This is the only reason: God wills something, and it is. There are no natures that exist separate from this will. God does not create things with natures that then determine the scope of their existence and their relations with each other and so effectively bind his power. According to nominalism, if God created dogs with the nature to fetch, and then if he decided he didn't want them to fetch, he would have to "intervene," to do violence to their natures. This problem could be avoided, the nominalists maintained, if we understood that God merely wills continuously that certain individual creatures, such as Rover, like to fetch. Then, if he willed that they no longer did, they wouldn't, and there would be no inconsistency or violence at all. To a nominalist, God's power was absolute. The nominalists thought that the realist insistence on the reality of universals, of natures, was an attack on this absolute power. Against the realists, the nominalists maintained that the cosmos was made up of radically individual entities. All that existed were the particular things that we see and interact with. Rover did not exist as a dog. Rover just existed as Rover. "Dog" was just a *name* of convenience, hence "nominalism."

Nominalism maintained that people observe the individual things around them, recognize useful similarities, and then group things together accordingly and give those groups names. This means that human reasoning, which relies upon categories, is not about the world as it is in its nature, but is about merely our systemization of the world. Our logic is self-contained in its own definitions. Here we see man pushing himself away from nature, opening up a gap. A gap opens up between man and God as well. Because human reason is not participating in the reason of God through the natures of creation, there is not even an analogous connection between man and God. God is entirely unknowable by human capabilities. This is a fragmentation of the High Medieval, and indeed biblical, vision of the cosmos.

However, for the nominalists, this did not lead to nihilistic despair, as we might expect. Rather, they maintained that God was good and gracious and that God had ordained the world to behave in a certain way and that he maintained it accordingly. The world operated, then, not through the indwelling rationality of the creatures themselves but through the external law of God. Rover played fetch because God ordered him to do so. He also ordered Fido and Rex to do so. We notice this and call Rover, Fido, and Rex "dogs." This is not a mistake on our part. God has ordered these animals to behave in a similar way, and we are right to notice this. We can perhaps see here the beginnings of the modern scientific perspective. In the traditional realist view, things become more themselves as they move toward their end. Our own rationality becomes more reasonable as we move toward the fulfillment of our natures in virtue. This means that the world remains always mysterious; it is always moving and changing, and we can be always surprised by what comes next. To the realist, no matter how much truth we learn about the natures of the world, there is always more to learn because the final truth is the truth of God himself in which all natures participate. In medieval realism there was, therefore, a profound confidence in human reason within an even more profound humility. St. Thomas Aquinas, who argued so passionately in favor of man's ability to know the universal essences of things, also wrote: "Our manner of knowing is so weak that no philosopher could perfectly investigate the nature of even one gnat."[14] For the nominalist, on the other hand, the world is as we see it. There are no partially hidden natures moving toward their fulfillments. Rather, God ordains certain behaviors, and we can see them clearly and sort the world accordingly. There is no reason in creation; there is no reason *for* or *in* the dog. Rather, God just wills it. Now, of course, God could arbitrarily change his will at any moment. If he did so, the cosmos would not undergo any sort of violence. It would just change. God, though, has promised us through a covenant, which is a sort of contract, that he will not change his will. His laws will remain the same. We can count on them in faith.

This logic holds true for the moral life as well. For the extreme nominalist, there is no such thing as human nature. Mankind is not being prompted through his reason to steadily fulfill his nature. Rather, he is moving through the world in total freedom. There is no natural law in the sense of a law that emerges from within human nature itself and which provides a guide to how people ought to behave. Rather, there is a moral law that is given by God. In the same sort of way that God orders the behavior of things in the world through his will, he commands people to behave in certain ways. This is law not because it corresponds to eternal truth or eternal reason but because God in his infinite power says it is. God's will alone determines what is good and what is evil, and he could, theoretically, reverse them. He could declare murder to be moral. But, as with the laws of nature, he will not do this. God has made a covenant with mankind. He is a good and loving God who is not interested in hurting us through arbitrary whims. He is stable and predictable and has made promises that he will keep.

For the nominalist, we can only learn about God through revelation. We only know about God from what he tells us about himself

---

[14] Thomas Aquinas, *Expositio in Symbolum Apostolorum*, Prooemium.

and in the manner in which he tells us. We have no way of working ourselves toward a knowledge of God, even an analogical knowledge. Similarly, we can only learn about the moral life from God's revelation. We know what is right and wrong because we are told. The virtue we achieve in life, then, is not a matter of perfecting our own natures but a matter of conforming ourselves to God's external commands. This means we don't move into salvation through achieving the perfection of our natures, but rather that we are saved through obedience. The High Medieval vision of a social ascent to God, into perfection and freedom, is swept away. Rather, the world of men and the world of God are wholly different, as is the world of men and the world of animals, plants, and things. All these worlds are united only through external law and language and not through a harmony that flows out of what they actually are. Law becomes a permanent and fixed institution.

This was a metaphysics that was appropriate to the new reality in Europe. The temporal power had always been the particular power that resided in certain individual principalities and was wielded by particular men. The spiritual power, on the other hand, was the universal power that united all the various temporal powers together through something that was greater than each of them and yet radically different and therefore, not a threat. Now, though, the temporal powers had managed to push the spiritual below them. The particular had taken precedence over the universal. This fragmentation mirrored nominalist metaphysics. The various individual kingdoms were bound together now not through spiritual communion at the level of their natures, but rather through external law, through agreements and contracts. Christendom was held together externally through positive constructs. What is more, nominalism had made God a distant, sovereign lawgiver. The newly powerful kings of Europe mimicked this. The kings of the High Middle Ages had not been primarily lawgivers. The law flowed out of the natures of things. Rather, they were primarily judges. They tried to discern the law of justice and to act accordingly, restoring society to the peace of the harmonious interaction of the various things and people of creation. The kings of the Late Middle Ages, however, became primarily lawgivers. Their will was law, and their law structured society itself. Like God's law in nominalism, the law of the king was increasingly absolute and always present. This was a new political conception, which, as we will discuss later, came eventually to be known as absolutism, but which we often just call sovereignty.

Nominalism

In the Late Middle Ages, gaps opened up throughout society. In the midst of the great suffering of the period, of the corruption, and in the theology of the time, God and heaven were pushed further away. The world was not a part of a grand, dynamic dance toward its elevation into the wholly transcendent. The transcendent was distinct and distant. God was unknowable and his will inscrutable. Man knew his law through revelation, and man's only hope of escaping the world and crossing over into heaven was to obey that law. Similarly, gaps opened up between people. The Church was not so much a communion of people moving toward ever-greater peace and harmony as it was a collection of nations united through external rules and treaties. These nations themselves were not so much large families, united in faith and charity, as they were small cosmoses, united and ordered by the will of their increasingly godlike kings. The papacy had been reduced to little more than another one of these kingdoms. To top it off, the power of Islam was on the rise. In 1453, the Turks conquered Constantinople itself. This was the final fall of the eastern half of the Roman Empire. By 1500, the Middle Ages were coming to a close and what was left of Christendom was hanging by a thread.

IV

The Early Modern Church

1. The Reformation

The Trigger

The Protestant Reformation is of incalculable importance. The Reformation was a profound reordering of Christendom. It was similar, perhaps, to the fall of the Roman Empire in the fifth century. Like with the fall of the empire, the world that came out of the Reformation was very different from the world that had gone into the Reformation. It might even be said that modernity itself was born of the Reformation. The Reformation is commonly asserted to have begun in 1517 when Martin Luther nailed his 95 *Theses* to the door of Wittenberg Cathedral, but, like all such events, the ground was being prepared long before. We have already discussed much of this preparation at the level of theology and politics, but popular piety was being equally prepared.

Catholicism is a sacramental religion. It asserts the intimacy of the divine and the spiritual with the human and the material. What we do on earth has eternal consequences, and the eternal, God himself, works on earth through what we do. Salvation is historical and material. Grace works in time and through events, people, and things. This sacramentality takes on a highly ritualized form in the life of the Church. In the sacrament of penance, for example, the penitent seeks forgiveness for his sins, and he does so in a ritualized manner that is laid down by the Church. The priest, for his part, acts *in persona Christi*, in the person of Christ, forgiving the penitent though a highly ritualized procedure. In the sacrament, God himself does the forgiving, and the penitent himself must be contrite for his sins and approach God with true sorrow. But this intimacy between God and man is necessarily mediated through the Church, through her sacraments. The sacrament is not some sort of an empty shell of symbolism, encasing a purely spiritual event which is what is really going on, on the inside. The sacrament *is* what is really going on. The symbol effects what it symbolizes. Nevertheless, at no point does a person control God's grace or dictate God's favor. Properly understood, sacraments and the rituals that surround them are not magic. Saying certain words or performing certain actions do not in and of themselves affect the universe or compel God to certain actions. To believe that they did would be superstition.

However, such superstition is a constant temptation in Catholicism, and in the period leading up to the Reformation, large swaths of the Church had indulged in it. We have already discussed how the fourteenth century was a time of general suffering. This understandably led to an increased desire for people to figure out some way of controlling their environment. At the same time, God had been pushed a little further away and was increasingly imagined more as a sovereign lawgiver and less as a loving father. The Church itself and society as a whole were increasingly legalistic, increasingly organized and driven by authorities and the commands of their wills. We can perhaps understand, then, why popular piety took on a magical flavor, as if the external structures of ritual and sacrament were what produced the result, as if the priest were casting spells and the Eucharist were a talisman, as if one could just say the right words, assert the right beliefs, or perform the right actions and curry God's favor. This tendency was not helped by the bureaucratic understanding of the Church that led the clergy to increasingly think of themselves as technicians of God's grace, pushing the right papers and saying the right prayers, rather than living conduits of the living God. These were just tendencies. These were just the particular temptations of this particular period as all periods have particular temptations. But it was here that the Reformation was ignited.

Perhaps nowhere were these tendencies more pronounced than in the practice of indulgences. Indulgences had first been widely issued in connection with the Crusades. Crusaders were granted a plenary indulgence by the pope. What this meant was that on account of their remarkable act of charity, they were forgiven all the penance that they owed for their sins, penance that otherwise would have to be performed either in this life or in purgatory after death. The theology behind indulgences was sound. The Church was a body, and members of that body could benefit from the health of other members. When the Church gave an indulgence, it was declaring that the merit of Christ and his saints was imputed to the penitent as if it were his own. The sinner was wrapped in the garments of their justice. Over the course of the Middle Ages, the practice of indulgences spread beyond the Crusades as the Church awarded indulgences for many acts of penance or charity and started to award partial indulgences as well. Partial indulgences did not remit all the penance that was owed but only a portion of it.

The practice of indulgences was often corrupted in the late Middle Ages. Giving alms had, for centuries, been a practice that could earn an indulgence, but increasingly these alms became, more or less, prices. If you gave more money, you could get a better indulgence. Indulgences had always had certain spiritual prerequisites, such as contrition for sin. These were sometimes downplayed or just forgotten. Therefore, indulgences were sometimes mistaken for magic, and what is worse, it was magic that was for sale. This was a real corruption, a combination of superstition and simony. Many reformers in the Church knew this, but the practice was hard to eradicate, especially in parts of Germany, where princes had made deals with the Roman Church to split the proceeds from indulgence sales.

This corruption was the immediate context for Martin Luther's *95 Theses on Indulgences*. Martin Luther was an Augustinian friar and intellectual. A product of the religious tendencies of his day, he was extremely anxious about the state of his soul and had tried to perform the external works necessary to become assured of his salvation. This had led him to despair and drove him in the opposite direction, away from good works. He became convinced that the Church was using the scruples and theological errors of people such as himself in order to exploit them; it was claiming to have powers that it did not really have, such as the power to remit penances that were owed to God himself. But he went well beyond criticism of indulgences. Luther developed a whole new theological system around an intense distrust of all human works, of all ritual, and of all sacramental mediation.

The Theology of Martin Luther

Luther's thought as it developed in the decades after 1517 and even more so among his followers rested on three principles: *sola fides* (faith alone), *sola gratia* (grace alone), and *sola scriptura* (Scripture alone). Luther's central concern was how a person could know whether he was saved. No matter how many good works he did, he still sinned. Did this mean that everyone was rightly going to hell? Wouldn't that be justice? Luther's solution was his formulation of salvation through faith alone. According to Luther, we did not become better people through years of working into virtue, through a lifetime of struggle to achieve some degree of perfection and so merit before God. Rather, God infused faith into those whom he chose to save. This infusion of faith, which saves, was a pure, gratuitous gift of God. One was saved through faith alone, which one could acquire through grace alone. But the content of faith came only through an encounter with Scripture. Revelation was through Scripture alone. The three *solae* were, therefore, united: through an encounter with Scripture, one attained the faith which saved through grace. For Luther, a person was not saved (or justified) through becoming actually holy. This was the Catholic understanding. To the Catholic, salvation also required grace. But this grace enabled one to achieve actual virtue, actual holiness. For the Catholic, grace, leading to faith and charity, actually healed fallen nature and elevated it beyond itself. Perfection itself would await in heaven, of course, but in this world, real progress into true holiness was made. This was the soul's justification.

Luther denied this. Properly understood, no justification was possible in this world. He wrote: "We put in place two worlds, as it were, one heavenly, the other earthly. Into these we place the two kinds of righteousness, which are separated and maximally distant from each other."[1] For Luther, justification was not the product of a slow movement into righteousness. It was a legal verdict that was received passively. The sinner was acquitted of the guilt for his sins externally, and the merits of Christ were imputed to him as if they were the sinner's own. Christ's holiness was treated as if it were the Christian's holiness, even though it wasn't. For the Catholic, the moral law was slowly fulfilled in a person as he became more virtuous. Grace did not destroy the law; it allowed the faithful person to fulfill the law. For Luther, the law was a standard of perfection that could never be satisfied. The law's purpose was to humble a man into despair, which was the first step toward conversion to faith. Luther argued that mankind could do

---

[1] Martin Luther, "Commentary on Galatians," in *The Essential Luther*, ed. and trans. Tryntje Helfferich (Indianapolis, IN: Hackett Publishing, 2018), 254.

nothing on his own except sin. As he wrote: "Free will, after original sin, is a thing in name only, and as long as it does what is in it, it commits a mortal sin."[2] For Luther, all efforts at holiness were ultimately pride. Indeed: "It is certain that man must utterly despair of his own ability before he is prepared to receive the grace of Christ."[3]

In this theology, there is a mixture of timeless spiritual truth and true novelty. The belief that man can obey the moral law without grace is the Pelagian heresy that St. Augustine had rebutted more than a thousand years earlier. Luther was clearly right to condemn such error. Man was dependent on grace. However, Catholicism maintained that dependence on grace did not mean that a person played no part in his own salvation. Rather, he had to respond to God's grace and work with it and through it; he had to work to make progress. This ability to cooperate with grace was itself a gift from God, mysteriously a product of grace. Grace was first; grace was necessary; but nevertheless, the Christian chose grace. He somehow moved into grace, through grace. For the Catholic, merit and righteousness were not merely imputed to a person while his sinful, fallen nature remained unchanged. Rather, he was himself changed through grace, through faith working through charity. This patristic and medieval understanding maintained that sanctification was a lifelong process that led, finally, to justification. For Luther, on the other hand, sanctification happened now because of justification: "Good, pious works never make a good pious man, but a good pious man does good pious works."[4] There is an irony here. Martin Luther began his protest with an attack on indulgences, which were the Church's imputation of Christ's merit to the sinner in return for an act of faith. The Church taught that such imputation was merely a part of the path to salvation, which rested more profoundly on actual inward transformation. Luther, however, absolutized such imputation. For Luther, in a manner of speaking, all of Christianity was an indulgence, a massive imputation of another's merits to the sinner in response to an act of faith.[5]

There were many consequences that followed from Luther's theory of justification. One of them was that the hierarchical Church

---

[2] Martin Luther, *Disputation Held at Heidelberg*, 13.
[3] Luther, *Disputation Held at Heidelberg*, 18.
[4] Martin Luther, *On the Freedom of a Christian*, 23.
[5] See Mary C. Moorman, *Indulgences: Luther, Catholicism, and the Imputation of Merit* (Steubenville, OH: Emmaus Academic, 2017).

was not strictly necessary. For Catholics, the clerical Church mediated grace to the faithful through outward actions and rituals. But for Luther, grace was direct, and faith was the immediate consequence for each individual. He had no strict need for mediation. Individuals were saved not by being grafted onto the body of the Church, which was Christ, but by Christ entering them one at a time, so to speak. This means that for Luther, the Church could only be finally understood as an invisible communion of the saved. The saved make up the Church rather than the Church being the place where people were saved. The social aspects of humanity were accidental for Luther.[6] For Luther, the Church was still necessary in the sense that Scripture had to be preached and the sacraments administered. But the sacraments for Luther were not themselves efficacious, as they were for Catholics. Rather, they were signs or testimonies of God working immediately through grace.[7] In our essence, we stand alone before God.

Luther asserted that all Christians were equally priests, that all the baptized were the spiritual power. However, what he was really doing was denying the existence of the spiritual power. Luther repudiated the Catholic understanding of Holy Orders and of the sacraments its recipients confected. Likewise, he denied the importance of the monastic vocation—such pursuit of perfection was equally available to all through grace since it was equally impossible to all through even a lifetime of effort. For Luther, then, the three orders of Catholicism—the clergy, the laity, and the religious—were reduced to one: everyone was just a baptized Christian, just a layman. He wrote, "There is fundamentally no other true difference between laymen and priests, princes and bishops, or between what [Catholics] call spiritual and secular, except on account of their office or work."[8] And again, "What then are priests and bishops? Answer: Their government is not one of authority or power, but of service and office, for they are neither higher nor better than other Christians."[9] This was a dramatic flattening and laicizing of the Church. The preaching of bishops and priests was not somehow intrinsically different from the preaching of

---

[6] Luther, *On the Freedom of a Christian*, 26.
[7] Martin Luther, "The Babylonian Captivity of the Church," in Helfferich, *The Essential Luther*, 71–72.
[8] Martin Luther, "To the Christian Nobility of the German Nation," in Helfferich, *The Essential Luther*, 51.
[9] Martin Luther, "On Secular Authority: To What Extent It Must Be Obeyed," in Helfferich, *The Essential Luther*, 139.

anyone else whom God chose to use. Likewise, there was no special sacramental power. The spiritual power, we will recall, was the universal power, the power that united particular, time-bound people to the universal truth and to eternity through its teaching and its administering of grace. Through the spiritual power, the temporal power received the teaching and the grace necessary for it to build societies of peace in time that led mankind to their ultimate end, which was union with God in eternity. In denying the true existence of the spiritual power, Luther, in effect, asserted that the only human power was the temporal power—the power of the sword, the law, which became the universal power that "should be allowed to perform its office unhindered throughout the entire body of Christendom, with no one excepted, whether it affects the pope, bishops, priests, monks, nuns, or whoever else."[10] For Luther, ultimate justice came only through grace that was not mediated through men. Civil justice and a worldly peace, however, could be enforced by the sword; this was the role of all properly human authority.

For Luther, every man was *simul justus et peccator*: at the same time a just man and a sinner. For Luther, and even more so for his followers, injustice and justice, therefore, lived together in each of us. This is an impossibility to the Catholic for whom justice is achieved in degrees, and we are moving either up or down, either toward more perfect justice or toward less perfect justice. For the Catholic, where there is justice, there cannot be, as a matter of definition, also injustice. The Catholic perception integrates the temporal power, therefore, into the process of salvation. Its law and authority were fulfilled as men moved into virtue, into justification. For the Lutherans, though, the sword had nothing to do with salvation. At its best, it was merely the force to stave off anarchy and to provide some semblance of peace and order, allowing the space for the grace of God to work on men directly. But more often, the sword was simply violence and injustice. There are, therefore, for Luther two kingdoms, the earthly and the heavenly, that have essentially nothing to do with each other:

> Christians know, I say, that there are two kingdoms in the world, which are in great conflict with each other. In one kingdom Satan reigns, who is thus called "the ruler of the world" by Christ, and "the god of this world" by Paul. He holds captive to his will all who

---

[10] Luther, "To the Christian Nobility of the German Nation," 52.

have not been seized from him by the Spirit of Christ, as Paul also testifies.... In the other kingdom Christ reigns, who constantly resists and fights the kingdom of Satan. We are transferred into Christ's kingdom not by our own strength, but by the grace of God, which frees us from the present wicked age and rescues us from the power of darkness.... We are forced to serve in the kingdom of Satan unless we are rescued by the divine power.[11]

These two kingdoms were in stark contrast to St. Augustine's two cities. For Augustine, salvation was a man's movement from being a citizen of the City of Man to becoming a citizen of the City of God. For Augustine, the City of Man was left behind in history as men converted to the City of God, a dynamic that was ongoing and never final but in which humanity could make real progress. This was the very "process" of salvation, the mission of the Church in history. For Luther, the heavenly kingdom was invisible, and its subjects, even if they no longer needed the law strictly speaking because of their faith, nevertheless submitted to the sword along with everyone else. This means that the sword, which was no longer a power that operated from within the Church, governed all things in this life because all in this life was governed by sin: "The world and the multitudes are, and always will be, unchristian, even if all are baptized and called Christian."[12] The true Christian, then, was only spiritually free from the law. In externals, he was properly as servile to Caesar as was the rest of humanity. All men were subjects of the fallen kingdom. As Luther asserted, "Frogs must have their stork."[13]

Above, then, this kingdom of magistrates and judges was the kingdom "in which God rules the hearts of men, and which is a kingdom that one cannot see, for it consists only in faith and it will continue until Judgment Day. These then are the two kingdoms: the secular, which governs with the sword and is seen externally; and the spiritual, which governs solely with grace and the forgiveness of sins. This latter is a kingdom that one cannot see with bodily eyes, for it can only be comprehended with faith."[14] This amounted to the denial that the Old

---

[11] Martin Luther, "The Bondage of the Will," in Helfferich, *The Essential Luther*, 175.
[12] Luther, "On Secular Authority," 131.
[13] Luther, "On Secular Authority," 139.
[14] Martin Luther, "How Christians Should Regard Moses," in Helfferich, *The Essential Luther*, 193.

Testament was fulfilled in the New Testament, a denial of the temporal efficacy of grace, a denial that the law was fulfilled through the virtue made possible by the Gospel in favor of the idea that salvation occurred over and against the law, that the law and Gospel operated independent of each other, really that the law and the Gospel were opposed: "Thus we see that in faith a Christian has enough, and no works are required to make him pious; and if he requires no further works, then he is certainly released from all commandments and laws; if he is released, then he is certainly free. That is Christian freedom."[15] Such freedom was perfectly compatible with complete and utter "political" subjugation:

> For Christians the law must be exercised spiritually, as was said above, for the recognition of sin. But for the brutish people, for the common man, it must be exercised physically and coarsely so that they perform and allow its works. And so, compelled to be under the sword and the law, they must be externally pious, just as one restrains wild animals with chains and cages, so that external peace shall continue among the people. This is why the secular authority is prescribed, and God will have us honor and fear it.[16]

This is a vision of a static world, a world without real history. It is a world ruled by an extrinsic force, the sword, that is essentially pre-Christian. It is, in short, a world trapped in the Age of Nature. Salvation for Luther did not move the world out of the Age of Nature into the Age of Law and on to the Age of Grace. The Age of Nature was the condition of the world. Law came from without to convict a man of sin, and grace came from above to save him *in* the fallen world, rather than to save the world itself.

We can see, no doubt, the nominalism that is present in Luther's conceptions. Men stand before God not as sharers in a nature that is being redeemed in the Church, as Christ's Body, but rather as radical individuals. We do not move into our natures as we are perfected. We, rather, are declared perfect by an all-powerful lawgiver. Law for Luther becomes, ironically, absolute. It is nothing other than a command, an order. It does not lead people deeper into their own natures.

---

[15] Luther, *On the Freedom of a Christian*, 10.
[16] Martin Luther, "Against the Heavenly Prophets," in Helfferich, *The Essential Luther*, 155.

It, rather, leads them to despair and then to faith. It makes sense, then, that Luther placed so much more emphasis on faith than on charity. St. Thomas had described the Age of Law as characterized by faith while the Age of Grace was characterized by charity. Law comes from without and instructs the intellect, an action perfected in faith. Grace comes from within and shapes the heart, an action perfected in charity. Of course, the two movements can't be separated, but the appropriateness of Luther's emphasis on faith even as he absolutized law is striking. For Luther, furthermore, the laws of the princes begin to resemble the law of the sovereign and distant God. Realism and the Catholic theology that it supported was rooted in an ultimate unity of all things through their own natures in God. Nominalism and the Lutheran theology that it ultimately supported was rooted in an ultimate fragmentation and disunity of things and men, and men with God. Catholicism led to the conviction that, by rights, all of humanity in their various political arrangements, run by their various temporal powers, ought to be united under one spiritual power—their natures being fulfilled in a higher harmony. Lutheranism led, eventually, to the conviction that the temporal powers were themselves absolute in their own kingdoms and that the spiritual power did not finally exist at all among men. Heaven was not anticipated, even analogically, on earth.

The Spread of Lutheranism

Luther quickly gained a large following and the support of many German princes. There were several reasons for this. The most important is probably that the Church really did need reform. Remember how after the fall of the Carolingian Empire, a period of decadence set in, and then a reform movement formed and grew and led to the civilization of the High Middle Ages? The sixteenth century was perhaps a similar time. Medieval civilization had crumbled. As we have already discussed, there was corruption, not only institutionally but also spiritually. There was, no doubt, too much emphasis on outward actions and rote ritual. There was, no doubt, too much superstitious treatment of works and too much of a magical understanding of the sacraments. There was, no doubt, too much of a legalistic understanding of papal and priestly power. A reform was, no doubt, needed. There were at this exact time, therefore, many reformers and many people who

The Spread of Lutheranism

were waiting for the rise of reformers. Fittingly, much of the emphasis of these reformers was on personal faith, on an individual's conformation of himself to Christ, and less upon outward devotions. Luther was embraced by many such reformers as a needed corrective to the errors of the period. Even Luther thought of himself at first as only a reformer within the Catholic Church.

The Church in the West had been unified for so long that it initially did not occur to people that it could be permanently torn in pieces. Many people, therefore, supposed that Luther's movement was a welcome development. In each of the Church's previous reform movements, there had been extreme elements that went too far. In these movements, the Church had slowly determined which aspects of the reform went too far and condemned them, even while many of the ideas and much of the impulse of the reform were integrated into the Church, successfully reforming her. The Lutheran movement was initially dealt with in just this manner. Nevertheless, as Lutheran ideas spread rapidly, and as Luther's theology became better understood, more people put up a progressively stronger resistance. Finally, in 1521, the pope excommunicated Luther, and Emperor Charles V declared him an outlaw.

This should have been the tempering that the reform needed. This should have pulled people from the extremes of the reform movement and back into the center of orthodoxy, where real and proper reform was badly needed, and this did happen for many who had initially supported Luther. Many early supporters of Luther abandoned him. But Luther's movement overall was not tempered. Rather, the opposite happened. It became more extreme, and it gained ground. Why? To answer this question, we have to understand the political situation in Germany.

Germany was not a united country in the sixteenth century. It was still the Holy Roman Empire. It was made up of hundreds of relatively small principalities, free cities, bishoprics, and even single estates that all had various degrees of independence from each other and from the imperial government. The imperial government had very loose and limited authority over most of these little states. The centralization of government into powerful monarchies that had occurred in Spain, France, and England had not occurred in Germany. Also, the monarchical control of the Church that had occurred in these other kingdoms did not occur to the same degree in the empire. Rather, in all of Europe, the Holy Roman Empire was the one place where the old medieval idea of the temporal and the spiritual powers governing together over largely independent small states most endured. The pull to the universal remained a constant limitation to the ambitions of the many princes of Germany. They could not get too powerful temporally because they were eventually checked by the emperor. They could not get too powerful spiritually because they were eventually checked by the papacy. In Germany, local, particular power was loosely integrated into a larger whole. This was a check to the power of both local and universal authorities.

Luther's movement was very attractive to many of these German princes. The reformers called for a decentralized Church that was submissive to temporal rulers. As we have seen, the Lutherans claimed that the universal bond between Christians was invisible. Neither the emperor nor the pope represented universal Christendom. Lutheranism, then, gave the princes an opportunity. They could sever ties with the universal principles of Christendom, with the emperor and the pope, but without denying the reality of the Church itself or the truth of Christianity. In fact, Lutheranism asserted that their power was instituted by God as supreme over all things that happened on earth. Lutheranism allowed them to break free from Catholic universalism without giving up the fundamental connection between their power and Christianity. This was attractive. What was also attractive was that breaking free from the Roman Church meant that the princes could stop sending portions of Church revenues to Rome. In fact, it meant that all the revenue and all the property held by the Church in their territories could effectively become theirs. Luther taught, of course, that in all things temporal and material the clergy were not different from anyone else and so were completely subject to the temporal power. Many princes, therefore, supported the spread of Lutheranism in their territories. We don't have to attribute merely cynical motives to these princes. It is perfectly reasonable to suppose that many of these princes sincerely believed that what they thought was right in politics and what they thought was right in theology were compatible. It would be strange for things to be otherwise. They no doubt sincerely believed that the emperor and the pope were tyrants, and Luther showed them why.

What the reformers and their princely supporters were proposing was not a divorce of the temporal and the spiritual but, rather, a new understanding of their unity. Nowhere was there a conception of religious diversity or pluralism, and the reformers certainly had no notion of modern religious liberty. Rather, truth remained understood as necessarily unified and the source of all legitimate authority. There was no room in this period for the convenience of relativism. Theological revolt was necessarily a revolt against the basis of social cohesion and against a ruler who based his legitimacy on the theology that was being undermined. The Reformation was not, therefore, a questioning of authority itself; it was an attempt at establishing a new system of authority. This, unsurprisingly, led to bloodshed.

Serious violence first broke out in 1524. Not only the princes but also hundreds of thousands of poor and struggling peasants saw the revolutionary potential in Luther's thought. They extended Luther's logic to include not only the hierarchy of the Church but the temporal hierarchy as well. If the princes were to be free from the emperor and the pope, why should the peasants not be free from the princes? They, therefore, revolted and called for the support of the Lutheran reformers. This support was not forthcoming. Instead, Luther wrote a book titled *Against the Robbing and Murdering Hordes of Peasants*. He urged the nobles to "smite, slay, and stab the rebellious."[17] For Luther, submission to worldly power was the counterpart to spiritual freedom. Spiritual freedom was not freedom from domination, quite the opposite, in fact. The princes were not just justified in putting down the peasants, therefore, but this was demanded by God; it was a type of crusade: "Thus it may be that whoever is slain fighting on the side of the authorities would be a true martyr to God ... for he proceeds in obedience to the divine word. On the other hand, whoever dies fighting on the side of the peasants is one who will eternally burn in hell."[18] The princes agreed, killing over one hundred thousand peasants as they put down the rebellion.

Things in the empire were bad and were certainly going to get worse. The emperor, Charles V, could not enforce his law against Lutheranism. He was bogged down in wars with the French in the West and with the Ottoman Empire in the East. The war with the Ottomans was particularly consuming. The Ottoman Empire was the largest Muslim power in the world, and it had been aggressively expanding into southeast Europe. In 1529, the Ottomans laid siege to the city of Vienna itself, in the heart of central Europe. Charles V had

---

[17] Martin Luther, "Against the Robbing and Murdering Hordes of Peasants," in Helfferich, *The Essential Luther*, 165.
[18] Luther, "Against the Robbing and Murdering Hordes of Peasants," 167.

no choice but to expend most of his resources in trying to stop them. The French saw in Charles's troubles an opportunity to weaken him as a rival, and so they supported the reformers in his lands and blocked his attempts to hold an ecumenical council to resolve the theological disputes. The king of France could do this because he had almost complete control over the French Church, and he simply forbade his bishops from attending any such council. In the end, too much time passed. Through the 1520s and 1530s, Protestants and Catholics vilified each other until compromise was all but impossible.

War broke out in 1546 between a coalition of Lutheran princes and the emperor with his allies. The emperor technically won the war, but his victory had little effect on the ground, and a second war broke out in 1552. This war went on for nearly three years. Exhausted, in 1555 the two sides ended hostilities through compromise, agreeing to the Peace of Augsburg. The agreement maintained the unity of the Holy Roman Empire but reduced the imperial power. It also declared the principle of *cuius regio, eius religio*, "whose region, his religion." What this meant was that Lutheran princes could enforce Lutheranism in their lands and Catholic princes Catholicism in theirs, and that neither would concern themselves with the other. This was an uneasy compromise, and it was not destined to last.

The Reformation in France and England

The forces of radical reform were not limited to the German-speaking lands of Europe. In France, a theologian named John Calvin published his *Institutes of the Christian Religion* in 1536. Calvin was heavily influenced by Lutheran thought, taking certain themes within Luther's work to their logical conclusions. Calvin emphasized the helplessness of man in the face of the power and inscrutable justice of God. God, for Calvin, became an absolute sovereign placed at such a distance from mankind that humans had no way of making sense of his will. Calvin explained that the act of faith itself could not be an act of the human will, for the will was totally depraved. Choosing faith would itself be a work.

In this way, Calvin absolutized law. For him, justification was the result of righteousness as it was understood in the Old Testament. Such righteousness was nothing short of complete obedience to the law.¹⁹ Rather than reading the Old Testament through the New, as was the Catholic practice, Calvin read the New Testament through the Old.²⁰ For Calvin, Old Testament-style righteousness was how man was saved. If man obeyed the law, he was justified. But man could not obey the law. He was not capable of righteousness. Therefore, he could not be saved and was rightly damned, "since God by his Law prescribes what we ought to do, failure in any one respect subjects us to the dreadful judgment of eternal death, which it denounces."²¹ God, however, through a unilateral and unmerited act, willed to see in some people, called the elect, the righteousness of Christ *as if* it were their own righteousness. This was faith. Calvin wrote:

> A man will be said to be justified by works, if in his life there can be found a purity and holiness which merits an attestation of righteousness at the throne of God, or if by the perfection of his works he can answer and satisfy the divine justice. On the contrary, a man will be justified by faith when, excluded from the righteousness of works, he by faith lays hold of the righteousness of Christ, and clothed in it appears in the sight of God not as a sinner, but as righteous. Thus we simply interpret justification, as the acceptance with which God receives us into his favor as if we were righteous; and we say that this justification consists in the forgiveness of sins and the imputation of the righteousness of Christ.²²

The elect were, therefore, still saved through obedience to the law. It just wasn't their obedience, but Christ's, that saved them. As Calvin wrote, "man, who had lost himself by his disobedience, should, by way of remedy, oppose to it obedience, satisfy the justice of God, and pay the penalty of sin. Therefore, our Lord came forth very man, adopted the person of Adam, and assumed his name, that he might in his stead obey the Father."²³

The New Testament did not, therefore, fundamentally transform the Old, elevating the law into a higher law of grace that fulfilled it. Rather, through Christ, the law was obeyed and, through faith, man

---

[19] John Calvin, *Institutes of the Christian Religion*, trans. Henry Beveridge (Peabody, MA: Hendrickson Publishers, 2008), bk. 3, chap. 11.15.
[20] See Calvin, *Institutes of the Christian Religion*, bk. 2, chap. 10–11.
[21] Calvin, *Institutes of the Christian Religion*, bk. 3, chap. 2.1.
[22] Calvin, *Institutes of the Christian Religion*, bk. 3, chap. 11.2.
[23] Calvin, *Institutes of the Christian Religion*, bk. 3, chap. 11.1.

shared in that obedience "so that though not righteous in ourselves, we are deemed righteous in Christ."[24] For Calvin, then, the Old Law was all there really was for man. Righteousness in works was the only path to salvation. We saw already the irony in Luther's position on imputation, through which all of Christianity became a single indulgence. Here we see the irony in Calvin's position on justification: justification through faith was the totalizing of justification through works, through the law. Indeed, even the sacraments of the New Law were the same as the sacraments of the Old Law.[25] They lacked all real efficacy. In and of themselves, they were mere works. All efficacy instead came from without, came from God unilaterally and arbitrarily, from above:

> The whole may be thus summed up: Christ given to us by the kindness of God is apprehended and possessed by faith, by means of which we obtain in particular a twofold benefit; first, being reconciled by the righteousness of Christ, God becomes, instead of a judge, an indulgent Father; and, secondly, being sanctified by his Spirit, we aspire to integrity and purity of life.[26]

According to God's justice, all should be damned. But through his inscrutable will, God saved some through Christ. For Calvin, these elect were predestined to glory through all of eternity through an act of pure unmerited election. Likewise, God predestined through all of eternity the reprobate to hell:

> We say, then, that Scripture clearly proves this much, that God by his eternal and immutable counsel determined once and for all those whom it was his pleasure one day to admit to salvation, and those whom, on the other hand, it was his pleasure to doom to destruction. We maintain that this counsel, as regards the elect, is founded on his free mercy, without any respect to human worth, while those whom he dooms to destruction are excluded from access to life by a just and blameless, but at the same time incomprehensible judgment.[27]

---

[24] Calvin, *Institutes of the Christian Religion*, bk. 3, chap. 11.3.
[25] Calvin, *Institutes of the Christian Religion*, bk. 4, chap. 14.23.
[26] Calvin, *Institutes of the Christian Religion*, bk. 3, chap. 2.35.
[27] Calvin, *Institutes of the Christian Religion*, bk. 3, chap. 21.7.

The Reformation in France and England

As for Luther, for Calvin the coming of the New Law of grace did not disrupt the temporal reign of the law, the Old Law, we might say. The New Law, rather, stacked on top of it, or worked through it, from outside it. Grace, in short, had nothing to say about the governance of this world, about the course of history, because salvation didn't happen in history. The church was invisible.[28] Calvin wrote of the spiritual and temporal powers:

> The former has its seat within the soul, the latter only regulates the external conduct.... Now, these two, as we have divided them, are always to be viewed apart from each other. When the one is considered, we should call off our minds, and not allow them to think of the other. For there exists in man a kind of two worlds, over which different kings and different laws can preside.[29]

The spiritual was real; therefore, it simply wasn't a power. It had no social efficacy. Rather, as for Luther, the temporal was the only power left to man. And what is more, grace did not disturb the juridical power that this temporal power wielded, rendering it remedial or provisional as in Catholic thought, but rather confirmed it as absolute.

Calvinism spread quickly, especially in France and the Netherlands. In France, Calvinists were called Huguenots. By the 1560s, there were around two million Huguenots. This was about one-eighth of the total population. Calvinism spread for several reasons. For many people struggling with the same late-medieval problems that had led Luther to reject works altogether, the idea of predestination could be profoundly comforting. If you were a member of the elect, it was because of nothing that you had done, and nothing that you did do could change it. All that was left was to throw yourself on the mercy of God. This could be liberating. As with Lutheranism in Germany, however, there were also political reasons for Calvinism's spread. The French monarchy based its legitimacy on being anointed Catholic kings. In the aftermath of the Hundred Years' War, France, like England, had grown into a strong monarchy that had extensive control over the ecclesiastical institutions in the kingdom. This control was one of the central mechanisms for the French monarchy's power. During the sixteenth century, the monarchy continued its

---

[28] Calvin, *Institutes of the Christian Religion*, bk. 4, chap. 1.7.
[29] Calvin, *Institutes of the Christian Religion*, bk. 3, chap. 19.15.

program of centralizing control. Both the legitimacy and the actual power of the monarchy, therefore, relied upon the kingdom's "catholicity." Many nobles and members of the middle class saw Calvinism as a way to resist this growth in centralized power. This was an obvious problem for the king. Calvinism spread widely, therefore, among the middle and upper classes in France and gained considerable economic and political power, putting great strain on the unity of the kingdom. Calvinism also spread into Germany, which placed strain on the Peace of Augsburg because it had recognized only Lutheranism and Catholicism as legitimate forms of Christianity.

Protestantism, whether Lutheran or Calvinist, offered a reinterpretation of Christianity that sought to make sense of both the suffering that accompanied the collapse of medieval civilization and the construction of strong states that marked the origins of modern civilization. Protestantism offered a version of salvation that did not demand the transformation of the world. Salvation was no longer about the redemption of all of humanity in history, no longer about the elevation of humanity out of the merely temporal and material through the spiritual. Rather, the spiritual was sealed off from the temporal. Grace didn't perfect the temporal; it counteracted the temporal; grace was a sort of *deus ex machina* that came down inexplicably from above to save some of humanity even while leaving the world itself alone, leaving it as a whole to its damnation and so to rule by the sword. The City of God and the City of Man could, therefore, coexist. The Reformation, then, offered a theology that reconciled the suffering of the Late Middle Ages with the growth of the monarchies and which made sense of the corruption and excessive legalism that infected the Catholic Church of the period. It was a theology that sought to show how Christianity could still fit in, and even justify, this increasingly non-Catholic world.

In England, the Reformation followed a very different course than it had in Germany or France. During the Late Middle Ages, the kings of England had gained near-complete control over the Church in their kingdom. Nevertheless, they were orthodox in faith and so not technically separated from the Roman Church. King Henry VIII was so orthodox that he wrote a book against the theology of Martin Luther and was awarded the title "Defender of the Faith" by the pope. However, Henry had a problem. He wanted to separate from his wife and marry another woman. The problem was that, for all his control of the English Church, he did not control annulments of such magnitude.

This power was retained by the pope. He asked the pope for an annulment. The pope refused it. This revealed to Henry and everyone else that the administrative control that Henry had was still ultimately tied to the universal idea of Christendom. Right and wrong, true and untrue, were still beyond the control of the king. He was still, at least in some respects, limited in what law he could pass; his will was still, at least in some respects, not absolute.

This was not acceptable to Henry VIII. In 1534, he issued the Act of Supremacy, declaring himself to be the head of the English church. It is important to understand this action. Henry was not saying that what the Church believes does not matter in politics or in private life. Rather, he was declaring himself to be the Church, with all of its powers intact, if not extended. This was a form of Caesaropapism. Henry was not at first heretical with regard to the rest of Catholic doctrine, and as far as most Englishmen were concerned, the change on the ground was at first minimal. The king, after all, had in practice been in charge of the Church for over a hundred years. Things changed, though, under Henry's son Edward VI (r. 1547–53). Edward was very young and came under the influence of more extreme Protestants. He instituted policies of persecution against people who remained loyal to Rome and what they called "the ancient faith." He went so far as to outlaw the Mass. His reign was short, and he was succeeded by Mary Tudor (r. 1553–58), who was still Catholic. Mary brought England back into communion with Rome, but she did not give up any of the crown's power over the Church. If anything, she sought to increase the monarchy's control. She died without an heir, and so the crown passed to yet another of Henry's children, Elizabeth (r. 1558–1603). Queen Elizabeth I attempted to moderate the religious conflicts that were tearing England in two. She was responsible for the establishment of the Anglican Church as we tend to think of it today. Her Anglicanism was a moderate Protestantism that made room for traditional forms of worship and even some traditional sacramental doctrine. Nevertheless, it was mandatory. Everyone in the kingdom had to attend Sunday services, and all clergy had to swear an oath recognizing Elizabeth as the head of the Church and the Church's independence from Rome. In 1570, Pope St. Pius V finally excommunicated Elizabeth and declared all Englishmen free of their allegiance to her. England was officially a Protestant country. This led to the systematic persecution of Catholics in the kingdom. During the reign of Queen Elizabeth, it become not just illegal to be Catholic; it became an act of high treason, an attack on the monarchy itself.

The Early Modern Church

The Counter-Reformation

Many of the complaints of the Protestants were based on real problems. The early reformers were not necessarily rebelling from the Catholic Church, and many of them did not break with Rome. Many reform-minded people stayed solidly within the Church and continued to seek its internal reform. The imperative of reform became obvious as the Protestant Reformation gained steam. If the Church was to stop the spread of Protestantism and bring its wayward flock back into the fold, it first had to get its own house in order. This movement of internal reform is, therefore, often called the Counter-Reformation, but it is probably better thought of as the Catholic Reformation.

One movement that had predated the Reformation and which continued to have influence within the Church was called the *devotio moderna*, or the Modern Devotion. This movement focused on individual spiritual growth, stressed the need for a personal encounter with Jesus Christ, and minimized much of the external devotions of the later Middle Ages. The *devotio moderna* had wide influence. A Spanish solider named Ignatius Loyola was influenced by the movement. Ignatius had been a worldly man until he was wounded. While recuperating, he had a powerful conversion experience. He became a priest and, in 1540, established the Society of Jesus, or the Jesuits. The Jesuits would become one of the most powerful forces of the Catholic Reformation. They sought intense, personal, spiritual communion with God and believed that individual holiness was possible to all Christians. They taught that the grace necessary for this growth flowed through the Church and her sacraments. For example, the Jesuits became masters of the confessional. They developed the practice of using the sacrament of penance as the means of spiritual healing and improvement, almost of spiritual direction. In the late Middle Ages, confession had often been approached as more of a transaction or legal arrangement. The penitent confessed, and the confessor gave a penance and absolved the sinner. The Jesuits, however, approached confession as an integral aspect of spiritual formation. We can see here how the impulses that animated many Protestants, such as an emphasis on the individual's encounter with Christ, could be brought into and so reinvigorate orthodoxy. The Jesuits were extremely disciplined and took a special vow of obedience to the pope. They were innovative, and to some they seemed dangerous, but they were on the front lines of the Counter-Reformation and established schools

The Counter-Reformation

throughout Europe to strengthen reformed Catholicism.

The most important event in the Catholic Reformation was the Council of Trent, which met from 1545 to 1563. Since the Protestant Reformation began, there had been calls for a council, and the popes had been in favor of such a gathering. However, political problems, especially complications resulting from France and the Holy Roman Empire's continual conflicts, made it nearly impossible until 1545. By this time, positions had hardened among the Reformation factions. The council was, therefore, largely about the Catholic response to now-formidable Protestantism and less about attempts at directly winning Protestants back to orthodoxy through compromise. In its first phase (1545–1549), the council approached the teaching of Luther systematically. It determined that Luther was mistaken about Scripture being the only source of revelation. Rather, Scripture was integral to a tradition that included the Church Fathers, the Councils, and the teachings of the bishops and popes. What is more, the council defined the books of the Bible to include the Greek books of the Old Testament, which Luther had removed. Luther's doctrine of justification without works was condemned. Justification was, of course, dependent on grace at every turn, but Christians' efforts toward a holy life were not in vain. Luther had maintained that there were only two sacraments: Baptism and the Eucharist. The Council countered by reiterating the ancient tradition that there were, in fact, seven. This was a wholesale repudiation of Luther's system and a dynamic restatement and development of orthodox doctrine. The Council also set out to reform the Church. It emphasized the importance of preaching, the pastoral duties of bishops, and prohibited clergy from holding multiple pastoral positions.

The second period began in 1551 and lasted only one year. It focused on the doctrine of the sacraments, confirming transubstantiation against various Protestant doctrines, and defining the Catholic doctrine on Confession and Last Rites. The third period did not begin until 1562. It dealt with the sacraments of Holy Orders and Holy Matrimony. It defined the doctrine of purgatory, a teaching repudiated by the Protestants, as well as that concerning devotion to the saints and the use of relics. As for reform, the council decreed that all bishops were to establish seminaries for the training of their priests. This was to have massive and far-reaching consequences. The ignorance of priests had been one the Protestants' most common attacks against the Church, and no doubt it often hit the mark. The

Council of Trent came to a close in 1563. It is one of the Church's great epochal councils, similar to the Council of Nicaea in 325 and Lateran IV in 1215. Like Nicaea, Trent had been called to deal with a doctrinal crisis and concluded by asserting orthodox doctrine in a manner appropriate to face the current danger. Like Lateran IV, it sought to institutionalize reform and construct a Church worthy of her universal calling.

In the early sixteenth century, the Church had been pushed back on her heels by the initial flurry of the Reformation. After Trent, she regained her footing. The popes of the next hundred years were almost all ardent reformers. Bishops became increasingly zealous for their pastoral responsibilities. New and reformed religious orders spread rapidly. There was a marked increase in the number of saints. There was also an explosion in missionary activity. Missionaries set out for India, China, Japan, Africa, and also the newly discovered Americas. They made countless converts to Catholicism and served as the constant conscience of European conquerors. Politically, the Church went on the offensive. In 1571, a league of Catholic kingdoms, headed by the pope, defeated a great Ottoman fleet at the Battle of Lepanto. This victory turned the tide against Muslim expansion and freed the Catholic powers to turn their attention to countering the spread of Protestantism. As we have already mentioned, in 1570, Queen Elizabeth I of England had been excommunicated and declared deposed. In 1588, the Spanish monarchy decided to overthrow her and sent a massive armada of ships to invade. It met with disaster off the cost of England, but it had been a bold undertaking. Catholic powers were more successful on the European Continent, with the emperor making progress against Protestants, especially in the Netherlands. The Catholic Reformation was the reform that the Church had needed, and the Church emerged out of the sixteenth century a different, more vital, and ultimately holier Church.

2. Confessionalization

Wars of Religion

The Catholic Reformation was one aspect of what historians often call the period of confessionalization, when the various kingdoms of Europe became "confessional states." One aspect of this movement was the creation of the confessions themselves. Before the Reformation, there was no notion of multiple "religions" or multiple distinct branches of Christianity. The Church was one, even though there was great diversity between different lands and among different peoples. During the first generation of the Reformation, this idea stayed pretty much intact. Everyone thought they were reforming the one Church and not breaking it into pieces. However, as the conflict wore on, people's positions began to harden. As factions increasingly defined themselves against each other, the hope of reconciliation faded, and a Europe of distinct Christian confessions emerged. At Trent, for example, the Catholic Church defined what it meant to be truly Catholic by pointing out where and how Luther was wrong. After Trent, Catholicism was, in a sense, defined against Lutheranism. The Lutherans did the same thing. In 1580, they issued the Book of Concord, which articulated a Lutheran system of belief that directly excluded the possibility of Catholicism. The Calvinists did the same thing in 1563 with their Heidelberg Catechism. By 1600, it was clear that there were multiple distinct forms of Christianity, known as "confessions," and each was defined as not being the other.

These confessions remained fundamentally tied to politics. In fact, it was largely the drive of princes to consolidate power in their realms and unify their people against each other that pushed the process of confessionalization forward. Within the various kingdoms and principalities of Europe, rulers were busy tying themselves ever closer to the churches of their realms, be they Catholic or Protestant. Everywhere, churches were increasingly becoming mere departments of state, and states were becoming more homogenous in their religion. A Lutheran prince, for example, increased his power by both making his people more Lutheran and by emphasizing how different they were from Catholics and how dangerous the Catholics were. The same was true in the inverse for Catholic princes. The dominance of the temporal power was not a secularization of society. The temporal power was understood as the God-given power of the sword. It was important to the wielders of this power that the people believed in its divine foundation.

Throughout Europe, then, in the late sixteenth and early seventeenth centuries, we see the construction of mechanisms of social discipline. These were governmental systems of making sure that the population was properly "confessional." In Calvinist regions, there was the establishment of consistories, which were a way to investigate, correct, and punish people for a lack of proper commitment to Calvinism. In Catholic countries, the old system of inquisition was revived and expanded. No longer was it merely interested in the salvation of souls; in the hands of confessionalizing, state-building monarchs who dominated the Catholic Church in their lands, the Inquisition became an instrument of ensuring proper devotion to both Church and State. The Lutherans built similar mechanisms through their princes. These confessional states were increasingly interested in religious observance as a form of submission to the State and not in the actual spiritual well-being of the believer. Discipline, therefore, often displaced the cure of souls, which was a far more subtle art that was less concerned with conformity and more concerned with the particular spiritual condition of individual believers or groups of believers. Confessionalization and the social discipline that it brought with it was, therefore, a process that both divided states from each other and worked to both eliminate diversity within states and to minimize the pursuit of holiness in favor of the pursuit of conformity. The temporal power is an external power. It makes sense, then, that the discipline that the temporal power enforced was more concerned with external actions and propositional beliefs than with the internal condition of the soul, which was, after all, the primary concern of the spiritual power. If the world was trapped in the Age of Nature, or at best the Age of Law, it was a world that was governed not by the movement into charity but by external law and conformity, even a taste of heaven being postponed until after death. The local specification of the human law that was possible through the coordination of temporal and spiritual powers had allowed for great diversity within a united Christendom. This was so because law came as much from below as it did from above. The confessional states, however, having subordinated the spiritual to the temporal, could not afford such a relatively hands-off approach.

The fragmenting of Christendom into competing confessions was identical to the fragmenting of Christendom into competing principalities. The destruction of the universal spiritual power led inevitably to increased division among the temporal powers. This led to terrible war. We have already seen how war erupted in the German-speaking lands. In 1562, it broke out in France as well. This civil war lasted until 1598 and is known as the French Wars of Religion. It was a vicious war, with both sides presenting the other as demonic and both sides stirring the populace to acts of large-scale mob violence. Over the course of the conflict, up to four million people died, possibly 20 percent of the population. The war ended in 1598 with the Edict of Nantes. Like the Peace of Augsburg in Germany, the Edict of Nantes was a compromise peace. The monarchy remained Catholic, but Calvinism was allowed in certain cities and in the lands of particular noble families. Generally speaking, the monarchy was weakened by the war.

The war in France was terrible, but the war that broke out in the Holy Roman Empire was worse. The process of confessionalization had been at work in the empire since the Peace of Augsburg, and the compromise between Protestants and Catholics began to break down as each side increasingly viewed the other as aggressive, dangerous, and beyond conversion. War broke out in 1618. It began as a Protestant revolt against the Catholic emperor. Catholic Spain entered the war, and by 1623, the rebels had been largely defeated. However, Denmark and England then entered on the Protestant side. This marked the beginning of the second phase of the war. The second phase saw the breakdown of the Protestant versus Catholic dynamic. For example, France, a Catholic country, entered the war by subsidizing the Protestant side. Why? The answer is that by this time, confessionalization had proceeded to the point that universal Catholic power was of less importance to a Catholic country like France than were its many other political concerns. France was more worried about the power of Spain and the Holy Roman Emperor than it was about the spread of Protestantism. The fragmentation of Europe had proceeded to the point that kingdoms did not perceive their internal unity as being bound up in the religious unity of Europe as a whole. Rather, the French Catholic Church was more like a national church than an integral part of a universal Church, and it was little affected by the national churches of other kingdoms, be they Catholic or otherwise. In 1630, Lutheran Sweden entered the war with great success against the imperial forces. France then began to fight with more conviction, as did the Spanish. The war raged on until 1648.

Extending from 1618 until 1648, this conflict is known as The Thirty Years' War. It was a devastating war. As we have discussed, during the Late Middle Ages and the Reformation period, governments had been growing stronger and stronger. Confessionalization had added ideological commitment to administrative centralization. The governments could not only field and arm and feed large armies; they could also motivate them with what amounted to Crusade rhetoric. The soldiers were fighting the enemies of God, and their kingdoms were God's chosen people, the true Church. The Thirty Years' War was ruthlessly fought. Some historians estimate that the population of German-speaking Europe was reduced by 30 percent. In some particularly ravaged regions of the empire, the losses may have been as high as 70 percent. One-third of all German towns were burned to the ground.

The Thirty Years' War is known to history as a war of religion. But was it? Were the states fighting over religion? The question itself misses what was really happening. As we have seen, in this period there was no distinction between politics and religion. All political fights were religious fights, and all religious fights were political fights. How could a faithful Christian go to war, after all, unless that war were against someone who was a terrible sinner, someone who was unjust and immoral, in other words, against a bad Christian, a non-Christian, or a heretic? Christians could only fight wars against the enemies of truth and justice. This meant that their wars were necessarily religious conflicts, even if they had nothing to do with theological disputes, because there was no notion of right and wrong outside of what we now call "religious" ways of thinking. To be the enemy of what was right and true was to be an enemy of God. This fact, however, rested on a lingering universal understanding of truth. The enemy was evil because he shattered the unity of humanity through his injustice. What happened over the course of the Reformation and the wars of religion was the creation of "the political" and "the religious" as distinct categories, at least with regards to international politics (though not internal politics). Through the wars of religion, we see the birth of what would become true national states and the birth of international politics that were far less concerned about we now call "religious" issues. Ironically, it was only after the so-called "wars of religion" that it became possible to talk about the difference between religious wars and nonreligious wars. In a real sense, the wars of religion were integral to the process through which "religion" was created as a distinct category of human action. They are wars of religion only in retrospect.

Divine Right of Kings and Absolutism

The Thirty Years' War ended in 1648 with the Peace of Westphalia. The treaty declared that the internal religious and administrative affairs of the various countries were of no concern to each other. It envisioned a system of sovereign states that interacted with each other as equals with no central point of unity. They were not united in some larger unit like a Church or an empire. Rather, each stood alone. This was the natural conclusion of the Reformation and confessionalization. It was the creation of "religion" as something that happens separately from international politics, as something that happens inside the various political units of the world, rather than something that united them, as something below the state rather than above the state.

After this period, the relationship between rulers and their subjects changed. Previously, people tended to have overlapping religious and political loyalties and associations. No one ruler could claim all of a person's obedience. Instead, societies tended to be diverse, with local authorities, such as the local lord and bishop, sharing most direct authority, and with these small groupings united into larger ones in similarly diverse ways. Any given person had a wide range of relationships with a wide range of authorities, including universal authorities, such as the emperor and the pope, that transcended all local power. Now, however, it was agreed that the people of each country were solely subject to a single state. This was not a division of religion from politics because nearly all the states of Europe were confessional states, with highly centralized churches, but it was the positioning of politics, of the temporal power, as the only real human power. The spiritual was entirely subservient to it and operated entirely within its bounds. Each country would decide what religion was and how it would function inside its own borders, and other countries were indifferent to its actions. Wars between countries, then, would no longer be over spiritual things but over merely temporal things like natural resources, power, or eventually ideology.

At the same time, diversity within countries became more and more of a threat, and reducing it was a means of extending central control. In the Middle Ages, connection to a universal standard and authority had allowed for significant local diversity because different people, who lived differently, were united through authorities that clearly transcended their particular ways of life and ways of worship. Now, though, with each country divorced from a universal authority, it became harder for them to tolerate local diversity. Thus, there emerged strong campaigns to enforce uniformity of belief and worship within each kingdom. The projects of social discipline accelerated after the wars of religion. The Peace of Westphalia did not cause but rather marked the end of Christendom even as an ideal, and it marked the birth of the sovereign-state system that remained in place through modernity. The universal spiritual power was effectively declared nonexistent and with it the legitimacy of local differences, and the temporal power, which was always the divided power, was declared all that there was. Europe, then, was fragmented into internally increasingly uniform states. The papacy, unsurprisingly, condemned the Peace of Westphalia as extremely harmful not only to Christian unity but to the independence of the local churches. In a formal papal bull, Pope Innocent X declared:

> By the present document that the aforesaid articles of these Treaties, ... which in any way injure or carry even the slightest prejudice ... to the Catholic religion, Divine worship, the salvation of souls, the said Apostolic Roman See, lesser churches, the ecclesiastical order and estate, and to their persons, members and affairs, possessions, jurisdiction, authority, immunities, liberties, privileges, prerogatives and rights of any kind, with all which has been deduced or shall be deduced from them, are and shall be from the legal point of view perpetually null, void, invalid, wicked, unjust, condemned, reprobated, futile, and without strength and effect.[30]

Pope Innocent X used every last bit of papal power in condemning the new order, and it is a clear testament to papal weakness that the consequences, in Catholic as much as in Protestant lands, were as if he had said nothing at all.

The settlement of 1648 confirmed the trends that had been developing for the past several centuries and which had accelerated after 1517. The temporal power was ascendant, and it was increasingly thought of in terms of absolute monarchy. The problem that rulers and their theoreticians faced as Europe fractured was how monarchies could claim both to have a mandate directly from God and to have independence from each other and from any sort of universal spiritual power that might limit their particular control. The solution was the invention of the idea of the divine right of kings. This theory maintained that kings were appointed directly by God and that they were answerable only to him. The king was God's representative on earth,

---

[30] Innocent X, *Zelo Domus Dei*, in *Church and State through the Centuries: A Collection of Historic Documents with Commentaries*, trans. and ed. Sidney Z. Ehler and John B. Morrall (New York: Biblo and Tannen, 1969), 196.

Divine Right of Kings and Absolutism

and his word was law. This theory worked as well for Protestants as it did for Catholics. In a speech to Parliament, King James I of England explained divine right, stating:

> The state of monarchy is the supremest thing upon earth; for kings are not only God's lieutenants upon earth, and sit upon God's throne, but even by God himself they are called Gods . . . Kings are justly called Gods, for that they exercise a manner or resemblance of divine power upon earth. For if you will consider the attributes to God, you shall see how they agree in the person of a king. God hath power to create, or destroy, make or unmake at his pleasure, to give life or send death, to judge all, and to be judged nor accountable to none. To raise low things, and to make high things low at his pleasure, and to God are both soul and body due. And the like power have Kings: they make and unmake their subjects: they have power of raising, and casting down: of life and of death: judges over all their subjects, and in all causes, and yet accountable to none but God only.[31]

Here we see the nominalist idea of God as lawgiver merging with human political theory. The king made laws through his mere will, and his will was not subject to evaluation by those he ruled. As one Catholic theorist wrote: "All the other attributes and rights of sovereignty are included in this power of making and unmaking law, so that strictly speaking this is the unique attribute of sovereign power."[32] He continued, "The principal mark of sovereign majesty and absolute power is the right to impose laws generally on all subjects regardless of their consent . . . There are therefore in each case two parties, those that rule on the one hand, and those that are ruled on the other."[33] Those ruled could not determine if the king's will was just or unjust, right or wrong, because his will was the source of these concepts' content. Indeed, the same theorist wrote: "He who contemns his sovereign prince, contemns God whose image he is."[34] It was not that the king was not capable of sin. Most divine right theorists thought that

---

[31] King James I of England, *Speech Before Parliament*, March 21, 1609, in G. W. Prothero, ed., *Select Statutes and Other Constitutional Documents Illustrative of the Reigns of Elizabeth and James I*, 3rd ed. (Oxford: Clarendon Press, 1906), 293–294.
[32] Jean Bodin, *On Sovereignty*, trans. M. J. Tooley (Oxford: Basil Blackwell, 1955), chap. 10.
[33] Bodin, *On Sovereignty*, chap. 8.
[34] Bodin, *On Sovereignty*, chap. 10.

he was. It was, rather, that there was no one in his kingdom capable of judging him. Rather, the king could only be judged by God. All order descended from God through the king. There was no work-around, no alternative route to God's justice. As the famous Catholic theorist Bossuet explained: "Princes act as ministers of God, and his lieutenants on earth. It is through them that he exercises his Empire ... the royal throne is not the throne of a man, but the throne of God himself."[35] Indeed, he continued, "the judgments of sovereigns are attributed to God himself ... One must, then, obey princes as if they were justice itself, without which there is neither order nor justice in affairs ... Only God can judge their judgements and their persons."[36]

Through this theory, the universal was preserved even as it was rendered practically meaningless. In theory, the spiritual remained higher than the temporal, but its contact with the world had been reduced to the person of the king. As far as the kingdom was concerned, all was below him. The temporal power was supreme. We are very far from the Christian monarchs of the High Middle Ages, who were, first and foremost, judges of the law and not the sources of law. Their power had been a mediation of God's power, but it had been a power that worked in and through the peaceful life of the multitude. The order of a kingdom came from below as well as from above. Order was found in harmony and mutual peace. The High Medieval king was the guardian of a peace and order that found it source in the life of the faithful, a life in which he participated along with his subjects. The divine right kings, on the other hand, were the source of peace and order. Their will structured what order even meant, at least in theory. As Bossuet explained:

> God is infinite, God is all. The prince, in his quality of prince, is not considered as an individual; he is a public personage, all the state is comprised in him; the will of all the people is included in his own. Just as all virtue and excellence are united in God, so the strength of every individual is comprehended in the person of the prince ... The power of God can be felt in a moment from one end of the world to the other: the royal power acts simultaneously throughout the kingdom. It holds the whole kingdom in position just as God holds the

---

[35] Jacques-Benigne Bossuet, *Politics Drawn from the Very Words of Holy Scripture* (Cambridge: Cambridge University Press, 1990), 58.
[36] Bossuet, *Politics*, 82.

whole world. If God were to withdraw his hand, the entire world would return to nothing: if authority ceases in the kingdom, all lapses into confusion.... Thus God enables the prince to discover the most deep-laid plots. His eyes and hands are everywhere ... He even receives from God, in the course of handling affairs, a degree of penetration akin to the power of divination.... You have seen a great nation united under one man: you have seen that secret reason which directs the body politic, enclosed in one head: you have seen the image of God in kings, and you will have the idea of majesty of kingship.[37]

We are not far here from the god-kings of antiquity.

How, though, did one become king? This was a problem. Traditionally, kings had assumed their power after being anointed by an archbishop, similar to how a priest was made a priest. This, though, implied that there was some king-making power on earth, that kingship emerged out of the liturgical life of the body of the faithful. This wouldn't do. So, many theorists emphasized the idea of divine bloodlines, the idea that royal blood was somehow different from normal blood and that it passed from father to son. Kings were not made; they were born. This political form was called absolutism, or sovereign monarchy, and it came to dominate European politics and political thought, both Catholic and Protestant. It is the clear triumph of the particular, the temporal, the legal over the universal, the spiritual, and the gratuitous, which is in no way the same thing as some sort of division of religion from politics. Nothing could be further from the case. The absolutist monarchs needed God. It was just a hypothetical God, a God who established them in their offices and then faded from the scene, a God who was present to the kingdom only as the king.

Theories of absolute monarchy were being built while the Renaissance was occurring in literature and the arts. While we cannot go deeply into the Renaissance here, we must at least note that the heart of its "humanism" was a retrieval of ancient, pagan forms—both artistic and intellectual. Divine right monarchy obviously retained a formally Christian character and therefore had to maintain the theoretical superiority of the spiritual. However, there emerged from within this humanism an alternative. This alternative is most closely associated with Niccolò Machiavelli (d. 1527). Machiavelli developed a theory

---

[37] Bossuet, *Politics*, 160-162.

of politics in which Christianity was largely irrelevant. Machiavelli viewed human society as broken up into small units that were ruled by their various princes. These princes had to protect their power and, through their power, the general safety and prosperity of their subjects. In order to do this, however, the princes needed to understand that Christianity and morality in general were not universal things, even in theory. Rather, right and wrong, true and false, just and unjust functioned only within the political units that the princes ruled. The princes themselves not only were not subject to the demands of morality but couldn't be, or they would be beaten by other princes or by their own people, and the safety and prosperity of the people would suffer. Princes had to have the courage to face the facts: what mattered in their world was strength and resolve, not right and wrong. That was how "right and wrong" could be preserved for the common people.

Machiavelli placed religion completely within politics. Religion was extremely useful, even necessary, for a happy society. Morality governed the people for their own good. But it did not apply outside that society. The princes operated in the dangerous realm that was found outside and between particular societies. This realm was necessarily free from religion or morality. It was a realm of heroic strength. This was the destruction not only of the spiritual power, but of the temporal power—both of which, we must remember, came from God. For Machiavelli, the power of the sword was not a power given by God and subject to his law, which was the medieval understanding of the temporal power and which had carried over in its own way into absolutism. Rather, the power of the sword was just plain power, and it was ultimately governed not by the law of God but by the pursuit of glory in a battle against fate. This was a return to a pagan understanding of politics, a form of politics that had been driven out of Europe with the conversion of the Roman Empire.

This was a political philosophy for a resurgent City of Man. Here the "universal" operated completely within and below the particular and so was rendered truly relative. The particulars of law and power were the source of the content of justice and peace as universal concepts instead of the other way around. This was an inversion of the City of God, an aiming down rather than up, a positing of the will of man as the highest power in a cosmos closed in on itself. Over the course of the early modern period, Machiavellianism grew in influence. Over time, many of the people who claimed divine right became, in fact, Machiavellian.

The most penetrating political thinker of the period, however, was Thomas Hobbes (1588–1679). Hobbes built a science of politics that sought to explain the genesis and functioning of all regimes, regardless of their historical forms or theories of legitimacy. Within this science, Hobbes, unlike Machiavelli, did not endorse any strategy for ruling, nor was his system a plan of action or an attempt at a theory of legitimacy. Rather, he described his work as a geometry of politics, as a true science that simply described how regimes functioned. Hobbes compared regimes to pieces of architecture. Men had been constructing buildings without a worked-out science of architecture for most of their history, but this did not mean that such a science was impossible. It just needed to be worked out by studying existing buildings, determining their principles, determining how and why they were built and how they worked. This was what Hobbes was doing with politics. He sought merely to explain how polities worked. Men, Hobbes reasoned, could then take that knowledge and build better in the future.[38] Like geometry, Hobbes's political science relied upon certain axioms from which he deduced the total system. These axioms were that the spiritual power did not really exist, that true gifts were impossible, that power, force, was the only fundamental social reality. As Hobbes put it: "So that in the first place, I put for a general inclination of all mankind, a perpetual and restless desire of power after power, that ceaseth only in death."[39] Society simply was competition over power.

Hobbes imagined a primordial state of nature in which every man was at war with every other man, in which "life is solitary, poor, nasty, brutish, and short."[40] Immediately within this anti-Eden, however, certain men conquered other men and compelled them to submit to their will. These more powerful men then warred with each other, resulting in bigger groupings of men under the victors. This process continued until humanity was organized into kingdoms and countries. But the war was ongoing: kings were themselves engaged in a continuing war with each other and with rebellious factions within their own kingdoms.

Hobbes referred to the power that held these groupings of men together as sovereign power. His idea of sovereignty is very simple, and yet penetrating. Men's ability to kill each other leads directly to

---

[38] Hobbes, *Leviathan*, II.30 (221).
[39] Hobbes, *Leviathan*, I.11 (58).
[40] Hobbes, *Leviathan*, I.13 (76).

preemptive war. These battles lead directly to weaker parties "cutting their loses" by submitting to the will of stronger parties—making these powers even stronger. Because he is only one man, who can be killed by any other man, a strong man's strength can only be augmented through such submission. He must be able to deploy the power of others. This, however, is tricky because any two of them are stronger than him. He must, therefore, play them off each other so that each assumes, or at least suspects, that everyone else is on the strong man's side. In the end, additional people and groupings of people submit to his will only because they believe others to have done so, only because he is now the combined will of a multitude, in the face of whose combined power they must cut their losses. Each person within this multitude, therefore, continues in his submission to the sovereign only because of its corporate power, only because so many other people are submitting to this power. The strong man himself, then, is increasingly merely one actor within the actual power structure, which is this corporate thing, which Hobbes calls a mortal god, a man-made god, which loses its center as it grows ever more powerful. The sovereign will is no longer the will of a natural man but is the will that emerges from this deep and perpetual struggle of wills. It is the Leviathan, who demands the submission of everyone it encounters.

For Hobbes, then, sovereignty is not something that a society ought to have. Rather, sovereignty is what constitutes society. To the extent that society is, to the extent that it holds together, to that very extent, there is, necessarily, sovereignty. This sovereignty is the source of right and wrong, true and false, just and unjust, mine and thine. This is important. The struggle of wills is the most fundamental social phenomenon. All other aspects of society emerge out of this struggle. To the extent that a society holds together, it has a notion of just and unjust, which is, by definition, a manifestation of sovereign power. For Hobbes, to be a member of society is to sincerely believe in its notion of justice, to see the world through the sovereign will, which is to submit to its ordered power structure, to submit to it as one's god.

Political legitimacy, therefore, was not the source of power but its consequence. In the end, for Hobbes, the cosmos was nothing but material things bumping into other material things. Everything was particular and temporal, and nothing was transcendent or universal. All religion, then, was a form of (cynical) paganism. The gods, even the Christian God, were simply a part of the mechanisms of power that structured society. Hobbes's science of politics was indifferent to the reality of the existence of the God of Christianity. Whether or not he existed did not affect the structure of regimes or the way in which their power worked. Indeed, for Hobbes, all regimes ultimately took the form of divine right regimes because man feared spirits. This meant that control of the spirits was a form of power and so, was necessarily an aspect of all sovereign power. In fact, all gods were, in the end, unknowable other than as regimes of power.[41] Men knew who their gods were because the priests and kings who ruled them told them who their gods were. If there appeared a god or religion that operated outside of the power of the sovereign power, this was a demonstration that that power was not yet sovereign, that it was still warring with rival, would-be sovereigns. This was a final, theoretical, destruction of the spiritual power. The so-called spiritual power to Hobbes was just a name for one way in which temporal power, the only real power, was manifested. What Hobbes was doing was explaining how paganism worked, how the gods were nothing more than the power of men over other men, and at the same time asserting that this cynical paganism was all there was. Even if the God of Christianity really existed, he was only politically relevant as the particular god of particular regimes.

No would-be ruler was a Hobbesian in the sense that he might be a Machiavellian. The Machiavellian was himself a type of neo-pagan. He desired glory and thought it was good and right that he should achieve it. Such thoughts amounted to his claim to legitimacy. The Machiavellian prince ruled "legitimately" because he was heroic, because he conquered fortune and determined his own fate. He believed himself worthy of rule. Hobbes sought to explain such behavior. He sought to place the Machiavellian prince within the same set of political equations as he placed the Islamic sultan, the democratically elected city council, the absolutist Christian monarch, or the temple-states of the ancient world. All were merely different historical manifestations of sovereign power. Hobbes was, therefore, not a pagan himself but rather a theorist of paganism. He knew the gods were nothing more than the assembled power of men, illusions through which men enslaved other men. For Hobbes, though, this was all there was or ever could be.

For Hobbes, man was trapped in an absolutized Age of Nature, as described earlier in this book. He imagined the downward spiral

---

[41] Hobbes, *Leviathan*, I.16 (103).

into depravity and so slavery to false gods that characterized that age as reaching its theoretical terminus, as being complete. Hobbes took seriously the total depravity of man as described by the Protestants and simply worked out logically what it meant. If this world was the kingdom of Satan and man was irredeemably vicious, Hobbes seemed to have reasoned, we can set aside grace and the kingdom of God as something that may or may not happen in the next life and get to work understanding the mathematics of pure, raw, violent power. Hobbesian thought, therefore, did not animate the City of Man but rather sought to explain the forces that did. It was perceived as odd and dangerous and was held in suspicion by even the most power-hungry of would-be despots. As Hobbes himself had explained, after all, sovereign power needed the people to believe that it truly represented divine power on earth, and the masters of sovereign power tended to believe their own claims to legitimacy. Hobbes was cynical about the cynics. This made him dangerous and widely condemned, even if more secretly studied.

V

The Modern Church

1. The Twilight of Christian Civilization

The Enlightenment

During the eighteenth century, the papacy found itself in a very difficult position. The Counter-Reformation had succeeded in reforming the morals of much of the hierarchy, in establishing a strong doctrinal basis against Protestantism, and in increasing the devotion of the faithful. However, Europe was divided into absolutist nations of various confessions. Even the Catholic kingdoms, such as France, paid little attention to the papacy. In fact, it was in Catholic countries that monarchical control of the Church was often most complete. The papacy was so weak that it was compelled to enter into a series of concordats, or agreements, with countries such as Spain, Portugal, and the states of Italy, that ceded most ecclesiastical jurisdiction to their princes and that essentially handed institutions such as the Inquisition over to the state to be operated as an instrument of centralized control. Things were particularly bad in France. The French Church was torn in two by a vicious fight between the Jansenists, who practiced an extremely austere form of Catholicism that emphasized the depravity of man, and the Gallicans, who believed that the government of the Church was most properly an episcopalian (run by bishops) and national affair and that the papacy had only the minimal role of maintaining doctrinal unity. The monarchy and its episcopal allies used this conflict and the constant threat of France breaking away from Rome in order to gain more and more control over the ecclesiastical hierarchy. Gallicanism had a German counterpart in

Febronianism. Febronius was an official of a German prince-bishop, and he argued for a revived from of conciliarism, for episcopal control of the universal Church. Like Gallicanism, Febronianism emphasized the power of the Catholic princes and asserted that the ecclesiastical hierarchy was ultimately subject to their rule. Unsurprisingly, the temporal powers and the bishops who supported them tended to support these doctrines and had books propounding them translated and spread throughout their lands.

Papal weakness vis-à-vis the monarchs was so pronounced that in 1773, Pope Clement XIV gave in to extreme pressure and abolished the Jesuits as a recognized religious order. The Jesuits were too committed to Counter-Reformation spirituality, too international in orientation, and not loyal enough to the monarchs to be suffered. Their suppression was an indication of the shifting ground in Europe. The Jesuits had been, of course, one of the primary forces of the Counter-Reformation. Now, with the Westphalian settlement firmly established, such continued emphasis on the reality of the universal spiritual power was a threat to the monarchs' control over their own territories. This is not because the monarchs were secularizing. Indeed, the Catholic monarchs of Europe were largely more committed to the uniform enforcement of Catholic orthodoxy in their territories than ever before while simultaneously wanting to drive the Jesuits out and minimize the power of the papacy. This situation might appear as a paradox or contradiction at first. But an understanding of the dynamic of confessionalization clarifies the situation. The monarchs needed a strong national Catholicism in order to increase their legitimacy and strength internally, and they needed a weak universal Catholicism for the same reason. During this period, then, we have to understand Catholicism as having a primarily national flavor, and it might even be appropriate to talk about national "Catholicisms."

In addition to these difficulties, there was an increasing tendency among intellectuals toward skepticism, rationalism, and empiricism. This tendency would develop over the course of the eighteenth century into what we call the Enlightenment. We have seen already how the relationship between the temporal power and the spiritual power broke down as Christendom crumbled, leading to the superiority of the material and the temporal over the spiritual and eternal. The same type of thing was happening in thought. The material world was increasingly broken away from the spiritual world and declared independent. Christianity is inherently sacramental. It proposes a world in which the material and temporal are united with the spiritual and the eternal, in which the particular is real and solid and yet finds its intelligibility and full realization in the universal. The drive of modernity was to undo this profoundly realist, and yet ultimately mysterious and incarnational, worldview. Rather, the Enlightenment thinkers tended to maintain that the material and temporal operated in a realm that was wholly independent of any spiritual reality that might or might not exist.

The rationalists among them argued that "unaided" or "natural" human reason could perceive and understand fundamental reality. Starting from a position of extreme doubt about physical experiences, philosophers such as René Descartes (1596–1650) built systems of thought that rested entirely on reason. If faith was valid, as Descartes thought it was, it was nevertheless not needed to gain an understanding of the material world, which was nothing more than objects in motion. Empiricists, such as John Locke, argued that our knowledge of the world comes directly from our experience of things. What we see is what we know and nothing more. Faith, if it was a legitimate source of knowledge at all, operated on an entirely different level and about a different subject matter. Early scientific thinkers such as Isaac Newton constructed intricate and mathematically sophisticated models that could predict the behavior of the observable world of things in time but that did not attempt to explain why things happened or what these things themselves really were. What these thinkers had in common was the conviction that the material world was separate from the spiritual world and that the rules that governed the material world were laws that we could discover and then use in order to manipulate our environment. Regardless of their philosophical disagreements, their work amounted to an extreme flattening of the universe. Everything that existed was really of the same kind of stuff, and it all obeyed the same kinds of laws, and human reason was capable of understanding this as an objective observer. Once we understood the laws of things and of thought, we could use this understanding to gain power over the world. Francis Bacon, the father of the scientific method, for example, claimed simply that knowledge was power, that the purpose of research was the dominance of nature.

Even among serious Catholic thinkers, a new type of realist scholasticism came often to replace the old medieval realism. This new realism was more Aristotelian than Thomistic. Rather than a thing's nature being an idea of God and so always aiming beyond itself to the supernatural, natures were imagined as operating in a closed "natural" order. Human beings had access to these natures through their "unaided" or "natural" reason and so could understand and work within the natural world without the necessary involvement of the supernatural or spiritual. This natural world was flat, operating according to its own metaphysical laws, and tended toward its own natural ends. These modern scholastics, of course, maintained the reality of the supernatural end of mankind and so of the necessity of revelation and grace, but these things came from above to work upon a natural world that, strictly speaking, did not need them in order to be itself. These thinkers maintained the superiority of the spiritual over the temporal, therefore, even while minimizing the two orders' essential relationality and giving the temporal, material world a theoretical space without an active God.

Not without a degree of similarity, many Enlightenment thinkers posited some form of Deism. Deists maintained that a creator god existed. He made the universe and was the source of its laws. After this initial creation, the universe ran on its own without his intervention. Some, but not all, Deists maintained that we would be held accountable to this god after death. The Deist god was a minimal god that they believed any rational person could come to acknowledge, but that this acknowledgement had little bearing on this person's understanding of the world around him. Deism was not far from extreme skepticism or atheism, and many thinkers, such as David Hume, pushed beyond it into these more radical positions. If the world simply obeyed disinterested laws, after all, and if our reason operated in an unaided and natural way in order to understand these laws, why did we need a god at all? Couldn't we just drop this nominalist, law-giving god and merely have the laws instead? What is the difference between having faith in an unknowable god who gives us knowable laws and just having faith in the laws, just knowing them and trusting them? What proof could we have of the reality of an entirely spiritual being when the spiritual itself was what was precisely beyond the realm of proof? But what is more, what need have we of the spiritual realm at all? If the material world is the one in which we encounter objects and in which we experience happiness and sadness, pleasure and pain, isn't it the only one we can really know anything about and, what is more, isn't it the only one that really matters? If the spiritual world were a realm that was merely stacked on top of the material realm, like the second story on a building, why couldn't we just drop it altogether and live comfortably in the first story? When Pierre-Simon Laplace, an important Enlightenment mathematician, was asked why he did not mention God in his work on the structure of the cosmos, he is reported to have responded, "I have no need for that hypothesis."

Enlightenment thinkers applied these ideas to society and politics as well. As with the world of things, they reasoned that the world of people must obey certain laws. By studying human beings, they could come to understand these laws. Then, in the same sort of way that a machine is designed and built, a better society could be designed and built. Reason was the measure of all things, including social things. Enlightenment thinkers thought not only that better governments could be designed but also that, through schools, education, and other social institutions, better people could be produced. There emerged, then, the modern idea of progress. The Enlightenment notion of progress rested on the notion that in the past people had been scared and vulnerable, with no understanding of the causes of the phenomena that they observed around them. This had led them into superstitions, religions, and systems of social oppression. Over time, however, human reason was peeling back these layers of obstruction, and truth was slowly emerging. Eventually, this progress would lead to the triumph of truth and, with it, humanity would achieve the peace and prosperity that it sought. Tradition was the drag on this process. Tradition had to be overthrown and everything exposed to the disinterested eye of reason. Reason could determine what should be kept and what should be discarded. Reason would build a perfect, or at least a much better, world. We should remember that the "religion" that they were observing was the religion of the divine right monarchs, the religion of social discipline, the religion that, in hindsight, seemed to be the source of the immense bloodshed and oppression of the previous two centuries. They were looking at the "religion" that was a product of the early modern period and not at historical Christianity. Their criticisms, then, were often not far from the mark, even if their optimism in progress was naive. Thinkers such as Voltaire popularized this sort of thought through both academic writing and popularly through novels, plays, and poetry.

In our history books, the Catholic Church is often presented as a solid opponent of the Enlightenment. It is very true that the popes of the period were highly suspicious of most Enlightenment thought. However, among the clerical elite, the theologians and the bishops, this was not so much the case. Many accepted a great deal of Enlightenment thought and tried to apply it to the Church. For example, it was common to believe that the traditional devotions of the faithful were simply superstition that had little spiritual value and that they should probably be eliminated. It was common to believe that the traditional understanding of monasticism as a properly contemplative vocation was misguided and that all monks should have an active vocation. It was common to believe that faith should be submitted to reason. It was common to believe that the spiritual power ought to be subservient to the temporal power in all but narrowly defined doctrinal matters. In fact, by the mid-eighteenth century, it was probably the case that most of the Church's clerical elite were proponents of one form of Enlightenment thought or another. Such "Enlightened Catholicism," we might call it, was, by the end of the century, the norm among the upper classes throughout much of Catholic Europe. This was not true, however, of the common people, who overwhelmingly retained a traditional piety along with a profoundly traditional way of life.

Similarly, many historians have been tempted to treat Enlightenment thought as at odds with the political systems of the eighteenth century. This is because many Enlightenment thinkers criticized monarchy and championed religious tolerance and individual freedoms that were not common in the absolutist, confessional states of the period. While this is true, it misses the more fundamental connection between eighteenth-century thought and eighteenth-century politics. At root, they shared a conviction in the superiority of the temporal and the material. For the absolutist monarch, the spiritual certainly existed, but it existed as his "religion" that operated within his state and according to his laws. For the Enlightenment thinker, the spiritual may exist, but if it did, it was either subservient to reason, as in Deism, or it was irrelevant to the functioning of the material world. In both cases, the temporal and material and, by extension, the "rational," became the universal principle at the expense of the spiritual. In politics, absolutist monarchs interacted with each other without reference to religion but, rather, according to the universal laws of power politics. In Enlightenment thought, the material world functioned without reference to the spiritual but according to universal physical laws. Both are totalizing or absolutist materialist visions.

What is more, the truth is that most Enlightenment thinkers supported some form of sovereign monarchy. The famous philosopher Immanuel Kant, who was completely dependent on the king of Prussia, articulated his understanding of free speech by writing, "Argue, as much as you want and about whatever you want, but obey!"[1] Most Enlightenment thinkers were very wary of democracy and suspicious of the masses, whom they thought to be too deeply religious and prejudiced. Rather, most preferred the idea of an "enlightened absolutist" who had the power to implement a comprehensive plan for a more perfect and rational society. Many eighteenth-century absolutist monarchs attempted to oblige them. Frederick the Great of Prussia (r. 1740–1786), for example, sought to organize his kingdom along strictly rational lines. He invited many philosophers, including Voltaire, to his court and patronized their work. His main interest, however, seems to have been the construction of the most effective army possible, and he was clever enough to understand that Enlightenment thought could be very helpful in this regard. Catherine the Great (r. 1762–1796) in Russia was also known as an enlightened absolutist. She brought Western concepts of government and education to Russia and reformed the empire, greatly expanding it and making it a true European power. But perhaps the best example is Joseph II of Austria (r. 1765–1790).

In 1780, Joseph II launched an ambitious reform effort throughout the Austrian Empire. The overriding principle was that there existed no aspect of life outside the purview of the state. For Joseph and his advisors, society ought to be organized like a giant machine, and the state was duty bound to build, tweak, and fine-tune this mechanism toward the end of general welfare. The institutions of traditional society, the customary liberties, obligations, and representative and regulatory mechanisms had to be reformed and rationally organized toward the interests of the state or else be eliminated. This included all aspects of religion. It was not that religion was unimportant or that Joseph believed Catholicism to be untrue. Rather, Joseph, like most of his peers, was an "enlightened Catholic." He believed that a proper Church would serve the strength of the state and that the practice of the Church, like anything else, was open to disinterested reason. If it wasn't serving the state in an optimally efficient manner, it must not be true religion.

He thought the Church's primary function was to educate and care for the population, to lead them to be better subjects. It was import-

---

[1] Immanuel Kant, "What Is Enlightenment?," in James Schmidt, trans., *What Is Enlightenment?: Eighteenth-Century Answers and Twentieth-Century Questions* (Berkeley, CA: University of California Press, 1996), 59.

ant, therefore, that the clergy taught the right things. For this reason, all the seminaries were taken over by the state and their curriculum directly controlled. Like many enlightened Catholics, Joseph couldn't make sense of contemplative religious orders. Contemplative monks and nuns make sense, of course, only within a traditional, corporate understanding of society, the understanding that underwrote the medieval idea of the three orders of society. Within this understanding, society is like a body with many parts. The parts are fundamentally different, and yet all benefit from each other's proper functioning. The prayer and the penance of the religious are, in traditional thought, not a waste of energy but rather serve all the faithful. For the enlightened mind, on the other hand, this makes little sense. Society is not a body but a machine. Each piece needs to work like a cog, moving the machine forward. In this line of thinking, the monks don't help the peasants unless they leave their cloister and actually serve them directly as pastors or teachers. To the enlightened thinker, such an active life would better serve society both religiously and politically, making society as a whole more efficient. And so, Joseph II abolished all contemplative orders which, as he said, "being utterly and completely useless to their neighbors ... could not be pleasing to God."[2] The substantial wealth confiscated from the abolished houses was diverted to finance Joseph II's other reforms of the Church. The institutions of the Church should be reformed, as Joseph said, "for pious purposes which would be at the same time useful to the state, such as the education of children who, while becoming Christians, would become good subjects."[3] Within Joseph's "flat," Enlightenment way of thinking, the interests of the state and the spiritual interests of the people had to be the same. What was good for the state would be good for their souls, and what would be good for their souls would be good for the state. This is why his "reform" wasn't just about property or power but was extended to even the smallest detail of worship, including candles, draperies, the number of Masses, music, pilgrimages, processions, feasts, indulgences, and preaching. Indeed, to Joseph II's mind, "the service of God is inseparable from the service of the State."[4]

There was, however, an inherent contradiction in such "enlight-

---

[2] Quoted in Derek Beales, *Prosperity and Plunder: European Catholic Monasteries in the Age of Revolution, 1650–1815* (Cambridge: Cambridge University Press, 2003), 476.
[3] Quoted in Beales, *Prosperity and Plunder*, 168.
[4] Quoted in G. P. Gooch, *Maria Theresa and Other Studies* (London: Longmans, Green and Co., 1951), 24.

ened absolutism." The arguments that it used against the authority of tradition and against established institutions and in favor of disinterested reason could, of course, be easily applied to the authority of kings. Perhaps having an absolute monarch was the most rational form of government, but perhaps it wasn't. Were monarchs such as Joseph II willing to open their own authority to such questioning? Of course not. In fact, the authority of such kings depended finally on the old understanding of society. Even to monarchs such as Joseph II, subjects needed to obey the king because he was the king, instituted by God, and not because they had concluded that his power was useful to them. Enlightened absolutism was really only an option when the Enlightenment remained an elite way of thinking and the masses retained a pre-Enlightenment, inherently sacramental worldview. Throughout the eighteenth century, this remained mostly the situation. The real world of real people remained rooted in faith and traditional in devotions. As modernity pressed on, this world would come under increasing strain.

The French Revolution

History is slow. Cultures change over the course of generations, not years. And yet, every once in a great while, there is an event of immense importance, an event that seems not only to emerge out of long-term trends but also to propel society suddenly in a particular direction, to accelerate change rapidly and decisively. The French Revolution was such an event. The French Revolution was such a decisive event that historians call the world that came before it the *ancien régime*, the old regime, in a way similar perhaps to how Christians talk about the Old Testament. It is not that the Old Testament slowly transitions into the New. Rather, a decisive event, the Incarnation of Christ, comes as a total surprise and yet clearly flows out of all that came before it. This surprise establishes the New in such a way that the world would never be the same. With not a little exaggeration, we can say that the French Revolution was like this. In fact, we often find ourselves talking about pre-revolutionary history in terms of how the revolution happened and talking about post-revolutionary history in terms of the consequences of it having happened.

France was the most powerful Catholic kingdom in Modern Europe. Like the rest of Europe in the aftermath of the wars of religion,

France had set about building itself as a confessional state. Indeed, in 1685, King Louis XIV revoked the Edict of Nantes, which had ended the religious civil war in France through toleration of Protestants. Louis XIV was a model absolutist, claiming at one point, "I am the state," and at another, "A thing is legal because I will it." Louis's absolutism rested on the theory of divine right, according to which he and no one else had been placed on the throne by God, and God ruled directly through him. Louis needed religious homogeneity in order for his power to be legitimized and maximized. He needed the Church. This is why he revoked the compromise with the Protestants. In the decades after Louis XIV's death in 1715, this ideology did not change, and the Church in France was steadily integrated more fully into the royal regime.

However, it is important not to imagine *ancien régime* France as a big, centralized, bureaucratic, and administrative state that was run by a theocratic dictator. We carry around with us images of twentieth-century totalitarianism and sometimes mistakenly read that form of government back to the absolutists. Instead, while the French monarch was absolutist, the state as an institution was most certainly not totalitarian. The government of France was a crazy quilt of different jurisdictions and different regions and cities with their own laws and customs. The law in one part of the country was not the same as the law in another part of the country. There was an aristocratic hierarchy of nobles, which had certain powers and certain rights, that terminated with the king. There was a commoner hierarchy that moved from the peasants up through the middle class and the officials of the government, which had its own powers and rights that also terminated with the king. There was a clerical hierarchy, stretching from the common parish priest through the monastic houses and to the most powerful archbishops, and it, too, more or less terminated with the king. Each of these hierarchies had different manifestations in different parts of the kingdom and interacted with each other in vastly different ways at different levels. Their rights and powers had largely grown up over centuries of custom and negotiation. The king's theoretically absolute power necessarily worked through these structures. The Church was wholly integrated into this rule.

The system began to break down in the last quarter of the eighteenth century. The kingdom was in massive debt, and the crown needed more tax revenue. The nobles and the commoners, represented by the wealthy middle class called the *bourgeoisie*, resisted. What is more, the economy was in shambles. There had been years of bad harvests, and peasants were actually starving in the countryside. Many poor people flooded into the cities seeking food and work. This growing urban class increasingly blamed the whole system for their plight. Enlightenment ideas had spread, and notions of equality and natural rights were increasingly popular with the middle class. These ideas severely undermined the theory of the divine right of kings and convinced many people that they could design a better government. Unlike the monarchs in other countries, such as Joseph II in Austria, Louis XV, who ruled from 1715 to 1774, had not co-opted Enlightenment ideas, defusing their radical implications. His heir, Louis XVI, followed in his rather inept footsteps.

By 1789, the kingdom was in crisis. Louis XVI gave in to pressure and called a meeting of the Estates General. This was an old medieval institution that had not been summoned since 1614. It was a sort of representative body for the kingdom that could be called in times of crisis so that the kingdom could work together in order to overcome the trial. The absolutists, for obvious reasons, had not been interested in invoking this body, and so it was a sign of serious weakness when Louis XVI did so. Everyone knew this. The Estates General was organized into three groups, or "Estates": the nobility, the clergy, and the commoners. Representatives from the three Estates started fighting immediately. The Estates General was organized according to the traditional corporate idea of society, with each of the three orders having one vote. This seemed grossly unfair to the Third Estate, the commoners, who, of course, made up the vast majority of the population. The representatives of the Third Estate were entirely made up of the middle class (there was not a single peasant among them), and they were the most imbued with Enlightenment ideas. With the support of enlightened members of the two other estates, they clamored for constitutional government. Finally, convinced that the Estates General was incapable of enacting the reforms they wanted, the Third Estate and its allies broke with it and declared themselves the National Assembly. It was clear that the *bourgeoisie* were now the most powerful group in the kingdom.

Rumors started flying that the king was going to use the army to disband the National Assembly. In response, an urban mob marched on the Bastille, an old fortress and prison. They killed the commander and marched around Paris with his head on a pike. At the same time, peasants in the countryside rose up and attacked their lords. This was called the Great Fear, and many nobles fled France. This outbreak of violence was the beginning of the Revolution.

The revolutionaries rallied around the slogan "Liberty, Equality, and Fraternity," and the National Assembly took immediate action, publishing two sweeping decrees. The first was the *Decree Abolishing the Feudal System*. This decree's purpose was to end the system of diverse rights, privileges, and jurisdictions and replace it with a uniform, centralized system. It called for a single judicial system and a single law code. It called for a uniform tax administration. It called for the end of class privilege and the opening of every office to every man. It called for the end of all customary land and other property rights and the turning of all property into, essentially, private property that could be owned by anyone. Remember, the Church had been nearly completely integrated into the system of the *ancien régime*, and so it was directly implicated in nearly every aspect of this decree. Priests were now to be paid by the state, becoming essentially government employees. The tithe was abolished. This is important. The tithe was not voluntary as we think of it now. Rather, it was a tax that was paid directly to the Church. With this money, the Church not only ran the parishes but also was the chief social services provider. It cared for the poor; ran education, hospitals, and orphanages; and performed countless other services. All of this was now centralized into the revolutionary state. The abolishing of the feudal system was a reduction of the three hierarchies of society—the aristocratic, the clerical, and the commoner—to one. Everyone would be a commoner, and there would be one central state that managed their rights and responsibilities.

This result was buttressed with the second degree of the National Assembly, the *Declaration of the Rights of Man and Citizen*. This document advanced a radical version of enlightened thought. It declared "Men are born and remain free and equal in rights," and that "the principle of all sovereignty resides essentially in the nation," and that "liberty consists in the freedom to do everything which injures no one else." Law, rather than being the will of the king, the document declared, "is the expression of the general will." Taken together, these two decrees represented the radical restructuring of French society. They called for its flattening and its standardization. Everyone would be equal, and everyone would live under one uniform and ubiquitous government. Here, perhaps, we see the inconsistency that had lain beneath the efforts of the Enlightened Absolutists coming to the fore. The full centralization and rationalization of government didn't need a king, let alone the nobles or clergy.

Unsurprisingly, Louis XVI declined to sign the decrees. A mob marched on his palace and placed the king and his family under a type of house arrest. The National Assembly established a constitutional monarchy. They then set about establishing the new order. They radically reorganized the country into departments, similar to American counties, of roughly the same size; they established a centralized and universal court system; they established uniform taxes. They established that all tax-paying males could vote, ensuring that the middle class would retain power. In 1790, they also established the Civil Constitution of the Clergy and other laws concerning the Church. They unilaterally abolished the existing dioceses and established in their place one diocese for each department, aligning Church jurisdiction directly with civil jurisdiction. They declared that bishops were to be elected, just like any civil official, and the pope's only role would be to be informed after the fact. They dissolved all convents and monasteries and forbade the taking of vows in the future. They confiscated the property of the Church in order to pay the country's debts. They declared that the people would elect their own pastors and that the state would pay their salaries according to a fixed and universal pay scale. And, perhaps most importantly, they required all clergy to swear an oath of loyalty to the National Assembly. This was a direct attempt to "nationalize" the Church.

We are seeing here the ironic realization of the Gallican tendencies that the monarchy had been fostering for well over a hundred years. The Westphalian settlement had essentially asserted that each kingdom had one sovereign power, the temporal power, and that the clergy operated under that power. The absolutists had fostered this idea even while trying to maintain that their royal power came from the universal and transcendent, from the spiritual side of reality. They were trying to maintain that their power was still the temporal power of the Church, as it had been understood for over a thousand years, but that the temporal power was now, somehow, superior to the spiritual power. This was not tenable: Christian temporal power could only finally make sense if it operated below the spiritual power. The particular, the temporal, simply could not both assert the existence of the universal and at the same time trump the universal. It was a contradiction. The revolutionary government solved the contradiction by essentially denying that the new state was the temporal power. The state was no longer the temporal power of Christianity; it was just the civil power, just the state, and its sovereignty came not from above, but from below, from the nation or from disinterested reason. Similar to the material world in Enlightenment thought, their rule simply operated in a different realm than any truth that there might be to Christianity or any consequences that might result from grace, and their realm encompassed all of human governance. In nature, there was no rock that was exempt from the law of gravity, and in revolutionary France, there were no men that were exempt from the law of the state. The state's power, therefore, was not conditioned by the Church at all, and the clergy were just another batch of citizens with a job to do.

About half of the clergy refused to swear the oath to the new state. They became known as the nonjuring clergy. Out of 134 bishops, only 5 gave in. Those who refused the oath were removed from their positions to make room for government clergy. Pope Pius VI quickly condemned the actions of the government, calling the Civil Constitution of the Clergy "heretical," "sacrilegious and schismatic," and "devised and published with the sole design of utterly destroying the Catholic religion." Pius exhorted the faithful priests to stand firm against the state, and he called on all the faithful Catholics to not abandon the faith of their fathers, "for it is the one true religion which both confers eternal life and makes safe and thriving civil societies." Pius continued:

> Carefully beware of lending your ears to the treacherous speech of the philosophy of this age which leads to death.... Listen carefully to the message of your lawful pastors who are still living ... Finally, in one word, stay close to us. For no one can be in the Church of Christ without being in unity with its visible head and founded on the See of Peter.[5]

The pope declared that every priest and bishop who swore the oath was suspended from his office and that all elections which occurred according to the new law were null and void. The French Church was officially rent by schism. This schism opened up divisions among the revolutionaries and their sympathizers. Many, especially the peasants, now moved to defend the old order. They had been opposed to corruption and to the oppression that they had been subject to under the old regime, but they were not radicals. Their opposition to the nobles had largely been in defense of their old rights and liberties and not based on an aggressive desire to establish entirely new rights, and they were

---

[5] Pius VI, *Charitas* (1791), §32.

certainly not ready to abandon their priests.

Up to this point, the revolution had been mainly in the hands of the well-to-do *bourgeoisie*. They had instituted massive changes, but overall they wanted stability. This was why they hadn't deposed the king outright but rather had established a constitutional monarchy. They were not the only faction on the revolutionary side, however. There was another group made up of radical intellectuals and urban tradesmen and workers who were known by their nickname, *sansculottes*, and were organized in what were called Jacobin clubs. They were far, far more radical and felt that the revolutionary leadership was too moderate. In 1792, France went to war with Austria and Prussia, who were worried that the revolution might spread. The war went initially very poorly for France. The mob in Paris blamed the weakness of the government, and they started murdering clergy who hadn't sworn the oath and any nobles they could find. The government was compelled to hold elections, and the radical Jacobins were swept into power.

They declared France a republic. King Louis XVI was tried and found guilty of treason and on January 21, 1793, he was executed. Ten months later, they executed the queen, Marie Antoinette. These actions sent shockwaves through the royal courts of Europe. Britain, the Netherlands, Spain, Portugal, Sardinia, and Naples all joined Prussia and Austria in the war against France. The war, though, became a part of the French revolutionary ideology. For the radicals now running the government, the revolution wasn't just for France. Rather, the French army would free all the peoples of Europe. Animated with revolutionary zeal, the French army had remarkable success on the battlefield.

Internally, the government declared a state of emergency. They suspended the legislature and the Committee of Public Safety was set up to secure the republic against all enemies, internal and external, and to carry out the radical republican program. The committee took dictatorial powers. They launched what became known as the Reign of Terror. They arrested anyone suspected of being counter-revolutionary or not radical enough. Hundreds of thousands of people were arrested. Around fifty thousand people were executed. During 1793 and into 1794, the guillotine in Paris worked nearly nonstop. This was how the war internally was being fought. The war externally was another problem. The government issued the *levée en masse*, the mass levy, which was a general call to military service of all able-bodied men. They raised an army of 850,000 soldiers and propagandized them with an intense patriotism. One man wrote home to his mother: "When the fatherland calls us to her defense, we ought to fly there . . . Our life, our wealth, and our talents do not belong to us. It is to the nation, the fatherland, that all that belongs."[6] This worked. The tide of the war turned in France's favor.

The radical government was simultaneously attempting to build a utopia of reason and "public virtue." In this "Republic of Virtue," as they called it, nothing traditional or established mattered. Everything was eligible for a complete restructuring. This most especially included the Church. The nonjuring clergy were directly persecuted and liable to end up in jail or executed. But now the traitorous clergy who had sworn the oath to the revolutionary regime came equally under persecution. Priests were compelled to marry in order to prove their loyalty to the new order. Under intense pressure, twenty-three of the remaining eighty-five bishops apostatized; twenty-four of them abdicated; the remaining thirty-eight accepted persecution. Monasteries and Church buildings were burned, resulting in both a horrifying loss of life and of priceless medieval texts and artifacts. Christianity was effectively abolished. Theophilanthropy was to take its place. This was a deistic religion designed to be both rational and to inculcate the docility and "virtues" that would form people into good citizens. The churches were transformed into "temples of reason," and new festivals were made up and new liturgies devised to replace the devotional life of the masses. Education became the sole responsibility of the state. Marriage became a merely civil contract, and divorce was legalized. The unbelievable hubris of these "enlightened" thugs led them to "rationalize" the calendar itself. They made the weeks ten days long, with one day of rest, abolishing Sunday altogether (the seven-day week, of course, stretched all the way back to Genesis). They changed the months to equal lengths and changed their names. They started the years over, with year 1 being the first year of their republic. All people were known simply as "citizen."

We see here, clearly, the radical implications of the total flattening of the world and of society. If everything is the same and all is open to the power of unaided human reason, then nothing lies beyond our control. There is no justification for tolerance of the "irrational." There is no justification for respect for the mystery of tradition, of

---

[6] Quoted in Dennis Sherman, *Western Civilization: Sources, Images, and Interpretations*, 2nd ed. (New York: McGraw Hill, 2008), 61.

religion, of institutions of immemorial duration. All is the same. All is clear. People resist only because they've been deluded into superstition and servility. They had to be woken up! They had to be compelled to move into the brilliance of enlightenment, into the clarity of reason and "public virtue." All resistance had to be destroyed because all resistance was merely entrenched tyranny. Law structured society, as natural laws structured things, and law could be changed.

There was insurrection in the countryside. The peasants and their noble allies were mostly not interested in such excesses, and when the revolutionary government shut down and sold off their parish churches and arrested or drove into hiding their priests, it was too much. When the government came for their sons in order to force them into the army, they rebelled. In one region known as the Vendée, they actually formed an army made up of tens of thousands of volunteers and fought toe-to-toe with the revolutionary military machine. The republicans sent in overwhelming force and adopted horrendous tactics of total war, killing and burning all that stood before them. The rebellion was finally crushed, and the republican general wrote to his masters in Paris:

> The Vendée is no more... I have buried it in the woods and marshes of Savenay... According to your orders, I have trampled their children beneath our horses' feet; I have massacred their women, so they will no longer give birth to brigands. I do not have a single prisoner to reproach me. I have exterminated them all. The roads are sown with corpses. At Savenay, brigands are arriving all the time claiming to surrender, and we are shooting them non-stop... Mercy is not a revolutionary sentiment.[7]

Even though the republican government was having military success both internally and externally, resistance continued to grow. The excesses of the Terror and absurdities of the Republic of Virtue had gone too far. The republican government was eventually overthrown by more moderate revolutionaries. The Terror was turned against the radicals and then was shut down. Similarly, much of the Republic of Virtue's more extreme legislation was scaled back, and many people who had initially apostatized returned to the Catholic Church. To

---

[7] Quoted in Norman Davies, *Europe: A History* (Oxford: Oxford University Press, 1996), 310.

many, the nonjuring priests who had stood up to the republican government were heroes, even though many, maybe most of them, had been either killed or driven into exile. In response, the new government afforded some degree of toleration to Catholicism.

The new government could not restore order, however. There were constant revolts from royalists on one side and radicals on the other. The people wanted order. They demanded an end to the chaos. Napoleon Bonaparte gave it to them. Napoleon was a young, successful general who was a hero of the revolutionary army. In 1799, he outmaneuvered a group that was attempting to overthrow the government and swept in to "protect" the revolution. He quickly drew up a new constitution that provided him immense powers and put it up for a vote. It passed overwhelmingly. Napoleon emerged as both a dictator and as the "Savior of the Revolution."

Napoleon set about moderating the ideology of revolution even while consolidating many of the changes that had been implemented. His was a practical form of rationality rather than an arrogant and inflexible form of rationality. To Napoleon, what worked was what mattered. He launched a major legal reform, instituting a universal code of law. His education reform centralized and standardized education throughout the country: every child would have the same education, and every child would learn Parisian French. He centralized the monetary system, giving the government control of the economy. At the same time, he built a massive system of secret police forces and informers. His government heavily censored political speech. Napoleon was a new type of "enlightened absolutist." The old absolutists had been trapped by their need for transcendent religion in order to justify their divine right rule. Napoleon had no such need. As he said, "My political method is to govern men as the majority of them want to be governed. That, I think, is the way to recognize the sovereignty of the people. It was by making myself Catholic that I ended the war in the Vendée; by making myself Muslim that I established myself in Egypt; by making myself ultramontaine that I won over the minds of the Italians. If I had to govern a nation of Jews, I should rebuild the temple of Solomon."[8] Religion for Napoleon was not necessary, but it might be practical. As he stated, "Religion is excellent stuff for keeping the common people quiet."

In 1802, Napoleon, therefore, made a concordat, or treaty, with

---

[8] Napoleon Bonaparte, *Documents sur la Negociation du Concordat* (Paris, 1891), 1:76–77.

the papacy. This agreement allowed Catholicism to again function legally in France. However, it was in no way a restoration of Catholicism in anything like its pre-revolutionary form. Rather, the Church would now operate entirely within the state administration itself. Its property still belonged to the state or whomever it had sold it to. The clergy were still paid by the state and still had to take an oath of loyalty to Napoleon and his regime. But the seminaries could reopen. The parishes and cathedrals could again sing Mass and baptize and marry and bury their faithful. The agreement officially instituted the principles of Gallicanism and mandated that they be taught in all seminaries. Under this agreement, the pope had merely doctrinal authority, and even that authority was tempered by councils and by tradition. The government appointed bishops, though now, significantly, the papacy would have veto power. The papacy had to agree to the terms offered because it had to ensure that the great mass of faithful Catholics in France could practice their faith and receive the sacraments. Napoleon didn't mind the return of Catholicism. He didn't care either way about whether peasants could say their rosaries. He wanted control of the institutions of his nation. He wanted the power. The pope had to concede this control because he *did* care about the peasants and their rosaries. Again, though, we can see how absolutism as a political theory and Gallicanism as an ecclesiological theory had laid the groundwork for Napoleon. In Napoleon's regime, the practice of religion became a private affair of the devout even while the temporal aspects of religion—its officials and pastors, its property, its processions down the street, even the ringing of the bells—became affairs of state, and none of it could be done without Napoleon's permission. As long as he was willing to allow orthodox teaching in faith and morals and the practice of the sacraments, the papacy had to concede.

Napoleon's regime was not a confessional state in the absolutist mold. This was put on shocking display when, in 1804, Napoleon held another popular vote. This time it concerned whether France should be declared and empire and Napoleon its emperor. The people voted yes. How are emperors made, however? Charlemagne had been crowned by the pope in the year 800, as had every emperor in the West since. Napoleon, therefore, invited Pope Pius VII to Paris for the coronation. The pope came. Everyone expected a normal imperial coronation. However, things did not go as expected. The ceremony was held in Notre Dame Cathedral. Pius was seated before the altar, and Napoleon approached. Rather than kneeling before the pontiff to receive his imperial crown, Napoleon strode up to the pope, picked the crown up from the table to his side, and crowned himself emperor. Napoleon was emperor, indeed, but he was not a medieval Christian emperor, nor was he an absolutist king claiming some sort of divine right for his rule. Napoleon was the emperor because he had the power and the people wanted him to have it. He needed nothing more than this. This was a move into the pagan, into the Machiavellian, and it should not surprise us that Napoleon's empire was self-consciously modeled not on the Christian Holy Roman Empire of Charlemagne but on the pagan Roman Empire of Diocletian. Christianity, for Napoleon, operated within his regime. For him and his supporters, in reality everything was temporal and particular; nothing was real about the spiritual or the universal except the felt reality of the power that they justified. With Napoleon, the Machiavellian strand of modern politics displaced the absolutist strand. This was the beginning of a return to a form of paganism.

Assuming the office of the ancient Caesars, Napoleon was happy to tolerate Christianity as long as it was a Christianity that buttressed his power and did not undermine it. This cynicism was flagrantly apparent in 1806 when Napoleon issued a universal catechism that he ordered be used in all the dioceses of the empire. After stating that every Christian owed love, respect, obedience, fidelity, military service, and taxes to Napoleon, the catechism read:

Question: Why are we subject to all these duties toward our emperor?

Answer: First, because God, who has created empires and distributes them according to his will, has, by loading our emperor with gifts both in peace and in war, established him as our sovereign and made him the agent of his power and his image upon earth. To honor and serve our emperor is therefore to honor and serve God himself. Secondly, because our Lord Jesus Christ himself, both by his teaching and his example, has taught us what we owe to our sovereign. Even at his very birth he obeyed the edict of Caesar Augustus; he paid the established tax; and while he commanded us to render to God those things which belong to God, he also commanded us to render unto Caesar those things which are Caesar's....

Question: What must we think of those who are wanting in their duties toward our emperor?

Answer: According to the apostle Paul, they are resisting the order established by God himself and render themselves worthy of eternal damnation.[9]

Like the ancient pagans, Napoleon was driven by the pursuit of glory. "I am an upstart soldier," he declared. "My domination will not survive the day when I cease to be strong, and therefore feared." Napoleon, therefore, sought conquest. His armies became devastatingly effective. They were rationally organized with an officer corps based purely on merit. They used experimental new tactics. But what was most important was that Napoleon had built, for the first time in centuries, a citizen army. This army was motivated not by money or by the threat of violence but by intense love of country and pride in their prowess. They were motivated by the conviction that they were right, that France had the right and even the duty to spread its revolutionary system throughout Europe. And they were willing to give their lives for their country. Under Napoleon, we see the first flowering of what would become modern nationalism.

In the High Middle Ages, the Crusaders had been drawn from all parts of Europe, from all kingdoms and language groups, and they fought together as a universal Christian army against the enemies of the faith, dying as martyrs. After the Reformation, this aspect of Christianity was divided up into particular confessional kingdoms. It wouldn't be much of a stretch to say that the wars of religion were fought by crusaders on both sides. The armies were particular, but the ideal was still universal and Christian. Now, the zeal and the sacrifice of martyrdom was shifted away from Christianity altogether and toward the nation. France was, in a sense, now holy, and to sacrifice for France was the height of glory and honor. The nationalism that grew out of the French Revolution and blossomed under Napoleon demanded the homogenization of the interior of the country: everyone had to become, first and foremost, a Frenchman with all other identifications either eliminated or reduced to secondary importance. It also demanded a break from any sort of universal solidarity. France provided its own legitimacy, and expansion of its power was a part of this legitimacy.

---

[9] *The Imperial Catechism*, in *Readings in European History: From the Opening of the Protestant Revolt to the Present Day*, ed. James Harvey Robinson, vol. 2. (Boston: Ginn and Co., 1904–1906), 509–510.

Napoleon fought nearly all the powers of Europe and won victory after victory. By 1809, his empire stretched from Spain to the borders of Russia. Napoleon abolished the Holy Roman Empire as an institution. The Holy Roman Empire had been established by Charlemagne more than one thousand years prior. It was largely powerless by the nineteenth century, but it was symbolic of the unity of Christendom, as was the papacy. That unity was now even theoretically finished. When the papacy refused to support Napoleon in his conquests, he conquered the papal territories in Italy and took pope Pius VII hostage. Bringing the pope to France, Napoleon held him as a prisoner for four years. Napoleon demanded that the pope approve of his rule; the aged pontiff refused. In response, Napoleon essentially disbanded the Roman Church. The pope hadn't given in, but it was clear that Napoleon was in charge. The French armies imposed their revolutionary form of government everywhere they went, abolishing the old order and establishing Napoleon's system of rationalized and centralized administration and universal citizenship. Everywhere they went, they flattened, they standardized, and they centralized.

But Napoleon began to face a problem. The very sources of his strength, as they spread through Europe, became equally sources of strength to his opponents. The nationalism of a conqueror has the predictable consequence of strengthening the nationalism of the defeated. The mechanisms of centralized control that gave French nationalism its material and human strength worked just as well for Napoleon's opponents. As the French spread the fruit of their revolution more thoroughly, they found themselves facing resistance of a more effective design. Finally, Napoleon miscalculated. In 1812, he launched an invasion of Russia, sending six hundred thousand men to conquer the vast eastern empire. It was a disaster. As the French army retreated, Russia, along with just about every other country in Europe, went on the offensive. Only thirty thousand French soldiers made it back to Paris. Back in France, Napoleon tried to compel Pius VII to support him. The now-weakened pope refused, giving moral authority and conviction to Napoleon's enemies both inside France and without. Finally, in 1814, Napoleon was defeated and was exiled to the island of Elba. However, this was not quite the end. Less than a year later, Napoleon escaped from Elba, returned to France, and took control once again. He was finally defeated for good at the Battle of Waterloo in 1815.

The French Revolution and the Napoleonic Wars changed the

face of Europe. The *ancien régime* was overthrown not only in France but also effectively throughout Europe. Everywhere, rationalized and universal law codes, tax systems, administrative apparatuses, and massive armies of highly trained soldiers came to dominate. Society was no longer viewed through the corporate idea of different orders with different levels of rights and responsibilities that culminated in the king, who answered for his divine right to God himself. The Enlightenment's flattening of reality began to change society into a great mass of interchangeable people, of citizens with identical, abstract rights. The laws of nature had once needed a God, first nominalist and then Deist, in order for people to accept their universal validity. But once the laws were accepted, God could be done away with. Similarly, modernity had first needed absolutist monarchs as the source of the law, the sovereignty, that governed and organized and marshaled all the resources of man's temporal existence. But once sovereignty was accepted as the basis of social order, divine right, like God himself, could be done away with.

Christianity had been the basis of political authority. The confessional states needed its universality for their legitimacy. They needed a transcendent good and truth to motivate men to fight for their particular causes. This was now changing. For the intellectuals, the Enlightenment had provided universal reason as a substitute, and for the masses, nationalism looked promising as a replacement for Christianity. Christianity was no longer the basis of institutions. Even the hospitals and schools and orphanages that the Church had run for centuries generally became departments of the state, and the tithes, the taxes that had been paid directly to the clergy, now went to the civil powers, with only voluntary donations going to the now-marginalized Church. The Church was no longer the universal bond that held all the nations of the baptized together but was, rather, an aspect of domestic policy of different relative importance in different countries. The victors hated Napoleon, no doubt, but they generally came to share his Machiavellian understanding of the state and the proper role of the Church. Even after his defeat, for example, Napoleon's concordat with the pope remained the law in France and became the model for the concordats demanded by rulers throughout Europe as they reestablished their governments. While clearly unfavorable to the Church, these agreements did maintain a limited place for the papacy in episcopal elections, and so papal involvement remained, even if the clerical hierarchy as an independent source of social order was generally replaced with unitary states throughout Europe.

These changes did not happen all at once. Napoleon had been defeated by a coalition of monarchs who still claimed divine right and still saw themselves as defending Christian civilization. In fact, in the aftermath of the Revolution, a type of conservatism came to dominate. But these powers and the societies they ruled had been definitively changed by the Revolution, and the consequences of this change would be increasingly felt over the next hundred years.

2. The Nineteenth Century

The Industrial Revolution

The nineteenth century was a century of rapid and expansive change. In history, we often find ourselves talking about governments and intellectuals, about wars and ideas. This is mostly because it is easy to find out about these things. There are lots of books, newspaper articles, and government documents that tell us about what the social elite were up to. It is harder to see the common people. In the centuries between 1500 and 1800, there had been changes to the lives of common people. There are always changes. But these changes had not been dramatic. In 1800, the vast majority of Europeans were still peasants, working the land in a manner that was not that different from the way peasants had been working the land since the fall of the Roman Empire. The vast majority of these peasants never traveled far from the village of their birth, and they knew by name nearly everyone with whom they interacted. The vast majority of these peasants retained a traditional Christian faith and worshiped through liturgies and devotions that had not changed much over the centuries. They continued to live in a sacramental world.

All this changed over the course of the nineteenth century. The entire economic and social landscape changed dramatically, catching up with the quickly advancing ideas of the Enlightenment and the political structures of the French Revolution. The blueprints for the new social architecture had been drafted over the course of the previous several centuries, but it was during the nineteenth that the edifice itself was constructed. It was during this century that the new "laws" of thought and action were internalized into a new culture, a new way of life. We call the economic transformation the Industrial Revolu-

The Industrial Revolution

tion because its most dramatic manifestation was the construction of immense industrial cities that produced an unprecedented volume of goods. But the change's roots began before the first modern factories were built. The economic transformation began in the countryside. The premodern agricultural economy was profoundly local. Most food was consumed by the people who produced it. This means that the crops of any given region had to be diverse and that the work of the peasants had to include not only farming but also animal husbandry, forestry, fishing, and other forms of small-scale production. This lifestyle was predominately carried out according the customary practices and customary rules.

To generalize dramatically, in premodern Europe the countryside was typically divided up into estates. These estates each had a lord, a noble who held title to the estate. This was absolutely not the same as owning the land. Instead, he had certain rights over the land and was owed certain things from the peasants who lived on the estate. So, for example, he might be able to demand a couple days a week of work from the peasants in his fields, or he might be able to demand certain payments to him in eggs or pigs or chickens. He was also generally the local judge and magistrate, what we would think of as the police and judiciary system. When there were local conflicts or disputes, it was his job to adjudicate. The peasants, however, also had rights. They had a right to work the land that their families had worked. They had a right to owe to the lord what they had customarily owed. He could not just increase his extractions. Most importantly, they had rights to the use of the resources of the estate. So, for example, if there was a forest on the land, they would have rights to collect a certain amount of firewood every year. If there was pastureland, they would have the right to graze their flocks and herds on it. If there was a river, they might have rights to fish in it. If there was a mill on the estate, they would probably have a right to use it on certain days a month in order to grind their flour. Nobody could just change these rights because nobody was in charge of them. They were the laws of the estate because they were the way the people on the estate lived and had lived for as long as anyone could remember. This was a very stable and very, very local way of life.

The problem, of course, was that this traditional way of life was terribly inefficient. It was not easily adapted to new methods. It was not capable of taking advantage of the comparative advantage of certain regions over other regions. For example, it might be the case that the weather and soil of a certain estate made it perfect for the growing of grain and the conditions on another estate made it perfect for the raising of cattle. The most efficient thing would be for the one to produce nothing but grain and the other to produce nothing but beef and then for them to trade; the traditional way of life, however, could only accommodate a little bit of such commercialized agriculture. This way of life began to change in the seventeenth and especially in the eighteenth centuries. The tendency was to increasingly treat the estates as the private property of their lords and the peasants as mere renters. The traditional way of life was based on custom and tradition. Custom and tradition, though, were not considered by the enlightened mind to be rational. So, they were steadily undone by positive law that was created by the sovereign states that were growing in the period.

Predictably, these new laws favored the powerful at the expense of the weak. As the lords gained property rights, they started to use the property in a manner that maximized its efficient production. Sometimes, this movement is called "enclosure." It is called this because the commons, the land and resources that everyone had a certain right to, were enclosed by fences and turned into the private property of the lord. As this movement gained steam, agriculture became more and more commercialized. Comparative advantage could be maximized, and so overall agricultural production increased. However, the peasants' way of life was completely destroyed. Instead of having customary rights that no one controlled, they were turned into hired farm workers who rented their own cottages and plots. In the traditional way of life, if a peasant was born into a community, he was a member of it, and the community would share the resources that it had in order to give him the work he needed to support his family. As agriculture was commercialized, however, this changed. The farm owners only needed as many workers as they needed; to pay for more would be inefficient. This meant that many peasants became unemployed, something that was basically impossible in the traditional way of life. There emerged for the first time a class of rural poor. This has to be understood properly. In the traditional way of life, in a sense, everyone was poor. They lived a basically subsistence lifestyle that was rather precarious. If there were a couple bad harvests, for example, famine was a real possibility. Their community, though, was a unit that cared for each other, and they always had certain rights to certain resources. In commercialized agriculture, however, while overall wealth and agricultural production increased, many peasants had no right to any share of it. These peasants, desperate, often went to the cities looking for work.

Commercialized agriculture, therefore, produced both the food necessary and the surplus population necessary to build cities, and what was built in the cities were factories. The factory was the great invention of the period. The idea was fairly simple. All the steps in the production of a particular good would be brought under one roof. Then, the labor would be subdivided into the smallest units possible so that the workers could do each step very quickly. The key to the factory was thinking of production as a single machine, with both mechanical and human components. The theorists of the factories thought of the workers as just cogs in the larger machine, and their drive was to minimize the effects of human imperfection through increasing automation and through a reduction in the need for skilled labor. Compared to the peasants and tradesmen of the old order, the factories were incredibly efficient. In the 1780s, Britain produced forty million yards of cotton cloth a year. In 1850, they produced two billion yards, fifty times as much. Commercialized agriculture spread, cities grew, factories were built, and the whole social world changed. In the mid-eighteenth century, 90 percent of the population had been farmers. By 1850, in England, more than half of the population lived in cities. This was the Industrial Revolution.

The Industrial Revolution was, first and foremost, about machines. As we have seen, during the Enlightenment, it became normal to think of the world as a giant machine. It was made up of many little pieces that all followed the same laws, and if you just assembled them correctly, you could produce a new machine that performed some new task. This notion animated both the commercialization of agriculture and the construction of states. During the Industrial Revolution, though, the machine took on a whole new importance. The steam engine was really what made it possible. Before the invention of the steam engine, machines had serious limitations. Their sources of power were directly tied to the natural world. In fact, there were only a few such sources: muscle, either human or animal; wind; and water. These sources of power had limitations. Muscle had to rest and be fed. Wind and water were either there or they weren't. Machines, therefore, had to be integrated into nature. The population of people and animals had to be fairly widely distributed across the land that supported them. Every once in a while, when the environment allowed it, a wind or water mill would be built. But these machines could not be concentrated, and neither could populations of men or animals. But this all changed with the steam engine. The steam engine could be placed anywhere. Its fuel, coal, was dug out of the ground and shipped to where it was needed. Coal could be stored, bought, and sold. The fuel was a commodity. Wind and water could not be owned, neither could the muscles of other men. In a sense, the old machines took from nature's abundance. The steam engine, on the other hand, broke free from nature.

Because of the steam engine, factories could be concentrated in cities. Because of the steam locomotives and steam ships, the human populations that the factories required could be concentrated and fed by farms far away. Before steam transportation, things were moved by animals or by wind power. Goods normally traveled by river or sea. Their movement was limited and still tied to geography and the natural world, which no one owned. This changed with the railroads and the steam ships. Steam power tied the whole economy together. The raw materials could be transported to the factories. The factories themselves could run. The food for the workers could be shipped into the cities. The goods from the factories could be shipped to markets far away. The constraints of nature became less and less relevant. The Industrial Revolution was marked by an increase in power, an increase in production and efficiency, as more and more aspects of the economic machine became commodified. One pound of coal was as good as another; one hour of labor was as good as another; one yard of finished cloth was as good as another. As everything became property that could be converted to money, everything became a commodity capable of efficient allocation through prices, and the machine that was the economy became more and more efficient. This was the birth of capitalism.

The Industrial Revolution started in England and spread throughout Europe over the course of the nineteenth century. The increased production was staggering. Britain's national product tripled between 1780 and 1850. The population of Europe exploded from 175 million to 266 million in the same period. The middle class, the class of people who manage things and move money, ballooned. As the philosopher James Mill said, "The heads that invent . . . the hands that execute, the enterprise that projects, and the capital by which these projects are carried into operation all come from the middle class."[10] There

---

[10] James Mill, "Article IV" *Westminster Review* 1, (1824): 68–69.

were other consequences as well. Europe was deforested as commercial agriculture spread and the need for wood increased. Mines and factories produced waste that was dumped into the soil and rivers. This was the genesis of pollution and environmental destruction. But the most shocking consequence was the creation of the poor, urban working class, a brand-new social class.

The urban working class was made up of people who had once been farmers and artisans but were now factory workers and miners. They lived a brutally hard life. To generalize, they worked twelve to sixteen hours a day, earning just enough for food and shelter. They were treated as little more than pieces of the machines, and efficiency was all that mattered. Because most factory work was unskilled and did not require strength, women and children were put to work and earned far less than men. Labor was treated as just another commodity. Wages were determined by market supply and demand. There was no job security, and a worker could be hired or fired as the fluctuations in the market demanded. If he got sick or injured, he was fired. There was little concern for safety. The working class largely lived in terrible slums that grew steadily as the cities exploded in size. What is more, the work itself was, in many ways, miserable. The work of the factories never stopped, and it was completely divorced from the rhythm of night and day and of the seasons. Workers toiled to keep pace with the relentless machines. There were children who almost never saw the sun. Alcoholism became a major social problem as men tried to find escape. Morals and family life deteriorated. Faith declined.

The Industrial Revolution was the economic counterpart to the Enlightenment's revolution in thought and the French Revolution in politics. The mechanical and flattening logic of modernity is fully present. The economy was imagined as following laws that no one could change. Like the laws of physics or the laws of society, all one could do was learn what they were and then use them to build a better machine. In capitalism, everything was a piece of property of some kind, subject to the same legal definitions. Every person was a citizen with the same rights and legally the same powers. So, the child working twelve hours a day in the mines for pennies was "the same" as the mine's owner for whom he worked. Relationships of duties and obligations were replaced with relationships of contracts and rights. There was no doubting the amazing power this worldview had produced in science, no doubting the remarkable strength of the states that had been built according to its principles, and similarly there was no denying the unbelievable wealth that was produced by the factories. But, at the same time, people everywhere were horrified by the consequences. The urban working class had developed so quickly and in such a horrid way that everywhere elites were trying to figure out what went wrong and how to fix it.

Modern Ideologies

Worlds built by human beings are capable of being described and manipulated through systems of human thought. In contrast, human beings can only ever just begin to understand a natural thing, like an animal. An animal's real nature is an idea of God, and ideas of God are not open to us in their totality. We can participate in them, certainly, and we can know them in our own way, through analogy. We can describe a dog truthfully and so in a way congruent to how God sees it, which is the way it really is, but this human knowledge is never more than a truthful likeness. An animal's complete nature, in the final analysis, eludes us, and so there is always more to a dog than what we can say about it. There is always something symbolic, something that points beyond what we know to what God knows. Natural things have meaning that we don't give them, and the meaning we do give them points inadequately, even if truthfully, to this final meaning. A machine that we have built, on the other hand, can be understood by us completely insomuch as it is merely a machine. A system made up of categories that we have invented and that obeys laws that we have laid down can be understood by us insomuch as it is merely this system. If we are god, a nominalist account, an account of our ideas and our categories, becomes a total account. Things are what we declare them to be, and they follow the rules that we lay down for them to follow. This idea is crucial to understanding modern ideological thought. The Enlightenment idea, if we dare to reduce it to one, was that the world in which we live is a world that we can describe fully and which we can manipulate. It is a world that is itself without mystery, without inherent symbolism or sacramental implications. It is the merely material and the merely temporal. That is to say, the world is nothing more than what is below us, made up merely of things that we can master. We are the gods of this world, denying the existence of anything that we don't command.

The ideologies of modernity are attempts at speaking coherence into this world. They are attempts at categorizing the things within it so that the world can be seen to function within our thought, without remainder, with nothing left over. They are machines of thought, architectures for the City of Man. In a proper ideology, everything that we encounter can be described and can be put in its right place in the system. Ideologies make sense of this world, and they give us the power to manipulate it, or at least, they give us the illusion that we can. Ideologies are religious systems for the faithless, for people who deny mystery and refuse humility. There were three main ideologies that emerged out of the Enlightenment and the French Revolution: liberalism, socialism, and nationalism. We have already had a chance to discuss nationalism a bit, and we will revisit it again below. But first we need get a handle on liberalism and socialism.

LIBERALISM

Liberalism was born in England in the thought of Thomas Hobbes and John Locke and developed by thinkers such as Adam Smith, Jeremy Bentham, and John Stuart Mill. The idea starts with the assumption that society is not a natural or even a real thing. Rather, human beings are autonomous individual actors who seek their self-interest. They encounter each other and attempt to maximize their advantages, and society is no more than the sum of these encounters. People form themselves into organized societies because it is in their mutual self-interest to combine their power to pursue more complex benefits and to defend themselves from other individuals who would take what they have. Organizing as a society allows for reliable trade and contracts rather than fighting over resources. For the liberal, then, the purpose of government is to maximize the individual's freedom to pursue his desires and to maximize his ability to retain the property that helps him do so. The state, then, must be neutral toward subjective desires, toward the ends of human action. Different people find happiness in different things, and the purpose of the state is merely to facilitate the individual pursuit of these individual ends. Government does this by establishing a universal legal system that grants every actor identical rights and which defines all objects as forms of private property. Every person and every thing is made to fit into this universal categorization system, which determines beforehand how they can interact in the pursuit of their various ends. Individuals can, therefore, approach each other from within this legal system, each seeking his own gain and without knowing anything particular about each other, and instead of fighting over their property, they can make legal contracts, legal trades, which are enforced by the disinterested state, which also doesn't have to know anything particular about them.

Within liberalism, freedom is understood in an entirely negative sense. Freedom is freedom from bodily coercion and not freedom for something. This means that law is always a negation of freedom. The purpose of law, therefore, is to set up a framework that minimizes the scope of coercion. John Stuart Mill expressed the dominant ethical sentiment:

> The sole end for which mankind are warranted, individually or collectively, in interfering with the liberty of action of any of their number, is self-protection. That the only purpose for which power can be rightfully exercised over any member of a civilized community, against his will, is to prevent harm to others. His own good, either physical or moral, is not a sufficient warrant. . . . In the part which merely concerns himself, his independence is, of right, absolute. Over himself, over his own body and mind, the individual is sovereign.[11]

Liberalism, therefore, maintains a hard distinction between the public, which is governed by law, and the private, which is the realm of individual thoughts, beliefs, and desires. The private is where values, morality, and religion function because this is where the ends or desires that a person pursues are determined. Once they are determined, the individual enters into the public space made up of universal, objective categories in order to try to satisfy them. This public space is governed by a disinterested, minimal, and yet ubiquitous law.

At its best, liberalism emphasized the dignity of the individual and was outraged by unjustified social inequality. A liberal thought that the peasant was as much a man as the noble and that he should have the same rights, most importantly, the right to think whatever he wanted and speak it publicly and without fear. Liberals valued the free exchange of ideas and believed, therefore, in democracy, free speech, and freedom of religion and conscience. At its best, liberalism empha-

---

[11] John Stuart Mill, *On Liberty* (Indianapolis, IN: Hackett Publishing, 1859), 9.

sized merit. It advanced the notion that a man's value was in what he did and not in which family or class he came from. Liberals believed that every man had the right to determine his own future in his own way. As long as someone does not infringe on the rights of another individual, he can pursue the fulfilment of whatever desires please him. On the other hand, if society privileges certain ends and handicaps others, it violates the agreement that brought society into existence to begin with. It is violating some people's freedom in order to help other people fulfill their desires. This is the liberal's notion of injustice.

There were many different versions of liberalism, but generally liberals were utilitarian in their ethics. This means that they wanted the maximum amount of pleasure for the maximum number of people. The success of a society could be determined by adding up all the pleasure and subtracting all the suffering. The social project, then, was to steadily increase total pleasure. Capitalism was the economic system liberals built to do this. Capitalism was very efficient, and it sought to fulfill the subjective desires of individuals in the most cost-effective way possible. The basic idea is very simple. If one man has a loaf of bread and another man has a dollar, and the man with the dollar desires the loaf more than his dollar, and if the man with the loaf desires the dollar more than his loaf, then they trade. Once they trade, both men have something that they desired more than what they had before the trade. Total pleasure has gone up. The liberals merely extended this principle to all human interactions. If they could structure society so that every human interaction was contractual, so that every interaction was a voluntary exchange, that would mean that every interaction would result in an increase in society's total desire fulfillment. What is more, people would get very good at figuring out what they could trade in order to get more of what they want. If everyone did this, we would get more of everything, and we would get it more cheaply. As Adam Smith argued, if everyone pursued his own self-interest, we would all be better off, eventually.

We can easily see how this system makes assumptions about human nature—that we are rational, self-interested, and autonomous actors—and builds an ideological structure on them. Once it is built, anything that happens in society can be described and the proper course of action determined. So, for example, a leading liberal theorist, Herbert Spencer, was faced with the problem of the misery of so many in the working class. He responded:

> Pervading all Nature we may see at work a stern discipline which is a little cruel that it may be very kind. . . . It seems hard that an unskillfulness which with all his efforts he cannot overcome, should entail hunger upon the artisan. It seems hard that a laborer incapacitated by sickness from competing with his stronger fellows, should have to bear the resulting privations. It seems hard that widows and orphans should be left to struggle for life or death. Nevertheless, when regarded not separately, but in connection with the interests of universal humanity, these harsh fatalities are seen to be full of the highest beneficence—the same beneficence which brings to early graves the children of diseased parents, and singles out the low-spirited, the intemperate, and the debilitated as the victims of an epidemic.
>
> . . . We must call those spurious philanthropists, who, to prevent present misery, would entail greater misery on future generations. . . . That rigorous necessity which, when allowed to operate, becomes so sharp a spur to the lazy and so strong a bridle to the random, these paupers' friends would repeal, because of the wailings it here and there produces. Blind to the fact, that under the natural order of things society is constantly excreting its unhealthy, imbecile, slow, vacillating, faithless members, these unthinking, though well-meaning, men advocate an interference which not only stops the purifying process, but even increases the vitiation—absolutely encourages the multiplication of the reckless and incompetent by offering them an unfailing provision, and discourages the multiplication of the competent and provident by heightening the difficulty of maintaining a family. And thus, in their eagerness to prevent the salutary sufferings that surround us, these sigh-wise and groan-foolish people bequeath to posterity a continually increasing curse.[12]

We can see here clearly both utilitarian ethics and the idea of society as a collection of competing individuals whose competition is the essence of society. Capitalism, no doubt, results in winners and losers. But, as Spencer would have us see, the beauty of liberalism is that the winners, the strongest, actually win. The losers have little of value to trade. To give them anything, therefore, would be for society as a whole to take a loss, for the machine to lose efficiency. The overall

---

[12] Herbert Spencer, *Social Statics* (London: George Woodfall and Son, 1851), 323–324.

strength of the machine, and so the total amount of desire fulfillment, requires instead that we allow it to function without interference. Therefore, we ought to let the poor starve.

This logic is inescapable once the premises have been accepted. Let's return to our example of the man with the loaf and the man with the dollar. What if the man without bread is starving? He desires the loaf of bread beyond all else. He would rather have the loaf of bread than anything else he might have. So, the man with the loaf asks not for $1 but for $1,000. The starving man, of course, pays it, and they both walk away richer than they had been, right? They both have something that they value more than what they had before the trade. Total pleasure has gone up. The trade was voluntary. No one's rights were violated. Therefore, as a matter of definition, total wealth has increased, and the ideological liberal would have to say nothing is wrong. This is the market working. The price of the loaf of bread was properly $1,000 because that was what the customer was willing to pay for it given the circumstances in the market.

To name another example: say there is a famine in a certain region. In liberal theory, as the hungry people scramble to acquire some share of the limited supply of grain, the owners of the grain would be fully justified in raising their prices. At some point, there would be a single bushel of grain left, and it would be offered at a price that was so high that the last customer with the means would just be willing to pay for it. In this example, the principled liberal would conclude that there was not a shortage of grain. Supply and demand had met perfectly at the market price: there was no one else left who was willing to pay the going price for a bushel of grain at the exact moment that there was no more grain to be sold. They could say this—that there was no shortage of grain—even as people starved. This logic was actually put into practice, perhaps most horrifically during the Irish Potato Famine (1847–1852). Because of a fungus, the potato crops that fed the poor tenant farmers of Ireland failed for several harvests in a row. As more than one million peasants starved to death, Ireland continued to export massive amounts of livestock, peas, grain, and other crops to England. The price was just better in England and so feeding the peasants would have meant a loss of profits. If the peasants had been able and willing to pay the going price, the exporters would have sold the food to them. There was, therefore, technically no shortage. The market was working. These extreme examples point out a fact about every real exchange. Real exchanges are almost never actually between equals; one party always has an advantage. The type of injustices that famines reveal are, therefore, almost always present, even if rarely in so striking a manner. Often the real inequalities that result in some level of exploitation in even the most voluntary of transactions are subtle or are obscured. Ultimately, the equality that liberalism relies upon is a legal fiction, a matter of definition, which is how ideologies work.

We can see clearly, then, the consistency of the ideologically liberal response to the plight of the working class. True liberals viewed no proper distinction between the factory owner and the factory worker. They were just two men with equal rights making a deal, like the man with the loaf and the man with the dollar. The worker would not make the deal if he did not believe that it made him better off, and neither would the factory owner. Therefore, while we might find the plight of the working class to be upsetting, we have to conclude that the workers are better off than they would have been otherwise and conclude that their condition is maximizing total pleasure in society, like when the starving man buys a loaf of bread for $1,000. If we are heartless, we might take the line of Spencer or the exporters in Ireland; if we are not heartless, we might concede that other individuals ought to increase their own pleasure by giving charity to the poor, which would increase the poor's pleasure, and so would be a profitable exchange. But we wouldn't want to push that idea too far, or we would disrupt the market's efficiency, and it could only be condoned if such charity were totally voluntary and private and so could be considered as just more self-interested exchanges. If we did otherwise, if we introduced notions of duty or of substantive justice, we would be introducing ethical imperatives that would reduce the scope of voluntary transactions and so the total amount of subjective utility in society, and once this is done, the whole system starts to lose its coherence.

Religion did not have a particularly important place in the liberal system. Someone like John Locke could argue that every individual ought to be more concerned about religion than anything else because nothing could be more important than eternity, and then turn around and argue that society ought to dictate almost nothing about religion. This is completely consistent within liberalism. From a liberal's point of view, pursuing the goods of religion might be smart in one's pursuit of pleasure maximization, but that is a private affair, like all subjective desires. For liberals, the goods of religion had to be pursued within the same "neutral" legal framework as all goods. If it is legal for me to gather with friends to watch football, it should be legal for me to gather with friends to pray to God. The point is that our gathering together voluntarily to pursue some common pleasure doesn't inhibit the freedom of anyone else, and so we can do it. An individual's relationship with God was his own affair and, to liberals, did not affect the similar relationships or lack of relationships of others. The pious liberal would argue that only a fool would not value the relationship with God more than all others, but society must suffer the fool. Didn't the pious person appear foolish to the impious? That's the way subjective desires work.

We can see clearly, in this treatment of religion, that liberalism was an ideological outgrowth of Protestant thought, and it is not a coincidence that liberalism flourished in predominately Protestant countries. It is Protestant for a number of reasons. First, it supposes man to be fundamentally selfish. In its most extreme versions, such as that of Hobbes, man is totally depraved. But even someone as moderate as Adam Smith maintained that man's selfishness was a given, and that is what made the liberal system work. Second, in Protestantism, Christianity doesn't change man's fallen state. Grace does not fundamentally change men into virtuous men of charity. Rather, it saves them in spite of their sinfulness. In the end, religion, even true religion, is of little social importance. If this weren't the case, if religion actually changed the social situation, it would have to be recognized as politically relevant and integrated into the legal regime in some way. It was this basic theology that allowed liberalism to suppose that the religion of individuals was not a matter of true social importance. Thirdly, and perhaps most obviously, Protestant ecclesiology was fundamentally individualist. Individuals were saved directly by God, and the Church was merely the association of the saved. Liberals, of course, shared this basic anthropology. Fourthly, in both liberalism and Protestantism, the association of the saved, the Church, had nothing to do with the governing of this world. In Luther's two-kingdom theology, the world in all its temporal aspects was the kingdom of Satan, and it was properly governed by the sword only to keep men from preying upon each other. This could be done as well by a Muslim as by a Christian as by a pagan. The kingdom of God, on the other hand, had no physical, political presence. Christianity was "private," invisible. Fifthly, liberalism envisioned a society that was governed by external laws, as the Protestant God governed the universe. For Protestants, law was fundamental and universal, descending from a sovereign God, and human salvation came only through obeying that law perfectly, something that only Christ could do. Liberalism similarly envisioned a universal and seamless law that governed all men and all things—some of that law was made positive through the state, and some of it was experienced as the "laws of economics," but either way, one prospered through understanding and obeying this law. In much of Protestantism, as in nominalism, contracts or covenants form the basis of peace, as they also do in liberalism. What is more, for Protestantism, heaven is not something that is anticipated on earth through the hierarchy of orders and the steady elevation of what is lower to what is higher. Rather, life in history is flat, and all men are essentially the same. It would be hard to be more liberal. For both, heaven is something that happens after you die. Christianity, therefore, is not political and is, rather, just another "religion."

Liberals often advanced tolerance, therefore, toward all types of religion, with the exception of Catholicism. Catholicism embraced the notion of the common good and argued that grace was efficacious in the here and now. It maintained not only that real differences between people existed but also that those differences, these levels or orders in society, were beneficial and that justice was defined as each deploying its resources in pursuit of the common good of the whole. Such justice, and so true peace, was possible only through the inflow of grace, which was real and efficacious, changing people and making them capable of virtue. In other words, to the liberal, Catholicism wasn't a proper religion at all but a political agenda. This is why John Locke, who argued that a man's religion was absolutely no business of the state, in nearly the same breath, argued that Catholicism should be outlawed. Liberalism was a protest against Catholicism and so was fundamentally incompatible with Catholicism. It was a sort of anti-Catholicism. Both liberals and Catholics in the nineteenth century understood this.

SOCIALISM

If liberalism was an outgrowth of Protestantism, socialism was a heretical form of Catholicism. Socialism, like liberalism, was a very diverse ideology, and so we must generalize. Here, we are going to follow the thought of Karl Marx, who developed the most historically significant form of socialism in the mid-nineteenth century. Marx couldn't disagree more profoundly with the liberals. Socialism posited that society was not made up of individuals pursuing incommensurable subjective desires but, rather, was made up of classes of people who were competing with each other over power and resources. Socialists were materialists. They believed the only thing that was actually real was the physical stuff of the world. What we are, what we think and feel, is ultimately the result of the way we encounter this stuff. The way the stuff is encountered is what they mean by the economy. The economy is the total organization of the material world as encountered by people. Different people, however, encounter the economy in different ways. The economy is big and complicated, and so some people interact with the economy as workers and others as farmers and still others as factory owners. The socialists called these encounters the person's "relationship to the means of production." One's relationship to the means of production constituted one's class, and because of fundamental materialism, one's class necessarily constituted one's consciousness: the way in which one thought about one's life and about the economy. The worker lived in a different material environment than did the factory owner, and so he actually saw and understood the world in a different way. He had a different consciousness. As Marx put it: "Consciousness is, therefore, from the very beginning a social product, and remains so as long as men exist at all."[13] The socialists added to this materialism the insistence that these classes were necessarily antagonistic to each other. The class with the most power, in fact, sought to construct and maintain an economic organization that enriched itself through subjugating the weaker classes. This subjugation was economic, but because of their materialism, the socialist understood it as simultaneously psychological.

Let's revisit our example of the man selling a loaf of bread in order to see how this works. A socialist would present the example, perhaps like this: The man with the dollar is a worker. He works all day in a field growing grain. He then harvests the grain and mills it and makes it into loaves of bread. Let's say he makes three loaves of bread. But he does not own the land or the harvesting equipment or the mill or the ovens—what the socialists would call the "capital." This is all owned by another man, the capitalist. As a result, the worker doesn't own the three loaves of bread that he produced. Rather, the capitalist owns the bread. The capitalist pays the worker a wage for his labor, let's say $1.

---

[13] Karl Marx, *The German Ideology* (1847).

Now the worker has $1, and he is hungry. So, he goes to a shop that is owned by the same man who owns all the capital and buys a loaf of bread for $1. He goes away with no money and one loaf of bread. The owner of capital, the capitalist, on the other hand, has his dollar back to pay the same man tomorrow, and he still has two loaves of bread to sell to other workers who are manufacturing other things through his capital. In this way, he amasses wealth through the workers' labor.

For the socialists, this is a scam. The capitalist did none of the work, and yet he ends up with two-thirds of the wealth that was produced by the worker. The socialist would expand this basic analysis to society as a whole. The class of capitalists is perpetrating this scam on the class of workers. It is not normally the same man who owns the land and the mill and the store, and it is not normally the same worker who grows the grain, who mills it, and who bakes the bread. Because of this, the scam is obscured through many transactions. But the complex scam works essentially the same as the simple example. If we look at it in terms of class, the capitalist class, together, is scamming the working class as a whole. For the socialist, this was capitalism.

Why does the worker go to work every day and do all the work and accept worthless money as payment in order to buy back some of the fruit of his labor? Why does he fall for it? The socialists argued that he had been convinced that the system is right or at least that it is merely the way the world works. He doesn't see the system as something that could be different. To him, it seems natural or at least inevitable. The way he is convinced of this is through what socialists call the superstructure of society. Let's look at private property. The whole example given above turns on private property. The capitalist owns the means of production. He gets to keep the loaves of bread because they were produced on property he "owns." But what does it mean to "own" something? Why do we say that the capitalist "owns" a field if he never works in it or maybe has never even seen it? How do we know that he owns it? To "own" a field must mean merely to be able to *legally* keep the loaves of bread that were produced on it. We know he owns the field because the law asserts that he gets the bread. But, obviously, we find ourselves back to where we started. He gets the bread because he owns the field, and he owns the field because he gets the bread. The capitalist gets to keep the fruit of the labor of the workers because he owns the capital and owning capital means getting to keep the fruit of the labor of the workers. For the socialist, this amounts to a circular dogma, the dogma of private property, which is the unjustified belief that all things are a form of private property and that private property has certain essential and timeless properties (it is really the belief that, like truth, goodness, and beauty, "property-ness" is a transcendental). Socialists point out that liberals argue their case from the concept of private property, as if it were a given, when the legitimacy of private property is exactly what is at issue.

The socialist wants us to see that such dogmas are fictions that are created in order to benefit one class at the expense of another. The worker goes to work every day only because he, too, believes in private property. He, too, believes that he is working "for" the capitalist who "owns" the field in exchange for a dollar that he then "owns." He believes that he "owns" his labor in the same way that the capitalist "owns" the field and that they are making a trade. He would like to "own" more property and so is motivated to work harder for the capitalist in order to acquire more of his "own." In other words, the worker forges his chains as much as does the capitalist. The capitalist, for his part, really believes, as a part of his class-bound consciousness, that he really owns the means of production, and the worker believes, as a part of his class-bound consciousness, that the capitalist really owns the means of production. The idea of private property is, for the socialist, a part of the superstructure of society. The "structure" is made up of the actual mechanism of production and distribution. The "superstructure" is made up of the ideas that make it work. The superstructure included all cultural productions, it included all politics, it included philosophy, and it especially included religion. All of this was part of the mechanism that kept the workers going to the factories every day and therefore increasing the accumulated wealth of the capitalists.

The socialist claimed, though, that this scam wouldn't ultimately work. They claimed that the capitalists couldn't maintain this system forever but that it would, in the end, undermine itself. It does this in a number of ways. The capitalists are, of course, competing with each other. As they do so, their numbers dwindle. The winners drive the losers down into the ranks of the workers. This meant that more and more property would become concentrated in the hands of fewer and fewer people. At the same time, as the superstructure of capitalism more deeply converted the working class, they would become more anxious for property acquisition and more aware of the fact that the capitalists have a lot and that they have very little. Ironically, as they became more capitalist themselves, the more adversarial they would become to the capitalists. Next, as the capitalists more perfectly exploit the labor of the workers, they actually reduce the amount of private property that the workers own, to the point where they own nothing but their labor and are forced to rent everything else. This creates a new material environment for them and so eventually changes their consciousness. The socialists claimed that when nearly all of society was reduced to workers who did not own any property, the working class would start to gain true "class consciousness." They would come to see the capitalists for who they were, and they would be prepared to overthrow the capitalist regime and establish a socialist regime.

The socialist regime would be the rule of the working class, as the capitalist regime had been the rule of the capitalist class. However, because capitalism had eliminated all classes except the capitalist class and the working class, which consisted of nearly all the population, the consequence of the rule of the working class was essentially the elimination of class rule itself. Everyone ruled, and so no one did. The regime of private property would be overthrown. The greed and acquisitiveness that underwrote the superstructure of capitalism would be eliminated. Instead, society would construct a superstructure that supported a community of universal work and universal sharing in the fruits of that work. Instead of wealth being produced and distributed through the dogma of private property, it would be produced and distributed according to the principle of "from each according to his ability and to each according to his need." This would be the end of history. History was driven forward by class conflict, and once there were no more classes, history would stop. Instead, people would live on indefinitely in peace and prosperity. There would be no more manipulative superstructures, such as religion or morality. Rather, people would live in total freedom and total brotherhood. This would be perfect Communism, the final utopian end of socialist ideology.

In order to get there, though, there would have to be violence. The capitalists obviously weren't going to give up control easily. Once enough of the workers gained true class consciousness, they would have to overthrow the regime through violent revolution. No amount of reasoning would work. Once they came into power, the workers would face another problem. Society would be full of people who had not yet achieved proper consciousness. Many people would still be mired in the superstructure of capitalism. The socialists, once in power, would change this by changing the environment. They would get rid of private property by law and create an economy that operated without market mechanisms. They would outlaw, or at least starve out of existence, aspects of the old superstructure that lingered and replace them with a new, socialist superstructure. This would be the period of "socialism" or what would come to be called the "dictatorship of the proletariat." Through these changes, the socialists would change everyone's relationship to the means of production and so, ultimately, finish the revolution through building the new "socialist man." They would have to use the state in order to do this, but the state itself was ultimately a part of the capitalist superstructure. This means that as socialism succeeded, as the state became less and less necessary, it would, in fact, wither away. In Communism, there would be no state.

Socialism is a Catholic heresy. It is an attempt at rearticulating the Catholic corporate conception of salvation, of the Church as the Body of Christ, within materialist and rationalist metaphysics. Catholicism teaches that we are each members of societies that are integrated wholes. Mankind fell on account of the sin of one man and was redeemed through the sacrifice of one man. We are corporate in our nature. Socialism understands this in a way liberalism simply doesn't. However, because socialism denies the existence of the soul and of transcendence, it cannot understand that this corporate reality is not absolute but that, rather, each society is open to what is above it, and each society in its particularity is capable of participating in the universal. For the same reason, it cannot understand the individual as both entirely a member of a society and yet at the same time a unique and transcendent whole on his own account. Rather, it has to posit each corporate grouping as only intelligible to itself and as fundamentally at conflict with other groupings, and each individual as only meaningful as a member of these groups.

Socialism understands that mankind actually changes through the influence of his society. In fact, in some of its forms, socialism expounds an understanding of social habit that is very close to St. Thomas Aquinas's treatment of virtue and vice. For socialism, like Catholicism, law is pedagogical, moving from the external to the internal, from the mind to the heart. However, socialism denies the existence of grace. It denies the power of the free gift of God that enables man to freely choose to move into virtue. Without grace, force must rule. Socialism, like Catholicism, had little patience for the liberal's simplistic flattening of society. Of course, some people had more real power than others. However, the socialists saw in such hierarchy only injustice. They could not imagine a hierarchy of love and service. Here, like the liberals, they seem to accept an anthropology of depravity. Socialism, like Catholicism, maintained the reality of history. For the Catholic, history started with Adam and Eve and moved through biblical history and continued into the history of the Church. This history had not stopped, and mankind was moving toward the eschaton, toward the end, when all things would be restored and peace would finally be accomplished. For the Catholic, this peace was approximated and approached in time, but in the very end, it would be found perfectly only in eternity. For the socialist, history, too, was real. It moved mechanically, however. Its path was necessitated by the laws of matter in motion and not laid down through the providence of a loving God and the free actions of men. It moved forward toward its goal not through conversion to peace but through war, through revolution and conflict. It would achieve its goal of heaven on earth only once all enemies had been destroyed and once the final intense and all-encompassing suffering of capitalism had been endured. Nevertheless, like Catholicism, socialism was universal in its outlook. All men would ultimately be united into one society. However, socialism could not see how that unity is compatible with diversity. Rather, national and regional cultures were aspects of the reigning superstructure. Socialism shared with Catholicism a real concern for the poor and an abhorrence of injustice. It, like Catholicism, thought that a society dominated by money and greed was a bad society and that the poor did not somehow deserve their plight. But the socialists' response was not to consider the duties of the wealthy or to inquire into the just uses of property for the common good. Rather, they thought that wealth had to be destroyed and that all property was unjust.

Socialism was closer to Catholicism than was liberalism. But this does not mean that it was more benign. Often being closer to the truth enables one to be, in fact, more evil. Satan believes in God, after all, and worshiping the devil is worse than being an atheist, even though such worship acknowledges the reality of the supernatural. Socialism wanted justice and peace in this world without God. This, as St. Augustine taught us fourteen centuries earlier, was a recipe for unspeakable violence. The liberals at least, like their Protestant counterparts, settled for a social world of mitigated violence and tamed injustice, saving heaven for the next world. Socialism became a great danger and temptation to the Catholic regions of Europe, largely because it was a materialist response to liberalism that retained much of the Catholic disposition. Even the materialism of socialism echoed the sacramental vision of Catholicism—external things affect us internally. But, by the time socialism rose to real prominence, Catholicism had become minimally relevant as far as politics and economics were concerned, and the socialists were fighting against the liberals, not traditional Catholicism. As we'll see in a later chapter, however, the Church would come to engage them directly.

NATIONALISM

The third ideology that we need to understand is nationalism. We have already been exposed to nationalism in our discussion of the French Revolution. Liberalism posited that the fundamental unit of society was the individual. Socialism maintained that it was the class. For the nationalist, the fundamental unit was the nation. What is a nation? This is a difficult question to answer. To the nationalists, the nation was the organic whole of a people. It was the natural "living" unit of society. It is important not to confuse the nation with our idea of a country. For the nationalists, there were many nations that did not have a state and many states that were not nations. Nations, instead, were constituted by a shared culture, by a shared religion, by a shared language, by a shared spirit. For the nationalist, the French were a nation because they were all Frenchmen and not because they lived under the same government. But nationalism is not just some vague understanding that we, as individuals, belong to social bodies. Rather, nationalists had a certain understanding of what these social bodies were. For example, to argue that one was a member of his village or his town, even to argue that the culture of these little places was what made him what he was, was not to be a nationalist. Similarly, in the other direction, to claim that every individual was a member of humanity as a whole and that this identification ought to constitute his social being was not to be a nationalist. Nations were not so small. Nor were they so big. Nations were about the size of France, Spain, or England. Nationalism grew up as these kingdoms fragmented from each other and consolidated their internal rule, a story that we have told above, and the definition of what it meant to be a nation was formed in this process.

The formation of the nation was the process of both homogenizing kingdoms internally and separating them from all external subordination. In order for France to have legitimacy separate from any larger organization, such as the Church, and in order for France to be able to marshal the resources of its territory and population, France had to exist as a nation. This meant the suppression of internal differences, as we saw in our discussion of the French Revolution's centralizing efforts, and it meant the total divorce of the nation from international bodies, as we saw with the revolutionaries' treatment of the Catholic Church. For a modern nation to really be a nation, the people must understand the nation itself as their basic social unit. They must understand that their smaller organizations, such as towns or villages, are components of the nation, and that the nation itself is what acts at any level larger than the nation. Politics smaller than the nation are "local" politics, governed by national politics, and politics larger than the nation are "international" politics, where only nations are actors. The nation is what stands alone.

In contrast, a traditional Catholic kingdom both understands itself as a part of something larger and is capable of accepting dramatic diversity within its borders. This is so because the ultimate measure of right and wrong, just and unjust, lies beyond it. A little town someplace could participate in true justice in a way that was very different from another little town someplace else, and yet they could both have just laws. This is because justice is bigger than particular laws. Laws are particular and justice is universal. This allows for a kingdom to accommodate far-ranging diversity internally precisely because it is itself integrated into something that is universal—the idea of justice itself. The unity of Christendom, therefore, allowed for local diversity. This can easily be seen in the Crusades, when people from all over Europe, people with different languages and customs, fought together in defense of a more fundamental truth, a truth that they participated in through their differences. The growth of nationalism was a part of the process of undoing this.

Having broken from the universal truth of Christendom, the kingdoms could no longer accommodate local diversity. Local diversity implied a lack of unity, and the kingdoms had to be unified in order to justify and maintain their power. In the modern period, then, what had once been the vague medieval notion of "nationality" assumed a dramatically new level of importance, taking on wholly new layers of meaning as royal power became national power and as national power came to dominate. A man who, in the Middle Ages, might have thought of himself first as a Christian and then as a member of a certain family and then of a village, would have asserted only somewhere far down the line that he, too, was a Frenchman. Now, under the influence of nationalism, the order was reversed. He was a Frenchman first of all, and his other attachments now became attachments that happened within France, within their French-ness.

Nationalism came into being, then, as an integral aspect of the construction of unitary politico-cultural states, what we now call nation-states. Part of the construction of these nation-states was the representation of the nation, the cultural element, as something that had always existed, even as it was, in fact, being assembled. Nations were built with histories, with mythologies. Part of their construction was the construction of their past. So, once a nation was built, it was hard to see that it had not always been there, and most moderns came to believe that nations were natural, timeless, and essential aspects of humanity when, in fact, they had been born only recently.

Nationalism spread through Europe, carried first by the French revolutionary armies. It had different consequences in different regions. In Central Europe, the Germans were divided into many smaller states, and nationalism became a force for unity under the powerful Prussians. In the Habsburg's Austrian Empire, however, nationalism was increasingly a force for disunity. The Austrian Empire was made up of many ethnicities, which coexisted under one state that was dominated by German-speakers. Nationalism became a means of opposing such an empire. In other parts of Europe, such as Italy, there was no central government at all. The Italians were divided into several little kingdoms and independent city-states. Nationalism, for them, became a part of the drive to unify as a nation-state in order to become strong enough to resist the other burgeoning nation-states of Europe.

Ideologically, nationalism took two basic forms. In one, the nation was understood as the natural unit of human society. In this form, conflict between men was understood as the product of nations not respecting each other's nationhood. If each nation just had its own state, there would no longer be any justification for war. God, according to this way of thinking, had created mankind as nations, and we did violence to his plans when we either assembled nations into empires or divided nations into little, subnational states. Either way, we got violence. The solution was a Europe of independent nation-states. As a leading nationalist theorist wrote:

> Even as a wise overseer of labor distributes the various branches of employment according to the different capacities of the workmen, [God] divided Humanity into distinct groups or nuclei upon the face of the earth, thus creating the germ of nationalities. Evil governments have disfigured the Divine design. Nevertheless you may still trace it, distinctly marked out—at least as far as Europe is concerned—by the course of the great rivers, the direction of the higher mountains, and other geographical conditions. They have disfigured it by their conquests, their greed, and their jealousy even of the righteous power of others; disfigured it so far that, if we except England and France, there is not perhaps a single country whose present boundaries correspond to that design.[14]

The second form of nationalism was more belligerent. This form agreed that humanity was naturally divided up into nations. However, it posited that it was human nature for these nations to war with each other. Only the victory of one nation over another brought any break to this conflict. War was not, therefore, to be avoided. Rather, it was a sort of hygiene for humanity that kept the strong getting stronger and eliminated the weaker. This second form of nationalism gained ground in the second half of the nineteenth century and merged with racism under the influence of Darwinian theories of evolution.

Nationalism at its best promoted solidarity and fraternal love. It sought to instill into men the idea that they were a part of something bigger than themselves and to encourage them to sacrifice for each other. These are vestiges of Christian fraternal charity. In the end, however, nationalism is a form of paganism. It advances a mystical unity of a people that is not rooted in the transcendent or the universal but is, rather, tied to concrete historical reality—blood and soil, as some nationalists would come to call it. Nationalism sees the strength of the nation in a heroic sense as the goal of human existence, and each individual exists ultimately to serve this strength and finds his fulfillment in a participation in this strength. Nationalism is romantic, but it is not transcendent. Its gods, the nations, are not truly divine. Like the gods of the pagan pantheon, they live in history and yet are more powerful than any single man. While there were various theories of nationalism, it was not overly intellectual; rather, it manifested itself in intense, participatory love for one's nation. A national-

---

[14] Joseph Mazzini, *An Essay on the Duties of Man* (1858).

ist wasn't someone who necessarily had a well-thought-out answer to every social problem, like a liberal or a socialist. Rather, a nationalist identified with his nation; he loved his nation; he intuitively believed that everything should be directed to the strength and well-being, the glory of his nation; and he was willing to sacrifice for his nation, even to die for it. Nationalism was accessible to everyone. Nationalism was an ideology that was truly for the masses.

The French Revolution's slogan was "Liberty, Equality, and Fraternity." The Revolution then progressed through three distinct phases. The first phase was dominated by the middle class, by the property owners, and it was the most liberal phase. This, we might say, corresponded to the "Liberty" aspect of the slogan. This phase, though, couldn't maintain power because it failed to address the concerns of the new urban working class. This class, dominated by the *sansculottes* and the Jacobin clubs, took control in the second phase of the Revolution and implemented a radical program of complete social reengineering. This, we might say, corresponded to the "Equality" aspect of the slogan and was clearly the most socialist of the phases. The third phase began when Napoleon took control. Napoleon did not outright reject the first two phases. He didn't need to. He could adopt their attractive elements and reject their extreme elements precisely because he had a unifying principle. That principle was the nation. Napoleon's rule, we might say, corresponded to the "Fraternity" aspect of the slogan. It was "Fraternity," love of brother and love of nation, that managed to pull the various ideological strands together. Now, the common man who was fighting in Napoleon's army could love liberty and equality not because he understood the complex philosophy of Enlightenment thinkers but because he was a good Frenchman, and good Frenchmen loved liberty and equality. The ideological content became an aspect of nationalist commitment rather than standing on its own. This was the Machiavellian turn. The "universal" ideas of justice, of reason, of right and wrong, became an aspect of the particular. The divinity was divided up into the gods, destroying all true transcendence. This is how nationalism is ultimately a form of paganism.

Throughout the nineteenth century, we will see this same basic dynamic play out on a larger scale. Liberalism and socialism vied for ideological dominance. But really it was nationalism that pulled it all together. Liberal and socialist ideologies were Christian heresies. Ultimately, Christian heresies cannot resist paganism. Heresy must either convert back into orthodoxy or drift forward into paganism because, in the final analysis, there are really only two options: sin or redemption. The City of Man or the City of God. There isn't a place for anything in between.

The Alliance of Throne and Altar

In the aftermath of the Napoleonic Wars, when industrialization and the ideologies were just beginning to take root, conservativism ruled Europe. The conservatives were suspicious of the ideologues' conviction that they could redesign society. After the chaos of the Revolution, the conservatives contended that the willy-nilly tearing down of institutions was clearly a mistake. Rather, change should be slow. Change should happen "organically." Perfectly expressing the sentiment, a leading conservative, Edmund Burke, wrote: "It is with infinite caution that any man ought to venture upon pulling down an edifice which has answered for ages the common purposes of society."[15] Conservatism was an anti-ideology. Leading conservatives, such as Klemens von Metternich of Austria, viewed ideology as pure presumption, as an almost adolescent foolishness. In 1820, Metternich wrote:

> Religion, morality, legislation, economy, politics, administration, all have become common and accessible to everyone. Knowledge seems to come by inspiration; experience has no value for the presumptuous man; faith is nothing to him; he substitutes for it a pretended individual conviction, and to arrive at this conviction dispenses with all inquiry and with all study; for these means appear too trivial to a mind which believes itself strong enough to embrace at one glance all questions and all facts. Laws have no value for him, because he has not contributed to make them, and it would be beneath a man of his parts to recognize the limits traced by rude and ignorant generations. Power resides in himself; why should he submit himself to that which was only useful for the man deprived of light and knowledge? That which, according to him, was required in an age of weakness cannot be suitable in an age of reason and vigor amounting to universal perfection.[16]

---

[15] Burke, *Reflections on the Revolution in France* (1790), para. 97.
[16] Klemens von Metternich, *Secret Memorandum to Czar Alexander I* (1820).

Conservatives were practical and not idealistic. They had defeated Napoleon, and they had learned a great deal from him. Even though many conservatives were royalists, the monarchies they wanted to preserve were no longer the monarchies of the *ancien régime*, and they certainly weren't the monarchies of premodern Europe. Instead, they were the highly centralized and authoritarian monarchies that only came into full being during the Revolution and its aftermath. They wanted a highly organized and centralized society that supported big armies and that could collect massive revenues. Conservatives were almost all personally devoted to Christianity, but Christianity was increasingly seen less as the justification for all political power and more as socially useful because it created moral and obedient subjects. For conservatives, it was increasingly the case that Christianity happened inside a political world rather than politics happening inside a Christian one.

Underneath the stability that the conservatives produced, the Industrial Revolution advanced, and the ideologies grew in strength. In the first half of the nineteenth century, liberalism and nationalism were the strongest ideologies. They often combined into a sort of liberal-nationalism in order to undermine the conservative order. Socialism, in varying forms, was being developed, but it remained the weakest of the three ideologies. Socialists often joined with liberals to oppose the status quo. Ideological discontent culminated in a series of revolutions in 1848. While conservative government almost everywhere managed to withstand these rebellions, they largely did so by conceding to many liberal demands, by flattening society, by granting universal rights, by extending the ubiquity of private property. In the aftermath of 1848, the conservatives also began to recognize that extreme nationalism could serve as a potential bulwark against extreme ideology, and so they attempted, with some success, to co-opt its power in support of their own governments. Conservatism was extremely hard to unseat. It was, in its nature, adaptive and flexible, willing to compromise and absorb some of the revolutionaries' positions and so steal some of their thunder. The ideologues, on the other hand, were often rigid and had a very difficult time working together. Even when the revolutions had initial success, infighting among the revolutionaries allowed the conservatives to regain control. In addition, the Industrial Revolution was just starting to gain momentum, and the majority of the population retained a traditional way of life. These farmers may have wanted change; they may have wanted reform and justice; but they were not really susceptible to ideology. Peasants almost always want stability, not revolution. Their way of life, after all, relied on the predictability of multiple-year cycles of weather, planting, harvest, and crop rotation.

Faced with this reality, the papacy found common cause with the conservative monarchies. The popes were primarily concerned with protecting the great majority of Catholics who remained traditional and faithful in spite of the upheavals of the previous decades. The conservatives generally supported the Church in these efforts, even if on their own terms. They wanted the people to remain devoted to the Church and for the Church to remain integrated into their rule. The papacy, who in the aftermath of the French Revolution had made deals with many of these rulers, agreed. This situation is often referred to as the Alliance of Throne and Altar. For the papacy, this alliance was primarily defensive. The Church had real, concrete Catholic ground to defend in the way of life of normal people. As Pope Pius IX described the situation, there was "a very bitter and fearsome war against the whole Catholic commonwealth . . . being stirred up by men bound together in a lawless alliance."[17] The ideologues were actively attempting to undermine this ground by spreading their doctrines, which necessarily included the rejection of traditional Catholicism. As Pope Gregory XVI wrote, "They enter the hovels of the poor, traverse the countryside, and seek the acquaintance of the farmers and the lowest classes. They try every method of attracting the uneducated, especially the youth, to their sects, and of making them desert the Catholic Faith."[18] The popes, therefore, sought to limit the spread of the ideas of liberalism and socialism, especially the idea that all religions are the same and that Catholicism is just one among many. The popes called this "indifferentism," and they recognized it as seductive and, therefore, extremely dangerous. They believed that calls for "liberty of conscience" or for the freedom to publish any ideas and spread them were clearly aspects of the ideologues' larger strategy. What benefit, they asked, could be expected by the publication and distribution of untruths? Would this not result in scandal, leading the faithful astray? They, therefore, wrote sternly against the propagation of such "freedoms," which they believed to be based on a false notion of freedom that was divorced from truth and that was, in fact, part of a larger

---

[17] Pius IX, *Qui Pluribus* (1846), §4.
[18] Gregory XVI, *Probe Nostis* (1840), §1.

strategy to destroy the hold that Christianity still had on the populace. As Pius IX wrote:

> As the result of the unbridled license to think, speak and write, We see the following: morals deteriorated, Christ's most holy religion despised, the majesty of divine worship rejected, the power of this Apostolic See plundered, the authority of the Church attacked and reduced to base slavery, the rights of bishops trampled on, the sanctity of marriage infringed, the rule of every government violently shaken and many other losses for both the Christian and the civil commonwealth.[19]

However, because the popes' primary focus was the preservation of the faith, their writings were not merely lists of condemned errors. In fact, they understood that strengthening the faith of the people was as important as protecting them from error. They, therefore, exhorted the bishops and priests to lead holy lives, to preach, to teach, and to give the sacraments more often. The grace that flowed through the Church was, of course, what really mattered. It was, after all, the reason that the Church was worth defending in the first place. The imperative to keep preaching and to ensure the availability of the sacraments was, of course, the reason the papacy had conceded so much ground to princes in the previous centuries. Preaching and the sacraments were the faith, and it was these more than anything else that had to be protected and extended because they would strengthen the faithful against the assault of ideology. As Pope Leo XII wrote to the pastors:

> Strive with all your ability to saturate youth with Catholic customs and rule of life, demanding this of them, of their parents, and of their teachers. Especially however, see that they are on their guard against seduction, so that they may shudder at the evil opinions propagated by these miserable times and at the books inimical to religion, morals, and public peace, from which this foul crop of wickedness has grown. . . . If the faithful are nourished with the word of God, if the frequent reception of the sacraments is stressed, if pious societies are promoted wherever they are, or established where they do not yet exist—if these things are done, the needs of

---

[19] Pius IX, *Qui Pluribus*, §18.

every age, sex, and human condition will be met.[20]

What is more, the popes had not accepted the Protestant and liberal notion that religion was somehow distinct from the peace and prosperity of nations. Far, far from it. Rather, without true religion, civil society itself would crumble. Pope Gregory XVI asserted that through the new teachings, "the restraints of religion are thrown off, by which alone kingdoms stand. We see the destruction of public order, the fall of principalities, and the overturning of all legitimate power approaching. . . . When all restraints are removed by which men are kept on the narrow path of truth, their nature, which is already inclined to evil, propels them to ruin."[21] Christianity resulted in better and more just princes. As Pius IX remarked, "The faithful should reckon it to the credit of our most holy religion that princes in Christian times feared the 'stern judgment in store for governors,' and the eternal punishment prepared for sinners, in which 'the strong will suffer strong torments.' Because of this fear, they have ruled the peoples subject to them more justly and clemently." The pope was here understating his case. In fact, it was the preaching of the Gospel and the distribution of the sacraments that enabled Christian princes to be just, to be better than "the old kings of the pagan nations."[22] The popes knew that the spread of error was the demise of kingdoms.

The popes explained that the ideologies were based upon false notions of liberty and equality. The ideologues sought a flattened society, when, in fact, it was "a mark of the natural, and so of the immutable, condition of human affairs that even among those who are not in higher authority, some surpass others in different endowments of mind or body or in riches and such external goods."[23] There was a natural hierarchy in society. The ideologues were, therefore, doomed to fail: "For man is not empowered to establish new societies and unions which are opposed to the nature of mankind. If these conspiracies spread throughout Italy there can only be one result: if the present political arrangement is shaken violently and totally ruined by reciprocal attacks of citizens against citizens by their wrongful appropriations and slaughter, in the end some few, enriched by the plunder

---

[20] Leo XII, *Charitate Christi* (1825), §15.
[21] Gregory XVI, *Mirari Vos* (1832), §§5, 14.
[22] Pius IX, *Nostis et Nobiscum* (1849), §23.
[23] Pius IX, *Nostis et Nobiscum*, §20.

of many, will seize supreme control to the ruin of all."[24]

The papacy likewise resisted calls for the separation of Church and State. Pope Gregory XVI wrote: "Nor can We predict happier times for religion and government from the plans of those who desire vehemently to separate the Church from the state, and to break the mutual concord between temporal authority and the priesthood. It is certain that that concord which always was favorable and beneficial for the sacred and the civil order is feared by the shameless lovers of liberty."[25] The princes were rightly placed "as if they were parents and teachers of the people," and "they will bring them true peace and tranquility, if they take special care that religion and piety remain safe."[26]

During this period, the practical power of the papacy grew within the Church. This may seem unexpected, but there is a logic to it. As the conservative governments consolidated power, they knew that Catholicism was a bulwark against revolution. They wanted to strengthen it. At the same time, however, the established power of bishops within their kingdoms was a threat to the increased centralization of their power. Gallicanism, for example, asserted the real ecclesiastical power of the episcopate underneath the monarchy as a check to the monarchy. They did not want to strengthen the bishops. In order to strengthen Catholicism without strengthening local power, therefore, the monarchs empowered the papacy. Through a series of concordats in the middle decades of the century, the state in most Catholic countries gave up much of the control that it had won over the Church during the revolutionary period. But they transferred this power not to the local churches, run by the bishops and monasteries of their countries, but to the Roman Church that was increasingly run by the papacy. As the papacy became relatively more powerful within the Church, the faithful looked increasingly to it rather than to their own bishops when they had religious problems with their governments. The papacy was, then, in a better position to negotiate, and the princes, for their part, were more inclined to do so precisely because the papacy had more power. The papacy's support for the power of the princes dramatically reduced the likelihood of revolution in their kingdoms, while the Alliance of Throne and Altar helped the papacy consolidate its own jurisdictional power over the

---

[24] Pius IX, *Nostis et Nobiscum*, §25.
[25] Gregory XVI, *Mirari vos*, §20.
[26] Gregory XVI, *Mirari vos*, §23.

clerical hierarchy. Ironically, then, the growing centralization of the power of the princes was crucial to final papal victory over Gallican or conciliarist sentiment within the episcopate and the priesthood. The centralization and standardization of government that was happening in the kingdoms was mirrored in the clerical hierarchy itself.

We can clearly understand why the popes pursued the Alliance of Throne and Altar. However, it did sometimes lead them into perhaps misguided positions. The popes, faced with revolution and upheaval, were sometimes excessive in their apparent support of all established power. They sometimes deployed too freely the biblical texts in support of the God-given authority of earthly powers and sometimes exhorted the oppressed to suffer in patience with too much inflexibility. This could give the impression that the Church called on the faithful to submit blindly to whoever happened to have power. In their defense of a Christian order, the popes sometimes mistook the "legitimacy" claimed by the heirs of the absolutist monarchs for legitimacy itself, as if the divine right of kings were a real thing, which it wasn't. In fact, unjust law was no law at all, and the legitimacy of temporal rule was tied always to the propagation and defense of true justice and proper morals. The papacy had asserted this repeatedly through the Middle Ages and the Reformation. For example, during the Reformation, the papacy released English subjects from all obedience to the monarchy on precisely these grounds. The papacy did not contradict established teaching, of course, but it certainly blurred lines that led it to be seen by many as merely a propaganda arm of the established governments.

The popes necessarily move and act in whatever time they happen to live. They do not have prophetic insight into the working of history or perfect vision of the world in which they are thrust. Throughout history, this has led to mistakes or miscalculations. But even these mistakes are often providential. The Alliance of Throne and Altar may have included such mistakes, but it almost certainly also preserved the faith of countless souls.

National Unifications and Mass Politics

The pope was the monarch of his own state, centered in the city of Rome and extending through much of central Italy. Through the Age of Absolutism, this state had secured the papacy's independence, and it continued to serve in that capacity through most of the nineteenth century. After Napoleon, the religious policies of most states became increasingly cynical, but because the bulk of the population was still traditionally Christian, Christianity remained politically important. In the first half of the nineteenth century, then, many kings, fighting for survival against the forces of modern ideology, would have loved to get control of the papacy. The papal state was not finally lost, however, to one of the powerful monarchies. Rather, it was lost to the new forces of nationalism.

The papal state was one of several small states that made up Italy. Most of these states were dominated, in one form or another, by the major powers—normally France or Austria. Nationalism in Italy grew, then, as a movement for unification that was, at the same time, a movement for liberation from foreign dominance. Nationalism and liberalism, or republicanism, tended to go together in Italy. In the revolutions of 1848, a nationalist force in Italy made a bid for unification. One of the consequences was the short-lived Republic of Rome. The pope was driven out of the city, and an independent republic was declared. The French, however, sent troops in, and the pope was restored. This experience led the papacy to strengthen its alliance with the conservative monarchies and to grow in its suspicion of liberal ideas.

The fight for Italian unification, however, continued. Under the leadership of King Victor Emmanuel of Piedmont and Giuseppe Garibaldi, a popular revolutionary, in 1861 most of Italy was united and the Kingdom of Italy declared. While most of the papal state had been conquered and incorporated into the new kingdom, the province of Rome had been left under the direct rule of the papacy. This changed in 1870. The pope's position in Rome had been buttressed by a French force. With the outbreak of the Franco-Prussian War in 1870, however, the French troops were recalled to fight the Prussians. The Italian nationalists saw an opportunity and marched on Rome. Pope Pius IX had about fourteen thousand troops, including his Swiss Guard and volunteers from all over Europe. He faced a force of about fifty thousand men. The city fell with minimal fighting, and the papal forces pulled back to the Vatican. The papal state, which had existed since the 600s, was no more. All that was left was the little island of land surrounding St. Peter's Basilica. The Italian state was moderately liberal in ideology, but the papacy's defeat meant the end of clerical control of most of the social departments of Italian life:

marriage, education, health care, and so on.

The movement for the unification of Italy was one of several national unification movements of these decades. North of the Alps, most of the German-speaking regions of Europe were divided up into many small states, which were dominated by either Prussia in the North or Austria in the South. In 1848, nationalists had attempted to establish a unified state, but they ultimately failed. The rivalry between Prussia and Austria made a state that unified them seemingly impossible. In the 1860s, Otto von Bismarck was prime minister of Prussia. He was convinced that unification of the German states was possible through an alliance of nationalists and conservatives. Nationalism, Bismarck realized, was compatible with the state centralization and military might that he believed necessary for dominance in contemporary Europe, whereas liberalism and socialism were ultimately internationalist in their thinking and so tended toward national weakness and a limited state. An alliance of conservatives and nationalists could marginalize these ideologues. Bismarck was a master of the new way of doing politics, called *Realpolitik*. *Realpolitik* is simply the notion that all that really matters in politics are outcomes. What matters is the successful attainment of practical objectives and little else: ideology, morality, honor, and other such trifles could be useful and had to be used, but they could not be mistaken for the actual substance of politics. *Realpolitik* is just modern Machiavellianism. As Bismarck remarked, "Not by speeches and majority resolutions are the great questions of the time decided—that was the mistake of 1848—but by blood and iron."

In 1866, Bismarck provoked a war with Austria. The Prussians defeated Austria in seven short weeks and annexed all the territories that had allied with their rival. Prussia formed an autocratic government called the North German Confederation that included most of the German states. There was resistance among the Catholics of Southern Germany, however. Northern Germany was, of course, dominated by Protestants, and the Catholics in the South did not see themselves as naturally united with them. Bismarck concluded that nationalism had simply not yet overpowered religion; there were some lingering, old-fashioned notions in the South that had to be overcome. The solution was another war. In 1870, Bismarck provoked France into war. His plan worked. If there was one thing all the German speakers could agree on, it was dislike for the French. The Southerners and the Northerners united against the common enemy. The Prussian military defeated the French with relative ease. And in 1871, the Prussian King William I was declared emperor of the Second German Reich, or empire. This is the birth of Germany as a full-fledged nation-state.

It is often overlooked, but this movement of national unification was happening in America as well. Not only were there many revolutionary movements in South America, but the American Civil War really must be understood within this larger context. Before the war, the country was extremely decentralized, really a fairly weak alliance of independent states. The North was far more industrialized than the South and wanted a stronger central government. The South was agricultural and, of course, relied upon slavery as its economic base. In the North, nationalist sentiment had increasingly attached to the United States. In the South, nationalist sentiment had increasingly attached to the individual states. Slavery become the trigger because it was an issue that, in the long term, did not allow compromise. The Northerners tended to think of slavery as grossly unjust and therefore, unacceptable in the Southern states as well as in the Northern. The Southerners thought that if the Northerners thought slavery was wrong, they should go ahead and outlaw it in their states and leave the Southern states alone. We see, then, a conflict that is rooted in rival nationalisms. The North's victory was a major step toward the establishment of the United States of America as a true nation-state, as a single political entity that governs a single people.

As we have seen in Italy, Germany, and America, nationalism pulled states together. In other parts of the West, it tore them apart. For example, the Austrian-Hungarian Empire was one of the major powers that emerged after the defeat of Napoleon. It was an empire made up of many different peoples—Czechs, Serbs, Romanians, Magyars, and, of course, Austrians—who were governed by the Habsburg monarchy. The Habsburgs managed to retain the empire through the nineteenth century, but it could not, obviously, harness the power of nationalism like its neighbors. Instead, the growth of nationalist sentiment slowly but relentlessly weakened the Habsburg Empire.

The growing force of nationalism also compelled well-established states to reach out to their people in new ways in an attempt to channel nationalist energy into state building. In France, in 1848, Napoleon's nephew Louis-Napoleon Bonaparte was elected president. In 1851, he took control of the country directly. As his uncle had before him, he held a general election, and more than 90 percent of the voters supported the establishment of the Second Empire with him as emperor, and he took the name Napoleon III. His empire was ultimately defeated in the Franco-Prussian War, and liberals retook control of France, declaring the Third Republic. But the country was not the same. Napoleon III had continued his uncle's construction of a single "French" nation-state. Nationalism had thrust him into power, and he stoked it and developed it even further. In fact, France's weakness in the face of Prussia's might was such an affront to French nationalist sensibilities that it was largely responsible for Napoleon III's downfall.

What we are seeing in all these countries is the growth of what we call "mass society." The people, the masses, increasingly mattered. States of immense power, highly centralized states that could mobilize the resources of entire countries, were the invention of Napoleon and the nineteenth century. Such states required the support of the people. Previously, things had been small. The central states were weak, even if they claimed absolute power. They may have claimed divine right, but kings who had only have a few thousand officials and a relatively small professional army in actual fact only ruled over a fairly small part of people's everyday lives. Most of the things that we think of the government doing now were handled by other social institutions: the Church, guilds, fraternities, the village and town communities, and various communes. Before the nineteenth century, the central state was just one institution among many. This is what changed decisively in this period.

The advance of commercialization and industrialization weakened local social structures as regional economics were centralized into one system and as populations moved from their traditional communities to anonymous cities. The central state was the power capable of regulating this depersonalized economic and social reality, and the central state encouraged its growth and extension. This economy allowed for the amassing of centralized wealth and material power, something that was necessary for the construction of modern military machines. But just as important were the ideas of the people. The people, moving out of their traditional ways of life and traditional ways of thinking, had to have those traditions replaced with something. In the villages, most relationships were personal and governed by friendship, a shared morality, and, ultimately, a shared faith. The people were committed to the truth of Christianity, and Christianity was what ultimately governed most of their social life, including things that we would now associate with the government. When they moved to the cities and into an industrialized economy, this changed.

There, most interactions were commercial and were governed by contracts and laws, that is to say, by the state. When there was a conflict of some sort, instead of turning to tradition and to a shared morality, in the industrial cities, people turned to the central government. It makes sense, then, that the people became more and more interested in national politics. As the states centralized and became more powerful, controlling steadily more of everyday life, what was happening politically increasingly mattered to normal people. In this world, the modern ideologies, which concerned themselves directly with economics and politics, seemed to have more to say about the everyday lives of urban workers than traditional Christianity.

At the same time, the people had become increasingly literate. Governments throughout Europe set up public school systems. These schools were set up for a number of reasons. The liberals believed that everyone was the same, that everyone had a right to a basic education, and that such an education would lead to increased economic competitiveness. They believed that democracy was the best form of government and that democracy required an educated citizenry. The socialists largely agreed with them on these points. The conservatives realized that education was necessary for national power and saw in the public schools a mechanism for the inculcation of patriotism, for the production of good citizens, workers, and soldiers. More schools meant more readers, and this, coupled with their increasing interest in politics, lead to the birth of journalism. In 1850, newspapers were rare. There were tens of thousands of them by the end of the century. Newspapers shaped public opinion. They provided hubs of communication through which people could form their political opinions, and they provided mechanisms for the effective use of propaganda. The rise of journalism was coupled with the rise of political parties, through which the newly informed and engaged public organized for political action. Mass society combined mass politics with mass economics and mass culture.

The material resources of a nation-state and the cultural "essence" of the people had to be united in some way. This is what makes a nation-state a nation-state. There were various mechanisms for doing this. Democracy funneled the power of the people into the state through the mediation of political parties. So, in theory, every person in a democracy had the same political power. But in actuality, people became loyal to political parties and voted accordingly. So, most democracies became types of oligarchies run by party leaders and their financial backers, with the masses' loyalty maintained through the parties' journalism arms. This was the route taken in Britain and France, for example. Mass society, however, could just as easily be molded into nondemocratic regimes, where the people's loyalty centered on the nation as a whole or on its leader rather than on a political party. This was the route ultimately taken in Germany. In either case, however, more and more aspects of life were coming under the rule of the dual power of the state and the market, while smaller and traditional structures withered away. The centralized mass society greatly increased the power of political leaders, but those leaders now had to monitor and navigate the shifting tides of public opinion and had to try to direct that opinion. The power of the public was indispensable, but it was also fickle. It had to be both manipulated and placated.

By the 1860s, the papacy found itself in a tricky situation. It had built its defense against the forces of modernity through the Alliance of Throne and Altar. It was through its concordats with the conservative states that the Church continued to function with any degree of liberty. The problem was that these states were growing stronger and stronger, and the ideas that underwrote strong central government were likewise growing stronger. This strength could only mitigate the importance of the Church in the eyes of the states and increase their relative power against the papacy. The irony, of course, was that the papacy itself had buttressed the strength of these states in the aftermath of the French Revolution. The liberal, socialist, and nationalist ideas that the papacy had fought through its alliance with the conservative states became more statist themselves, and the states became more inclined to use these ideologies in their own state-building projects. States began, therefore, to encroach again on the "liberty" of the Church, only it was now a Church that was more directly organized under the papacy as its head.

The papacy was under attack from all quarters. In 1864, Pope Pius IX famously issued an encyclical, *Quanta Cura*, and attached to it a list of modern errors called the *Syllabus Errorum*. The tone of these documents was profoundly defensive, the tone of a Church struggling to keep its head above water. Pius presented a pessimistic picture of a profoundly unhappy age. The foundations of Christian society themselves were being undermined. The chief error was the idea that society could function well independently of true religion. This idea manifested itself in many ways. For example, the call for freedom of conscience and freedom of worship assumed that it didn't matter for civil order what religion people had or what ideas they held to be true. This was clearly false. Likewise, calls for the separation of Church and State assumed that civil society could be run without the help of the sacramental system and the preaching of the Church, also clearly false. In short, the idea was that religion was a merely private affair with little social significance. This thesis would be disastrous. As Pius wrote:

> And, since where religion has been removed from civil society, and the doctrine and authority of divine revelation repudiated, the genuine notion itself of justice and human right is darkened and lost, and the place of true justice and legitimate right is supplied by material force, thence it appears why it is that some, utterly neglecting and disregarding the surest principles of sound reason, dare to proclaim that "the people's will, manifested by what is called public opinion or in some other way, constitutes a supreme law, free from all divine and human control; and that in the political order accomplished facts, from the very circumstance that they are accomplished, have the force of right." But who, does not see and clearly perceive that human society, when set loose from the bonds of religion and true justice, can have, in truth, no other end than the purpose of obtaining and amassing wealth, and that (society under such circumstances) follows no other law in its actions, except the unchastened desire of ministering to its own pleasure and interests?[27]

Catholicism, as the true faith, was not merely an add-on nicety to otherwise self-sufficient secular rule. Rather, the royal power was given for "the governance of the world, but most of all for the protection of the Church."[28] The civil order was not the universal order. But the spiritual order was the universal order. The Church was "a true and perfect society, entirely free." Her rights and powers were not defined by the civil power and neither were the limits within which she could exercise those rights.[29] Under the papacy, the Church operated according to her own laws. Pius defended the authority of the papacy against not only national governments but against lingering Gallican or conciliarist theories.

---

[27] Pius IX, *Quanta Cura* (1864), §4.
[28] Pius IX, *Quanta Cura*, §8.
[29] Pius IX, *Syllabus Errorum* (1864), §19.

In these documents, we find the pope compelled to argue both for the social importance of Christianity and for clerical institutional independence from the state. This combination had been possible in a pre-sovereign state world. But, in the age of centralized, nationalist states, it was a dangerous line to take. Independence from the state could mean only two things to the modern regimes. Either the Church was merely private and so operated completely within the space of civil society governed by the state, or it was a foreign power that had to be driven out of the state. The old notion of communion and harmony between the dual temporal and spiritual powers was no longer an option. The particular and the universal were no longer joined in a rightly ordered hierarchy. This, though, was what the pope was calling for. He even harkened back to the medieval notion of the three orders of society, defending the importance of the contemplative orders to society as a whole in the face of vulgar utilitarian and materialist understandings of economic value. However, even the pope's vision had, in many respects, moved into modernity. The spiritual power that he was defending, for example, was not so much the power of the national episcopates as it was the power of the papacy.

When Pius asserted that revelation was not merely an optional addition to self-sufficient reason, but that it rather proposed necessary truths without which reason itself was handicapped, he was denying the validity of the Enlightenment project as a whole. Pius IX was making one last defense of the Christianity of Europe, one last plea for the survival of a Christian civilization. He ended the *Syllabus Errorum* by condemning the proposition that "the Roman Pontiff can, and ought to, reconcile himself, and come to terms with progress, liberalism and modern civilization."[30] Much of Europe laughed at the pope. Many Catholics scrambled to explain away his intransigent positions. What was clear, however, was that the era of the Alliance of Throne and Altar was coming to a close. The ideologies were taking over the state, and the growth of mass society was transforming the people, slowly but surely.

Germany emerged from this period as the strongest power in Europe, and its growth allows us the opportunity to see mass politics at work. Bismarck's bid to build a strong, autocratic state rested on the support of the lower classes against the more educated middle class, who tended to be ideological liberals. With wide popular support,

---

[30] Pius IX, *Syllabus Errorum*, §80.

fired up with German nationalism, Bismarck's government solidified Prussian control of the new empire through a standardized legal code and the extension of public education. The public schools were used to reduce regional diversity and unite everyone to the center, which included standardizing the German language. By the early 1870s, centralization had advanced remarkably.

The Catholic Church, however, was a problem. Catholicism was a rival loyalty, a rival basis for determining just and unjust, a lingering reminder that the state and the mass society that supported it were not absolute. Catholic Germans were not, in Bismarck's mind, German enough. Bismarck, therefore, launched the *Kulturkampf*—the struggle for culture—against the Church. The papacy under Pius IX had opposed Bismarck's increase in state power, especially the state's claim to regulate all aspects of life, including marriage and education. During the *Kulturkampf*, the state asserted absolute power in these departments, and the clergy resisted. Bismarck launched a persecution campaign against them. The Jesuits were expelled. The seminaries were nationalized. All religious orders were dissolved. Clergy could only be ordained and invested with positions through the state. Thousands of priests were thrown in prison or went into exile. The Catholic faithful overwhelmingly supported their priests. Pope Pius IX understood rightly that the Church in Germany's "final extinction now threatens. For the new laws, to be sure, have as their intent its destruction."[31] The pope attempted to reiterate the terms of the Alliance of Throne and Altar, arguing that the civil order depended on the spiritual order. He wrote:

> If no other laws than these of the civil authority existed and if they were of the highest order, it would be wrong to transgress them. If, moreover, these same civil laws constituted the norm of conscience, as some maintain both impiously and absurdly, the early martyrs and their followers would have been worthy of reprehension rather than honor and praise. Indeed it would have been against the laws and the wish of princes to hand down the Christian faith, propagate it, and found the Church. Nevertheless the faith teaches and human reason demonstrates that there is a twofold order of things. Two kinds of powers must be distinguished on earth—one natural that looks to the tranquility and secular business of human society;

---

[31] Pius IX, *Etsi Multa* (1873), §14.

the other, whose origin is above nature, which is in charge of the Church of Christ, divinely instituted for the salvation and peace of souls. The offices of these two powers are wisely coordinated so that things which belong to God are returned to God and, because of God, those of Caesar to Caesar, who "for this reason is great because he is less than heaven for he belongs to Him whom heaven and all creatures belong."[32]

In the end, the *Kulturkampf* failed to destroy Catholicism, but not because of Pius's arguments in favor of cooperation between Church and State. Rather, in the era of mass politics, the outcomes of such initiatives were unpredictable. The *Kulturkampf* strengthened Catholicism in Germany as Catholics bound together with common cause and looked to the papacy for leadership. One consequence of the *Kulturkampf*, for example, was a rallying of Catholics to a new political party, the Catholic Centre Party, which became a real force in Germany. Bismarck started rolling back his persecution of the Church by 1878.

He had bigger problems because of the rise of socialism. As industrialization had spread in Germany, so, too, did socialist ideology. This was a problem because socialism was spreading among the common people, who were the foundation of the state's power. Bismarck outlawed socialist publications and meetings. This didn't work. Again, mass politics was a tricky thing. Oppression often leads to the spreading of movements. Bismarck, however, was a master of *Realpolitik*. If he couldn't defeat the socialists directly, he appropriated the most popular aspects of their political program. Faced with the massive and obvious injustice of early industrial capitalism, the workers were demanding reform, and in the new political reality, that meant state-initiated and state-enforced reform. This was why socialism was growing. The socialists promised the workers better conditions. They explained to the workers why and how they were being exploited and showed them a political path to improving their lot. Bismarck understood this. To steal the socialist's wind, he started building the first modern welfare state, within which the state provides basic social services and a basic social safety net to the whole population.

This worked. The German state grew in power, and the German people grew in their nationalism. It was this nationalism that eventually mitigated the political significance of the Catholic population's religion.

---

[32] Pius IX, *Etsi Multa*, §16.

In a sense, *Kulturkampf* was a mistake for Bismarck not because it was impossible to reduce Catholic loyalty to the supranational Church, but rather because it was unnecessary to do so through such old-fashioned, direct persecution. This type of behavior was from another era, from the era of Joseph II or Napoleon. In the era of mass society, you defeat opponents through culture, through the shift in loyalty, through the slow marginalization of Catholicism until it is just the private religion of some of your citizens and not a political force of any real significance. This was the real lesson from *Kulturkampf*.

The *Kulturkampf* demonstrated that religion didn't much matter anymore. Nationalism was where the power was found. Nearly everyone came to understand this. In the same period, therefore, the liberals became nationalists in order to advance some of their political program. The conservatives became nationalists in order to control reform and to retain power. Even the socialists found themselves becoming nationalists, increasingly giving up their insistence that socialism could only be an international movement and that nations were just a part of the capitalist superstructure. Nationalism, in its purest forms, as was remarked earlier, should be seen as a new paganism. What became clear in the nineteenth century was that this paganism, like ancient paganism, was capable of incorporating a wide variety of particular ideologies and religions. This is the nature of paganism. It is not transcendent, and is not universal. It focuses on particulars and sees in them great power. Liberalism was a development of Protestantism, and it slowly became incorporated into pagan nationalism. Socialism was a heretical form of Catholicism, and it was more slowly and more incompletely incorporated into pagan nationalism. Christianity itself, as it became merely a private religion and not a worldview, could be incorporated into pagan nationalism. Nationalism could accommodate these belief systems as long as their believers gave proper reverence to the nation and its state, which they were increasingly inclined to do. The state and nationalism became the glue that held society together. They became the true focus of unity.

The papacy lost its state in precisely this period. There is a providential appropriateness to this. The papacy had needed its state because the states of Europe cared deeply about Christianity, which meant they would be tempted always to appropriate the power of the papacy for themselves. The papal state had protected the popes. Once the states of Europe no longer cared much about Christianity, there was really no need for a papal state, and so it passed out of existence.

The papacy was no longer a sovereign Christian monarch among a Europe of sovereign Christian monarchs. Now, the pope was an independent voice among industrialized nation-states and the mass societies that supported them. This was a new situation.

Mass society created a new political dynamic. Politics became both increasingly popular and increasingly ideological. To generalize, we could map ideologies on a spectrum. On the extreme left, we would find the anarchists. Anarchists believed that all power structures were part of the superstructure of oppression and believed that they had to be destroyed in order for people to find freedom. After them, we have the Communists, and then various types of socialists. As we move from left to right, we would come to the trade unionists and to the progressive liberals. Liberals and conservatives occupy the center of the spectrum. Then, as we move on the right, we would come to the monarchists, the nationalists, then to the ultranationalists, who believed that nations are necessarily in conflict, and then on the far right we would come to the anti-Semites and the racists. (Racial theory was new in the late nineteenth century. It was the attempt to make nationalism scientific by incorporating Darwinian theories of evolution and survival of the fittest.)

The political dynamic of mass politics tended toward the extremes of this spectrum in both directions. This is so because as the majority of the people fought it out in the center of the spectrum, they needed as many allies as they could find, and they needed to demonize their opponents as much as possible. This means that their rhetoric tended to adopt the more extreme positions from their own side of the spectrum, and they tended to paint their opponents as the most extreme elements on the other side of the spectrum. Everyone on the left became an "anarchist" to those on the right, and everyone on the right became a racist or chauvinist to those on the left. Over time, this led to increasingly radical ideological commitments as the extremes got stronger. The moderate nationalist liberals and nationalist conservatives managed to maintain control throughout most of Europe for the rest of the century, but political radicalism was on the rise everywhere.

Vatican I

There had not been an ecumenical council for three hundred years when Pope Pius IX called the First Vatican Council in 1869. This is remarkable when we consider the sheer magnitude of the changes that had occurred in Christendom during those centuries. No council was called during the Wars of Religion, during the Age of Absolutism, during the Enlightenment, or through the revolutionary period. Why? The answer, at least in part, is that the Church's unity was severely weakened during these centuries. The Catholic Church was, in practice, divided up into national churches that were dominated by their princes. The pope could not have called the bishops of the Church together without the permission of the princes, and once they arrived, most of them would have come as representatives of a kingdom more than as pastors in the universal Church. There was a very real danger that the bishops would have tried to impose upon the universal Church a Gallican ecclesiology. In the period of confessional states, an ecumenical council was a practical contradiction. The Council of Trent had been held before confessionalization had really taken effect. By 1869, the period of confessional states was coming to an end. The ideologies, especially nationalism, were taking the place of Christianity as the glue that held societies together, even if they continued to espouse a more or less nominal Christianity.

By 1869, an ecumenical council was possible again. The unity of the Church could be asserted again largely because the unity of the Church didn't matter much to the independent nation-states that were then emerging or being solidified. Increasingly, the Church was becoming just another private institution that operated within the borders of states. That it claimed some sort of special status for itself didn't really matter to those states as long as its members obeyed the law, went to work, and fought in the army. The heads of state of the countries of Europe were not invited to this council, as they had been to the councils of the fifteenth and sixteenth centuries, and they didn't seem to care. The papacy no longer recognized any state as a properly Catholic state, and the states, for their part, seemed to agree.

There were two main issues dealt with by the council. The first was the relationship between reason and faith, and the second was the office of the papacy. Against the full spectrum of modern thought, the council asserted that reason and faith were not in contradiction and that they, in fact, "mutually support each other, for on the one hand right reason established the foundations of the faith and, illuminated by its light, develops the science of divine things; on the other hand, faith delivers reason from errors and protects it and furnishes it with knowledge of many kinds."[33] The council refuted rationalism and naturalism with the assertion that faith was a necessary path to truth and that the truths of faith were not available to unaided reason, and it refuted fideism (the belief that faith had nothing to do with reason) with the assertion that the content of faith was reasonable and that reason itself was capable of attaining truth, even some limited truth about God.

The council asserted, dogmatically, that God could be known in some capacity through reason. This was an assertion about the very structure of the cosmos. The cosmos was structured in such a way, and human beings were situated within it in such a way, that we could come to some knowledge about God on our own. However, that knowledge was profoundly rudimentary. In fact, even enlightened by faith, our intellect was only capable of grasping the mysteries of God analogically and indirectly, and this limited ability was wounded by sin. Faith, then, was a remedy that restored us first to our natural abilities before elevating us beyond them: "It is indeed thanks to this divine revelation, that those matters concerning God which are not of themselves beyond the scope of human reason, can, even in the present state of the human race, be known by everyone without difficulty, with firm certitude and with no intermingling of error."[34] The council asserted as the basis of this understanding of faith and reason that God was the creator of all things out of nothing.

The council refuted the Enlightenment notion of reason not by denying the power of the human intellect but by confirming it and elevating it. Reason was *so* capable that it, through faith, could reach beyond its own powers. The council also refuted the fideistic notion of revelation as something unconnected with the world of experience, as something that comes from above in an entirely unpredictable way and that must simply be believed through a blind faith. Rather, revelation was supremely reasonable because it came from the very reason of God, and we participate in that divine reason. What both Enlightenment rationalism and fideism had in common was the dividing of faith and reason into sealed-off compartments. Both made a space for the life of man that did not necessarily involve God and a space for "religion" to operate that did not necessarily

---

[33] Vatican I, *Dogmatic Constitution on the Catholic Faith* (April 24, 1870), Session 3, Chapter 4, §10.

[34] Vatican I, *Dogmatic Constitution on the Catholic Faith*, Session 3, Chapter 2, §3.

involve the life of man. Either way of thinking can buttress secularized society and privatized religion. The council refuted them both by reasserting the integral nature of faith and reason. They were distinct, of course, but they were intertwined. There was *one* "twofold created order, that is the spiritual and the bodily."[35]

The council's work on faith and reason was important. But the most hotly debated topic among the seven hundred or so assembled bishops (out of the approximately thousand worldwide) was the question of papal infallibility. The Church, of course, had always taught that the pope, as the successor to St. Peter, was the head of the Catholic Church. It had always taught that the pope had a special teaching office and bore a special authority. The question before the council was whether this authority should be defined: should the papacy's universal governance of the Church be defined juridically, and should his teaching authority be defined as infallible in matters of faith and morals? We have already seen how the practical power of the papacy within the clerical hierarchy had increased during the nineteenth century. In the post-revolutionary period, the papacy had been increasingly looked to in order to lead the universal Church, both by the faithful and by the princes. The Gallican, national-Church way of thinking about Catholicism was on the wane.

Those who wanted to emphasize the power of the papacy and give it the most robust reading possible were called Ultramontanes. Ultramontane literally means "beyond the mountains" and is a reference to Rome being beyond the Alps from the rest of western Europe. The Ultramontanes made up the majority of the bishops. They saw a strong papacy as necessary for the assertion of the Church's rights against power-hungry governments and necessary for the condemnation of modern ideological and theological errors. Some Ultramontanes wanted the pope to take control of the Church as an absolute monarch. Some wanted the doctrinal infallibility of the pope to be defined so broadly that he would appear more as an oracle than a pastor. The Ultramontanes were opposed by a minority that was itself divided. The minority included bishops who believed in the infallibility of the pope but who thought it was an inopportune time to emphasize and define this infallibility. It also included those who doubted papal infallibility altogether and who were still inclined to a Gallican understanding of the Church.

---

[35] Vatican I, *Dogmatic Constitution on the Catholic Faith*, Session 3, Chapter 1, §3.

In the end, the council confirmed the Church's traditional assertion that the pope had universal ordinary jurisdiction. The pope has "full and supreme power of jurisdiction over the whole church, and this not only in matters of faith and morals but also in those which concern the discipline and government of the church dispersed throughout the whole world."[36] This means that the pope could act anywhere in the Church directly and under his own power. He could act always and everywhere to affect governance and discipline in the Church. However, the council also asserted that the bishops governed their local churches directly and as successors to the Apostles. They held not merely delegated papal power; rather, they wielded their own power as bishops. Nevertheless, the council asserted papal governmental power in very strong terms. This included denying the civil power any proper role in the governance of the Church. Even rights that some princes had successfully held for centuries, such as the right to approve all communications from the papacy to the bishops, were denied. The civil power had no direct power to govern the Church. This is an important assertion because it assumes a difference between the Church and the social world governed by the princes. This was a condition that neither the popes nor the princes would have recognized just a hundred years earlier. The Church is here understood as a distinct society from the society of economics and politics, a society so distinct that it is capable of separate governance. We can see in the language of the council a perception of this new reality. The fact that the council's statements engendered little protest shows that the princes had the same perception.

The most controversial act of the council, however, was the definition of papal infallibility. The minority was overcome, and the council taught and defined

> as a divinely revealed dogma that when the Roman pontiff speaks *ex cathedra*, that is, when, in the exercise of his office as shepherd and teacher of all Christians, in virtue of his supreme apostolic authority, he defines a doctrine concerning faith or morals to be held by the whole church, he possesses, by the divine assistance promised to him in blessed Peter, that infallibility which the divine Redeemer willed his church to enjoy in defining doctrine concerning faith or morals. Therefore, such definitions of the Roman pontiff are of

---

[36] Vatican I, *First Dogmatic Constitution on the Church of Christ* (July 18, 1870), Session 4, Chapter 3, §9.

themselves, and not by the consent of the church, irreformable.[37]

This was a robust definition of papal infallibility, but not as robust as it could have been. The pope is infallible only in matters of faith and morals and only when he is exercising his office of universal shepherd and teacher. We have already seen that the pope's power extended far beyond his teaching in faith and morals, and yet his infallibility did not. What is more, by asserting infallibility *when* the pope exercises his office as teacher, the definition implies that he is not always doing so. Sometimes, it seems, he speaks without exercising this office. It also asserted that the pope's infallibility was not a different infallibility than was held by the Church as a whole. Rather, it was exactly the Church's infallibility that the pope exercised. The Church, in a sense, speaks through him.

In this way, a moderate Ultramontanism carried the day. The papacy emerged from the council theoretically stronger within the hierarchical Church than it had perhaps ever been. However, that Church was now accepted to be something other than Western civilization itself. The pope was stronger within a Church that was itself far, far weaker. The Church as posited by Vatican I was again the universal Church of the Council of Trent, but it was a universal Church that existed within a dramatically fractured West. It was no longer integrated into society from top to bottom and therefore, wrapped up in affairs of economy and state. Rather, ironically, the Church could find its unity again only through an implicit acknowledgement of its distinction from society, an implicit acknowledgement that society seemed to be operating according to some other logic than the logic of Christ. The pope could assert seamless power over the Church as a whole precisely because the Church was no longer the whole. The victory of Ultramontanism was premised on weakness.

The pope ruled the Church directly and without sharing authority with governments, but if he declared a king deposed, what would happen? If he declared an economic venture immoral, what would happen? If he called for a crusade, what would happen? Not much. The papacy's power was consolidated as it shifted and shrunk. The papacy's power would now be found in its teaching office. The pope emerged in the late nineteenth century primarily as a preacher of the Gospel in a world increasingly governed by the logic of the machine,

---

[37] Vatican I, *First Dogmatic Constitution on the Church of Christ*, Session 4, Chapter 4, §9.

by the logic of ideology and power, that is to say, a world that was increasingly pagan. But it was not yet pagan through and through. Liberalism and socialism were Christian heresies, after all, and still contained much truth. The majority of people were still Christian, even if Christianity was becoming something private. There was still hope of redirecting society from within.

The Formation of Social Doctrine

Pope Leo XIII came to the papal throne in 1878. He was the first pope elected after the loss of the Papal States, after Vatican I, and after the rise of the militantly secular regimes of Otto von Bismarck in Germany and the Third Republic in France. What is more, the Industrial Revolution and the mass politics that it brought with it had definitively spread throughout Europe, challenging traditional ways of life almost everywhere. Leo came to power over a different Church that was facing a different Europe than had his predecessors.

Leo took on the office of preacher rather than governor. He at least implicitly understood that the Roman Church was no longer a political power in its own right; rather, its power and its duty lay in calling the baptized to a reconversion. Leo understood that he had to reformulate Christian teaching using the language and the social realities of his time. The world had changed too much for the still-lingering but tired language of the *ancien régime* and the Alliance of Throne and Altar. The papacy was not faced with generic "revolutionaries," "free thinkers," or "innovators." Rather, Leo was faced with true ideological opponents. Indeed, Europe was caught between liberal and socialist interpretations of what was going on and what needed to be done, while non-ideological, yet power-hungry, conservatives attempted to play one off the other. The ideologies were, at root, intellectual; they were about ideas. To counter these ideologies, Leo set about formulating Catholicism as a type of rival ideology, really an anti-ideology, an antidote to ideology. He sought to formulate Christian doctrine in such a way that it provided answers to ideological questions even as it attempted to point beyond these questions to a fundamentally Christian understanding of who mankind is and of what a just social order looks like. The result was what we now call Catholic Social Doctrine.

Of course, Catholicism had always been concerned about society. It had always proposed a critique of the way society functioned and made proposals and exhortations concerning how it ought to function. We have seen this throughout its history. But beyond such teaching, Catholicism is, in its essence, social. Catholicism is about the fall and redemption of mankind, and mankind fell and is redeemed together. As St. Paul wrote: "For as by one man's disobedience many were made sinners, so by one man's obedience many will be made righteous" (Rom 5:19). The Church then, throughout its history, has not merely "taught" about society; it has also been itself the means of society's healing and ultimate salvation. The Church is society being saved. So, what was new in the teaching of Leo XIII was most certainly not the recognition that social problems are real and relevant for salvation. No notion could more completely miss the thrust of all of salvation history, which, of course, is the profoundly social movement from slavery to freedom. Rather, what was new with Leo was a systematic ideological engagement with the intellectual foundations of liberal, industrial nation-states and those of their socialist enemies. Catholic Social Doctrine is simply the name that we have given the Church's engagement with the ideologies of political modernity.

The Church had launched similar initiatives in every age where it found itself faced with a non-Christian order. The Church Fathers, for example, had done so with paganism and had given the Church the formulation of her foundational dogmas in classical modes of thought in the process. Similarly, the emergence of Social Doctrine was the emergence of the Church's dialogue with late modernity's non-Christian order. Leo was attempting to reformulate Christianity for this new post-Christian reality. He was attempting to describe a vision of the City of God for a society that had largely forgotten that there was anything other than the City of Man. Christianity, of course, was still culturally present throughout Europe. But it was increasingly understood as a mere religion, as a mere private affair that had to do with morality or heaven or other such domains that were defined as politically and economically irrelevant. Society itself was organized along very different lines, and the political fights that were raging were between factions seeking to control those lines, and no faction was really Christian. Christianity was no longer the basis of political order. This was so much the case that many Christians mistakenly came to believe that Christianity wasn't essentially concerned about politics or economics at all, a notion that would have seemed extremely strange to the premodern Church.

Leo's central argument against the ideologies was that some

degree of goodness is, in fact, possible in the midst of the suffering of the world. Brotherly love does not have to wait until the final elimination of all inequality and all suffering, as the socialists thought, and neither does it have to be dismissed as a mere fairy tale in favor of the cold, hard reality of rational self-interest, as the liberals thought. Rather, in spite of our ever-present imperfection, we can move deeper into justice and love. At the heart of this argument is the idea of hierarchy, of "inequality," as the ideologues would put it. For liberalism, inequality between individuals' means and abilities must be ignored in favor of a pretend equality through a universal law code: men are equal as a matter of legal definition, regardless of their actual, obvious inequality in both ability and property. For the socialists, such real inequality must be exposed and acknowledged, but it must be interpreted always to be the result of exploitation and injustice. In stark contrast to both, Leo maintained that inequality is not merely undeniably present, nor is it merely inevitable, nor is it necessarily unjust, but it is, in fact, desirable.[38] For Leo, hierarchy was what made a just society possible. Against both the liberals and the socialists, he asserted that man's power over man was the very foundation of justice, but only if that power was a mediation of the power of God, only if it was true authority, an authority rooted in service. The alternative was not some sort of utopia of equality but rather oppression and tyranny. Justice and injustice turn on the use of power. Power itself, though, was not optional.

This seems like a complex idea, but it is based on a series of rather simple premises. The first is that mankind has a real nature and so a real end, something after which we are striving. We have a way that we are supposed to be, and being that way is what makes us happy and what, ultimately, leads us to heaven. This end, this way we are supposed to be, can be described in many ways. It is peace. It is blessedness. It is happiness. Actions that lead us closer to this end can likewise be described in many different ways. They are moral. They are rational. They are in keeping with the natural law. They are just. Human beings fulfill their natures when they behave in ways that lead them closer to their end. When Leo says that society ought to be rooted in justice, he means it ought to be rooted in this real human nature and directed toward the human end of social happiness. This happiness is finally found only in brotherly love, or charity, which

---

[38] See Leo XIII, *Quod Apostolici Muneris* (1878), §§5–6.

itself is only found through the love of God and the grace he makes available. Charity is, therefore, the final content of justice, and this content is prior to any particular state or political arrangement. Its maintenance is, in fact, the reason for any particular political arrangement. This means that every state can be judged by the standards of justice. Justice stands outside and prior to human power even as it is the principle that orders that power.

The second idea was that justice is implemented in human society through law. Law, if it is true law, is a particular instance of a just ordering of society. For example, it is an aspect of justice that children respect their parents and that parents care for their children. This immutable "natural law" is made a concrete law when human beings legislate that, for example, people must care for their parents in old age. Such particular laws can vary, but they must always relate back to the more fundamental and universal law. If they don't—if, for example, a society makes a law that mandates the opposite, perhaps that children be taken away from their parents and put in state schools—then such laws are not, in fact, laws because they are unjust. For Leo, then, there cannot really be unjust laws because an unjust law is no law at all. It is tyranny. What this means is that the particular governments and the particular laws of different people can be both diverse and unified in a single concept of law that is itself rooted in human nature. This was a profoundly Thomistic understanding of law.[39] Within it, it is possible that the so-called "law" of a particular state can be highly "illegal" if it is irrational or morally wrong. In other words, immoral law is a logical contradiction. This means that governments can do things that are illegal, which is really another way of saying that they can work against the happiness of their people, that they can be unjust. The State, then, is not self-sufficient; it must be a participation in the universal. Particular states must be oriented toward the universal end of human beings—happiness—which is, ultimately, to be found only in union with God. The purpose of true, just law is to lead people deeper into their union with God, which is at the same time deeper union with each other. True law is both disciplinary and pedagogical. Politics, then, are both totally necessary and at the same time dependent upon what is higher than them.

The third idea, which pulls the first two together, was the idea of authority. The laws that guide a society deeper into justice, and so

---

[39] Leo XIII, *Libertas Praestantissimum* (1888), §7.

happiness, must be made by men who have the authority to do so. This authority flows not from society itself but, for Leo, from God. This is the case because the law that they are making is nothing short of the particular application of the very law of God. Men with true authority work within God's authority. They mediate it to mankind. This idea of authority permeates the hierarchical ordering of human society. The family is governed by the authority of the father. The community is governed by the authority of its older and venerable members. The city is governed by its mayor and city council. The kingdom is governed by its king. But the principle is always the same. All true authority flows from God and through the hierarchies of power that are everywhere in society. As Leo wrote:

> For, He who created and governs all things has, in His wise providence, appointed that the things which are lowest should attain their ends by those which are intermediate, and these again by the highest. Thus, as even in the kingdom of heaven He hath willed that the choirs of angels be distinct and some subject to others, and also in the Church has instituted various orders and a diversity of offices, so that all are not apostles or doctors or pastors, so also has He appointed that there should be various orders in civil society, differing in dignity, rights, and power, whereby the State, like the Church, should be one body, consisting of many members, some nobler than others, but all necessary to each other and solicitous for the common good.[40]

Through these innumerable hierarchies and the laws they create, just authority flows into every nook and cranny of human social life. These hierarchies are not arbitrary. Rather, hierarchies of true authority are simultaneously hierarchies of prudence and even, in an ideal society, of holiness. Proper authority, at every level, leads men to their true happiness through the creation and application of true law. This is social order itself. As Leo wrote:

> In political affairs, and all matters civil, the laws aim at securing the common good, and are not framed according to the delusive caprices and opinions of the mass of the people, but by truth and justice; the ruling powers are invested with a sacredness more than

---

[40] Leo XIII, *Quod Apostolici Muneris* (1878), §6

human, and are withheld from deviating from the path of duty, and from overstepping the bounds of rightful authority; and the obedience is not the servitude of man to man, but submission to the will of God, exercising His sovereignty through the medium of men."[41]

What this means is that the presence of inequality is not proof of corruption. Far, far from it. In fact, there must be authority in order for justice to be lived. Without hierarchy, the natural law cannot be applied in a particular time and place through human law, and so man cannot live justly as a political society.[42]

Perhaps even more penetrating is Leo's assertion that hierarchy is not only desirable, it is unavoidable. If power is not working toward the good, it is working toward evil. But every society is permeated with hierarchies of power, one way or the other.[43] If a society pretends that it doesn't have hierarchy or tries to eliminate it, in fact, what it will do is obscure the mechanisms of power and provide cover for wicked men to oppress the weak. Rather, society should elevate authority, should recognize it, should sanctify it, should be very clear as to who has it and why and what their responsibilities are. Leo wrote: "Then, truly, will the majesty of the law meet with the dutiful and willing homage of the people, when they are convinced that their rulers hold authority from God, and feel that it is a matter of justice and duty to obey them, and to show them reverence and fealty, united to a love not unlike that which children show their parents."[44] In this way, authority can be empowered to perform its essential task and, at the same time, can be held accountable when it fails. Indeed, within this line of thought, if a state acts unlawfully, it becomes the duty of citizens to resist and a crime for them to obey.[45] Legitimate authority, for Leo, is the mechanism through which true law guides society to its proper end. Illegitimate authority, on the other hand, is the mechanism through which false law leads society deeper into sin and so misery. These are our options, options that neither liberalism

---

[41] Leo XIII, *Immortale Dei* (1885), §18.
[42] Leo XIII, *Libertas Praestantissimum*, §8.
[43] For Leo, the primordial social contract that underwrote most modern political theory was clearly a fiction that distorted the nature of real societies. Men do not set up inequality from a position of equality. Men find themselves always already in hierarchical society. Leo XIII, *Diuturnum Illud* (1881), §12.
[44] Leo XIII, *Immortale Dei*, §5.
[45] Leo XIII, *Sapientiae Christianae* (1890), §10.

nor socialism comprehend.

For Leo, this notion of authority was not a challenge to human liberty, as both liberal and the socialist ideologues would insist. The ideologues understood law and liberty to be diametrically opposed. Men had freedom when the law let them do whatever they wanted. For Leo, though, this didn't make sense. The law, as we have seen, was nothing else than reason itself directed toward the fulfillment of human nature in a particular time and place. For a person to act in an unlawful way, then, was an act of irrationality, an act that he would never choose on his own if he had not been in some way misled, manipulated, or dominated (including by his own disordered passions and vices). If a person really knew the truth and really wanted his own happiness, he would act in keeping with the fundamental law. He would act rationally. This, for Leo, was true freedom. If a person voluntarily acted in violation of the true law, and so in a way detrimental to his own well-being, the only possible explanation was that he was under the sway of sin, of vice, and so was a slave to a force foreign to him. It was precisely the elimination of such slavery that was the task of true law and so true authority. What this means is that true authority was not opposed to freedom but was the precondition for it. Liberty could only be obtained through the rational and prudent application of true law.

An example might help us understand. An alcoholic is a slave to his vice. The pursuit of drink dominates the rest of his life. Because of his slavery, he acts in ways that hinder his own happiness. He also hurts those around him, most especially his own family. For Leo, even if the "law" of the state allows this man to drink himself into depravity and misery, he acts illegally, immorally. What is more, this immorality is a mark of his servility. He is dominated by his vice, indeed, but he is no less dominated by the men who control him through his vice. The men who prey on him and use his vice in order to make money, in order to take from him what is his, to get him to abuse his authority over his family and its property for their own benefit, these men are his true masters. Slavery to vice brings with it slavery to other men. It brings false hierarchies. When proper authority, therefore, uses law in order to restrain such behavior, they are "inhibiting" the liberty of neither the alcoholic nor the wicked men who would prey on him. Quite the opposite is the case. Through law, they are increasing the liberty of both. Proper law is the application of the law of God, which governs men in their very natures whether they like it or not. Compliance with this law is the meaning of liberty. As Leo wrote:

> Therefore, the nature of human liberty, however it be considered, whether in individuals or in society, whether in those who command or in those who obey, supposes the necessity of obedience to some supreme and eternal law, which is no other than the authority of God, commanding good and forbidding evil. And, so far from this most just authority of God over men diminishing, or even destroying their liberty, it protects and perfects it, for the real perfection of all creatures is found in the prosecution and attainment of their respective ends; but the supreme end to which human liberty must aspire is God.[46]

This understanding of law and liberty had implications that most people in our day find troubling. One is that everything that is wrong, either morally or intellectually, is, by definition, potentially illegal. What this means is that one cannot have a right to do anything that is itself wrong, including saying things that are untrue. It is impossible to have an intrinsic *right* to speak or publish lies, for example. Therefore, the very notions of "freedom of speech" or "freedom of conscience" are based on a flawed understanding of liberty.[47] Freedom of conscience and freedom of speech cannot be understood as rights that somehow reside within human nature itself. Error has no rights. Nevertheless, a particular state might decide that it is in the interest of the common good to tolerate some degree of error, and so institute merely positive and provisional "rights" to free speech, but it could never recognize the maintenance of error as a truly legal right, as some sort of "human right."[48] What is more, the perfection of a society is necessarily reduced to the extent that error flourishes within it.[49] It must, therefore, be the objective of legitimate authority to steadily eliminate error in the most prudent way possible. Indiscriminate "free speech" can only be a remedial compromise.

For the same reasons, religious liberty cannot be understood as a human right. For Leo, Catholicism was the true religion, and all proper law was the articulation of truth. Freedom of worship, if it is

---

[46] Leo XIII, *Libertas Praestantissimum*, §11.
[47] Leo XIII, *Immortale Dei*, §32; *Libertas Praestantissimum*, §23.
[48] Leo XIII, *Libertas Praestantissimum*, §§33, 42.
[49] Leo XIII, *Libertas Praestantissimum*, §34.

understood as a human right, must, therefore, entail religious indifferentism, the idea that one religion is as true as another.[50] But the entire basis of human rights rests on the idea that there is, in fact, a true and universal "law" that ultimately descends from God. Catholicism, as the true religion, is our only complete access to this law. Leo wrote: "For, since God is the source of all goodness and justice, it is absolutely ridiculous that the State should pay no attention to these laws or render them abortive by contrary enactments."[51] To effectively act as if there were no God, or to act as if Catholicism were merely one religion among many, would be to undermine the very notion of true justice and so of legitimate authority. Therefore, "it is a public crime to act as though there were no God."[52] If the true religion were undermined, justice itself would necessarily be undermined, and society would descend into tyranny, which is exactly what Leo claimed was happening. As with free speech, however, a particular state might decide that it is conducive to the common good to tolerate religious error to various degrees. Such tolerance is probably nearly always prudent. But, for Leo, it must be understood as a compromise and not as rooted in fundamental "rights."

As is clear, Leo's entire social understanding rested on the truth of Christianity. True law was important not only because it dictated what people ought to do as a matter of positive duties, but also because obedience to it necessarily worked the best in the pursuit of human happiness. As Leo reminded those in power, fear is not enough to produce a stable state. Rather, a prosperous state required true obedience to its laws, and true obedience came only through a deeply felt duty toward God, which led to affection toward neighbor and social good will.[53] Without true religion, authority could not be real authority and could be only violence, only tyranny. This sounds hard to our ears. But we would do well to think it through. Leo was arguing that in Christian states, in actual fact, and in our lived experience, rulers were more just and the people were happier than in non-Christian states. He was arguing that Christian states, because they are in conformity with human nature and because they are animated by grace, actually work

---

[50] Leo XIII, *Libertas Praestantissimum*, §§19–21.
[51] Leo XIII, *Libertas Praestantissimum*, §18. See also §§39–40.
[52] Leo XIII, *Immortale Dei*, §5.
[53] Leo XIII, *Diuturnum Illud*, §24.

better.⁵⁴ This was, of course, a restatement of the Church's perennial understanding of itself as the only means of salvation. Institutionalized Christianity was a governments' only hope against the dysfunctional misery that the ideologies necessarily bring.⁵⁵ Our own experiences bear this out. Communities of true Christians are obviously more honest, more caring, more forgiving, more oriented toward each other's good than communities based upon ideological or commercial principles. Leo is clearly right that this fact is applicable to polities generally. It is based on the reality of the supernatural. The Catholic Church teaches the truth, but it also dispenses grace through the sacraments. This grace enables fallen mankind to live out the dictates of this truth, of the true law. The Church is not perfect, of course. Far from it. But faithful Christians living sacramental lives were obviously, to Leo, closer to living lives in conformity to the eternal law than were non-Christians. They were, therefore, capable of a greater happiness. Even from a utilitarian point of view, Christianity is the best policy.

Without the Church, mankind was reduced to its condition before Christ, reduced, ultimately, to the condition of paganism. Paganism, we should remember, was capable of order. It was capable of immense power and the accumulation of immense wealth. But these were built on fear, injustice, and cruelty. For Leo, then, this was the danger to which liberal or socialist calls for the separation of Church and State inevitably led. As Leo wrote:

> When Christian institutions and morality decline, the main foundation of human society goes together with them. Force alone will remain to preserve public tranquility and order. But force is very feeble when the bulwark of religion has been removed, and, being more apt to beget slavery than obedience, it bears within itself the germs of ever-increasing troubles. The present century has encountered memorable disasters, and it is not certain that some equally terrible are not impending.⁵⁶

If the Christian basis of law is suppressed, eventually the pursuit of pleasure would become the basis of law, and this, Leo says, "is simply

---

⁵⁴ Leo XIII, *Libertas Praestantissimum*, §22.
⁵⁵ Leo XIII, *Quod Apostolici Muneris*, §10.
⁵⁶ Leo XIII, *Sapientiae Christianae*, §3.

a road leading straight to tyranny. The empire of God over man and civil society once repudiated, it follows that religion, as a public institution, can have no claim to exist, and that everything that belongs to religion will be treated with complete indifference."[57] Governments that are in this way unconcerned with man's final end should not "be accounted as a society or a community of men, but only as the deceitful imitation or appearance of a society."[58] Ultimately, their order can rely only on mere force.[59]

Through this framework, Leo approached contemporary problems and attempted truly Christian solutions. No problem was more pressing than the plight of the working class. As we have already discussed, the Industrial Revolution turned the common man's world upside down. Millions of people found themselves crowded into cities, working in inhumane conditions for pennies. Leo addressed this problem in 1891 in his most famous encyclical, *Rerum Novarum*, which means *On Revolutionary Things*. *Rerum Novarum* is one of the most-cited papal encyclicals and one of the most misrepresented. Because Leo attempted a Christian solution that opposed the errors of both socialism and liberalism, both socialists and liberals have been able to manipulate the text and weaponize it against each other. The truth, though, is that Leo was neither a liberal nor a socialist. He was a Catholic, and *Rerum Novarum* is a Catholic rebuke of both ideologies.

Leo understood the situation quite well. As he described it, in the past hundred years all the traditional protections of the poor had been swept away. All the institutions, all the laws that had regulated the relations between the orders of the hierarchy of society had been overthrown, including the moral protections provided by Christianity. In the process, Leo contended, the workers "have been surrendered, isolated and helpless, to the hardheartedness of employers and the greed of unchecked competition." Indeed, "a small number of very rich men have been able to lay upon the teeming masses of the laboring poor a yoke little better than that of slavery itself."[60] This situation was intolerable.

As we have already seen, the intellectual integrity of liberalism and so the coherence of capitalism rested on the institution of ubiq-

---

[57] Leo XIII, *Libertas Praestantissimum*, §16.
[58] Leo XIII, *Sapientiae Christianae*, §2.
[59] Leo XIII, *Libertas Praestantissimum*, §16.
[60] Leo XIII, *Rerum Novarum* (1891), §3.

uitous private property. For the liberals, the right to private property was not just one right among many. It was, rather, the paradigm of all rights. It was a universal right. For liberals, everything was ultimately a piece of property, and what it meant to own something was to be able to do what you wanted with it, especially to trade it freely. For them, the factory owners and the factory workers were merely exchanging their private property in free transactions. The socialists, of course, understood capitalism in more or less identical terms. They understood clearly that capitalism rested on the institution of universal private property, and this, they believed, was the mechanism of its unbearable injustice. The socialists, therefore, advocated for the abolishment of private property in favor of state ownership. Leo pulls the rug out from under both ideologies.

Leo maintained that the right to private property was an aspect of the natural law. This was merely an aspect of the naturally hierarchical makeup of society. For Leo, it was right that the material goods of society be distributed through society in an unequal manner in the same sort of way that all goods, such as intelligence or health, were distributed in an unequal way. In a just society, certain people had control over more property than did other people, and this variation was part of what determined their relative position in the social hierarchy because, obviously, more property was the equivalent of more power. Like all hierarchical power, the power that property brought could only be justified if it was a mediation of God's loving power. At the bottom of the hierarchy, individual men had a duty to provide materially for themselves and for their families. They, therefore, had a right to the power necessary to perform this function, including the right to produce and retain the material means necessary, and no one had the right to take that property away from them. When the socialists, therefore, called for the elimination of all private property, Leo understood immediately that this was an attack on the rightful authority of the simple working father. It was an attack on his rightful place in society and his rightful authority. A father had a right to private property because he had the duty to rule his family well. This was his responsibility within the social hierarchy. For the same reasons, the socialist attack on all private property would disrupt higher orders in the social hierarchy and their relative responsibilities. Those with greater responsibilities needed greater means, including material means, in order to fulfill them. The socialists were after material equality, and, as we have already seen, Leo believed that this foolish endeavor would lead inevitably to its very opposite, the most extreme forms of tyranny. Private property, for Leo, was inviolable because hierarchy was both inevitable and desirable.

However, this most certainly did not make him a liberal. As we have already seen, the average working father had a right to private property only so that he could satisfy his responsibilities toward himself and the common good of his family, over which he ruled. The exact same principle applied to those higher in the social hierarchy, those with more property, only to a heightened degree. As Leo wrote:

> Therefore, those whom fortune favors are warned that riches do not bring freedom from sorrow and are of no avail for eternal happiness, but rather are obstacles; that the rich should tremble at the threatenings of Jesus Christ—threatenings so unwonted in the mouth of our Lord—and that a most strict account must be given to the Supreme Judge for all we possess. The chief and most excellent rule for the right use of money . . . rests on the principle that it is one thing to have a right to the possession of money and another to have a right to use money as one wills. Private ownership, as we have seen, is the natural right of man, and to exercise that right, especially as members of society, is not only lawful, but absolutely necessary. "It is lawful," says St. Thomas Aquinas, "for a man to hold private property; and it is also necessary for the carrying on of human existence." But if the question be asked: How must one's possessions be used?—the Church replies without hesitation in the words of the same holy Doctor: "Man should not consider his material possessions as his own, but as common to all, so as to share them without hesitation when others are in need." . . . Whoever has received from the divine bounty a large share of temporal blessings, whether they be external and material, or gifts of the mind, has received them for the purpose of using them for the perfecting of his own nature, and, at the same time, that he may employ them, as the steward of God's providence, for the benefit of others.[61]

The factory owners, then, owned their factories *for* those lower than they in the hierarchy, for their workers, and for society as a

---

[61] Leo XIII, *Rerum Novarum*, §22.

whole, and not merely for themselves. At every level in the vast complexity of the economy this simple principle holds. People own property for the common good, and especially for those who happen to fall immediately under their power. Property gives them power, and this power is justified only if applied to the common good. This is merely the meaning of justice. A just man is a man who perceives and acts in favor of the common good from his particular position within society. This is, of course, directly related to the proper meaning of the law. True law orders society toward the common good. Nothing could, therefore, be more unjust than "the cruelty of men of greed, who use human beings as mere instruments for money-making."[62] Leo is, therefore, asserting the Christian concept of justice against the liberals and their absolutist notions of private property. For Leo, private property was not *for* the person who held it. It wasn't really "his" in the liberal sense, in the same sort of way that the power that he held in society wasn't really "his." Property was a form of power, and power was always a mediation of God's power, directed always in service, and was never possessed outright.

This is why notions such as the "just wage" make sense in Leo's thought. Leo understands fully the liberal argument that wages are determined by free consent, that wages are a free contract. Therefore, for the liberal, injustice can only mean that either the employer does not pay the agreed-upon amount or that the worker does not do the agreed-upon work. This notion, Leo asserts, is entirely wrong. It is wrong because it rests on the liberal fiction of equality. In fact, the employer almost always has far more power than the workman, a power that is demonstrated in his control of far more property, including the factories. In a very real sense, this power is for those below the factory owner: the factories are *for* the worker and so *for* the little bit of society over which the worker rules, his family. This is how hierarchies work, and it is the basis of the doctrine of a just wage. A just wage is a wage that properly distributes control of property through the hierarchy of social authority. A worker must be able to support himself and his family in a manner that is appropriate for his dignity. This is a primary reason for which power higher in the hierarchy exists, why the factory owner's property exists. Leo writes:

> Let the working man and the employer make free agreements, and in

---

[62] Leo XIII, *Rerum Novarum*, §42.

particular let them agree freely as to the wages; nevertheless, there underlies a dictate of natural justice more imperious and ancient than any bargain between man and man, namely, that wages ought not to be insufficient to support a frugal and well-behaved wage-earner. If through necessity or fear of a worse evil the workman accept harder conditions because an employer or contractor will afford him no better, he is made the victim of force and injustice.[63]

At the same time, Leo argued that the great mistake of the socialists was to refuse to see that the social classes could work together for the good of society as a whole. They insisted on seeing all inequality as injustice. But, as we have repeatedly seen, this is just outright wrong. Justice rested on the distribution of goods, including the goods of power and property, through society in unequal and yet totally dependent ways. The working class and the capitalist class ought to work together as a single social organism in order to build a more harmonious and happier society.

Leo, of course, understood that this harmony was only finally possible through Christianity. The Church "alone can reach the innermost heart and conscience, and bring men to act from a motive of duty, to control their passions and appetites, to love God and their fellow men with a love that is outstanding and of the highest degree and to break down courageously every barrier which blocks the way to virtue."[64] Nevertheless, the entire social hierarchy ought to work for justice. This means that if people somewhere in the middle, such as factory owners, were abusing their power over those lower than they, the highest authorities, such as the State, must step in and protect the weaker parties. In general, the weak needed special concern because "when there is question of defending the rights of individuals, the poor and badly off have a claim to especial consideration. The richer class have many ways of shielding themselves, and stand less in need of help from the State."[65] The powerful's power was *for* the weak. If it was used otherwise, the weak had little recourse.

In his treatment of the plight of the working class, Leo imagined a just society consisting of as many people as possible owning as much property as possible with all of them using that property for

---

[63] Leo XIII, *Rerum Novarum*, §45.
[64] Leo XIII, *Rerum Novarum*, §26.
[65] Leo XIII, *Rerum Novarum*, §37.

the common good. It would be in such a society that true equality could be found because "the true worth and nobility of man lie in his moral qualities, that is, in virtue; that virtue is, moreover, the common inheritance of men, equally within the reach of the high and low, rich and poor. . . . If Christian precepts prevail, the respective classes will not only be united in the bonds of friendship, but also in those of brotherly love. . . . Would it not seem that, were society penetrated with ideas like these, strife must quickly cease?"[66] This vision posed a direct challenge to both socialism and liberalism by recombining the bits of truth that both heresies contained within a reframed orthodoxy. Leo was reframing for modernity the understanding of hierarchy and justice that had underwritten Christian thought since its beginning. True hierarchy, hierarchy that opened up to God, was the hierarchy of the City of God, the hierarchy of peace. False hierarchy, hierarchy that was closed downward, was the hierarchy of the City of Man, the hierarchy of domination and war. Both liberals and socialists proposed closed hierarchies. Leo was showing the alternative.

There was a penetrating brilliance to Leo XIII's work. Nevertheless, there were also significant limitations. One was the lingering consequences of the Alliance of Throne and Altar. Leo seemed to hold that a proper social order would be constituted at the top through a treaty or agreement between two more or less independent powers, the temporal and the spiritual, the king and the pope, rather than as a single, integrated, sacramental whole.[67] This idea maps nicely onto what appears to be a metaphysical assumption that the supernatural realm is stacked on top of the natural realm, as if reality were a two-story structure.[68] In this way of thinking, the state is natural and rules over the realms of bodies and of reason, directing man toward a fully "natural" end of temporal peace and security. The Church, for its part, is supernatural and rules over the realms of the soul and of faith, directing man toward the supernatural end of beatitude. The problem with this way of thinking is that while it seems to elevate the Church in importance, it actually makes it possible to imagine the world without the Church. If nature is self-sufficient and can deal with its own problems through

---

[66] Leo XIII, *Rerum Novarum*, §§24, 25.
[67] Leo XIII, *Sapientiae Christianae*, §§30–31.
[68] Leo XIII, *Sapientiae Christianae*, §6.

so-called "natural" reason, what do we really need the supernatural for? Heaven? If that is all, if the Church is not directly political, why not relegate it to the private lives of people? Why not structure society as if the supernatural doesn't exist? Couldn't such a secular society still pursue the natural ends of man, peace and prosperity, which happen to be the exact ends that the ideologues were after? Of course, Leo would refuse these suggestions. He would insist that the supernatural is not just a kind of bonus given on top of the natural but is, rather, what the natural is for, that the natural is for its elevation into the supernatural, where beatitude, the final end of man, is found. He would also insist that human nature is wounded and that grace is needed to heal as well as elevate. But his thinking does sometimes seem to lead in the two-tier direction, and those inclined to see the natural, political world as independent from the supernatural were able to use some of his writing in defense of their position.

Leo's writings also have an almost constant top-down orientation. He normally imagines law as being imposed from above by either the State or the Church, and the subject's primary response is one of simple obedience. Individual virtue comes from what appears to be a merely external obedience to law, through "submission." As Leo writes, "The political prudence of private individuals would seem to consist wholly in carrying out faithfully the orders issued by lawful authority."[69] But this authoritarian tendency almost certainly misses that political virtue does not consist merely in obedience. Rather, the character of the people itself, the people's collective virtue or vice, is the wellspring from which comes their leaders' legislation. St. Thomas understood this. St. Thomas asserted that the multitude was the ultimate legislator and that particular rulers merely stand in for them and work within their more fundamental, customary "law."[70] Leo seems to deny the multitude any legislative ability.[71] He also fails to adequately recognize how virtue opens up true freedom in the sense of increased scope of action. As we will see, later popes will pick up and develop these themes.

These shortcomings are significant, and they point to Leo's membership in the conservative milieu of his time and place. Leo was, in the final analysis, a profoundly orthodox conservative, clinging to

---

[69] Leo XIII, *Sapientiae Christianae*, §36.
[70] *ST* I-II, q. 90, a. 3.
[71] Leo XIII, *Quod Apostolici Muneris*, §2.

aspects of the early nineteenth-century Alliance of Throne and Altar, and not a radical—even as his thought was creative and often profound. Sometimes, people from the political left mistake Leo's criticism of capitalism for sympathy with their cause. They make this mistake because we have largely forgotten that the aristocratic conservatives of the nineteenth century disliked the grasping and money-grubbing that they perceived in the middle class-dominated, new economy as much as did the socialists, if not more. One often catches echoes of Metternich in the writings of Leo XIII. Indeed, even Leo's understanding of natural hierarchy and his understanding of property as being always tied to social duty are natural developments from very old notions of aristocracy and *noblesse oblige*. This is, perhaps, the genius of the first generation of Catholic Social Teaching: the integration of what was, at that time, already old-fashioned conservativism with the language of liberalism and socialism in a restatement of orthodox social doctrine.

The pontificate of Leo XIII marked a shift in the Church's orientation. The Church was now something clearly and obviously distinct from society itself. Politically, this had occurred through the unification of nations and the final end of Christendom, socially through the creation of non-Christian mass culture, and intellectually through the development of Catholic Social Doctrine. The Church was now a critic of society, operating as an organization that stood somehow outside particular societies, even as a "private" association with a "private" agenda, like a political party, a club, or an industrial concern, operating within a public world of economics and politics that behaved as if the Church didn't exist. As was appropriate to this new setting, the Church now proposed an "ideological" doctrine that competed with the modern ideologies more or less on their terms. This was necessary if Christianity were to have anything to say to the new order.

And yet, Leo was missing something profound. Leo and most other Churchmen were missing the profound importance of the swelling nationalism in the West. They were concerned with ideas, with systems of thought, with truth and error, with doctrine. Nationalism, however, was concerned with glory, with pride, with the heart. Nationalism stirred passions, and increasingly the ideologies served as little more than intellectual trappings for a deeper nationalism. Throughout Leo's writing, we get the sense that he mistakenly thinks that the ideologies are what is stirring the populace to "new things," when, in fact, those ideologies themselves were being steadily incorporated into rival nationalisms. Leo was arguing against the heirs to the rationalist Enlightenment. History, however, was shifting in favor of the heirs of Machiavelli, Napoleon, Bismarck, and Garibaldi, even if those heirs were slowly breaking into ideology-inspired factions: liberal-nationalism, socialist-nationalism, and racial-nationalism. The next hundred years would be about nationalism's victory over its ideological rivals and then its self-destruction in the unprecedented horrors of modern warfare.

3. The End of the Modern World
Radical Ideologies and the First World War

Perhaps better than anyone else, the philosopher Friedrich Nietzsche (1844–1900) articulated what was happening. God, he declared, was dead, and we had killed him. What he meant was that the sway of the Christian God, the sway of Christianity itself, was over. Christ had been overthrown. The world no longer needed him and was no longer submitting to his rule. Nietzsche at least partially understood what this meant. He understood, as did Leo XIII, that without God, Christian morality would eventually fail. Eventually, the momentum of Christian notions of right and wrong would dissipate. Without God's rule, it was mere prejudice, mere aesthetics, that kept people living more or less in the manner he demanded. As this Christian prejudice slowly withered, nihilism, the belief that there is no right and wrong, no meaning, no truth, would gain ground. But nihilism, for thinkers such as Nietzsche, was merely the death rattle of Christian morality, dependent as it was on the Christian notion of morality for its own definition. It, too, would give way to a new morality, one focused on glory and power and beauty, a new paganism dominated by the "overmen," the new heroes. Nietzsche understood the Enlightenment to be a sort of self-destruction of Christianity. What would ultimately come to take its place was not unaided reason, disinterested science, or any other tedious rationalism, which ultimately rested on a lingering Christian cosmology. In the end, what would take Christianity's place was a culture of struggle, conquest, victory of the strong, and the glory of power. This was the final undoing of Christianity with its "slave morality." This, for Nietzsche and his followers, was exciting; it was an opportunity for the strong to rise to the top and for the weak to finally be dominated. As Nietzsche wrote to his disciples:

> You higher men, learn this from me: in the market place nobody believes in higher men. And if you want to speak there, very well! But the mob blinks: "We are all equal."
> "You higher men" – thus blinks the mob – "there are no higher men, we are all equal, man is man; before God we are all equal."
> Before God! But now this god has died. And before the mob we do not want to be equal. You higher men, go away from the market place!
> Before God! But now this god has died. You higher men, this god was your greatest danger. It is only since he lies in his tomb that you have been resurrected. Only now the great noon comes; only now the higher man becomes—lord.[72]

This was the return of the glory of the ancient pagans, a return to the unchallenged dominance of the City of Man. Nietzsche asserted without hesitation that Christianity had destroyed the "tremendous deed of the Romans," the *imperium Romanum*, and that "until today nobody has built again like this, nobody has even dreamed of building in such proportions *sub specie aeterni*."[73] But the time was quickly approaching for the reconstruction of such pagan magnificence, for the return of the god-men and the power that they made possible. As Nietzsche asserted, "The time for petty politics is over: the very next century will bring the fight for the domination of the earth – the *compulsion to large-scale politics*."[74]

Nietzsche was a pagan, and as such, he could not understand Christianity. For him, Christianity could only be just another strategy of power because power was the only thing that was real. For Nietzsche, Christianity was nothing more than power in the service of bad taste and low culture, power in the service of the rabble, of the mass, and the degenerate politics and economies that they constituted. In the end, there was nothing other than the "will to power." The Christianity against which he railed bore almost no resemblance

---

[72] Friedrich Nietzsche, *Thus Spoke Zarathustra*, in: *The Portable Nietzsche*, Walter Kaufmann, ed., (Penguin Books: New York, 1982) 4: On the Higher Man, 1–2, (398).

[73] Friedrich Nietzsche, *The Antichrist*, in *The Portable Nietzsche*, Walter Kaufmann, ed., (New York: Penguin Books, 1982), 58 (648),

[74] Friedrich Nietzsche, *Beyond Good and Evil: Prelude to a Philosophy of the Future* (New York: Random House, 1989), 131.

to the Christianity of Christendom. But when it came to the privatized Christianity that he encountered in mass culture, when it came to Christianity as merely bourgeois "morals," he often hit much closer to the mark. This Christianity was hollow. It was on its deathbed. Something new, something big, something violent was brewing.

Nietzsche was putting into words what was actually happening toward the end of the nineteenth century. In the place of Christian notions of peace and harmony, of hope in a final and lasting justice, notions of fundamental conflict were on the ascendency. In science, Charles Darwin's theory of the survival of the fittest had, by the end of the century, definitely won the debate on the evolution of animal species. According to Darwin, life as we observed it was the result of unrelenting struggle and competition: the strong survived, and the weak died. Darwin's theories had been immediately applied to humanity. At the most extreme, there developed so-called "scientific racism" and eugenics. This was merely the idea that the races of humanity were in competition for survival and that the stronger races would and should defeat and hold in subjugation the weaker races. Particular races could make themselves stronger and so, more likely to win in the global contest through eugenics, which was the science of the selective breeding of human beings. For many, racism came to underwrite their nationalism. It was not just that they loved their nation; they wanted victory for their nation; they wanted their nation to be heroic, to win glory, in the old pagan sense of the term. While racism was its most extreme manifestation, such "social Darwinism" likewise penetrated more moderate ideological positions. Under its influence, liberalism's understanding of the competition between individuals became more ruthless, and socialism's understanding of class conflict became more violent and relentless. Everywhere the notion of conflict was displacing the decaying notions of harmony and virtue, and everywhere this was increasingly understood as a good thing.

Paganism had never had a sense of true transcendence. The gods had lived in the same world as their worshipers. They were merely far, far more powerful than mankind. Paganism lacked transcendence, but at the same time, it was not merely materialistic. It understood that power was more than matter in motion and that the forces of the world were more than the perfectly predictable and bland forces of physics. The pagan world was full of powers that could crush man but could also be harnessed by man. Indeed, the pagan gods were strong, stronger than any man, and yet they could be placated and even manipulated. These strong gods were integrated into the pagan struggle for survival. They were a part of the battlefield on which fortune could be overcome and glory could be won. The end of the nineteenth century saw the return of such gods. The nation, the race, the people, the class—these all took on the character of gods. They were powerful and had to be placated, but they could also be manipulated. They operated in the same world as the individual, but they could destroy him, or, conversely, greatly reward him. They were not themselves integrated into some cosmos of universal rationality or justice, a cosmos of ascending common perfection. Rather, they were integrated into an earth-bound cosmos of conflict, with winners and losers. The "forces" of mass society became actors in history as people forgot that these forces were really nothing more than the people themselves. The power of the ancient god-kings, as the Bible made clear, was never anything other than the alienated power of the peoples they enslaved. The slaves' own power became an "independent" force that held them in subjugation. The new gods, as they drove out God, were constituted in and through the construction of the mechanisms of mass society that made their power felt. Like the ancient gods, they were false because they were not what they seemed and not because their power was not truly felt.

Contending with these new gods on the social battlefield were the ideologies. But they, too, had undergone a transformation. They, too, had become powerful. As we saw earlier, both liberalism and socialism were based on an anthropology of conflict. For the liberals, society was fundamentally made up of individuals in competition. For the socialists, society was fundamentally made up of classes similarly in competition. In their early stages, however, both ideologies, as heresies, had retained many Christian intuitions and assumptions. Many liberals, for example, based their system on the sincere belief in universal human dignity. The liberals often assumed that basic Christian morality somehow persisted at the private level even within a society based on public self-interest. These earlier liberals seemed to imagine that they could unleash the gods on the world and profit from their power even while fortifying the private against them, as if such a house divided against itself could stand. The socialists, for their part, retained a strong sense of justice, even of charity, and optimistically believed that harmony was possible. They, too, believed in universal human dignity and hoped for its realization. Both liberalism and socialism in their early forms were universalist and rationalist. They had little use for the strong, arational loyalties that stirred men's hearts. A liberal world would have been a world where borders and languages would become mere window dressing to a seamless global system of trade and rational allocation of resources where the individual was free to pursue his version of happiness without hindrance. The socialists had looked forward to the breakdown of particular loyalties in the face of international class solidarity and finally of classless and nationless utopia. These "enlightened" and "disenchanted" forms of the ideologies were largely dependent on lingering vestiges of Christian morality and operated still within a Christian cosmos that had banished the gods of ancient paganism. As these vestiges faded, the ideologies shifted to systems of power, a shift that they could make through the steady extension of their ideological structures of the conflict that they had already posited as the foundations of their vision of society. Heresies only ultimately have two choices: they can either move back toward orthodoxy, or they can move forward into paganism. They can return to the City of God or advance to the City of Man. At the end of the century, the ideological heresies advanced.

Among the liberals, the market became both immensely powerful and profoundly dangerous. Rather than being the mere assemblage of men working toward the fulfillment of their needs, the liberals began to imagine it as a historical actor in its own right. The market had to be treated with care, it had to be grown, it had to be extended, fed, even, because in doing so, mankind would gain its favor and so grow wealthy. For the same reason, it must not be offended. If its laws were broken, it might turn against us, forcing us into poverty. All power, Pope Leo XIII had asserted, was the mediated power of God; no human power was able to account for itself, able to ground itself in anything other than raw force. The market was a power without God. It was made of men and yet did not obey them. Men became devoted to the market, both loving it and fearing it. But this devotion was not separated from their growing nationalism. Rather, the market became the particular god of certain nations—most especially the British and the Americans. Their national power and the power of wealth were tied directly together. For socialists, the socialist movement itself took on divine characteristics. History, for them, was unrelenting and was marching in the direction of socialism. No longer was socialism the mere assemblage of men seeking redress of injustice and a redistribution of productive property. Socialism was history itself, and the individual who stood in its way would be crushed. The movement, eventually "the party," became the object of devotion because it wielded great power, beyond the mere wills of the men who constituted it. It was both loved and feared. It obeyed its own laws and had its own motives to which the individual must submit or be destroyed. It became another god of power. As this transition occurred, the remnants of Christianity that had underwritten both liberalism and socialism were slowly driven out. The assumption of violence that had always formed their foundations came to dominate their entire ideological edifices. This was the paganization of the ideologies. More mundanely, but no less significantly, economics, sociology, and political science came to replace ethics and moral theory in the study of mankind. A new class of half-cynical social "scientists" attempted to understand the gods of mass society in order to manipulate them, like the priests and oracles of the ancient pagan cults. These were the emerging religions of the new paganism.

Like the ancient gods, these new gods were not at peace with each other. It was their mounting competition, for example, that underwrote the late nineteenth- and early twentieth-century construction of empires. Starting in the 1880s, the nations of Europe scrambled to conquer as much of the world as possible. By 1914, basically all of Africa and most of Asia were under European control. This "New Imperialism" was driven by many factors. As capitalism became more and more developed in western Europe, there emerged demand for cheap raw materials to feed the ever more efficient factories and at the same time, the need to find new markets within which to sell the products of those factories. Commercial interests were, therefore, almost universally in favor of expanding empires. At the same time, the mounting fervor of nationalism drove the imperial project forward. As one German politician said, "All the great nations in the fullness of their strength have desired to set their mark upon barbarian lands, and those who fail to participate in this great rivalry will play a pitiable role in the time to come."[75] The greatness of one's nation was on the line. If one country did not conquer a land and add it to its empire, its rival would. Tied closely to this motivation was the Darwinian notion that if one nation or race had the strength to

---

[75] Heinrich von Treitschke, quoted in M. E. Townsend, *Origins of Modern German Colonization, 1871–1885* (New York, 1921), 27.

conquer another, it had, at the same time, the right or even the duty to do so. And there remained still the Enlightenment notion that the more advanced peoples had a duty to bring the blessings of civilization, technology, and politics to the primitive and backward peoples of the world. Only the socialists, for the most part, found grounds to criticize the New Imperialism. But, while draped in ideological formulations, the real basis of their opposition was that they were nowhere in power, and so imperialism served only to strengthen their political rivals. Wherever socialists came to power, they, too, became imperialists. Pagans build empires.

Indeed, more than any other reason, imperialism was the result of the ascendency of the idea of power for power's sake. The elites of Europe found themselves in a world of powerful forces that had to be placated and manipulated, and they played them off each other in order to maintain the established power structures and to expand wealth accumulation. Imperialism was a mechanism that allowed them to do this. One theorist has gone so far as to ascribe imperialism to an "alliance between capital and mob."[76] Imperialism was both the consequence of the shift to power and the cause of its acceleration. Through imperialism, the elite classes were trained in governance through pure power. In the nation-states of the nineteenth century, power was necessarily tied to popular support. It was part of the very nature of nation-states that the "nation" underwrote the power of the "state." In the new empires, however, the nation used its state in order to dominate other nations, without any notion of those nations being assimilated or of their territories being "naturalized" into the imperial nation. The imperial governments were not *for* the people that they ruled; rather, they were *for* another people, often thousands of miles away. Unlike the government of a nation-state, an imperial government deployed power over a population without being answerable in any way to that population. In fact, the imperialist's power was diametrically opposed to the various social and economic powers of the lands over which he ruled. His project was the extension of his power at the expense of the powers that he found already infused into the subject peoples. Imperialism was a school in the use of raw power, a training in what it could accomplish, and an inculcation of the idea that society was ultimately merely a struggle for power and that power's primary function was the enrichment of

---

[76] Hannah Arendt, *The Origins of Totalitarianism* (San Diego: Harcourt, 1966), 155.

those who wielded it. Imperialism was driven by this shift to power, but it also accelerated it as the techniques and mentalities of imperial government returned to Europe to penetrate and transform domestic government. Imperialism was a seminary for the priests of the strong gods. At the same time, the elite's children were being "classically" educated in ancient pagan literature. Increasingly, such study of pagan thought was no longer a preamble to a Christian education but the culmination of elite education itself. An imperial frame of mind, a neopagan frame of mind, was becoming the norm.

Power is, of course, jealous. A politics of power is a politics of conflict, and while the established governments of Europe succeeded for some decades in directing the competing powers within their borders to a shared nationalism aimed at the imperialist endeavor, perpetual expansion could not be a long-term mechanism for the maintenance of national unity and wealth accumulation. The rivalry that had been present in Europe since the birth of nationalism and which had been accelerated through imperialism reached a fever pitch by the second decade of the twentieth century. Nationalism became militant and the construction of empires less capable of placating it. This nationalism was translated into domestic political power through mechanisms such as massive military buildups. In Germany, the liberals and the socialists, for example, joined with the conservatives in supporting an immense naval buildup. The most popular political program in Britain, uniting the ideological factions, was the policy of matching and surpassing the German buildup, ship for ship. All the major powers of Europe poured capital and political will into building gigantic war machines. This included the raising of huge armies. Most of the countries of Europe had near-universal conscription. Young men served in active service and then in the reserves through middle age. By 1914, mass society was increasingly a mass military society, made up of fiercely nationalist men who had been trained to fight, disciplined into military obedience, and were led by elites trained in the power techniques of empire.

Nevertheless, a general war was hard to imagine. The spread of capitalism had intertwined the economies of all the European powers to such an extent that some analysts argued that war would be basically impossible. The financial interests of the various countries would just not allow for a general conflict. Rather, steady and serious, but ultimately peaceful, competition seemed to be the order of the day. The French and German populations, for example, were no doubt becoming increasingly hostile to each other, but the integration of their economies and of the interests of their ruling classes would seem to serve as a reliable check to popular aggression. The buildup of military power itself was often, paradoxically, seen as prohibitive of large-scale warfare. As the thinking went, so long as the powers of Europe maintained some balance in military power, the increasing magnitude of that power could only make war less desirable and therefore, less likely.

Christianity had not become extinct from this world. In fact, in some countries, religious observance seems to have increased around the turn of the century. This seems a paradox. But the paradox dissipates when we understand that part of the reason for the rise of Christian observance was the decline of its social relevance. Because Christianity was of little importance to the great structures and powers of society, it was free to spread within the "private" lives of citizens. This was modern Christianity, however, Christianity as a mere religion and not as a civilization. This tended to be a sentimental Christianity of home and hearth and no longer the basis of social life itself. Most Christians' primary allegiance was now to their nation or perhaps their political party and not to a universal and global Christianity. By around 1900, in Europe, we should see Christianity as a particularly popular cult within the modern pantheon. Paganism is, of course, polytheistic, and so the gods of modern paganism were indifferent to the existence of the God of Christianity as long as Christians reserved ultimate devotion for them, as long as the most profound sacrifices, such as death on the battlefield, were made to them alone. In the modern regimes, there could be many religions but only one State, only one economy, only one society, and, increasingly, only one ideology. The Catholic Church alone retained even the pretense toward being a focus of international unity, and as we have seen, this was mostly theoretical.

World War I broke out in 1914 between the Triple Entente, made up of Britain, France and Russia, and the Triple Alliance, made up of Germany, Austria-Hungry, and Italy. This was a new kind of war. Industrialization led to the mass production of technologically advanced weapons such as machine guns, long-range artillery, tanks, airplanes, and poison gas. At the same time, mass society, motivated by militant nationalism, allowed for the mobilization of millions of people, of whole societies. The young men went to the front to fight, the old men and the women went to the factories to produce the weapons and material they needed in order to do so. The conflict quickly bogged down in a war of attrition, with each side trying to drain the other of resources, including human resources. The war became cynical, with battles launched and continued not for territorial gain or battlefield strategy but for the sole purpose of killing as many of the enemy as possible.

Most horrifying, however, was that the war wasn't really over anything. The ideological differences between the main combatants were not dramatic, and none of them had an ideology that demanded that they conquer all rivals. None of the powers wanted the territory of the other powers. Germany did not want to rule France; Russia did not want to rule Germany. Economically, the combatants' interests were so intertwined that there was no way the war was advantageous. It wasn't over ideology; it wasn't over territory; it wasn't over wealth. Why was it being fought? It was being fought because once it had begun, the only way for it to end was for one side or the other to concede, and no one was willing to do that. It was fought because the gods of nationalism, mass economy, and mass society demanded that it be fought, and no one was willing to oppose their will. Pride, seeking glory, was the cause of the slaughter.

As Pope Benedict XV wrote in 1914:

> On every side the dread phantom of war holds sway: there is scarce room for another thought in the minds of men. The combatants are the greatest and wealthiest nations of the earth; what wonder, then, if, well provided with the most awful weapons modern military science has devised, they strive to destroy one another with refinements of horror. There is no limit to the measure of ruin and of slaughter; day by day the earth is drenched with newly-shed blood, and is covered with the bodies of the wounded and of the slain. Who would imagine as we see them thus filled with hatred of one another, that they are all of one common stock, all of the same nature, all members of the same human society? Who would recognize brothers, whose Father is in Heaven? Yet, while with numberless troops the furious battle is engaged, the sad cohorts of war, sorrow and distress swoop down upon every city and every home; day by day the mighty number of widows and orphans increases, and with the interruption of communications, trade is at a standstill; agriculture is abandoned; the arts are reduced to inactivity; the wealthy are in difficulties; the poor are reduced to

abject misery; all are in distress.[77]

Pope Benedict XV tried to bring the war to an end. He tried to speak sense to the combatants, showing them the irrationality of their behavior. He pointed to the root problem: the eclipse of Christianity as the principle out of which flowed the governance of states and societies. The only solution was a return to the faith: "Such, moreover, has been the change in the ideas and the morals of men, that unless God comes soon to our help, the end of civilization would seem to be at hand."[78] Mass societies which had banished God molded children through their mass education and propagandized adults through their mass media into believing that God had nothing to offer, that all hope of happiness was to be found in the temporal enjoyment of riches, glory, and pleasure.[79] Only a return to the faith would finally end the violence. "In proportion to the growth of this faith amongst men will be the decrease of that feverish striving after the empty goods of the world, and little by little, as brotherly love increases, social unrest and strife will cease."[80]

None of the leaders of the belligerent nations had time for the pope and his talk of God and truth. They were dealing with the supposedly real world, the world of power and wealth, the world of frenzied mass nationalism which the politicians could just barely contain and direct. The stirred-up masses were the source of their power but also the constant danger to that power. The war dragged on until 1918, when Germany and its allies finally surrendered. Over ten million soldiers had died. An estimated additional eight million civilians were killed. The great empires of Europe came to an end through popular revolution: the tsar in Russia was overthrown, and the Russian Empire collapsed into civil war as Communists slowly solidified control; the Austrian-Hungarian empire was dissolved into several nationality-based countries; the Ottoman Empire, which had existed since 1300 and had at one time dominated the Mediterranean, was broken up; Germany's monarchy was overthrown, and a liberal democracy was established.

---

[77] Benedict XV, *Ad Beatissimi Apostolorum* (1914), §3.
[78] Benedict XV, *Ad Beatissimi Apostolorum*, §5.
[79] Benedict XV, *Ad Beatissimi Apostolorum*, §§15, 17.
[80] Benedict XV, *Ad Beatissimi Apostolorum*, §18.

The Interwar Years and World War Two, 1920–1945

The Great War marked the definitive end of optimistic ideology in Europe. Through the previous hundred years, liberalism and socialism had each maintained a version of progress that assumed that things were going to get better and better. The nineteenth century was seen by many as a century of steady progress toward societies of freedom and prosperity, as the forces of tradition and religion were steadily undermined and eliminated. The First World War shattered what lingered of this optimism. The dream of the Enlightenment was over. Rather, it became clear to many that progress could be had only through violence. The "enlightened" dream had turned out to be a nightmare. The West came to despair of any notion of peaceful movement toward the fulfillment of human potential. Rather, to many, the war demonstrated that Nietzsche was right, that the world was a violent place, that movement toward social improvement could happen only through extreme violence, that only those willing to face the reality of history as brutal and heartless had any chance of realizing their goals. The war was followed by worldwide economic depression that thrust millions into unemployment and extreme poverty, confirming this dark vision of the world. It is an indication of just how weak the cultural influence of the Church was that these experiences did not lead to a return to the ancient faith. Instead, the great masses of the industrialized countries moved toward ever more extreme ideological systems in a seemingly desperate attempt to control the gods of modernity. Again, we see that depraved structures of power and order worked to produce vicious social habits, which reinforced and deepened the evil of the social structures. This was a return to the downward spiral that St. Thomas had identified as the historical dynamic of the Age of Nature, of the age of the god-kings.

The relatively mild socialism of the end of the nineteenth century gave ground to radical Communism, led by the newly formed Soviet Union in Russia. Throughout Europe, nationalism shifted into Fascism with the rise of Mussolini in Italy in the 1920s, and to extreme racism with the rise of the Nazi party in Germany in the 1930s. The liberal nations that had won the war shifted to a type of economic nationalism, with the State growing massively in size and scope and with "freedom" becoming a slogan of nationalist pride as much as it was a universal principle, while more and more emphasis was placed on the accumulation of material wealth. The American president, Woodrow Wilson, had hoped that the postwar dividing up of Europe into independent nation-states would reduce tension and lead to a lasting peace. But it seemed that just the opposite was happening. Moderation everywhere gave ground to ideological radicalism. Through the 1920s and 1930s, Europe was sorting into two totalitarian factions, neither of which had need for Christianity. Both left and right were shedding the lingering vestiges of Christianity in favor of late modernity's particular form of paganism, a totalitarianism that attempted to channel the raw power of mass society through cults of ideological extremism.

Benito Mussolini, the Fascist leader in Italy, wrote:

> Fascism conceives of the State as an absolute, in comparison with which all individuals or groups are relative, only to be conceived of in their relation to the State. The conception of the Liberal State is not that of a directing force, guiding the play and development, both material and spiritual, of a collective body, but merely a force limited to the function of recording results: on the other hand, the Fascist State is itself conscious and has itself a will and a personality.[81]

For the Fascists, the State, or in the case of the Nazis, the race, stood alone. Social units smaller than the State existed to serve the State, and social units larger than the State simply did not exist. This radical form of nationalism denied the validity of both the particular and the universal. Rather, all was in service to the State, which became, often explicitly, a god.

Pope Pius XI (r. 1922–1939) described Fascism as an "ideology which clearly resolves itself into a true, a real pagan worship of the State—the 'Statolatry' which is no less in contrast with the natural rights of the family than it is in contradiction with the supernatural rights of the Church."[82] Pius XI recognized directly the paganism that underwrote this movement and asserted definitively that it was incompatible with Catholicism. He wrote of the Nazis:

> Whoever exalts race, or the people, or the State, or a particular form of State, or the depositories of power, or any other fundamental value of the human community—however necessary and hon-

---

[81] Benito Mussolini, *Fascism: Doctrine and Institutions* (1935).
[82] Pius XI, *Non Abbiamo Bisogno* (1931), §44.

orable be their function in worldly things—whoever raises these notions above their standard value and divinizes them to an idolatrous level, distorts and perverts an order of the world planned and created by God; he is far from the true faith in God and from the concept of life which that faith upholds."[83]

Fascism and Nazism amounted to the denial of the transcendence of God, a lowering of the divine into the world, "substituting a dark and impersonal destiny for the personal God."[84] It attacked the particular rights of the family and the individual in one direction and denied the universal power of the Church in the other direction. The social world was reduced to mere power, and the most powerful thing was the absolute State channeling the forces of mass society. In the pursuit of heroic glory, the nation dominated all lesser powers and waged constant war against all equal or greater powers. This was a reconstituting in a new form of the slave-state, temple societies that Christianity had undone two thousand years before.

Against this violent paganism, the pope asserted the Church's ancient vision of unity within diversity, its vision of harmonious hierarchy that united in the Charity of the New Testament the most particular with the most universal: "The Church founded by the Redeemer is one, the same for all races and all nations. Beneath her dome, as beneath the vault of heaven, there is but one country for all nations and tongues; there is room for the development of every quality, advantage, task and vocation which God the Creator and Savior has allotted to individuals as well as to ethnical communities."[85] It was precisely the omnipotence of the divine that made peace possible in the particular. The only hope for peace was a return to Christianity. Pope Pius XI exhorted Catholics living under Fascist regimes to resist their power and to be willing to suffer persecution and even martyrdom in defense of their families and their faith, placing "evangelical humility" in direct opposition to fascist lies about "heroic greatness."[86] This was not pious exaggeration. When Hitler came to power, there had been some four hundred Catholic newspapers. Two years later, there were none. When Hitler came to power, millions

---

[83] Pius XI, *Mit Brennender Sorge* (1937), §8.
[84] Pius XI, *Mit Brennender Sorge*, §7.
[85] Pius XI, *Mit Brennender Sorge*, §18.
[86] Pius XI, *Mit Brennender Sorge*, §34.

of children attended Catholic schools. A few years later, almost all Catholic schools had been closed, and Catholic children were forced by law to join the Hitler Youth. Catholics were systematically intimidated and threatened into remaining silent. Those who dared speak out against the regime faced serious consequences. Over twelve thousand priests were sent to concentration camps, most of whom were murdered. Thousands of nuns faced the same fate.

Fascism's mortal enemy, however, was not the Church. Christianity had little real power. The relative ease with which Nazism spread through the most Catholic regions of Germany and Austria demonstrated this sad truth. Fascism's real enemy was Communism. The Leninist Communists in Russia had won their civil war by 1922 and set about building the Soviet Union as a superpower and exporting their version of militant Communism. For Lenin and his followers, the Communist revolution could only achieve the final classless utopia by passing through a period of the absolute, totalitarian rule of the Communist party. The party had to use its total power to liquidate all remnants of pre-socialist society. Communism, while resigned to working through existing nation-states, remained ideologically universalist. In the international Communist society that the Soviet Union sought to build, all national differences would ultimately be dissolved along with all cultural baggage like the family or Christianity. This universalism, along with its theoretical materialism and atheism, put Communism directly at odds with the Fascists. What is more, as Communism spread among the working class, the middle and ownership classes increasingly saw Fascism as an attractive alternative ideology that was capable of uniting the classes without disrupting the inequality in wealth and economic power that they enjoyed. Communism was, therefore, the mortal foe of Fascism.

The Church, of course, could take little comfort in this enemy of its enemy because the Communists were simply worse than the Fascists when it came to persecution of the Church. Fascists often maintained a weak, romantic respect for Christianity as an aspect of their nations' heritages. The Communists maintained no such nostalgia. For the Communists, Christianity was merely a particularly virulent aspect of the superstructure of capitalism. Christianity had to be destroyed, and the Communists of the 1920s and 1930s did everything within their power to do so. In the Spanish Civil War during the 1930s, the Communist forces murdered thousands of priests and religious and desecrated every church over which they gained control.

The socialist government in Mexico persecuted Catholics through the 1920s and 1930s to the point that the faithful peasantry organized into an ad hoc army to fight the government under the slogan *Viva Cristo Rey!*—"Long live Christ the King!" Many of the faithful and the clergy who served them were martyred. Of course, in the Soviet Union, Christianity was simply outlawed and systematically and ruthlessly suppressed.

Communism was, according to Pius XI, a "barbarism worse than that which oppressed the greater part of the world at the coming of the Redeemer."[87] It was worse than ancient paganism; it was a "satanic scourge."[88] Its appeal was found in its perversion of Christian notions:

> The Communism of today, more emphatically than similar movements in the past, conceals in itself a false messianic idea. A pseudo-ideal of justice, of equality and fraternity in labor impregnates all its doctrine and activity with a deceptive mysticism, which communicates a zealous and contagious enthusiasm to the multitudes entrapped by delusive promises.[89]

Communism destroyed all morality, and so social order could be maintained only through terror and through turning men into mere cogs in the political and economic machine. This was the consequence of the denial of all true authority and all true hierarchy.

Pius XI did not, however, spare the third modern ideology, liberalism, from his rebuke. Rather, the spread of both Fascism and Communism were the fruit of the seeds liberalism had sown: "If we would explain the blind acceptance of Communism by so many thousands of workmen, we must remember that the way had been already prepared for it by the religious and moral destitution in which wage-earners had been left by liberal economics."[90] Liberalism had de-Christianized society and turned man against man, subordinating "society to the selfish use of the individual."[91] As Pius wrote:

> There would be today neither Socialism nor Communism if the

---

[87] Pius XI, *Divini Redemptoris* (1937), §2.
[88] Pius XI, *Divini Redemptoris*, §7.
[89] Pius XI, *Divini Redemptoris*, §8.
[90] Pius XI, *Divini Redemptoris*, §16.
[91] Pius XI, *Divini Redemptoris*, §29.

rulers of the nations had not scorned the teachings and maternal warnings of the Church. On the bases of liberalism and laicism they wished to build other social edifices which, powerful and imposing as they seemed at first, all too soon revealed the weakness of their foundations, and today are crumbling one after another before our eyes, as everything must crumble that is not grounded on the one corner stone which is Christ Jesus."[92]

Liberalism had asserted that man's temporal prosperity had nothing to do with his spiritual progress, and so it sought to build a social order that pretended as if the spiritual simply did not exist, or at least was irrelevant. As Ludwig von Mises, one of the most sophisticated liberals of the period, explained:

"In the last analysis, [liberalism] has nothing else in view than the advancement of [mankind's] outward, material welfare and does not concern itself directly with their inner, spiritual and metaphysical needs. It does not promise men happiness and contentment, but only the most abundant possible satisfaction of all those desires that can be satisfied by the things of the outer world."[93]

With the ends of social life so reduced, he continued, "The organization of human society according to the pattern most suitable for the attainment of the ends in view is a quite prosaic and matter-of-fact question, not unlike, say, the construction of a railroad or the production of cloth or furniture."[94] The leader of the Bolshevik revolution, V. I. Lenin, basically agreed, saying of socialism: "The whole of society will have become a single office and a single factory with equality of labour and equality of pay."[95] The move from materialist liberalism to materialist socialism just wasn't that far. Indeed, as Mises himself succinctly put it: "Liberalism is distinguished from socialism, which likewise professes to strive for the good of all, not by the goal at which it aims, but by the means that it chooses to attain that goal."[96] The end of both was a merely worldly peace, the peace of the City of Man, even

---

[92] Pius XI, *Divini Redemptoris*, §38.
[93] Ludwig von Mises, *Liberalism: The Classical Tradition* (New York: The Foundation for Economic Education, 1996), 4.
[94] Mises, *Liberalism*, 6.
[95] V.I. Lenin, *The State and Revolution* (Penguin: New York, 1992), 91.
[96] Mises, *Liberalism*, 7–8.

if the disagreement on means was fierce.

Pius's critique of liberalism should never, therefore, be confused with an even half-hearted or implicit endorsement of socialism. Indeed, the solution to the "lamentable ruin" that liberalism had caused was "neither the class-struggle nor terror, nor yet the autocratic abuse of State power, but rather the infusion of social justice and the sentiment of Christian love into the social-economic order."[97] At the same time, his critique of socialism did not even resemble an endorsement of liberalism. To the pope, it was shameful that liberals had used Leo XIII's defense of private property as an excuse to "defraud the workingman of his just salary and his social rights."[98] This was a fundamental misunderstanding of property and justice. Indeed:

> In reality, besides commutative justice, there is also social justice with its own set of obligations, from which neither employers nor workingmen can escape. Now it is of the very essence of social justice to demand for each individual all that is necessary for the common good. But just as in the living organism it is impossible to provide for the good of the whole unless each single part and each individual member is given what it needs for the exercise of its proper functions, so it is impossible to care for the social organism and the good of society as a unit unless each single part and each individual member—that is to say, each individual man in the dignity of his human personality—is supplied with all that is necessary for the exercise of his social functions.[99]

Such an appeal to social justice, to distributive justice, however, was exactly what liberalism simply could not accommodate. Instead, liberalism had produced a situation where society was reduced to countless isolated and weak individuals who faced alone the power of the State and the Market.[100] With social justice ignored and more and more of society oriented to competition rather than cooperation, conflict had moved into the very center of social life.[101] The City of Man ruled. As one prominent liberal theorist, F. A. Hayek, unironically explained

---

[97] Pius XI, *Divini Redemptoris*, §32.
[98] Pius XI, *Divini Redemptoris*, §50.
[99] Pius XI, *Divini Redemptoris*, §51.
[100] Pius XI, *Quadragesimo Anno* (1931), §78.
[101] Pius XI, *Quadragesimo Anno*, §88.

the situation: "Unless this complex society is to be destroyed, the only alternative to submission to the impersonal and seemingly irrational forces of the market is submission to an equally uncontrollable and therefore arbitrary power of other men."[102] Pius was unwilling to accept the Hobbesian premises of this false choice: man was meant to submit to neither irrational, impersonal, *nor* arbitrary forces. As we have seen throughout this book, such submission was the constant demand of the gods and their priests, not that of just authority participating in the power of God.

The totalitarian movements of left and right were merely the outgrowths of the reality liberalism had produced. Devotion to the State or Party presupposed the elimination of competing devotions. The ground clearing performed by liberalism was prerequisite to their spread. Where this hadn't happened sufficiently, the totalitarians were forced to duplicate its effects through widespread and indiscriminate terror that resulted in the destruction of solidarity between friends and neighbors. As one scholar remarked: "Totalitarian movements are mass organizations of atomized, isolated individuals." The movements demanded total loyalty, "and such loyalty can be expected only from the completely isolated human being who, without any other social ties to family, friends, comrades, or even mere acquaintances, derives his sense of having a place in the world only from his belonging to a movement, his membership in the party."[103]

Against all three ideologies, Pope Pius XI called for a return to a social order that was oriented to the common good, one constituted by many social groups at different levels of power and size, but each with its own proper function and field of work, a principle that would come to be known as "subsidiarity."[104] He called for the return of the idea that property was held not for the good of its owner but for the good of society as a whole.[105] He called for a return to respect for work and to an understanding that work was not just another commodity to be bought and sold but was, rather, a duty to the social whole.[106] Greed and raw power could not be the basis of a stable and happy society:

---

[102] F. A. Hayek, *The Road to Serfdom* (New York: Routledge, 2006) 210.
[103] Arendt, *The Origins of Totalitarianism*, 323–4.
[104] Pius XI, *Quadragesimo Anno*, §§78–84.
[105] Pius XI, *Quadragesimo Anno*, §§45–54.
[106] Pius XI, *Quadragesimo Anno*, §69.

> For what will it profit men to become expert in more wisely using their wealth, even to gaining the whole world, if thereby they suffer the loss of their souls? What will it profit to teach them sound principles of economic life if in unbridled and sordid greed they let themselves be swept away by their passion for property, so that "hearing the commandments of the Lord they do all things contrary."[107]

Rather, "no genuine cure can be furnished for this lamentable ruin of souls, which, so long as it continues, will frustrate all efforts to regenerate society, unless men return openly and sincerely to the teaching of the Gospel, to the precepts of Him Who alone has the words of everlasting life."[108] This was a call back to the New Testament, back to the City of God, back to what grace—and only grace—made possible.

The liberal nations, however, had little notion of trading their pursuit of wealth and desire fulfillment for the pursuit of justice. The Communists had little notion of trading their class war for social harmony. And the Fascists had little notion of trading their power accumulation for humility and service. Christianity faced direct persecution from the far left and the far right. It was tolerated by the liberals on the condition that it confine itself to the private lives of individual citizens, that it surrender its civilizational claims and accept the rule of utility-driven, secular markets and states. In liberal states, privatization, the acceptance of social irrelevance, was the cost of toleration. The exhortations of the papacy toward a civilization of love seemed to be from another era, an era before industrialization, imperialism, and the First World War. The gods of the new regimes were too powerful to be turned back. Like all pagan gods, they demanded blood, and the fear of their power, coupled with the depraved desire to share in it, drove men to comply.

World War II broke out in 1939 and dragged on until 1945. The liberal nations, led by the United States and England, joined forces with the Communist Soviet Union against the Fascist and nationalist powers of Italy, Germany, Japan, and their allies. The war was like nothing the world had ever seen. The very notion of the person vanished. Tens of millions were killed as people became totally and

---

[107] Pius XI, *Quadragesimo Anno*, §131.
[108] Pius XI, *Quadragesimo Anno*, §136.

merely cogs in vast impersonal war machines. The strategic killing of soldiers that had characterized the attrition-based fighting of the First World War became the strategic killing of whole populations. The distinction between civilian and combatant vanished—what was the moral difference, after all, between killing a conscripted eighteen-year-old boy on the battlefield and killing his conscripted fifty-year-old father producing his weapons in the factory? What was the difference between bombing the supply lines that were the source of the soldier's ammunition and bombing his family back home that was the source of his motivation? Totalized societies fought total war within which the categories of old-fashioned morality simply no longer applied. All the threads of modernity converged into this conflict. It was an industrial and mechanized war, fought as much through factory output as through battlefield maneuvers. The mass societies of modernity were mobilized and organized as single mechanisms, merging men and machines, with the sole purpose of killing and destroying the enemy's identical machine. The warring machines were animated by radical and violent ideologies, spread and intensified by scientific propaganda, and backed by terror.

"Liberty, Equality, and Fraternity" had been the slogan of the French Revolution. The conceit of modernity was that these social goods could be had without the Christianity from which they had been derived. In the one hundred and twenty-five years between Napoleon and World War II, each part of this slogan had become increasingly perverted. "Liberty" turned into a liberalism that could justify the slums of industrial cities and the targeted killing of half a million Japanese civilians; "equality" turned into a socialism that killed tens of millions of its own people to achieve a "classless" society and that thought little of machine gunning its own soldiers if they dared retreat in the face of impossible odds; "fraternity" turned into virulent Fascist nationalism that turned hate into a virtue and that culminated in the killing of twelve million Jews and other racial undesirables in the Nazi death camps. Since the French Revolution, the Church had asserted that true liberty was found only in virtue and so through the moral law; that true equality was found only through the equal dignity of each person in their diverse functions, talents, and powers; and that true fraternity was found only in a social justice that sought always the common good. The Church had consistently taught that each of these three great social goods could be had only together and only through Christianity, only in the City of God, only in the truth of revelation and the power of grace. This had been the teachings of the popes since 1789, and the horror of 1939–1945 demonstrated, tragically, just how right they had been. By the end of the conflict, much of Europe and Asia lay in ruins, and eighty-five million people had been killed—such was the sacrifice demanded by the gods of modernity.

VI

The Postmodern Church

1. The Postwar Situation

World War II revealed just how post-Christian Western civilization had become, just how accurate Nietzsche had been when he declared God to be dead. Catholicism, for all intents and purposes, was powerless, not just politically but socially and culturally. Christianity lingered on only as a private religion that operated within a person's larger and more important loyalties. After the war, though, this reality was obscured in the liberal states. During the war, the liberal states had viewed themselves as the forces of goodness and truth fighting a crusade against the forces of evil and had propagandized their populations accordingly. Traditional Christian concepts of morality and justice had been appropriated by this liberal nationalism: the United States, for example, was worthy of the devotion of its citizens because it was the bulwark against pagan Fascist totalitarianism; it was the defender of home and hearth, of family, freedom, God, and decency. These moral concepts were portrayed as existing independent of particular denominational commitments, and so all Christians and Jews could commit themselves to fighting for the nation, which they did.

The war changed the people who fought it. The Allies' willingness to ignore Christian morality in the struggle for final victory demonstrated and confirmed the shift away from fundamental Christianity and toward a religiosity that instead flowed from liberal-nationalism. Hiroshima was a definitive decision against the priority of Christ. This decision was the price of victory. In the United States, a once crazy-quilt society of countless small ethnic and religious communities, was definitively reconstituted as a single nation, united in its fight against evil and in the shared justifications that this fight required. Through their deep sacrifices, the people of the liberal West came to believe profoundly in the liberal-nationalist cause and came home from the war to build "decent" and "moral," yet profoundly individualistic and increasingly homogenous, societies whose unity was found in the abstraction of "the country" or "the flag" or "the American way of life." Local loyalties and identities were increasingly replaced with national ones, and so the values that made someone a good person were increasingly derived from the nation and not these smaller loci of social cohesion, which had been where true, "thick" Christianity was still to be found, even in the midst of liberal ideological universalism. Men went away to war as Catholics who were members of small ethnic communities that revolved around the local parish. They came home as Americans, still Catholic, but Americans first. This is what they had in common with their neighbors in the newly built suburbs.

These trends accelerated in the 1950s. The defeat of the Fascists left the liberal-nationalist countries, led by the United States, facing down the communist-nationalist states, led by the Soviet Union. The Cold War between these onetime allies began as early as 1948 but took definitive shape in the early 1950s with the development of the Soviet Union's atomic weapons capability. Each side sought to spread their international power and influence in an attempt to restrain the power and influence of the other side, even while avoiding open warfare. The liberal West, then, continued to advance itself as the protector of morality and human dignity in the face of the barbarity of atheistic Communism. The ideology of liberal nationalism continued to contain exhortations toward a decency and morality that were clearly drawn from the Christian tradition. But the foundation of this morality was no longer Christianity; rather, this content had "migrated" to the nation. Morality was now built on national ideals. In the face of militant socialism, liberal societies added to this traditional morality the moral goodness of wealth accumulation. Capitalism became sacred and the pursuit of wealth a virtue, along with going to church on Sunday. Many Christians were now Christian because it was considered moral, rather than the other way around. Normal Americans were Christians, and so being a Christian was the right thing to do. The liberal West had fought and continued to fight for what it called truth and freedom, and as the veterans started families, they went to church and were good, upstanding citizens: that was what allowed the war to make sense, and those who questioned this commonsense morality and religiosity were seen as calling into question the legitimacy of that victory and of the continuing Cold War; they were bordering on cultural, if not quite political, treason.

This is why church attendance in the United States and the United Kingdom dramatically increased as their international conflicts mounted. In 1939, 37 percent of the American population attended church services once a week. In 1960, 50 percent did. In 1955, 75 percent of Catholics attended weekly Mass. The number of Catholic priests in the United States doubled between 1930 and 1965 and then started its long decline. In 1954, "under God" was added to the Pledge of Allegiance. In 1956, "In God We Trust" became the national motto. Against the Nazis and then the Communists, Americans, including Catholics, understood themselves as good and moral people; they were patriotic, honest, hardworking, freedom loving, and churchgoing. The citizens that weren't churchgoing, in spite of this minor fault, if they were patriotic, honest, hardworking, and freedom loving, could still be citizens in good standing. In this way, Christianity seemed to be growing in importance, but this Christianity was now derived from the unity of the nation rather than the reverse. Christianity was good because America was good. One believed in God because one was a good American, and that's what good Americans did. *We* were Christians because *they* were atheists. In the iconic 1950s sitcom *Leave It to Beaver*, for example, Ward Cleaver dutifully takes his family to church on Sunday, but his frequent moral lectures to his sons never include reference to Christ or even to God. To Ward, good men were honest and hardworking. They were financially responsible and materially comfortable. Good men also went to church and said their prayers. This religiosity was not cynical. In the same sort of way that the postwar work ethic was real, that people really did get up every day and work dutifully, in this same sort of way, postwar private religion was real: they really did believe in God, they really did say their prayers, and they really did think it was important for happiness of family life. It wasn't cynical, but it was derivative; a privatized Christianity was a part of the structure of postwar society, but it was not the foundation.

In this way, membership in a church was not categorically different from membership in other "patriotic" or "decent" clubs that good citizens joined with sincerity. For example, membership in the Freemasons started growing in the late 1930s and peaked in 1960. Political party affiliations grew, starting in the late 1930s and peaking in the early

1960s. Even memberships in bowling leagues increased by 30 percent between 1950 and 1960. Nearly identical dynamics happened in the United Kingdom and the other liberal democracies. Christianity was being "integrated" into liberalism in a way similar to how it had been integrated into feudalism after the collapse of the Carolingian Empire in the tenth and eleventh centuries. This integration reached a climax, perhaps, with the election of a Catholic, John F. Kennedy, as president of the United States in 1960. Politically, Catholics had always been held in suspicion in the United States because they had international loyalties and were a part of a social institution that transcended the borders of the nation and which sought to transform America into itself. By 1960, this was no longer the case. Catholics were good Americans, just like everyone else, and so a Catholic could be president.

This integration created an illusion of both Christian vitality and a true secular morality. For example, the newly formed United Nations was seen by many as a sort of reestablished Christendom, which enshrined in liberal language the moral truths of the faith. Catholics were very prominent in the drafting and codification of the UN's Universal Declaration of Human Rights. It seemed to many that the victors in the war were committed to establishing governmental regimes that looked to the natural moral law for ultimate guidance, even if they did so without explicit mention of God. Indeed, in the 1950s, the liberal democracies seemed to many to be living according to the moral law without an established religion, without the revelation and grace that the Church had always asserted was necessary. It seemed that perhaps the Church had been too harsh with the liberal strand of Enlightenment thought. Perhaps within liberal democracies, devoted to universal human rights, the faithful could indeed live side by side with the secular: they were all patriotic, honest, hardworking, and freedom loving. Liberal societies seemed to be living the natural law naturally, putting the lie to the long-standing Catholic claims that only Christ could provide true peace and social harmony, and allowing Christians to conceive of their "religion" as fitting seamlessly into the liberal-nationalist way of life. However, with morality and religion no longer founded on revelation and grace but on particular national mores, it was free to shift with those mores. It was, in a sense, arbitrary. Religion was now derived from what it meant to be a "normal" citizen. As "normal" changed over the rest of the century, so, too, would religious commitment. The strength of Christianity was, therefore, a chimera. And the optimism that it engendered was, sadly, sorely mistaken. This mistake, though, would not start to become clear until late in the twentieth century.

Accompanying these dynamics, among intellectuals in the West a new approach to politics and social theory began to emerge in the decades after the war. This approach would eventually coalesce into what is now called "postmodernism." Postmodernism tended to see through the ideological trappings of contemporary politics and claimed to explain the "economies of power" that actually underwrote social order. Taken as a whole, the movement was a revived Hobbesianism, an attempt to explain *how* competition for power and only competition for power explains human events. Like Hobbes before them, these thinkers should be understood as explaining, often with great insight, how paganism worked, how the "gods" were built and maintained by men as they competed for power. Among the intellectual elites of the West, lingering ideological rhetoric became, therefore, highly cynical, became the dogmatic "beliefs" that were integral to power politics, but which were never their actual content. Like the elites of the Roman Empire two thousand years before them, the elites of the late twentieth century understood that the masses needed to believe in the gods and in the myths, the narratives, that justified the status quo, even if they themselves understood their falsity. This explains why we see in the post-war West the seemingly bizarre combination of elite thought dismantling the "Enlightenment Project" piece-by-piece, exposing it for the fraud that it was, even while simultaneously buttressing the myths of "progress," "human rights," "freedom," and disinterested "science" within the popular culture. It seemed as if everyone was talking about freedom, as if a new humanitarianism was on the rise, at the exact moment that the elites of the West were "proving" in their academic presses that liberty and justice were nothing else than the trappings of a more fundamental domination. In the popular culture, it seemed that authoritarianism was definitively banished from acceptable political discourse in favor of democracy at the exact moment that political theorists were proving to each other that all politics was necessarily authoritarian and that democracy was nothing more than the most subtle among totalitarianisms. Starting in the early 1960s, postmodernism steadily gained ground among Western intellectuals until it achieved unquestioned dominance on university campuses by the 1980s. The highest intellectuals of the new paganism, the priests of the new gods, like the highest priests of the ancient gods before them, did not fall for their own ruses.

2. The Second Vatican Council

The Theological Background

In 1960, therefore, the Church was paradoxically both aware that Western civilization was, by and large, no longer Christian and optimistic about the "natural law" tendencies within liberal democracy. Many within the Church knew that the world had to be evangelized; they understood the emptiness that haunted a great deal of popular piety. Many Christians could feel intuitively that something was deeply wrong in the Church, that many of the faithful were "going through the motions," that somewhere along the line, the passion, drama, and excitement of a life truly in and through Christ had been lost. And yet, this pessimism was offset by an optimistic appraisal of the moral qualities of the liberal West. To many, the democracies seemed close to a true conversion. It seemed that they were coming to believe in many of the truths of Christianity, such as universal human dignity, through their own secular path. What was needed, it seemed to many, was for Christianity to be re-presented, to be "updated." *Aggiornamento* was the Italian word most often used. This was the background for Pope John XXIII's calling for a Second Vatican Council. The pope wanted the Church to "open the windows" and let in some fresh air. It was time, he thought, to consider a new approach to modernity.

The council's first session met in 1962. Immediately, it became clear that the bishops were divided. This division was rooted in theological controversies that had simmered in the Church for the past sixty years. On one side, there were the "conservatives." This group wanted to maintain the theological status quo, which was a particular form of neo-scholasticism that had dominated in the seminaries and Catholic universities since Leo XIII. Critics of this school of thought considered it excessively rationalistic. At is simplest, it was the combination of Enlightenment-style "unaided" reason, which operated within the sphere of "nature," with revelation and grace, which operated in the realm of "supernature." Supernature was stacked on top of nature, like two stories in a building. Nature (reason) could get us so far, and then Supernature (faith) could get us the rest of the way. Both reason and faith were seen to operate independently of, or at least prior to, culture or history. This school of thought had grown very strong institutionally during the first few decades of the twentieth century, partially as a response to a heresy called Modernism.

The Theological Background

The word "Modernism" should not to be understood to mean "any way of thinking that uses modern concepts or methods." Rather, Modernism was a particular theological movement of the late nineteenth and early twentieth century that tended to historicize Christianity to the point of denying any abiding truth. To the Modernists, the truths of Catholicism changed along with history. Doctrine had to keep up with the general thrust of historical developments. In response, many neo-scholastic thinkers became suspicious of all historical approaches to the faith. History, for many such scholastics, was properly understood as little more than antiquarianism, full of diverting anecdotes, no doubt, and marginally significant for establishing the context of dogmatic definitions, but really of little doctrinal importance. For these thinkers, "tradition" was understood primarily as the way in which the Church stood outside of history, stood against history, rather than the way in which the Church moved in history. This form of neo-scholasticism responded to the challenge of the twentieth century's turn to the social and linguistic by basically denying that the social, cultural, or linguistic aspects of humanity mattered much at all; they basically denied the reality of temporal change in favor of a static metaphysical system that was based on Aristotle and Aquinas but was really a part of the tradition of modern rationalism. As is the way with such conflicts, Modernism reacted in the opposite direction. For the Modernists, all that mattered was human history. God acted in history and could not break out of history. All was change; all was in flux. Therefore, Catholic doctrine could and must evolve with humanity. "Tradition" here dissolved into a vague, ever-changing Christian identity without any real, truth-bearing content. For many Modernists, then, the essence of Christianity became a feeling or intuition, a subjective religious "experience" that was had within the completely relative flow of history.

The neo-scholastics had used their institutional power in the decades leading up to Vatican II to suppress Modernism, and by the time of the council, the most extreme formulations of the heresy were all but extinct. But neo-scholasticism was a juggernaut, and its proponents tended to see "Modernists" or "Modernist tendencies" everywhere. In their zeal to protect what they believed to be timeless orthodoxy, these conservatives sometimes attacked any thinker who deviated from their line. Many conservatives came to mistake their clearly modern and historically contingent theological synthesis for orthodoxy itself.

There was a third school of theology, however, that had arisen in the 1930s and had gained influence in the decades leading up to Vatican II. This school would come to be known as the *nouvelle théologie* (French for "new theology"). These theologians had learned from the Modernists the importance of history and had learned to take seriously the social, linguistic, cultural, and temporal aspects of humanity that late modern philosophy had emphasized. For the thinkers of the *nouvelle théologie*, the Church was not a juridical institution that subsisted "on top" of secular, natural society. Rather, it was the People of God, traveling through history, grasping after the divine, responding through grace to God's revelation, reaching beyond history from within history. As one leader of the movement, Marie-Dominique Chenu, wrote: "Since Christianity draws its reality from history and not from some metaphysics, the theologian must have as his primary concern . . . to know this history and to train himself in it."[1] These thinkers called for a return to the sources of Catholic theology, to Scripture and to the Church Fathers, an imperative known as *ressourcement*.

The neo-scholastics were defending a system that had perhaps been appropriate for the Alliance of Throne and Altar period of Catholicism. It assumed a juridical outlook where order emerged from self-sufficient entities that were assembled into stable, reciprocal, and essential relationships through extrinsic authority or power. This system tended to forget that both the temporal power and the spiritual power were in the Church and received their authority and very identity through revelation and grace. They tended to forget that nature itself was fallen and could only be restored through the grace that flowed through the Church and tended to suppose that nature operated independently of the Church and yet in accord with the God-given natural law. They tended to forget that grace, the Church, was necessary for nature to be itself as well as necessary for it to be perfected beyond itself into the supernatural: nature was not simply "added to" through the supernatural; it was perfected; it was fulfilled. This was similar to how the social thought of the early nineteenth century had taken for granted that Europe was governed by Christian kings in alliance with the Church and had tended to forget that the monarchs, in fact, held a vocation *within* the Church.

---

[1] Marie-Dominique Chenu, quoted in John W. O'Malley, *What Happened at Vatican II* (Cambridge, MA: Harvard University Press, 2008), 36.

The core "forgotten" social reality was that the laity were as much the Church as were the clergy. The word "church" was used almost exclusively, for example, in reference to the clerical hierarchy. When people said "church," they were thinking "bishops and their priests," who dealt with supernatural matters, as opposed the natural matters dealt with in the world, where the laity worked. In response, the *nouvelle théologie* called for a reassessment of the relationship between nature and grace, between the human and the Divine. As one leader of the movement, Hans Urs von Balthasar, wrote, "We cannot carry on with natural metaphysics, natural ethics, natural jurisprudence, natural study of history, acting as though Christ were not, in the concrete, the norm of everything."[2]

The thinkers of the *nouvelle théologie* were attempting to reconstitute theology for the task of the conversion of post-Christian, neo-pagan nations. They looked back to the Fathers because the Fathers had similarly faced a non-Christian, yet powerful, civilization. And what they saw in the Fathers was the power of Christ to form a civilization of love through grace, from top to bottom. They turned their emphasis from law to grace, from the external to the internal. This allowed them to find in modern thought truth that they could then leverage in the explication of Christ. This strategy had been used before. St. Augustine had discussed at length the virtues of the pagans, their fortitude, their willingness to sacrifice, their pursuit of glory. But he did so only to point out their ultimate emptiness, to point out that the truth and goodness after which they grasped could only finally be had through Christ. The City of Man was fulfilled only in the City of God. Similarly, the great leader of the *nouvelle théologie*, Henri de Lubac, faced down the historical and cultural sophistication of collectivist ideologies, confirming their belief that man was intrinsically social and historical and confirming their condemnation of the Church when it acted as merely "a technician of individual salvation,"[3] even while demonstrating that their quest for communion and harmony pointed to and gained coherence from the temporal reality of the Church as the people of God. For de Lubac, "Catholicism is essentially social. It is social in the deepest sense of

---

[2] Hans Urs von Balthasar, *A Theology of History* (San Francisco, CA: Ignatius Press, 1963), 18.

[3] Henri de Lubac, *Catholicism: Christ and the Common Destiny of Man*, trans. Lancelot C. Sheppard and Sr. Elizabeth Englund (San Francisco: Ignatius Press, 1988), 14.

the word: not merely in its applications in the field of natural institutions, but first and foremost in itself, in the heart of its mystery, in the essence of its dogma."[4]

For Henri de Lubac, the socialist and nationalist repudiation of individualism and positivist rationalism were perversions of a truth that could find fulfillment only in Catholicism, just as for Augustine, the pagan desire for glory could be fulfilled only in Christ. As de Lubac wrote: "The whole history of the human race, which is transformed in its whole nature by the hypostatic union, cannot ultimately stand over against Christ as independent of him."[5] The *nouvelle théologie* developed an understanding of tradition that emphasized temporal change within transcendent truth. This conception of tradition put the Church back into history rather than imagining it floating along above history. History became the story of the Church making Christ ever new. To many neo-scholastics, this all smacked of Modernism. For them, tradition was fundamentally about things staying the same *in spite* of history, *against* history, and through the 1930s and to the start of Vatican II, many *nouvelle théologie* thinkers suffered censure and soft persecution.

When the council opened in 1962 with over 2,500 cardinals, bishops, and abbots in attendance, it became clear that the conservatives were not going to be able to control the drafting of the documents. Many, maybe most, of the assembled fathers had *nouvelle théologie* sympathies. Theologians who had suffered censure in the decades leading up the council emerged as major figures, helping the bishops to understand what was at stake and to draft their opinions and speeches. It became clear that the dominance of the neo-scholastic mode of theological discourse was largely founded on institutional authority and not on wide acceptance of its approach. Indeed, once the council began its work, there was no doubt that the documents it produced would have a different character. The *nouvelle théologie* looked to the Church Fathers and Scripture not only for its doctrine but for its style. This style was literary and pastoral. Indeed, as we discussed earlier in this book, most of the writings of the Church Fathers were sermons or pastoral commentaries on Scripture. The council quickly adopted a similar style and tone.

This was a break with conciliar tradition. The councils of the past

---

[4] de Lubac, *Catholicism*, 15.
[5] de Lubac, *Catholicism*, 114.

had been primarily juridical. They were law-making gatherings. They condemned error, decreed punishments, passed procedural rules, and defined disputed doctrine. Their theological expositions were normally minimalist; normally just enough explanation was given to make it clear what position or action was worthy of an anathema (excommunication). Councils had been primarily internal affairs having to do with the running of the Church, not unlike the feudal gatherings of the "Estates," of the nobles and other important people, that had helped the monarchs of Europe govern their kingdoms through the Middle Ages, especially in times of crisis. The fathers of Vatican II almost intuitively understood that times had changed. Unlike the theologians who were the major proponents of the conservative position, the bishops' vocations were dominated not by abstract theory but by concrete interaction with the faithful, with pastoral responsibility and troubles. They understood the mood of the times and knew that the Church had to reorient itself to the world because the world was no longer oriented to the Church.

As a result, the documents of Vatican II largely abandoned the scholastic style that had dominated since the thirteenth century. Scholasticism had been developed in Christendom for Catholics. It was a method of precise and rigorous reasoning based upon the premises of the faith that were so foundational as to be sometimes forgotten. Scholasticism was created to do the important work of developing the implications of the tradition from within the tradition. It filled in the missing pieces, building conceptual bridges between conclusions; it made use of definitions, arguments, refutations, and disputation in order to zero in on precise explications of the presupposed faith. Scholasticism had achieved remarkable syntheses of profound genius. It was not, however, appropriate for re-presenting Christ to a West which had forgotten who he was.

Scholasticism would never have converted the pagan Roman Empire, and it was not going to convert the new pagans of modernity. Catholic disputes with them were not over details; they were no longer, even as they had been under Leo XIII, about the proper way to apply shared categories. Rather, the postwar modern world was speaking a different language, operating in a new paradigm of thought and action. The only way to reach this world was to show them Christianity. This is what had converted the ancient Romans, not anathemas or creedal definitions, but the lives of Christians and the deaths of martyrs. Appropriately, then, as we discussed earlier, the literary work of the ancient Church Fathers had consisted mostly of sermons or commentaries for spiritual edification. They were mostly pastors, doing pastoral work. They were about making Christ known, making him visible, making him attractive. They were missionary. But the audience for their literary production was not first and foremost unbelievers. It was, rather, the baptized. The great works of the patristic period focused on leading the newly baptized peoples into the full implications of a life in Christ. The Fathers' work was about the pursuit of holiness. It was the holiness of the people of God that then attracted the pagans, that brought them finally to convert to this alternative and profoundly beautiful way of life. The bishops of Vatican II, with their fingers on the pulse of their flocks, knew that we had entered a period that demanded similar evangelization. Pope Paul VI, who ascended the papal throne just months after the council opened, referred to this universal call to holiness as "the most characteristic and ultimate purpose of the teachings of the Council." This drive unites all the documents.

The Liturgy

The first document promulgated by the council was *Sacrosanctum Concilium*, "On the Sacred Liturgy." The liturgy is the central experience of the Catholic life. To the Church Fathers, the liturgy, and the sacraments that were contained within it, was the very heart of the Christian life. Over the centuries, the Church had never compromised this tradition. What had happened in the modern period, however, was a sort of segregation within the liturgy between the laity and the clergy. Increasingly over the course of modernity, the priests became the ones who "did" liturgy, and the faithful became, increasingly, participants only through their presence and interior prayer. The exclusive use of Latin in the Roman Rite tended to exaggerate this division. The faithful watched the priests perform the liturgy in a language that they did not understand. For many Catholics, the Mass was most often experienced in the form of the Latin Low Mass. In a Low Mass, the priest and the altar servers recited the prayers and the responses in a low voice that the faithful could not even hear. During the first half of the twentieth century, research into the history of the liturgy and work on the theology of the liturgy had converged in such a way to challenge this status quo through a movement for liturgical reform.

The Liturgy

This liturgical reform movement maintained that the people should participate actively in the liturgy, and that things had been different in the past and so could be different in the future. This was indeed true. In the High Middle Ages, for example, the people's Mass was a loud, interactive affair, with the people singing the responses and sometimes displaying an almost pentecostal experience of the Holy Spirit. The modern Low Mass, on the other hand, had developed as a private Mass for priests to say by themselves. It was widely recognized by 1960 that its use as the people's Mass was in need of reform. Theologically, the centrality of the liturgical act to the life of faith was becoming more and more prominent, especially as modern anthropology and sociology demonstrated the profound importance of ritual to all systems of meaning. By 1960, many people had become aware that modern Catholic theology's tendency to emphasize propositions of the faith over actions of worship and prayer owed a great deal to Protestant influence and the influence of modern, rationalist philosophies. All of this animated the liturgical reform movement.

Sacrosanctum Concilium embraced this desire for liturgical reform but did so in a moderate manner. It called for lay participation, stating:

> Mother Church earnestly desires that all the faithful should be led to that fully conscious, and active participation in liturgical celebrations which is demanded by the very nature of the liturgy. Such participation by the Christian people as "a chosen race, a royal priesthood, a holy nation, a redeemed people" (1 Pet. 2:9; cf. 2:4–5), is their right and duty by reason of their baptism.[6]

It also called for more use of the vernacular and more sensitivity to local cultures. But, at the same time, it mandated that Latin remain the primary language of the liturgy and that Gregorian chant, a medieval musical tradition, retain pride of place. There had been many modest liturgical reforms in the long history of the Church, and a reasonable reading of *Sacrosanctum Consilium* would have predicted a similar reform. It simply did not call for dramatic changes in the liturgical celebration itself. What was more important than the outward reform of the rite itself was the council's theological emphasis on the importance of the liturgy in the life of the Church, including the life of the laity. This added an experiential, almost existentialist, element

---

[6] Vatican II, *Sacrosanctum Concilium* (1963), §14.

to the Christian life that many felt had been missing from official theology, even if it had been present in the lives of normal Catholics through the centuries. The Mass was not merely an obligation; it was not merely an edifying symbol or opportunity for private prayer; rather, the liturgy was the faithful's chief path to holiness. Through the Mass, the Word of God was read and preached, and through the Mass, the Body and Blood of Christ himself was consumed in the Eucharist, "the source and the summit of the Christian life,"[7] constituting the congregation as the very Body of Christ, as the People of God.

The Church

The idea of the Church as the "People of God" was perhaps the dominant theme in one of the council's most important documents: *Lumen Gentium*, the Dogmatic Constitution on the Church. *Lumen Gentium* was heavily influenced by the ecclesiology of thinkers such as Henri de Lubac. The Church was presented no longer as a juridical entity, a type of governmental regime, that operated on top of or alongside human society. Rather, the Church was humanity itself, moving toward its redemption through Christ. The Church was not merely the dispenser of sacraments; it was itself a sacrament. It made present the Divine within the human, made the eternal present in the temporal. The Church was God and man together *in* history:

> Already present in figure at the beginning of the world, this Church was prepared in marvellous fashion in the history of the people of Israel and in the old Alliance. Established in this last age of the world, and made manifest in the outpouring of the Spirit, it will be brought to glorious completion at the end of time. At that moment, as the Fathers put it, all the just from the time of Adam, "from Abel, the just one, to the last of the elect" will be gathered together with the Father in the universal Church.[8]

The Church was a living temple of the Spirit, and through the Spirit,

---

[7] Vatican II, *Lumen Gentium*, in *Vatican Council II: The Conciliar and Postconciliar Documents*, trans. Austin Flannery (Collegeville, MN: Liturgical Press, 1975), §11.

[8] Vatican II, *Lumen Gentium*, §2.

she advanced "the mission of proclaiming and establishing among all peoples the kingdom of Christ and of God, and she is, on earth, the seed and the beginning of that kingdom."[9] The Church was constituted not first by a juridical structure but, rather, as the very living body of Christ. This body was made up of all the baptized in their wide diversity of vocations and functions, from the common layman to the pope himself. But this mystical body was not to be placed in opposition to the external society. Rather, "the society structured with hierarchical organs and the mystical body of Christ, the visible society and the spiritual community, the earthly Church and the Church endowed with heavenly riches, are not to be thought of as two realities. On the contrary, they form one complex reality which comes together from a human and a divine element."[10] This is what it meant for the Church to be itself a sacrament: the spiritual and the temporal were united fundamentally.

Lumen Gentium asserted that this Church "subsists in the Catholic Church, which is governed by the successor of Peter" but it did not assert that it was simply identical with it. Rather, all the baptized were members, even those separated from the Catholic Church. What is more, "many elements of sanctification and of truth are found outside its visible confines. Since these are gifts belonging to the Church of Christ, they are forces impelling towards Catholic unity."[11] The council was extending the Church's long-taught doctrine that there was no salvation outside the Church. The doctrine was confirmed, but the meaning of the Church was broadened. All truth and goodness were, in a sense, in the Church already as they pointed to the unity and redemption found only in the Church.[12] "All men are called to this catholic unity which prefigures and promotes universal peace. And in different ways to it belong, or are related: the Catholic faithful, others who believe in Christ, and finally all mankind, called by God's grace to salvation."[13] But, the council was clear, all truth and all sanctification led to unity within the explicit Church of Christ. History was this movement into the Church. This was a return to a profoundly patristic vision of the Church. St. Augustine, after all, when trying to

---

[9] Vatican II, *Lumen Gentium*, §5.
[10] Vatican II, *Lumen Gentium*, §8.
[11] Vatican II, *Lumen Gentium*, §8.
[12] Vatican II, *Lumen Gentium*, §16.
[13] Vatican II, *Lumen Gentium*, §13.

explain the reality that was the Church, the City of God, had to write a history of the entire world, from creation to the final judgment, in which no human being, no nation among men was left out. "Hence that messianic people, although it does not actually include all men, and at times may appear as a small flock, is, however, a most sure seed of unity, hope, and salvation for the whole human race."[14] The Church was about all of us, but not all of us the way we are; it was about the perfection of all humanity in holiness.

Lumen Gentium was a wholesale rejection of any notion of an individualized faith. Rather, humanity was saved corporately, socially. The Church was the People of God: "Destined to extend to all regions of the earth, it enters into human history, though it transcends at once all times and all racial boundaries."[15] The Church was in history as that which reached beyond history. Here, then, was the antidote to modern collectivist ideology from either the left or from the right. They were wrong not because they rejected the insipid individualism of liberalism or of much of modern Christianity; they were wrong because the truth they were grasping after was the truth of the Church herself. It was also an antidote to both the rationalist creation of an a-historical Church, which would remove the Church from the living stream of history, and Modernist capitulation to pure historicism, which would relativize the Church out of existence. The Church was holiness present in its full truth in history, ever new, ever alive, ever calling out to all men; it was the People of God, the City of God, moving forward, gathering together humanity, to its consummation in glory.

The ecclesiology of *Lumen Gentium* is a missionary ecclesiology for a Church preparing to save the world. However, it was anything but a break with tradition. Rather, it took certain strands within the deep tradition that had been neglected in the modern period and brought them forward, front and center. It didn't compromise the hierarchical structure of pope, bishops, and priests. It, rather, bolstered it. It did, however, redirect the Church's understanding of this hierarchy from one of governmental authority to one of service. The powerful in the Church served the weak. They were *for* the weak. That was why their power was important and needed to be sustained. We see here again an antidote to modern ideology. The liberals and the socialists could see hierarchy only as exploitative. All hierarchy was domina-

---

[14] Vatican II, *Lumen Gentium*, §10.
[15] Vatican II, *Lumen Gentium*, §9.

tion, and so they sought to eliminate it. The nationalists agreed with their assessment of hierarchy but thought such domination was inevitable and embraced it. The Church challenged the premise, undoing ideology itself.

Reaching back to the High Middle Ages, the council asserted that the Church was divided into three orders: the laity, the clergy, and the religious. They each had an essential function, and only together was the Church constituted. Together, all of human experience was brought into the Church. The laity, for example, "are given this special vocation: to make the Church present and fruitful in those places and circumstances where it is only through them that she can become the salt of the earth."[16] The laity were the heralds of Christ in the "temporal order." They were called to sanctify the structures of society: the economies, laws, culture, and mores. No human activity could "be withdrawn from God's dominion."[17] Their holiness brought holiness directly into the world of men. The laity were, in a sense, the tip of the Church's missionary spear. It was the laity who would realize the preaching of the clergy through the grace of the sacraments by actually building societies of justice, love, and peace: "The laity consecrate the world itself to God."[18] This could only happen through their own holiness. Any notion, therefore, that holiness was set aside for the religious or for the clergy was definitively repudiated. All were called to holiness. This was a restatement of the deep tradition. As we saw earlier, the High Middle Ages understood the universal call to holiness. But, in the modern period, often through a naive acceptance that the laity were solidly Christian and lived lives structured through Christian authority, it had sometimes been forgotten that they, too, were called to radical holiness. It had sometimes been supposed that holiness was for the elite.

Vatican II presented an ecclesiology for the conversion of a civilization, top to bottom, with nothing but sin left out. The world of men, in its entirety, was to be brought within the Church because "in this kingdom creation itself will be delivered from the slavery of corruption into the freedom of the glory of the sons of God."[19] This is a missionary ecclesiology for a Church that sought to reach out into the

---

[16] Vatican II, *Lumen Gentium*, §33.
[17] Vatican II, *Lumen Gentium*, §36.
[18] Vatican II, *Lumen Gentium*, §34.
[19] Vatican II, *Lumen Gentium*, §36.

world, find the goodness that was in it, and pull it deeper into communion. It is an ecclesiology that "feathered" or "blurred" the edges of the Church, which sought to make the boundaries of the Church porous so that the faithful could reach out and unbelievers could move in. It was ambitious and appropriate for the Church's new position as missionary to what was once its own civilization. However, this vision often fell prey to the misplaced optimism discussed above. It perceived goodness in the non-Christian world of men, when often what it was actually seeing was the lingering inertia of Christendom.

Religious Liberty

One of the most controversial documents of the council was *Dignitatis Humanae*, the council's decree affirming an expansive notion of religious liberty. This was controversial because past popes had repeatedly and rather definitively condemned the very notion of religious liberty, going so far as to call it an "insanity" and merely a "liberty of perdition."[20] Following his predecessors, Pope Leo XIII had declared that "it is quite unlawful to demand, to defend, or to grant unconditional freedom of thought, of speech, or writing, or of worship, as if these were so many rights given by nature to man. For, if nature had really granted them, it would be lawful to refuse obedience to God, and there would be no restraint on human liberty."[21] Now, however, the Church seemed to reverse course, declaring "that the human person has a right to religious freedom," and that this right "is based on the very dignity of the human person as known through the revealed word of God and by reason itself."[22] How can we make sense of this jarring contradiction?

We can begin if we grant the council fathers a well-meaning optimism. The fathers seemed to see in all "religions" anticipations and movements toward the one true religion, which they acknowledged without qualification to be Catholicism. They seem to be extending even further *Lumen Gentium*'s extension of the notion of "no salvation outside the Church" to include the "religious" impulse itself. All

---

[20] Pius IX, *Quanta Cura*, §3.
[21] Leo XIII, *Libertas Praestantissimum*, §42.
[22] Vatican II, *Dignitatis Humanae: Declaration on Religious Liberty*, trans. Austin Flannery (Collegeville, MN: Liturgical Press, 2014), §2.

religion, it seems, has some positive relation to true religion, to the Church. They seem to be suggesting that *religion itself* is good and reasonable and, therefore, lawful. But the problem is that while this is true of some faiths, it is manifestly untrue of others. Is the Taliban's religion an anticipation or movement toward Christ? It seems, rather, on the whole, a movement away from the truth.

In order to make sense of this lacuna, we should assume that operative in *Dignitatis Humanae* is the assumption that the various faiths of the world are "religions," properly speaking, only to the extent that they resemble or move toward Christianity. This would mean that only adherents of these Christian-like religions have a right to religious freedom so that they can move closer to the one true religion through them. In this way of thinking, the Taliban could be outlawed precisely because it does not practice a proper religion at all. And yet, the document never comes out and states this. It, rather, allows the reader to suppose that all religions (even idolatrous paganism? even demon worship?) are movements toward the divine. It sometimes seems as if the council fathers had forgotten the fundamental evil of false gods, the evil about which the entire biblical narrative is concerned and to which the martyrs of the Church bear witness.

This forgetfulness is perhaps understandable. The great evils of the twentieth century were atheistic ideologies from the far right and the far left and the totalitarian states that they had built. Faced with such militant secularism, all "religions" seemed benign and good and worthy of toleration. There is, in fact, an unusual logical loop in the council's treatment of religious liberty. It calls for the equal liberty of all religions to be protected by the state, and yet it sets the boundaries of this tolerance at the defense of public order and the common good. It states that the civil authorities must act through legal norms "conformable to the objective moral order . . . for the adequate care of that honorable public peace which amounts to ordered life in common in true justice, and for the required protection of public morality."[23] Obviously, however, the question arises as to how the civil authority is to determine the content of the objective moral order and of true justice. Of course, as the Church's social doctrine has always taught, true justice and true morality leading to true peace is precisely the fruit promised by Christianity. It was exactly for this reason that the previous popes had condemned the very notion of religious liberty: man's

---

[23] Vatican II, *Dignitatis Humanae*, §7.

fallen nature was no longer capable of realizing true justice without Christ. Without Christianity, the temporal order, or "civil authority," could not, in practice, be peaceful, just, moral, or oriented to the common good. This was the reality that underwrote all of salvation history. The pagans, as we have seen, had their own notions of justice and the common good that involved the exposure of infants, a brutal slave economy, throwing people to wild beasts, and forcing slaves to fight to the death for entertainment. The modern post-Christian regimes were no different. Christianity, and nothing else, undid such "civil authority" in favor of "objective moral order," "public peace," "true justice," and "public morality." As Leo XIII had written, "The instruments which [the Church] employs are given to her by Jesus Christ Himself for the very purpose of reaching the hearts of men, and derive their efficiency from God. They alone can reach the innermost heart and conscience, and bring men to act from a motive of duty, to control their passions and appetites, to love God and their fellow men. . . . If human society is to be healed now, in no other way can it be healed save by a return to Christian life and Christian institutions."[24]

It is here that we can see both the naive optimism of the council and, ironically, its continuity with tradition. The council fathers seem to think that non-Christians, or at least non-Catholics, will, almost as a matter of course, agree on the content of objective morality and the common good. This assumption is certainly a result of the peculiar postwar situation discussed above. The liberal nations such as the United States seemed to be demonstrating that such agreement was possible and even easy, and it is no surprise that one of the chief drafters of *Dignitatis Humanae* was an American. And yet, it must be remarked that for the Council, the actual content of this morality remained decidedly Christian. Implicitly, Christianity remained the judge of what was the authentic justice and true morality that the civil authority had a duty to maintain. In a sense, the council seems to be saying that in order to protect the right to practice non-Christian religions within proper limits, which is to say, to the extent that they are movements into the truth, a civil authority must be, at least implicitly, Christian. The relative right to practice non-Christian religions must be judged by the Christian, non-relative understanding of morality, justice, and the common good. If the Taliban, for example, went against these norms and so were a threat to public

---

[24] Leo XIII, *Rerum Novarum*, §§26–27.

peace, which is another way of saying the peace of Christ, it seems they could be suppressed without violating religious liberty. Christian norms remained the standard, and so religious liberty remained most fundamentally the "liberty of the Church."

The drafters of *Dignitatis Humanae*, however, unlike the earlier popes, didn't simply call these norms "Christian" but instead used the language of natural law. The popes of the past had condemned the very notion of religious liberty precisely because Christianity was the only path to the truth through which a state could govern justly according to the natural law. Nevertheless, they had not condemned the notion that a Christian State could tolerate religious error for the sake of public peace and the common good. In fact, they stated such tolerance was often necessary, not only so that the individual was given space to grow, but also so that those public goods themselves were not disturbed.[25] The council fathers were placing this tolerance up front and expanding its importance. In short, *Dignitatis Humanae* seemed, in the end, to be saying that what Christianity teaches about right and wrong, good and evil, just and unjust, peace and war, are the standards by which the civil power ought to govern, and that the various non-Catholic religions should be allowed to function to the extent that they share these standards or work toward their realization, and that the faithful of these non-Christian religions had a right to practice their faith to this same extent because this was exactly the extent to which these religions were oriented to the truth. People had a right to practice goodness and believe truth, and there was much goodness and truth outside of explicit Christianity even if it always pointed toward Christianity and led people into its unity. Persons had a right to move into the Church through bottom-up dynamics of cultural diversity. But error as error still had no rights.

In order to understand *Dignitatis Humanae*, we have to be sensitive to the changing content of the concepts of "religion" and "the state." As we have seen in this history, the modern state-building project was constructing all-encompassing, top-down sovereign control. This project was initiated in absolutism and was consummated in the construction of the closed, ideologically driven nation-states of the twentieth century. As we have seen, to modernity, every aspect of humanity lay beneath the violence-based dominance of the state. *Dignitatis Humanae* implicitly attacks this notion of the state. Its decla-

---

[25] Leo XIII, *Libertas Praestantissimum*, §42.

ration of religious liberty can be read as an assertion that all that constitutes humanity does not lie beneath the control of modern states. Rather, there is a transcendent reality to humanity that reaches always beyond the merely historical, the merely particular, and to the spiritual, to the universal. Human politics can never be closed in on themselves, declaring themselves to have control over the very essence of humanity. Rather, politics must always be open upward, must always allow for the transcendent to break through their control. If every human being is called to a relationship with God, then the political community can never be a complete and seamless community. It must always allow for its own undermining through the breaking in of transcendent truth, often from below. In this sense, in the face of modern states, the council's insistence on religious liberty is a denial of the absolute sovereignty of man over man. In must be remembered that in the modern project, liberty was always understood in a negative sense. Liberty was where positive, coercive law was silent. The assertion of religious liberty within this context was the assertion that man's relationship with God was not directly governed by the laws of mere men.

In order to assert this position, however, the council did seem to accept, at least provisionally, modernity's understanding of religion. Over the course of modernity, as we have seen, religion was steadily reduced to the personal, private, internal, and reflective relationship of individual men directly with God. In a sense, the meaning of religion had been reduced to the individual aspects of what the word religion had once meant. "Religion" generally had come to mean what Protestantism tended to take religion to be. What this amounted to was the breaking up of the premodern understanding of religion into two unrelated fields. Premodern religion had, of course—as we have seen throughout this book—intrinsically included concepts of justice, morality, ethics, and peace. Now, those essentially social concepts had been annexed to politics, governed by the natural law. So, with only a little creative reading, we can reunite those two sides of premodern religion within *Dignitatis Humanae*. In the individual realm, man reached out to God through the resources that he had; he grasped after his own blessedness internally, through this new thing called "religion." In the social realm, man had to be governed by true justice and true morality, through this new thing called "politics," so that he could achieve true peace. *Dignitatis Humanae* asserted the importance of both realms. The document's drafters forgot to emphasize, perhaps, that the social, political goods, like the individual goods, were only attainable through Christ; nevertheless, the components of the traditional understanding are still present. And so, the document doesn't seem, in the end, to contradict tradition. Rather, it seems to emphasize the tolerance aspect of the traditional doctrine while maintaining that Christianity is necessary for social order.

This reading is confirmed if we turn to *Apostolicam Actuositatem*, the council's decree on the role of the laity. Following *Lumen Gentium*, *Apostolicam Actuositatem* asserts boldly that "the Church was founded to spread the kingdom of Christ over all the earth for the glory of God the Father, to make all men partakers in redemption and salvation, and through them to establish the right relationship of the entire world to Christ."[26] The laity's role in this mission was to "endeavor to have the Gospel spirit permeate and improve the temporal order," to make the "Christian spirit a vital energizing force in the temporal sphere."[27] This was a restatement of the Church's ancient understanding of the temporal power as a power that operated within the Church and not alongside it. Indeed, "God has willed to gather together all that was natural, all that was supernatural, into a single whole in Christ, 'so that in everything he would have the primacy' (Col. 1:18)." Because of sin, though, the temporal realm had become corrupted. In response, "It is the work of the entire Church to fashion men able to establish the proper scale of values on the temporal order and direct it towards God through Christ."[28] The document states clearly: "The apostolate in one's social environment endeavors to infuse the Christian spirit into the mentality and behavior, laws and structures of the community in which one lives."[29] It was through this work that the "true common good" would be advanced and laws formed in accord with true "moral precepts."[30] It's hard to read *Apostolicam Actuositatem* without wondering what has happened to the separation of Church and State that seemed to be advanced by *Dignitatis Humanae*. Reading them together, however, we must conclude that the council envisions in the ideal a civil power made up of faithful laymen and animated by the Christian spirit, and precisely for this reason, it would be capable of identifying goodness in non-Christian religions and allowing them

---

[26] Second Vatican Council, *Apostolicam Actuositatem*, in Flannery, *Vatican Council II: The Conciliar and Postconciliar Documents*, §2.
[27] Vatican II, *Apostolicam Actuositatem*, §§2–4.
[28] Vatican II, *Apostolicam Actuositatem*, §7.
[29] Vatican II, *Apostolicam Actuositatem*, §13.
[30] Vatican II, *Apostolicam Actuositatem*, §14.

to enrich the social whole, to further the Church's universal mission.

In this way, the council's teaching on religious liberty is a restatement of the tradition and is ultimately a form of the "liberty of the Church" that the Church had defended since its founding. But the tone and style of this restatement was dramatically different than those of its recent past. Motivated by evangelical zeal and the desire to pull all that is good into the Church, *Dignitatis Humanae* de-emphasized the importance of explicit Christianity and optimistically suggested that non-Christians, and even outright secularists, were living the natural law almost as a matter of course. Here we see, perhaps, the effects of a lingering neo-scholasticism with its notion of an independent realm of "pure nature." To those inside the Church as well as those outside the Church, this suggested that Christianity was properly a private religion that operated quite comfortably in the space afforded it by liberal politics. Such a conception of Christianity was profoundly flawed. It had been condemned by the pre-Vatican II popes in no uncertain terms, and the latter half of the twentieth century would demonstrate just how right they had been. Societies unmoored from Christianity descend ultimately into paganism. There is no "natural law" third way. This is the clear lesson of the totality of human history, including the biblical narrative which is obviously about the tragic inadequacy of fallen nature and about humanity's need for the healing and elevation that comes through Christ.

Dignitatis Humanae's optimism in nature also rests uneasily with the universal ecclesiology of *Lumen Gentium*, which, following Scripture, placed Christ in the center of all human activity. Within the vision of *Lumen Gentium*, it is hard to locate where exactly a realm of well-functioning "nature" would find a "non-Christian" place to operate. In *Lumen Gentium*, Christianity was not merely a superadded "religious" layer to an otherwise properly ordered humanity. Instead, all of human history, without exception, was about Christ. In the relationship, therefore, between *Lumen Gentium* and *Dignitatis Humanae*, we can see the tension that underwrote the council, the tension between evangelical zeal animating a patristic and medieval ecclesiology for the redemption of humanity and a misplaced optimism in fallen human nature in its modern liberal form. The tension permeates the council documents: Indeed, if much of the world was operating just fine without Christ, as the optimistic side of the council seemed to suggest, why was it so important that his Church come to encompass all the cosmos, as the missionary side of the council emphatically asserted?

The World

The same tension is clearly on display in the council's last and longest document, *Gaudium et Spes*, which dealt with the Church's mission in the world. *Gaudium et Spes* paradoxically oscillates between a maximalist ecclesiology that posits a Church that is destined to convert all the world, that leaves nothing of the world (or indeed, of the cosmos) "alone," and a treatment of Christianity as a minority religion, made up of a sort of spiritual elite, that has a lot to "offer" the independent "world" of the majority, a world that seems to be getting along pretty well on its own.

Along with *Lumen Gentium* and the main thread of the Catholic tradition, the document asserts a maximalist ecclesiology, stating boldly of Christ that there is no "other name under heaven given among men by which they can be saved. The Church likewise believes that the key, the center and the purpose of the whole of man's history is to be found in its Lord and Master."[31] The salvation that comes from Christ is total: "It is man himself who must be saved: it is mankind that must be renewed."[32] This is so because sin, the document argues, is real and penetrates all of human action: "The hierarchy of values has been disordered, good and evil intermingle, and every man and every group is interested only in its own affairs . . . man's swelling power at the present time threatens to put an end to the human race itself."[33] On account of the Fall, "man therefore is divided in himself. As a result, the whole life of men, both individual and social, shows itself to be a struggle, and a dramatic one, between good and evil, between light and darkness."[34] In clear continuity with the tradition, *Gaudium et Spes* argues that this tragic condition can find resolution only through Christ: "To the question of how this unhappy situation can be overcome, Christians reply that all these human activities, which are daily endangered by pride and inordinate self-love, must be purified and perfected by the cross and resurrection of Christ."[35] Indeed, the social consequences of sin "can only be overcome by unflinching effort under

---

[31] Vatican II, *Gaudium et Spes*, in Flannery, *Vatican Council II: The Conciliar and Postconciliar Documents*, §10.
[32] Vatican II, *Gaudium et Spes*, §3.
[33] Vatican II, *Gaudium et Spes*, §37.
[34] Vatican II, *Gaudium et Spes*, §13.
[35] Vatican II, *Gaudium et Spes*, §37.

the help of grace."³⁶ Here, the document presents Christianity as a civilization-building enterprise, an enterprise that encompasses all of history and all of human activity; it states, "The Lord is the goal of human history, the focal point of the desires of history and civilization, the center of mankind, the joy of all hearts, and the fulfilment of all aspirations."³⁷

But then it shifts. We read that in the world, "there is a growing awareness of the sublime dignity of the human person, who stands above all things and whose rights and duties are universal and inviolable."³⁸ This is the postwar optimism which seemed to give in to the temptation to imagine men achieving peace and justice without Christ. The document states, "We are witnessing, then, the birth of a new humanism, where man is defined before all else by his responsibility to his brothers and at the court of history."³⁹ The document sometimes conveys the notion that secular modern culture is engaged in uniting man under the ideals of brotherly love and communion and in deepening our movement into the true, the good, and the beautiful, and that Christians are called to serve as particularly helpful participants in this movement. Explicit Christianity seems sometimes to merely offer a religious "layer" to this world or a clearer explanation of the generally praiseworthy modern project.

Indeed, this tendency is so prevalent that the document actually uses the Augustinian category of "the Earthly City" in a positive light. It uses "the Earthly City" as synonymous with the temporal realm of politics, economics, and society and seems to suppose that the world is capable of true justice in these realms on its own terms, without the interference of "the Heavenly City," the Church. For Augustine, of course, the Earthly City was bound for perdition, and the Heavenly City included within it all human activity without exception, redeemed through Christ. For Augustine, the two cities were mutually exclusive. Where the City of God reigned, the Earthly City had been displaced. Where the Earthly City reigned, the City of God was persecuted. And yet, in *Gaudium et Spes*, we read, "Christ did not bequeath to the Church a mission in the political, economic, or

---

[36] Vatican II, *Gaudium et Spes*, §25.
[37] Vatican II, *Gaudium et Spes*, §45.
[38] Vatican II, *Gaudium et Spes*, §26.
[39] Vatican II, *Gaudium et Spes*, §55.

social order: the purpose he assigned to it was a religious one."[40] What happened to the laity of *Apostolicam Actuositatem*? We often get the impression that Christians are being envisioned as a minority that sees more clearly than others the good work that the world is engaged in and so is particularly helpful in getting that work done.[41]

The robust ecclesiology of *Lumen Gentium* presents humanity's movement into the true and the good as the same as its conversion into the Church, into the City or Family of God. *Gaudium et Spes*, however, asserts: "Thus the Church, at once a 'visible organization and a spiritual community,' travels the same journey as all mankind and shares the same earthly lot with the world: it is to be a leaven and, as it were, the soul of human society in its renewal by Christ and transformation into the family of God. . . . The Church, then, believes it can contribute much to humanizing the family of man and its history through each of its members and its community as a whole."[42] The sense here is not that the world is being turned into the Family of God as it is converted *from* the World *to* the Church, but rather that there is some sort of process of humanity's redemption that does not involve conversion to Christianity, that the "World" and the "Church" coexist permanently as a part of God's plan for salvation and with Christians fully members of both.[43] Are we now to suppose that "the World," which the writers of the New Testament unanimously declare to be the enemy of Christ, is, in fact, a partner of his Church, working toward the same ends? This is one possible reading, as the document states, "grace is active invisibly" in the hearts of "all men of good will. . . . For since Christ died for all, and since all men are in fact called to one and the same destiny, which is divine, we must hold that the Holy Spirit offers to all the possibility of being made partners, in a way known to God, in the paschal mystery."[44]

And yet, this tempting reading, verging on indifferentism, cannot finally stand, and the ecclesiology of *Lumen Gentium* wins in the end. As the document asserts, "The social order requires constant improvement: it must be founded in truth, built on justice, and enlivened by love: it should grow in freedom towards a more humane equilibri-

---

[40] Vatican II, *Gaudium et Spes*, §42.
[41] Vatican II, *Gaudium et Spes*, §56.
[42] Vatican II, *Gaudium et Spes*, §40.
[43] Vatican II, *Gaudium et Spes*, §43.
[44] Vatican II, *Gaudium et Spes*, §22.

um."⁴⁵ But this growth cannot happen outside of Christ. Ultimately, "the Church knows well that God alone, whom it serves, can satisfy the deepest cravings of the human heart, for the world and what it has to offer can never fully content it."⁴⁶ Indeed, without Christianity, humanity cannot even come to fully know himself because "Christ the Lord, Christ the new Adam, in the very revelation of the mystery of the Father and of his love, fully reveals man to himself and brings to light his most high calling."⁴⁷ Following *Apostolicam Actuositatem*, *Gaudium et Spes* states that it is the task of the laity "to cultivate a properly informed conscience and to impress the divine law on the affairs of the earthly city."⁴⁸ Of course, this means that the success of the lay vocation is nothing other than the conversion of the Earthly City to the City of God. Religion does not, in the end, operate in a special "private" realm. Rather: "Let there, then, be no such pernicious opposition between professional and social activity on the one hand and religious life on the other. The Christian who shirks his temporal duties shirks his duties towards his neighbor, neglects God himself and endangers his eternal salvation."⁴⁹ The laity's mission in the world is nothing less than ensuring "that God's design for man may be fulfilled."⁵⁰ Like the so-called virtues of the ancient pagans, the values of modernity that *Gaudium et Spes* sometimes naively praises are ultimately worthy of this praise only if they "afford a certain kind of preparation for the acceptance of the message of the Gospel and can be infused with divine charity by him who came to save the world."⁵¹

Gaudium et Spes is sometimes confusing. It is hard to keep up with its argument or track its overall message. In the end, however, it seems to be attempting to open the Church to the world. It seems to be trying to articulate how the Church can become porous. It seems to be grasping after an articulation of the Church's new missionary orientation. The question, though, is whether the boundaries of the Church were being made porous so that it could penetrate the world by converting it to Christianity or whether they were being made porous so the world could penetrate the Church by converting it to

---

⁴⁵ Vatican II, *Gaudium et Spes*, §26.
⁴⁶ Vatican II, *Gaudium et Spes*, §41.
⁴⁷ Vatican II, *Gaudium et Spes*, §22.
⁴⁸ Vatican II, *Gaudium et Spes*, §43.
⁴⁹ Vatican II, *Gaudium et Spes*, §43.
⁵⁰ Vatican II, *Gaudium et Spes*, §64.
⁵¹ Vatican II, *Gaudium et Spes*, §57.

modernity. *Gaudium et Spes*, like much of Vatican II, wrestled with this tension. In their extreme formulations, one approach sought total evangelization while the other sought little evangelization at all.

What seems to have been agreed upon was that Western civilization was no longer Christian. The modern popes had warned about this eventuality and had fought against it with all the authority they could bring to bear. They had argued that peace and justice could not continue if Christianity were abandoned, that civilizational apostasy would mean civilizational decline. The pervasive postwar optimism, however, made it possible to suppose that this prewar magisterium had perhaps been a bit unfair in its treatment of modernity. Perhaps modernity wasn't so bad after all. Perhaps modernity was finding a "natural" path to peace and justice that didn't need to be explicitly Christian. Perhaps Christianity could find a comfortable place as a "religion" in this burgeoning civilization modernity was building. Perhaps, from that comfortable place, it could provide wisdom and insight and help modernity become more fully and more completely what it aspired to be: a civilization of justice, freedom, and unity. Perhaps the New Testament was talking about a different "World" than the one the Church was then encountering.

This was the tempting approach that the ambiguities in the documents of Vatican II made possible. This amounted to deploying against modernity the first part of St. Augustine's strategy against the pagans without following it with the second part of his attack. It amounted to showing the people of the world what was good in their societies but without effectively showing them how that goodness could only be truly and finally good in and through Christ. It failed to show that without finding unity in Christ, the so-called virtues of the moderns, like those of the pagans before them, would lead them ultimately to perdition.

At the same time, however, Vatican II made possible the Church's breaking free from the defensive stance it had taken throughout modernity. This stance had been premised on the reality of Christian civilization. It had been premised on the existence of something to defend and so was totally appropriate while that something lingered on. That time had passed, however. It was time for bold evangelization, and this meant it was time to reformulate the truths of Christianity to put them on an aggressive footing within postmodernity. It was time to go on the offensive. Offense is inherently dangerous. We need only recall that it was during the aggressive conversion of the ancient world that the most formidable heresies were formed and widely propagated. Trying to articulate the Gospel into a pagan world inevitably leads to missteps, to mistaken tactics, to failed campaigns. It is a long-term project, with a distant goal and uncertain means, and so, fraught with danger. But it is no less necessary for all this. Through Vatican II, the Church initiated a move into this danger, a move to risk the world yet again.

3. After Vatican II

Turmoil and Confusion

The *nouvelle théologie* basically won the theological debate at Vatican II. However, as is often the case, victory revealed division within the ranks of the winners. The theologians of the *nouvelle théologie* split into two camps. One side emphasized the "missionary" aspect of the council. This group was centered on the academic journal *Communio*. The other side emphasized the "optimism about modernity" side. They centered on the academic journal *Concilium*. They disagreed profoundly on the proper interpretation of the council. The *Concilium* side, however, initially seemed to win the contest over how the council would be received on the ground, in the parishes. The *Concilium*-inspired "Spirit of Vatican II," as it developed in the years immediately after the council, was a spirit of innovation, a spirit of movement into modernity. At its most simplistic, this impulse was embarrassed by all things old and traditional and enamored with all things modern, new, or experimental. Pretending to be for the common people, it was, in fact, often profoundly elitist, supposing that the pieties that the simple faithful had lived for hundreds of years were misguided and a waste of time and could be suppressed or replaced with the creations of elite "experts." In the immediate aftermath of the Council, one can perceive, in some corners of Church leadership, an almost iconoclastic glee in the aggressive destruction of the "old" ways of being a faithful Catholic. To the innovators, those scandalized by the destruction needed to "get with the times," needed to fall into line.

The sophisticated liturgical reform movement that had developed in Germany and France over the previous century was pushed aside by a simplistic rush to throw out anything supposedly beyond the understanding of ordinary lay people.[52] The council had called for greater participation of the laity in the Mass. It had envisioned a greater use of the vernacular within a still-Latin liturgy. It had envisioned, in short, a reform of the Mass that reflected an ecclesiology of communion and mission. While it is debatable whether the new missal that was promulgated after the council went too far in its restructuring of the ancient rite along these lines, it is undeniable that a real break with tradition occurred in how the new liturgy was implemented in the parishes. Almost overnight, the Mass shifted from a high-culture experience of spiritual *gravitas* to a mundane experience of low-culture "togetherness." Not without a degree of cultural snobbery, the Catholic author Evelyn Waugh opined, "The Mass is no longer the Holy Sacrifice but the Meal at which the priest is the waiter. The bishop, I suppose, is the head waiter."[53] The theology that underpinned the council had imagined the Mass transitioning from a highly specialized transaction between the priest and God to a true event of sacramental communion, a communion both horizontal, among the faithful, and vertical, between the faithful and God. In the implementation of this vision, however, the vertical and sacramental aspects, which had been so heavily present in the old Mass, were often nearly completely lost in favor of horizontal "community building," of "meeting people where they were" and more or less leaving them there. The typical folk Mass of the 1970s was unrecognizable to those who had experienced the High Mass of the 1950s. It was experienced by the normal faithful as a hard break, and many, many Catholics stopped coming to Mass.

What happened with the liturgy was representative of a larger trend: the call to reform was often received as license to overthrow tradition and traditional authority in a scramble to catch up with the now postmodern world. For example, the United States had an extensive system of private Catholic colleges and universities. These had been built over the course of the previous century precisely because the Church had understood that Catholic education was unique, was different from the education of the world. The Church had understood that its young people needed more than a merely professional or academic training in the various secular disciplines. Rather, they needed to be formed in a Catholic worldview. They needed to be

---

[52] See Robert Royal, "Vatican II at 50," *Claremont Review of Books* 12, no. 4 (2012).

[53] Quoted in Dom Alcuin Reid, *A Bitter Trial: Evelyn Waugh and John Cardinal Heenan on the Liturgical Changes* (San Francisco: Ignatius Press, 2011), 65.

taught to see their world through the eyes of Christianity. However, in 1967, an influential group of leaders in Catholic higher education gathered at Land O' Lakes, Wisconsin. They issued a declaration of independence from all ecclesial authority. They envisioned Catholic universities that operated independently of the clerical hierarchy and that prized academic freedom over faithfulness. They sought to integrate Catholic universities fully into mainstream higher education, where Catholic scholars could finally win the prestige they coveted and Catholic schools could receive the funding that was increasingly flowing from government and industry. The result was the steady normalization of Catholic schools to the point of being largely indistinguishable from their secular counterparts. What is more, they were so thoroughly integrated into the mainstream government and funding apparatuses that the independence for which they had been established was all but eliminated.

This movement into the world was perhaps nowhere more damaging than in the area of catechesis. As fast as the progressive theologians in Europe could produce books justifying capitulation to modernity, publishers throughout the West translated them into catechetical materials, and educators began using them, while many priests preached the new approach from the pulpit. This new catechesis emphasized personal feelings and experiences over doctrinal content. It also minimized any notion that Christianity was the true religion, and, perhaps most devastatingly, it minimized the reality of sin. We can perhaps see this tendency as an overcorrection to the rigid, legalistic, and rationalist catechesis that had dominated before the council. It is no doubt true that this old catechesis needed to be reformed in the direction of a personal conversion to Christ, in the direction of a realization of the difference that God makes in our everyday lives, and in the direction of an emphasis on forgiveness and mercy. Likewise, it is probably true that the triumphalist tendencies of the older method lacked a proper humility in the face of the wide variety of humanity's good-faith attempts to reach God, attempts that were often manifested in non-Christian religions. But the new approach went far beyond such correction. Indeed, the pendulum swung so far the other way that belief in the necessity and uniqueness of Christ often dissolved into a generic call to kindness. The Christianity of the new catechesis was self-consciously not countercultural. Christianity was no longer a call to radical witness, even martyrdom, but was really just a way of being a particularly well-functioning, and yet profoundly normal, citizen of late modernity.

Perhaps unsurprisingly, many people stopped going to church. In 1955, in the United States, 75 percent of Catholics went to Mass every week; in 1975, 42 percent did. Similarly, thousands of priests left the priesthood, and tens of thousands of monks and nuns left the religious life. The seminaries, which had been bursting at the seams in the 1950s, steadily emptied. It is extremely tempting to simply blame Vatican II for these trends, and there emerged a "traditionalist" movement within the Church that did just that. However, the explanation is more subtle and more complicated. As we saw above, the shift in popular Catholicism from being a worldview in its own right to being a component of an essentially nationalist and ideologically liberal worldview had occurred over the course of the decades before World War II and was accelerated in the postwar period. Before the council ever met, Catholics were already thinking of themselves as good and normal citizens of their secular societies.

This trend was reinforced by the dominant preconciliar, neo-scholastic theology that tended to present politics, economics, and even ethics as having to do with man's "nature," and so, not in need of explicitly Christian revelation or the inflow of grace to be properly ordered. When simplified, this approach tended to reinforce the late 1940s and 1950s optimistic notion that the liberal West was building societies based upon the natural law and that Catholicism was basically a private endeavor for those who would go beyond mere nature and achieve a fullness of supernatural truth and happiness. It should be remembered, of course, that all the bishops that participated in Vatican II were the product of this sort of preconciliar theological training, as were nearly all the priests who implemented the council in a radical way in the parishes. We might say accurately that the 1960s and 1970s were the fruit of the 1950s. It is ironic but true that the preconciliar conservatives and the postconciliar radicals shared an optimism about nature. This was why so much of the Church could transition so quickly from one to the other. It was just not too far of a step. What happened after the council was the popular, vulgarized implementation of the simple idea that the world in its modern form, on the whole, was pretty good, and so Catholics could be normal.

However, the problem was that what constituted "normal" was shifting. The postwar consensus was short lived. The conjoining of intense nationalism, immense material prosperity, and a community-dissolving individualism with commitment to Christian moral norms and religious observance was not sustainable. This consensus, rather, flowed from the peculiar, context-bound personality of the World War II generation, and it began to pass away as the next generation grew up. The postwar consensus's contradictions began to manifest themselves in the 1960s and 1970s as the societies of the liberal West were hit with large-scale social upheaval and division. The two clearest demonstrations of this turmoil surrounded the so-called sexual revolution and the Vietnam War.

The sexual revolution was the widespread breakdown of traditional sexual morality that began in the 1950s and accelerated in the 1960s. To many in the West, the rules of sexual morality had lost all foundation and had become nothing more than rules. They were baseless and oppressive and could be easily overthrown without disrupting the real heart of social unity, which at its best was love of nation and at its worse was the pursuit of individual desire fulfillment. As we have seen, Christianity had already largely become a private moral code that lacked a hold on public order itself. In this environment, the postwar generation experienced their parents' sexual morality as arbitrary and tyrannical, and the sexual revolution was the widespread shedding of this oppression. The sexual revolution was empowered by the availability of the birth control pill, which reduced dramatically the connection between sex and children and so nearly eliminated the heavy responsibility that sexual activity had traditionally entailed. Once risk was removed from sex, once the social function of the old rules seemed to be eliminated, to many operating within a utilitarian ethical paradigm, the old rules appeared not merely unnecessary but, in fact, immoral. The sexual revolution was primarily a social movement that had to do with people's behavior, but it was enshrined in a number of laws. For example, "no-fault divorce" became the norm. This enabled someone to divorce his or her spouse for no reason, and so, legally, marriage was no longer understood as permanent. Most horrifying, however, was the United States Supreme Court's 1973 ruling in Roe v. Wade, which effectively legalized abortion. Abortion was similarly legalized throughout the West. Even the "moral" value of a human life was subject to the utilitarian calculations of pleasure fulfilment.

The Vietnam War triggered another front in the burgeoning battle against the postwar consensus. Integral to this consensus had been the notion that the United States was a force for good in the world. In this vision, the United States and its allies had fought a heroic fight against the Fascists during World War II and continued to fight an equally heroic battle against the Communists in the Cold War. American nationalism was directly tied up with its goodness. Americans fought the good fight because Americans were good and moral people. The Vietnam War called this goodness into question. The United States entered the conflict in Vietnam in the early 1960s in order to stop the spread of Communism into the country. It was argued that if Communism were allowed to spread into one country, this would increase the likelihood that it would spread to neighboring countries. If this process were not stopped, Communist expansion would snowball, and the liberal nations would be unable to contain it. Therefore, the best strategic option was to stop the spread of Communism at the beginning, before it could take root.

The Vietnam War was, therefore, presented to the American people as integral to America's heroic stand against Communism. The problem was that as the war progressed in the late 1960s, it became clearer and clearer that the North Vietnamese were not going to give up. To them, America was an imperialist power no different than the French Empire, which they had driven out of Vietnam in the 1950s. The war dragged on and become more and more costly in lives and money. In its bid to win, the United States relied upon its overwhelming superiority in technological power, especially air power and high explosives. This led to the killing of possibly millions of Vietnamese. The United States' moral superiority was called into question. In the late 1960s, the war led to the formation of a large protest movement throughout the liberal West. This movement challenged the notion of the inherent goodness of American foreign policy and fostered suspicion of American nationalism generally. In the face of the Vietnam War, could Americans really be sure that they were in the right? Could it be that the Communists had a point about capitalist imperialism? Such ideas directly undermined the postwar consensus.

The political parties in the West, especially the United States, quickly reconstituted themselves along the lines of these conflicts. The Republican Party became largely the defender of the postwar consensus. It was pro-American, pro-capitalist, and anti-Communist. It was also the defender of traditional sexual morality, and after 1976, opposed legalized abortion. The Democratic Party embraced the new movements. It became suspicious of capitalism and was anti traditional sexual morality, soft on Communism, and pro-abortion. The Catholic populations, now thoroughly normalized, split themselves up roughly along the same lines as society as a whole. Pope Paul VI's 1968 encyclical *Humanae Vitae*, which confirmed Catholicism's traditional belief that contraception was immoral, provided the necessary flash point for the sorting of Catholics with regards to the sexual revolution. Similarly, anti-capitalist and anti-American statements by such organizations as the United States Council of Catholic Bishops provided necessary flash points with regards to politics and economics.

To speak in sweeping generalizations, conservative Catholics became, for the most part, defenders of the 1950s postwar situation. They thought that Christianity was true and was essential to being a good and moral person and raising good and moral children. But they took for granted that the economic and political order in which they practiced their faith was secular, that it operated under its own laws that had little to do with revelation or grace. Christianity was envisioned as fundamentally private. This is why conservatives maintained the aspects of Christianity that most directly bore on the individual. They were concerned with sexual morality, with the explicit content of belief, with prayer and devotions. But they came to largely ignore the social aspects of Christianity. In individual matters, they confidently asserted objective moral standards that rested on notions of intrinsic right and wrong, and yet in regards to political and economic issues, they asserted consequentialist[54] or utilitarian belief systems: premarital sex was always objectively wrong, but dropping atomic bombs on Japanese cities had been justified because it ended up saving lives, and aggressive Cold War policies were justified to defend American "interests." Missing Mass on Sunday was a mortal sin, and yet businesses operated in an amoral realm where it was their job to seek profit and thereby increase total wealth, leaving value judgments to the individual consumer. One was to treat one's family with love and compassion, and yet, at the same time, one was to seek middle-class "success" in the competition of the marketplace.

There emerged, then, on the Catholic right a historically abnormal movement of seemingly conservative Christians who nevertheless embraced capitalism and liberal nationalism. Traditionally, of course, conservative Catholics had opposed liberalism as necessarily antithetical to a truly Christian society. This had been the thrust of the Church's entire social magisterium. In the post-Vatican II situa-

---

[54] Consequentialism is the doctrine that the morality of an action is to be judged solely by its consequences.

tion, however, conservatives were simply no longer pursuing a truly Christian society; they had lost sight of what that might even mean. They were, rather, defending the postwar consensus, a historically fleeting moment in which privatized Christianity had an important role within a decidedly non-Christian social order. The social doctrine of the Church, therefore, became an embarrassment to them, and they worked on justifying what amounted to more or less direct dissent from it. To their opponents, this made their position shallow and unconvincing. Their opponents quickly perceived that their commitment to Christian "morality" was not only not integral to the rest of their beliefs but also basically arbitrary and in the end just a matter of preference, or to use the word more often deployed, prejudice. Insisting on personal "morality" while ignoring Christianity's revolutionary call to social justice was transparently incoherent. It rested, then, not on a fundamentally Christian worldview but on the postwar liberal-nationalist worldview, which is why this group was so easily co-opted by center-right political parties.

The progressive Catholics, or liberals as they were known in the United States, did almost the opposite. They emphasized the social in Christianity to the point of the near total eclipse of the individual. Individual morality become almost nonexistent as they interpreted the Catholic mandate to follow one's conscience in a manner that dissolved objective right and wrong in private matters. Following one's conscience, apparently, could justify even abortion, the killing of millions of innocent children. This evaporation of the individual aspects of Christianity was most obvious in sexual matters, but it extended to nearly all aspects of an individual's participation in the Church. What an individual explicitly believed, for example, didn't really matter. Whether or not he obeyed the mandates of the Church didn't really matter. Indeed, the sense of individual sin basically evaporated. The privatized Christianity that reigned in liberal societies was relativized more or less out of existence.

However, these progressives dramatically emphasized the social aspects of Christianity. To them, it may not have been immoral to have premarital sex, but the Vietnam War, and by extension the Cold War itself, was a crime against humanity, a massive violation of justice. Whether to go to Mass or not was an issue of individual conscience, but social justice simply demanded that the welfare state be extended and the profit-motive curtailed. Human nature had little to say about our personal lifestyles, and so morality should not be legislated, but the protection of the environment, of non-human nature, demanded dramatic lifestyle changes, enforced by law. Individual sin was of little importance, but societal structures of sin had to be destroyed. In individual matters, the Catholic left seemed to adopt some form of moral relativism, while in social matters, it maintained the most dogged defense of objective right and wrong, of intrinsic good and evil. As with the conservatives, the position of the Catholic left was transparently incoherent to its opponents. The conservatives clearly saw that the progressives' Christianity was not necessary for their social program and so understood it as disingenuous.

The discord that rocked the postconciliar Church in the West was in large part, then, a fight that occurred within a general capitulation to the liberal notion that Christianity was merely a religion that operated within a secular world. Neither side thought that the entire social organism, the entire political, economic, legal, and moral order, from the largest of societal structures to the everyday actions of individual Christians, could find its end of true freedom and peace only through a top-to-bottom conversion to Christ and the acceptance of his healing and elevating grace. But what is worse is that Catholics became so "normal" that their religion was for many just a department of their political partisanship. In the United States, whether someone was a Republican or a Democrat was a better predictor of their stance on most issues than whether or not they were Catholic, and intra-Catholic fights became often little more than proxy battles for the two political parties. By 1980, the so-called "Catholic vote" disappeared as Catholic vote distributions came to be largely identical to that of the popular vote, as the boundaries of Catholicism became so porous that Catholics tragically dissolved into everyday liberal society.

At the same time, the institutional Church was being absorbed into liberalism. As we saw earlier in this book, in the aftermath of the fall of the Carolingian Empire, the institutional Church was absorbed into the feudal system. The Church was just a part of the complex system of governance and economics that reigned at that time. In the same sort of way, the postconciliar Church was steadily integrated into liberalism. The dioceses became multibillion dollar private corporations that employed thousands of lay people; they invested billions of dollars in for-profit enterprises, lobbied politically as special interest groups, and received massive amounts of government funding as well as funding from influential business interests. It is not that the institutional Church became a part of the government. That is not how liberalism works. Rather, it became just another actor in the public/private dance that characterizes a liberal society. The dioceses became massive providers of social services, services that often abandoned or minimized their direct connection to Christian mission. They increasingly operated according to the same practices as other private and public corporations, adopting their bureaucratic and administrative form much as the early medieval Church had adopted the form of feudalism, or the early modern Church had adopted the form of absolute monarchy. Lawyers and insurance companies became de facto policy makers, and bishops sometimes in practice transitioned from pastors to executives. This was the institutional side to the postconciliar move into modernity. All too often, the boundaries of the institution became porous, not to remake the world in the image of the Church, but the opposite.

Throughout history, the Church's integration into fundamentally non-Christian regimes has been accompanied by corruption within the clergy. For example, the post-Carolingian period saw the spread of concubinage and simony as the clergy were integrated into the feudal system; the Late Medieval and Early Modern periods saw the pursuit of wealth and worldly power as the clergy were integrated into the sovereign monarchy system. In both these cases, however, corrupt clergy were always a minority within the clergy as a whole. Even on the eve of the Reformation, the vast majority of parish priests were good and dutiful pastors, and the vast majority of monks and nuns were active in the pursuit of holiness. The moral corruption, however, is what is remembered. The corruption is what stands out and is noticed.

The Church's integration into liberalism was no different. Here, though, the worst of the moral corruption took the form of sexual abuse, especially of minors. The frequency of abuse began to increase in the early 1950s, shot up in the 1960s and 1970s, and peaked around 1980. In the United States, roughly 4 percent of clergy were implicated in over ten thousand allegations of abuse.[55] There are, of course, many compounding variables that account for these horrifying numbers. For starters, most of the offending clergy were part of the ordination boom that occurred in the 1940s and 1950s. As we discussed above, this boom was a part of the complex postwar cultural milieu. The central point, though, is that Catholicism was already being rap-

---

[55] John Jay College of Criminal Justice, *The Nature and Scope of the Problem of Sexual Abuse of Minors by Priests and Deacons* (Washington, D.C.: USCCB, 2004).

idly "normalized," and many of these priests were "normal" Americans who sought the prestige of the priesthood, or whose families had pressured them into the priesthood, or who had felt that the priesthood was a respectable place to hide from personality or socialization problems. Many of them should never have been ordained to begin with. What is more, their education had largely avoided sexual matters or had discussed them always in a negative light. This, too, was fairly normal for 1950s America.

As the sexual revolution gained ground in the culture at large, these priests were especially susceptible to its allures. The vast majority of priests who decided that celibacy was no longer acceptable to them left the priesthood to marry. Over twenty thousand priests did so. Disproportionately, however, those with abnormal sexual proclivities tended to stay in the priesthood, and many violated their vow of celibacy. Most of the sexual abuse cases involved this group. It should be remembered that in the 1960s and 1970s, across society the sexual revolution had often taken on an extreme, anything-goes personality that was only slowly reigned in during the 1980s, when the damage caused by sexual abuse became increasingly clear to society as a whole. While statistics are difficult to come by, it seems clear that sexual abuse of minors increased dramatically culture-wide during this period. The public school system, for example, suffered levels of abuse greater than in the Catholic Church. Pointing out that abusive priests were a part of an increasingly abusive culture is not to excuse them. Far from it. It is to acknowledge that their very "normalcy" was the problem.

During this period, sexual misconduct in the culture at large tended to be understood as a psychological problem rather than a predatory or criminal problem. Men who abused minors often underwent therapy in order to be "healed." In this, too, the Church acted "normally." Bishops tended to accept what "experts" told them and sought treatment for offending priests rather than turning them in to the police. Once the experts told them that a priest was again ready for pastoral work, they often took their word for it and assigned the priest to another parish. This is what large institutions across the culture were doing. This is, again, not an excuse, but an indication of the problem. As the Church was increasingly organized according to the forms of government and corporate entities, it took on many of their characteristics. One of these is rational, but heartless, risk management. There emerges in such institutions the desire to protect the organization against threats, and the best way to do this is to minimize problems, move problems, hide problems. When a problem does emerge, the bureaucratic, risk-management model then turns to the lawyers. This tendency is congruent with the tendency in such organizations for good managers or good "climbers" to reach the top of the organizational pyramid rather than good and holy men. Such managers attained their positions of power because they were good at protecting and growing the organization. The seeming unwillingness of the hierarchy to openly and effectively deal with the abuse problem is at least partly rooted in this phenomenon.

This was the culmination of the long, slow process of Christianity's transition from the basis of a civilization to a mere religion, from the architecture of society itself to window dressing on a structure built without Christ. The horror that we rightly feel in response to these developments is rooted in our deep, often obscured, knowledge that the Lord is more than the hearth god of a particular sect within a pagan pantheon, governing the private realm of family and friends. Rather, he is the Lord of all, the creator of the universe.

The New Evangelization

This was the general situation when St. John Paul II assumed the papal office in 1978. He immediately perceived that the missionary aspect of the council needed to be restored, and his pontificate was dominated by his attempt to give an official evangelical interpretation to Vatican II. This interpretation relied heavily on the *Communio* side of the *nouvelle théologie*. Indeed, the opening words of John Paul II's first encyclical were "The Redeemer of man, Jesus Christ, is the centre of the universe and of history."[56] In this truly Catholic understanding, there is no sphere of life that doesn't need Christ, and the Church could never rest as a comfortable minority. As John Paul II stated, "I sense that the moment has come to commit all of the Church's energies to a new evangelization."[57] This New Evangelization was not content to leave Christianity as a mere private religion that operated in a mass society that no longer needed Christ. It sought, rather, to reconvert humanity from top to bottom. What made it new was that it was

---

[56] John Paul II, *Redemptor Hominis* (1979), §1.
[57] John Paul II, *Redemptoris Missio* (1990), §3.

directed primarily at the already baptized. It was aimed primarily at the peoples who had once constituted Christendom, and it sought to show them anew the radical and all-encompassing call of Christ, the difference Christ makes in every aspect of life, individual and social. It was directed at the new pagans for whom Christianity had become merely one cult among many, for whom God had become merely a god within a pantheon of gods. As we have seen, for many, this god was still important when it came to family life or private life, but they had forgotten that he was, in fact, the God of all creation. Like the Church Fathers, John Paul II looked to the goodness in man as his starting point. His theology was not just a list of things that modern man was doing wrong. Rather, he sought out the deep yearnings of the modern heart and showed how Christ was the fulfillment of those yearnings.

In response to the sexual revolution, he gave the world his *Theology of the Body*. In this brilliant treatment of human sexuality, the pope asserted the fundamental goodness of human sexuality. He showed how men and women were intrinsically lovers and that the love that fulfilled them in their human natures was necessarily expressed bodily, sexually. The pope agreed with the proponents of the sexual revolution that any treatment of sex that viewed it as dirty, or as necessarily sinful, or as shameful, was opposed to human nature and was ultimately tyrannical. But, rather than an opening to sexual anarchy and infinite license, this recognition of the essential goodness of sex was simultaneously and necessarily a recognition of its immense importance and seriousness. Because it wasn't just a sin, sex was something that had to be ordered toward the ultimate end of man, which was happiness, a happiness that could only be had in communion, both horizontally between people and vertically between people and God. Sex, then, was connected fundamentally to truth, goodness, and beauty, to justice. It was not just a plaything. Treating sex as a toy was nothing more than the inversion of treating it as shameful. Nor was sex merely private. It, rather, implicated the whole person in his or her profound socialness. For the pope, the degradation of sex and the general degradation of man went hand in hand. Human nature was not split between "private" aspects and "public" aspects. Human nature was integral. The pope, therefore, addressed both sides in the sexual revolution and elevated the truth present in their intuitions into the far more profound truth that can only be had through Christ.

One of John Paul II's most important insights was that the errors of modernity were no longer primarily ideological. Rather, modernity had progressed to the point that ideological errors had become internalized into the moral life of the normal person. The Church no longer needed primarily to refute arguments; the Church needed, rather, to preach the Gospel. For example, since Pope Leo XIII, the papacy's criticism of capitalism had focused on the powerful's exploitation of the weak and on the intellectual errors that they deployed to justify that exploitation. This theme remained in John Paul II's work, but he added a popular dimension. He recognized that the greed and materialism that had motivated many of the owners during the Industrial Revolution had penetrated into the cultural life of the common people. He called this "consumerism." Consumerism was not merely about buying lots of stuff. Rather, it was an approach to life. "Consumers" approached the world concerned with what they could get, what they could take. They viewed their power, in whatever form it might take, as a resource to be deployed for the maximalization of their taking from the world. In a consumerist society, power was for the person who held it. This was, of course, a thorough denial of the Christian understanding of a social hierarchy of service and care.

Consumerism ran on the creation and fulfillment of new and self-destructive "needs." People wanted "more," even though this more was hurting them. John Paul II recognized that while the owners of capital bore a serious responsibility to justice, so, too, did the common person. His purchasing choices and his investment choices were as integral to unjust systems of production and distribution as was the organization of capital.[58] Social justice, therefore, could be achieved only through a society-wide re-conversion to Christ. John Paul II recognized that free market-style business and even profit could have an important place in a just society,[59] but only if businesses were ordered toward the common good and only if consumers were governed by temperance and motivated, ultimately, by charity; only, in other words, if the use of power was re-oriented toward the service of the relatively poor, of the relatively weak. Reasserting the Church's traditional claim that private property was justified only when it was used for the common good, the pope insisted that economics did not operate separately from morality.[60] He wrote of the right to private property: "Christian tradition has never upheld this right as absolute

---

[58] John Paul II, *Centesimus Annus* (1991), §36.
[59] John Paul II, *Centesimus Annus*, §35.
[60] John Paul II, *Centesimus Annus*, §§6, 30–32.

and untouchable. On the contrary, it has always understood this right within the broader context of the right common to all to use the goods of the whole of creation: *the right to private property is subordinated to the right to common use*, to the fact that goods are meant for everyone."[61]

The moral law must structure economic and political life, the realm of action. This is the only way to social happiness, and this way requires Christ. Thus, the two sides in the Cold War, the socialists and the capitalists, are really two sides of the same coin. These ideologies were based on a false materialism and ultimately on atheism, explicit among the Communists and practical among the capitalists. Indeed, because of their shared errors, the pope contended, socialism turns out to be merely "state capitalism," merely state ownership of all property.[62] What is more, both systems tend to reduce society to a sea of isolated individuals who stand alone before the immense power of the state and the economy. This massive violation of subsidiarity is an attack on the fundamentally social aspect of human nature. The damage is not assuaged through the construction of massive welfare programs. In fact, such programs often make things worse, further isolating individuals and undermining solidarity. Against this individual-state conception, the pope asserted the importance of real person-to-person communion,[63] the type of communion that is exemplified most clearly in the family. The pope asserted that the family "constitutes one of the most important terms of reference for shaping the social and ethical order of human work."[64] Such an assertion cuts in two directions. Against the Left, it asserts that the family is central to a proper anthropology, that social justice must include the stable well-being of the family. Against the Right, it asserts that family life shapes the economic order and vice versa, that the private and the public are not distinct realms. The maintenance of "family values" is consistent with neither the defense of value-neutral or profit-focused economics nor with the pursuit of power politics. If you want to protect the family, you must build and maintain a just economic and political order. And if you want to have a just social order, you must protect the family.

---

[61] John Paul II, *Laborem Exercens* (1981), §14.
[62] John Paul II, *Centesimus Annus*, §§14, 19, 35.
[63] John Paul II, *Centesimus Annus*, §48.
[64] John Paul II, *Laborem Exercens*, §10.

Central to this critique is the refusal to allow "morality" to become a merely private matter that concerns behavior that is of little social significance—the tendency of both the "conservative" and "progressive" branches of liberal Christianity. Liberals of both persuasions saw morality as rules or laws that limited freedom. This had also been the tendency in pre-Vatican II Catholic ethics, which emphasized obedience to law as the essence of morality. John Paul II, however, turned this on its head. He agreed with modernity that freedom was a supreme value, that maximizing freedom is the goal of human endeavor. However, he argued that freedom can only be realized through morality. He argued that morality is the experience of freedom. The argument is both elegant and simple. All human beings seek happiness. Their free will is used precisely in choosing the means toward achieving this happiness. Therefore, the more they know about the nature of happiness, that is to say, the more they know about themselves and the more they know about the relative goodness of the choices that lie before them, the more efficaciously they are able to choose a path through life that leads to happiness, and so the more efficaciously they are able to realize their will. Freedom is, therefore, dependent upon truth. It is not merely that those who know the truth feel less of the burdens of restraint; it is also that the positive scope of their action is increased. The more they know and desire the truth, the more possibilities lie open before them; the better they understand means and ends, the better they can execute their will, which is to say, the more they are free to do as they please. This is the meaning of Christ's assertion that "the truth will make you free" (John 8:32). He meant it literally. God's law is the communication to fallen humanity of truth. God's law gives us the possibility of freedom. This is so not because we "submit" to it as an outside force but because it is about us, about our natures, because God's revelation is the revelation of us to ourselves. It shows us how to get what we want.

Nevertheless, knowledge is not enough. We must not only know the truth; we must desire it; we must want the truly good. This ability we are given through grace. Through law, God tells us what is true. Through grace, God helps us want it. Freedom is, therefore, dependent on both law and grace. Freedom is the internalization of the law through grace.[65] To act in accordance with the truth, to see and desire the actual goodness of things, is what it means to be moral. Morality

---

[65] John Paul II, *Veritatis Splendor* (1993), §83.

is, therefore, not a check on freedom; rather, it is another word for it. The converse is also true, the immoral man is a man who does not understand himself or his world. He is unhappy and does not know why or how to change his condition. He can't act to satisfy his heart. His actions are futile and his choices barren. He cannot realize his own will. He is oppressed and calls out for freedom. Christianity, from the Old Testament Passover to the New Testament Paschal Mystery of Christ to the preaching and sacraments of the Church, is God's merciful response to this call, his leading of humanity out of bondage and into freedom.

While maintaining the supreme value of freedom, the pope pulled the rug out from under liberalism. Liberalism contended that freedom was merely the absence of coercion, that it was merely a negative condition. The pope asserted that it was a positive condition and that it was a gift from God. Morality, then, did not merely govern the life of family and friends while leaving the economic and political sphere "free." Such a conception misunderstood freedom fundamentally. Truth bore on all aspects of human action, and morality was the universal living in that truth.[66] Political and economic freedom could only exist through morality. The crisis of truth that modern civilization was experiencing was, therefore, necessarily the undoing of the economic and political freedom it so prized. Outside of truth, that freedom could not be maintained. Similarly, truth was the precondition of individual freedom, freedom of conscience. As the pope wrote, the "heightened sense . . . of the respect due to the journey of conscience certainly represents one of the positive achievements of modern culture."[67] But, he asserts, conscience does not determine right and wrong. Rather, it applies right and wrong to particular circumstances. A malformed conscience, therefore, hinders a man's ability to realize his ends, hinders his freedom. On the other hand, an individual conscience that is conformed to the moral law is a prerequisite to true freedom. A malformed conscience leads a man into bondage. The pope was reuniting the individual and the social within the true and the moral, within the gifts of God's law and God's grace, which is, of course, the New Testament.

The pope, then, was refuting the relativism that lay at the root of liberalism, both right and left, which would make morality simply a

---

[66] John Paul II, *Veritatis Splendor*, §5.
[67] John Paul II, *Veritatis Splendor*, §31.

private matter on one hand or embed it completely in a cultural context on the other. He asserted both the personal and the universal aspects of morality. The personal and particular always point beyond themselves to the universal and objective. What is moral in a particular situation is ultimately determined through reaching beyond the particular situation and to a universal norm. It is wrong, for example, to talk badly about a certain acquaintance in a particular circumstance because *that* would be gossip, and gossip *is always* wrong. It is not, then, that the particular circumstances of individual conscience are rendered meaningless in submission to an absolute norm. It is, rather, that the judgments of individual conscience always include appeal to an absolute norm. If these norms are properly ordered, it leads to freedom and happiness. If they are improperly ordered, it leads to slavery and misery. The objectivity of God's truth leads man, subjectively, out of bondage—but only through grace. Freedom can only be had through God's grace.[68]

The New Evangelization was a project of reintegration. It was a project of showing the modern world that its aspirations were largely derived from Christianity and were only realizable if they were reintegrated within Christianity. Truth and goodness were not private concerns but were, rather, the basis of all human society. If a society was based on the truth and pursued the good, it would move into peace, freedom, and happiness, into life. If a society was based on lies and pursued inferior goods, it would move into violence, misery, slavery, and death. As John Paul II wrote: "We are facing an enormous and dramatic clash between good and evil, death and life, the 'culture of death' and the 'culture of life.'"[69] This was a recasting of St. Augustine's two cities. Rather than merely criticizing particular errors, therefore, John Paul II's critique went far deeper. It was civilizational. Against modernity, the pope asserted, you cannot have freedom without law, and you cannot have reason without faith. You cannot have private happiness without public justice. Happiness is contingent on peace, and peace is the condition of justice. In spite of his pleas, however, by the end of the twentieth century, the paradoxes that underwrote the modern world had slowly resolved themselves in the direction of the culture of death.

This "resolution" was most cruelly manifested in abortion. Abor-

---

[68] John Paul II, *Veritatis Splendor*, §§22–24.
[69] John Paul II, *Evangelium Vitae* (1995), §28.

tion is the killing of the weak in order to maintain the so-called "freedom" of the strong. Abortion is a direct attack on the principles of solidarity and charity at their roots. It fundamentally denies that love can be a duty, that power can be *for* another. It is the definitive consumerist act, wherein the value of another human being is evaluated through the desires of the more powerful. In a sense, the weak become "worth" whatever the powerful are willing to pay for them, like any other product. Within its logic, even the relationship between a mother and her child can only be understood as a contract, as a deal. The rationality of absolutized private property becomes so pervasive that the unborn child is cast as a trespasser. Within this horrid logic, the inconvenient, helpless child becomes an aggressor. Through the logic of abortion, the powerful owe nothing to the weak. A society that cannot embrace the beauty of the imposition of the weak upon the strong at this most basic anthropological level, at the level of mother and child, is a society that no longer believes in the existence of love, of happiness, and of life. It is a society that is no longer open upward but closed downward. It is a society that has chosen death. As the pope wrote, "To claim the right to abortion, infanticide and euthanasia, and to recognize that right in law means to attribute to human freedom a perverse and evil significance: that of an absolute power over others and against others."[70]

Abortion is not, therefore, one issue among other issues. It is the most fundamental postmodern issue. As we saw earlier in this book, the gods of the ancient world demanded that their servants sacrifice their children to their power. This was the "abomination" that the Lord refused to Israel in the Old Testament and to which Israel was continuously tempted. In the Bible, this is not a random picture of evil meant merely to shock us. It is, rather, based on an anthropological insight: the willingness to kill your child and the consequent construction of a system of child murder is the only path to pure power, pure sovereignty. Pure power demands that keeping helpless people alive be a voluntary display of power, a whim of the strong; otherwise, if power is ever revealed to be *for* the weak, the social hierarchy is inverted, and the whole system is exposed for the lie that it is. This is why, as we saw earlier in this book, nearly all pagan societies condone the killing of babies. This is how human power can speak order into chaos without opening itself to what is beyond it, to the transcendent. Nowhere, then, is the West's final slide into post-Christian pagan-

---

[70] John Paul II, *Evangelium Vitae*, §20.

ism clearer than in the abortion regime, which kills around sixty million children every year, roughly 20 percent of all babies. As the pope wrote: "Where God is denied and people live as though he did not exist, or his commandments are not taken into account, the dignity of the human person and the inviolability of human life also end up being rejected or compromised."[71]

The culture of life is the inversion of the culture of death. Rather than beginning with self-interested power, property, and deals and then working back into the family, it begins with the logic of the family, the logic of love and sacrifice, and works out into the rest of society. This is why the family was of such profound importance to Pope John Paul II. The family was humanity at its most basic level. The New Evangelization, therefore, paid special attention to the family, not because it believed Christianity to be private, with nothing to do with politics or economics, but for the exact opposite reason, because it believed that the family was profoundly public, directly connected to just politics and just economics. Christian families, holy families, were a path to the re-evangelization of civilization. The defense of the family is the defense of the foundational principles of a Christian civilization.

Pope St. John Paul II was a charismatic man who took the New Evangelization to the people of the world. He made more pastoral trips than all his predecessors combined. He traveled to over one hundred thirty countries and spoke to some of the largest crowds ever assembled. In addition to his many encyclicals, homilies, and speeches, he oversaw the publication of a new *Catechism of the Catholic Church*, a definitive restatement of Catholic doctrine for the postmodern world. This was only the groundwork for the New Evangelization, for a new reform movement. Pope Benedict XVI followed in his footsteps, developing what he called a "hermeneutic of continuity" for understanding Church history. What this meant was that the post-Vatican II Church must be understood as consistent with the Church of the nineteen hundred years before Vatican II. This was a relativizing of modernity, a sort of "putting modernity in its place."

4. The Coming Reform

The Cold War ended in 1991 with the collapse of the Soviet Union,

---

[71] John Paul II, *Evangelium Vitae*, §96.

leaving only the liberal side in the ideological struggle still standing. But really, all three modern ideologies were spent. Their rhetoric was, by the end of the century, merely the language used for opportunistic, Machiavellian politics. Even the rhetoric of national greatness rang hollow. Nevertheless, nominal Christianity remained a part of the discourse. In 1970, 86 percent of the American population self-identified as Christian. In 1990, 85 percent did. Clearly, Western culture had grown considerably less pious, but Christianity remained an important part of the normal American identity throughout the Cold War. With ideological Communism defeated, however, there was just no longer much need to emphasize religion, and so by and large, people stopped doing so. The end of the Cold War freed the West to finally move past its lingering deference for Christianity and "morality," and both sides of the liberal spectrum set about shedding the remnants of religiosity and so-called "family values." The speed of the transition was shocking. By 2019, only 60 percent of Americans were Christian. During the same period, the number of atheists, agnostics, and the "unaffiliated" increased from only 8 percent of the population to nearly 30 percent. Among those who grew up after the fall of the Soviet Union, this number was closer to 40 percent. By 2016, Christianity was no longer an important focus of conservative concern, as conservatism shifted from a staunch anti-Communism to a sort of ethnic populism. Progressives, for their part, developed an outright hatred for the faith as they transitioned their focus from working class solidarity to identity politics and an exaggerated, often absurd, rhetoric of personal liberation. In an ultimate irony, "social justice warrior" (a term that historically would have been most accurately applied to Crusaders) became a term of reproach that conservatives hurled at progressives, and which atheist progressives claimed in the fight against traditional morality and truth.

It is an indication of just how quickly the twentieth-century American identity collapsed that by the second decade of the twenty-first century, those on the right were calling themselves nationalists and those on the left were calling themselves socialists. No one was an American "liberal" anymore—even the right's devotion to the ideological rhetoric of limited government and unfettered capitalism waned. The enemies of the Second World War, the nationalists, and of the Cold War, the socialists, were forgotten in a single generation, and so, too, were the key components of the postwar American consensus that had formed against them, which included, of course, the importance of Christianity as the cult of wholesome family life. In the first decades of the twenty-first century, Christianity became steadily more "abnormal," steadily weirder, and so steadily more antisocial. Anti-Christian bigotry became more acceptable, even the norm.

What Christians are currently witnessing is that the gods of burgeoning postmodernity are not, in the end, interested in sharing space with the Lord God. Even if Christians are willing to leave these gods alone, the gods themselves have no intention of leaving Christians alone. Pagans sooner or later realize that Christianity cannot really be just another cult, that the God of Abraham, Isaac, and Jacob can never really be just another god in their pantheon. Pagans recognize—often, it seems, before Christians themselves—that true Christianity just can't fit in. We saw this already in ancient Rome.

From the left, same-sex marriage, the transgender movement, and similar initiatives are designed as direct assaults on Christianity's comfortable "private" place in modern society. They say yes to family and marriage, in some modified form, while intentionally saying no to Christianity. They say yes to some form of justice while saying no to the most fundamental basis possible for social peace as understood by Christianity: "Male and female, he created them" (Gen 5:2). Similarly, from the right, an intensified social chauvinism asserts a yes to the notion of fraternal love while saying no to Christian universal brotherhood, a yes to unity while a no to justice and charity being the basis of that unity. This is the dismantling of the Christianity of modernity, which, for all its faults, retained some ability to mitigate power and control. This dismantling is making way, on both sides of the political spectrum, for the growth of the allure of wealth and pleasure, as a technocratic political and economic order of shocking power is steadily built behind the "right" and the "left's" empty rhetoric, almost without their noticing.

The twenty-first century will be the century of the Digital Revolution, as the nineteenth century was that of the Industrial Revolution. Through the Industrial Revolution, the machine came to dominate economics as ideologies came to dominate thought. Ideologies are mechanical thought-worlds that imagine human dominance over reality; they then attempt to force the natural world to fit into their molds in fact. This way of thinking and acting resulted in the shocking violence of the twentieth century, as men attempted to conquer nature, including human nature. These attempts failed because the real world always ultimately escapes man's total domination; it always resists man's self-deification because creation is necessarily ordered toward the true God. Man's proper—and so only truly possible—dominion is always an analogical mediation of and participation in God's final dominion. Man can know the truth, but he is not the source of truth. The violence of the twentieth century was man's futile and yet relentless and so horribly bloody rebellion against this reality.

The Digital Revolution is a different, more ambitious attempt at the same sort of project. Here, man is building a virtual world, a world where he is the sole creator. In this world, things do not have natures through which they participate in the ideas of God but are rather, merely, the ideas of men. It is a perfectly nominalist world in which man holds the *potentia absoluta*: the absolute power of God. In this virtual world, the logic of human sovereignty can be totalized because there is nothing pre-given, nothing resisting its closed "order" that descends from man. It can be a world, for example, of complete and seamless juridically-defined private property, where every interaction is transactional, where all "places" are under the unilateral control of fewer and fewer owners. It is a world in which every individual is nothing more than the "deal" he has made with the owners of the property on which he is allowed to move and act—renting from them his participation in the world they own. "Rights" vanish here because rights were always based on the predicament of human beings sharing a truth-bearing reality that was prior to them and their ideologies, a reality that they had to somehow negotiate together, and which no single person could quite completely dominate. Such difficulties evaporate in the virtual world. Here, the owners are exaggerated kings of the ancient variety, sons of gods. They create the world, order it, and, according to their own interests, manipulate the fate of those who inhabit it.

The Industrial Revolution began first in a traditional world that was ordered by custom and lingering medieval social forms. It steadily extended the logic of mass politics and mass economics into that world, steadily replacing the old order with a commercial, mechanized order, often subtly through the shifting of the meaning of words and the purposes of institutions, until the vast majority of people came to accept this new world as social reality itself. Politics shifted to the fight between liberals, socialists, and nationalists, a fight that occurred within and never against the new social "reality." People came to believe that anything that resisted the new order was odd and backward—even immoral and unjust. This habituation became so complete that people in our own day have largely lost the ability to even imagine a different order. Similar to the peasants, unaware that the sand had shifted beneath their feet, futilely advancing their traditional customs and privileges against the burgeoning mass powers of the Industrial Revolution, in the face of the contemporary politico-economic revolution, we advance naively the protection of "constitutions," "rights," and the public-private distinction upon which the modern order was based. Now, under the cover of that waning order, steadily more and more of reality is being read through the virtual world. Steadily, the virtual world is becoming, to more and more people, more real; the virtual is becoming the measure of the real, the architecture within which people live. It is becoming the structure that forms and organizes the world that they experience.

Within the confines of the virtual, the helpless individual—who "owns" next to nothing—is facing alone the creators of the world's very structure, those who manage what is true and false, just and unjust, right and wrong, good and evil, and who control its rewards and punishments. The builders of the virtual world need not violently conquer the physical, truth-bearing world of real relations. They need only shift social life into their domain—and allow reality to either assimilate into the structures of their control or simply fall out of view, simply be pushed outside the new world. Unlike the ideological totalitarians, they need not physically destroy rival centers of human solidarity—networks of friends, for example. They need only shift friendship onto their "platforms," where it becomes an extension of their power rather than a mitigation of it. They need not attack the family directly, removing children from the care of their parents, as did the totalitarians; they need only let parental authority decay in disuse as both children and parents increasingly live in the world of the screen. And this is indeed the path that the postmodern order seems to be taking. It is the most formidable strategy for victory that the City of Man has yet devised. It is a strategy of making mankind anxious and uncomfortable in the real, natural world—the world of human-to-human and human-to-nature contact, where bottom-up power can emerge and be maintained—and of making us desire instead the stability, the seamless order, the safety, of the virtual world: the "peace" of slavery.

Here, then, the final eclipse of the modern political architecture is occurring. The days of the dominance of the nation state—of ultimate power being the direct, political ability to marshal the physical and human resources of large geographical areas—are passing. Increasingly, these physical things are read through and ordered by virtual things that transcend them and connect them in new power structures: structures that stand above the persisting, but now demoted, political and economic forms. The old forms are not simply annihilated. That is not how history works. Armies, factories, farms, churches, courts—all continue. They are just re-ordered as pieces of something new, as they have been time and again through history. The deconstruction of old social architectures is the simultaneous construction of new social architectures: the inhabitants of old cities slowly disassemble the structures of their past to gain materials with which to build the structures of their future. This is a subtle process that mostly goes unnoticed unless it finally explodes in violence. (The Thirty Years' War, the Napoleonic Wars, and the First World War seem to be examples of such accelerationist conflicts, conflicts that finished in a flash what had been developing over long periods of time.)

It is fitting then, that the old ideologies themselves have become hollow trappings: bits and pieces of the old structure, now serving different purposes in the new structure. It seems clear, for example, that the "liberal" West, "nationalist" Russia, and "Communist" China are all converging with only slight modifications on this same technocratic order—within which the old divisions between private and public, between corporations and states, between the marketplace and the home, between economic and political action, between national and international, even between entertainment and news, are losing their old structural significance. It is quite clear that the various dimensions of social life are no longer under the umbrella of order provided by old-fashioned national "politics." Indeed, who could be so foolish as to mistake our politicians for the ones actually "in charge" of our social, political, or economic world? The rulers of the virtual world cut across all these old lines; and their rule is potentially more complete, more seamless, and more profound than anything the twentieth-century totalitarians could manage with their propaganda, bureaucracies, and armies. It remains to be seen whether this postmodern transition can be accomplished without the type of blood-letting that has accompanied similar changes throughout history.

Contemporary Christians are being forced into a fundamental decision. Will they allow the Church's already well-advanced integration into the postmodern world to become complete, or will they launch a reform? Will they extract themselves from a corrupt system so that they might turn and convert that system? Will they start to build again the City of God?

This is not, I think, some sort of hopeless endeavor. It seems to me that the power of the postmodern world is ironically being built on its weakness, on a foundation that rests on sand. The Church has encountered this before. Power that is not a mediation of the power of God, power that is not "undermined" through the humble recognition of a source that lies beyond its comprehension, becomes closed in on itself, justifying itself through its mere exercise. It becomes a god. This is all the gods of the pagan world ever were—man's own alienated power. The power of such gods is real, but it is always second hand, always based upon a promise to give something that they did not create or to take something that they did not give. It is parasitic reality because it is not a participation in the divine power that actually holds things in being.

Because of this, it is never seamless. It always has a weakness, a gap, a back door—a place to attack and to undo it. This is a constant problem for the priests and kings of the gods of power. The goodness in man, wherever it thrives, is a constant threat to their power, a constant potential rival, welling up from below as a participation in what is far above. And yet at the same time, the power of these false rulers flows from the continuing presence of the good because the good is what all desire, and without this desire, their redirection and manipulation of the good could have no force. What they must do is this: try to control man's pursuit of the good, contain it, limit it, funnel it into particular outlets, particular places that they have surrounded and that they thus dominate. But they can't finally dominate even these places because they cannot finally give men what they are looking for. If they try to, if, that is, they kill goodness, they destroy the source of their strength.

Men fight, for example, for the love of their families. Tyrants throughout history have used this love to build their power; and yet this love of family can as easily turn against the tyrant—and repeatedly throughout history, it has. Love of truth can motivate violent revolution; and yet as soon as the revolution settles into rule, the true believers are the most dangerous, the first to be purged. The powers of the world are, therefore, always engaged in a struggle of maintenance, of shifting love from one place to another, of countering its attempts to break free without finally killing it. Such worldly power is always fraught, always anxious, always paranoid. Such power is always the master of a half-restive population. Ultimately, men serve the gods because at a deeper level, they still serve God.

The gods are, therefore, in their nature cruel. They hurt without finally killing. And they must maintain the pain. For example, the mass anxiety that underwrites the liberal drive for wealth is the precondition for the power of the men who placate and manipulate the market. They must maintain the festering of this wound in society in order to provide the masses salve and bandages. Such power tends the wound even as it subtly tears it open again, maybe in a slightly different direction, maybe letting the wound heal in one place even as it cuts it deep in another direction. Such power demands that new desires be continuously created even as the old ones are relentlessly indulged, that relative abundance be played off an ever-deepening scarcity. This is a downward spiral.

Such power is ultimately self-defeating. The pagan priests and kings could amass power only because they, too, served the gods, whose power was, of course, nothing other than that of the people themselves. For the rulers to become more powerful, the combined power of the people must become more alienated, more unmoored from nature, more fanatical because it is less moderated by the real, more capable of centralization because it is less embedded in time and place. In order to maximize the rulers' power, the mass of people must be united in an ever simpler, ever greater, and yet ever falser, fear. But this collapses the free action of the rulers into a single possible course. The manipulation, the propaganda, and now marketing, that creates the power of the mob becomes, in the end, indistinguishable from pandering to it, from placating its hollow demands. At some point the rule of mass society becomes indistinguishable from obeisance to it. Unmediated power is extended in efficacy only as its freedom of scope is limited: such power gains more and more control over less and less until it controls everything of nothing. Absolute rulers emerge at the very moment when they can do nothing but serve the mass society that they have created, bound by the lie that holds it in being. This is the great paradox of so-called sovereign power. Its construction is its undoing. In the final analysis, sovereignty is held by the corporate thing, the Leviathan, who answers to no persons and who devours everyone it encounters. In the end, power without God, power closed in on itself, would enslave everyone. But such an end is not possible.

This is why the move to the virtual is both the most ambitious and the most foolish bid yet made for unmitigated human power. The domination that it advances is the most complete yet devised, and yet it is the least real. People can just turn away, just look at each other and at the world around them, just free themselves from the power of this most unreal of idolatrous systems. As the prophets of the Old Testament repeatedly declared, people need only realize the emptiness of these works of human hands, they need only stop and ask "Shall I fall down before a block of wood?" (Isaiah 44:15).

And this liberation is easier than we realize. Real people, in their real lives, love their families. They care about their friends. They want to have meaningful work that helps society as a whole. They want to experience true freedom in harmony with the real world and not against it. Real people are not as bad, as shallow or selfish, as political parties, global corporations, the media, academia, or Hollywood make them seem. Real people, in their real lives, like all people throughout all history, are pursuing happiness and have a great deal of goodness in their lives. They are good in their nature. As I have asserted, it is this goodness that evil preys upon, but it is also this goodness that provides an opening for the Gospel. This has been the situation since the beginning. This is the situation that the Church was made for. As with the ancient pagan regimes, the power of the burgeoning postmodern regime rests on slavery to sin, on consumerism, on the perversion of the truth and the goodness that it cannot itself provide. Converting people always from sin through the Gospel is today, as it was in the ancient world, the undermining of the concrete power of the City of Man, especially in its current iteration.

But the Church must first reform. Could it be that providence has allowed the Church to fall into the profound worldliness in which it currently finds itself so that the reform movement that will emerge will be a reform not only of the Church but of the postmodern world itself? Has the Church been exiled into the City of Man so that when she is called back, she can bring the goodness that is spread out in that City with her? The Israelites were left in Egypt for over four hundred years so that when God moved to save them, the society that they built could be a light to the nations because it had been pulled out of the nations. Its law, its cult, and its philosophy were wholly just and true, and yet they clearly bore the life of the pagans within them and so were intelligible to the world. Similarly, in the early Middle Ages, as society descended into violent feudalism, it dragged the Church with it. The papacy itself was mired in corruption, fully integrated into the world of feudal power. The reform movement that emerged did not create something totally new; it was not a total reversal of the ways of this world. Rather, it built a reformed feudal society, a society that brought with it the world out of which it was born.

The Church suffers the sins of the world so that she can redeem the world. And the City of God is the redemption of the City of Man, not its annihilation. The City of God is constantly pulled into the City of Man, as we see over and over again, because it shares in its humanity, because it is always looking at the world, always risking the world—because the City of God is for the world. Sometimes, the Heavenly City seems all but lost. But it isn't. The Church has already won the war, and tactical retreats are revealed to be part of a larger strategy. This is the Exodus story, the story of the Passover, of fall and redemption, that has been repeated throughout history and in the individual life of every believer. The reform that will come to the postmodern Church will no doubt be another chapter in this story. It will not be a return to an older form. The Church will not return to the thirteenth century, or to the Alliance of Throne and Altar, or to the 1950s. The coming reform will have the opportunity to bring the postmodern world with it because it will be born out of that world, and the Church that emerges will not be oriented backward but forward, driven not by nostalgia but by hope.

Nevertheless, we can learn from previous reforms. When the medieval reform came in the eleventh century, it did not come first from above. It did not come from kings, bishops, or popes. It came first from the religious orders, from those Christians whose lives anticipated most perfectly the true City of God. High Medieval Christendom was built because the laity founded, purified, and populated thousands of monasteries. The religious men and women of these foundations pursued perfection through grace. Not only was their example profound, but their prayer was also efficacious. The cloisters changed the world. The reform came pouring out of the monasteries as a vision of an integral life of peace, and charity became a real thing, as grace became once again credible. If the monks can find peace in Christ, why can't all of us? The religious life has collapsed in the Catholic Church. In 1970, there were 172,000 religious brothers and sisters in the United States; now there are 45,000, and most of them are elderly. Perhaps, then, it is not to the heights of political or ecclesial power that Catholics should be looking for reform, but rather, like the laity of the eleventh century, maybe they should be building monasteries for their sons and daughters to populate. Perhaps the Church won't break free from the world's domination until the faithful stop thinking of the Church as merely a little corner of the world and allow themselves to be led not by the powerful, but by the religious, by the meek. Israel defeated Nebuchadnezzar, "the king of all the earth," under whose power lived not only all men but "also the beasts of the field and the cattle and the birds of the air," only through the action of the weakest, of a widow (Judith 11:7):

> The Lord Almighty has foiled them
> > by the hand of a woman.
> For their mighty one did not fall by the hands of the young men,
> > nor did the sons of the Titans smite him,
> > nor did tall giants set upon him;
> > but Judith the daughter of Merari undid him
> > with the beauty of her countenance. (Judith 16:6–7)

This is, perhaps, how the New Evangelization will finally come to pass, how the Church can shine out again as the Light of the Nations, converting the desperate masses from fear to peace, from slavery to freedom. This is how it has happened before.

BIBLIOGRAPHY

Arendt, Hannah. *The Origins of Totalitarianism.* San Diego, CA: Harcourt, 1966.

Baldwin, Marshall W., ed. *Christianity through the Thirteenth Century.* New York: Macmillan, 1970.

Beales, Derek. *Prosperity and Plunder: European Catholic Monasteries in the Age of Revolution, 1650–1815.* Cambridge: Cambridge University Press, 2003.

Benedict XV. *Ad Beatissimi Apostolorum.* 1914.

Bernard of Clairvaux. *In Praise of the New Knighthood.* Translated by M. Conrad Greenia, OCSO. Kalamazoo, MI: Cistercian Publications, 2000.

Bodin, Jean. *On Sovereignty.* Translated by M. J. Tooley. Oxford: Basil Blackwell, 1955.

Bossuet, Jacques-Benigne. *Politics Drawn from the Very Words of Holy Scripture.* Cambridge: Cambridge University Press, 1990.

Calvin, John. *Institutes of the Christian Religion.* Translated by Henry Beveridge. Peabody, MA: Hendrickson Publishers, 2008.

Davies, Norman. *Europe: A History.* Oxford: Oxford University Press, 1996.

Deferrari, Roy Joseph, ed. *The Fathers of the Church.* Translated by Mary Melchior Beyenka. Washington, D.C.: Catholic University of America Press, 1954.

de Lubac, Henri. *Catholicism: Christ and the Common Destiny of Man.* Translated by Lancelot C. Sheppard and Sr. Elizabeth Englund. San Francisco: Ignatius Press, 1988.

Ehler, Sidney Z. and John B. Morrall, trans. and ed. *Church and State through the Centuries: A Collection of Historic Documents with Commentaries.* New York: Biblo and Tannen, 1969.

First Vatican Council. *Dogmatic Constitution on the Catholic Faith.* 1870.

———. *First Dogmatic Constitution on the Church of Christ.* 1870.

Flannery, Austin, trans. *Vatican Council II: The Conciliar and Postconciliar Documents*. Collegeville, MN: Liturgical Press, 1975.

Gooch, G. P. *Maria Theresa and Other Studies*. London: Longmans, Green and Co., 1951.

Gregory XVI. *Mirari Vos*. 1832.

———. *Probe Nostis* (1840)

Hayek, F. A., *The Road to Serfdom*. New York: Routledge, 2006.

Helfferich, Tryntje, ed. and trans. *The Essential Luther*. Indianapolis, IN: Hackett Publishing, 2018.

Henderson, Ernest F., trans. *Select Historical Documents of the Middle Ages*. London: George Bell and Sons, 1910.

Hobbes, Thomas. *Leviathan: With Selected Variants from the Latin Edition of 1668*. Indianapolis, IN: Hackett Publishing Company, 1994.

John Paul II. *Centesimus Annus*. 1991.

———. *Evangelium Vitae*. 1995.

———. *Laborem Exercens*. 1981.

———. *Redemptor Hominis*. 1979.

———. *Redemptoris Missio*. 1990.

———. *Veritatis Splendor*. 1993.

Lenin, V. I. *The State and Revolution*. New York: Penguin, 1992.

Leo XII. *Charitate Christi*. 1825.

Leo XIII. *Immortale Dei*. 1885.

———. *Libertas Praestantissimum*. 1888.

———. *Rerum Novarum*. 1891.

———. *Sapientiae Christianae*. 1890.

Mill, John Stuart. *On Liberty*. Indianapolis, IN: Hackett Publishing, 1859.

Mitchell, Margaret M., Frances M. Young, K. Scott Bowie, eds. *Origins to Constantine*. Vol. 1 of *The Cambridge History of Christianity*. Cambridge: Cambridge University Press, 2006.

Moore, John C. "The Sermons of Pope Innocent III." *Römische Historische Mitteilungen* 36 (1994).

Nietzsche, Friedrich. *Beyond Good and Evil: Prelude to a Philosophy of the Future*. New York: Random House, 1989.

———. *Thus Spoke Zarathustra*. In *The Portable Nietzsche*. Edited by Walter Kaufmann. New York: Penguin Books, 1982.

O'Malley, John W. *What Happened at Vatican II*. Cambridge, MA: Harvard University Press, 2008.

Pitra, J. B., ed. *Analecta Novissima*. Paris: Typis tuscalanis, 1888.

Pius IX. *Etsi Multa.* 1873.
———. *Nostis et Nobiscum.* 1849.
———. *Quanta Cura.* 1864.
———. *Qui Pluribus.* 1846.
———. *Syllabus Errorum.* 1864.
Pius XI. *Divini Redemptoris.* 1937.
———. *Mit Brennender Sorge.* 1937.
———. *Non Abbiamo Bisogno.* 1931.
———. *Quadragesimo Anno.* 1931.
Prothero, G. W., ed. *Select Statutes and Other Constitutional Documents Illustrative of the Reigns of Elizabeth and James I.* 3rd ed. Oxford; Clarendon Press, 1906.
Rahner, Hugo. *Church and State in Early Christianity.* San Francisco: Ignatius Press, 1992.
Reid, Dom Alcuin. *A Bitter Trial: Evelyn Waugh and John Cardinal Heenan on the Liturgical Changes.* San Francisco: Ignatius Press, 2011.
Robinson, James Harvey, ed. *Readings in European History: From the Opening of the Protestant Revolt to the Present Day.* Boston: Ginn and Co., 1904–1906.
Schaff, Philip, ed. *Nicene and Post-Nicene Fathers II.* Peabody, MA: Hendrickson, 1994.
Schmidt, James, trans. *What is Enlightenment?: Eighteenth-Century Answers and Twentieth-Century Questions.* Berkeley, CA: University of California Press, 1996.
Second Vatican Council. *Dignitatis Humanae: Declaration on Religious Liberty.* Translated by Austin Flannery. Collegeville, MN: Liturgical Press, 2014.
———. *Sacrosanctum Concilium.* 1963.
Sherman, Dennis. *Western Civilization: Sources, Images, and Interpretations.* 2nd ed. New York: McGraw Hill, 2008.
Spencer, Herbert. *Social Statics.* London: George Woodfall and Son, 1851.
Stevenson, James, ed. *A New Eusebius: Documents Illustrating the History of the Church to A.D. 337.* London: SPCK, 1987.
Tanner, Norman P., ed. *Decrees of the Ecumenical Councils.* Washington, D.C.: Georgetown University Press, 1990.
Townsend, M. E. *Origins of Modern German Colonization, 1871–1885.* New York, 1921.
von Balthasar, Hans Urs. *A Theology of History.* San Francisco: Ignatius Press, 1963.

BIBLIOGRAPHY

von Mises, Ludwig. *Liberalism: The Classical Tradition*. New York: The Foundation for Economic Education, 1996.

Whitcomb, Merrick, John Bach McMaster, Arthur C. Howland, William Fairley, and Dana Carleton Munro, eds. *Translations and Reprints from the Original Sources of European History*. Philadelphia: University of Pennsylvania Press, 1900.